Slavoj Žižek and Christianity

Slavoj Žižek's critical engagement with Christian theology goes much further than his seminal study *The Fragile Absolute* (2000), or his *The Puppet and the Dwarf* (2003), or even his discussion with noted theologian John Milbank in *The Monstrosity of Christ* (2009). His reading of Christianity, utilizing his signature elements of Lacanian psychoanalysis and Hegelian philosophy with modern philosophical currents, can be seen as a genuinely original contribution to the philosophy of religion. This book focuses on these aspects of Žižek's thought, with either philosophy and cultural theory, or Christian theology, serving as starting points of enquiry.

Written by a panel of international contributors, each chapter teases out various strands of Žižek's thought concerning Christianity and religion and brings them into a wider conversation about the nature of faith. These essays show that far from being an outright rejection of Christian thought and intellectual heritage, Žižek's work could be seen as a perverse affirmation thereof. Thus, what he has to say should be of direct interest to Christian theology itself.

Touching on thinkers such as Badiou, Lacan, Chesterton and Schelling, this collection is a dynamic reading and re-reading of Žižek's relationship to Christianity. As such, scholars of theology, the philosophy of religion and Žižek more generally will all find this book to be of great interest.

Sotiris Mitralexis is Seeger Fellow at Princeton University, Assistant Professor of Philosophy at the City University of Istanbul (İstanbul Şehir Üniversitesi) and Visiting Research Fellow at the University of Winchester. He has been a Visiting Fellow at the University of Cambridge's Faculty of Divinity and a Visiting Senior Research Associate at Peterhouse, Cambridge. He received a doctorate in philosophy from the Freie Universität Berlin, a doctorate in theology from the Aristotle University of Thessaloniki and a degree in classics from the University of Athens. His publications include *Ever-Moving Repose: A Contemporary Reading of Maximus the Confessor's Theory of Time*.

Dionysios Skliris is a Teaching Fellow at the Faculty of Theology, University of Athens. He received a doctorate from the Faculté des Lettres et Sciences Humaines of the University of Paris (Sorbonne – Paris IV). He studied classics and theology at the University of Athens and completed a master's degree in late antique philosophy at the University of London (King's College) and a master's degree in Byzantine literature at the University of Paris (Sorbonne – Paris IV).

Transcending Boundaries in Philosophy and Theology
Series Editors: Martin Warner
University of Warwick, UK

Kevin Vanhoozer
Trinity Evangelical School, US

Transcending Boundaries in Philosophy and Theology is an interdisciplinary series exploring new opportunities in the dialogue between philosophy and theology that go beyond more traditional "faith and reason" debates and take account of the contemporary reshaping of intellectual boundaries. For much of the modern era, the relation of philosophy and theology has been conceived in terms of antagonism or subordination, but recent intellectual developments hold out considerable potential for a renewed dialogue in which philosophy and theology have common cause for revisioning their respective identities, reconceiving their relationship and combining their resources. This series explores constructively for the 21st century the resources available for engaging with those forms of enquiry, experience and sensibility that theology has historically sought to address. Drawing together new writing and research from leading international scholars in the field, this high profile research series offers an important contribution to contemporary research across the interdisciplinary perspectives relating theology and philosophy.

Theological Philosophy
Rethinking the Rationality of Christian Faith
Lydia Schumacher

Renewing Spiritual Perception with Jonathan Edwards
Contemporary Philosophy and the Theological Psychology
of Transforming Grace
Ray S. Yeo

Wonder, Value and God
Robin Attfield

Slavoj Žižek and Christianity
Edited by Sotiris Mitralexis and Dionysios Skliris

For more information about this series, please visit: www.routledge.com/religion/series/APHILTHEO

Slavoj Žižek and Christianity

Edited by Sotiris Mitralexis and
Dionysios Skliris

LONDON AND NEW YORK

First published 2019
by Routledge
2 Park Square, Milton Park, Abingdon, Oxon OX14 4RN

and by Routledge
711 Third Avenue, New York, NY 10017

Routledge is an imprint of the Taylor & Francis Group, an informa business

© 2019 selection and editorial matter, Sotiris Mitralexis and Dionysios Skliris; individual chapters, the contributors

The right of Sotiris Mitralexis and Dionysios Skliris to be identified as the authors of the editorial material, and of the authors for their individual chapters, has been asserted in accordance with sections 77 and 78 of the Copyright, Designs and Patents Act 1988.

All rights reserved. No part of this book may be reprinted or reproduced or utilized in any form or by any electronic, mechanical, or other means, now known or hereafter invented, including photocopying and recording, or in any information storage or retrieval system, without permission in writing from the publishers.

Trademark notice: Product or corporate names may be trademarks or registered trademarks, and are used only for identification and explanation without intent to infringe.

British Library Cataloging-in-Publication Data
A catalog record for this book is available from the British Library

Library of Congress Cataloging-in-Publication Data
A catalog record for this book has been requested

ISBN: 978-1-138-10326-9 (hbk)
ISBN: 978-1-315-10290-0 (ebk)

Typeset in Sabon
by Apex CoVantage, LLC

Contents

List of contributors		vii
1	The Slovenian and the Cross: transcending Christianity's perverse core with Slavoj Žižek DIONYSIOS SKLIRIS AND SOTIRIS MITRALEXIS	1
2	Žižek and the dialectical materialist theory of belief AGON HAMZA	46
3	From psychoanalysis to metamorphosis: the Lacanian limits of Žižek's theology BRIAN W. BECKER	67
4	"No wonder, then, that love itself disappears": neighbor-love in Žižek and Meister Eckhart CHASE PADUSNIAK	86
5	Concrete universality: only that which is non-all is for all GABRIEL TUPINAMBÁ	104
6	Pacifist pluralism versus militant truth: Christianity at the service of revolution in the work of Slavoj Žižek HARALAMBOS VENTIS	117
7	Rethinking universality: Badiou and Žižek on Pauline theology JACK LOUIS PAPPAS	154
8	"Rühre nicht, Bock! denn es brennt": Schelling, Žižek and Christianity SINAN RICHARDS	167

9 Murder at the vicarage: Žižek's Chesterton as a way out of Christianity 188
BRUCE J. KRAJEWSKI

10 Žižek and the dwarf: a short-circuit radical theology 199
MIKE GRIMSHAW

Afterword: the antinomies that keep Christianity alive 219
SLAVOJ ŽIŽEK

Index 228

Contributors

Brian W. Becker is Associate Professor of Neuropsychology at Lesley University, Cambridge, Massachusetts.

Mike Grimshaw is Associate Professor of Sociology at the University of Canterbury, New Zealand.

Agon Hamza holds a doctoral degree in philosophy from the Postgraduate School ZRC SAZU in Slovenia.

Bruce J. Krajewski is Professor and Chair in the Department of English of the University of Texas at Arlington.

Sotiris Mitralexis is Seeger Fellow at Princeton University, Assistant Professor of Philosophy at the City University of Istanbul and Visiting Research Fellow at the University of Winchester, holding doctorates in philosophy and theology.

Chase Padusniak is a doctoral candidate in the English department at Princeton University.

Jack Louis Pappas is a doctoral student in systematic theology and philosophy of religion at Fordham University in New York City.

Sinan Richards is a doctoral candidate at Wadham College, Oxford. He currently teaches at the École Normale Supérieure, Paris.

Dionysios Skliris holds a doctorate in philosophy from Université Paris IV – Sorbonne and is a Teaching Fellow at the Faculty of Theology, University of Athens.

Gabriel Tupinambá conducts post-doctoral research at the Pontifícia Universidade Católica at Rio de Janeiro and is coordinator of the Círculo de Estudos da Ideia e da Ideologia (CEII RJ).

Haralambos Ventis is Assistant Professor of the Philosophy of Religion at the Faculty of Theology, University of Athens.

Slavoj Žižek is a cultural philosopher; he is Senior Researcher at the Institute for Sociology and Philosophy at the University of Ljubljana, Global Distinguished Professor of German at New York University and International Director of the Birkbeck Institute for the Humanities of the University of London.

1 The Slovenian and the Cross

Transcending Christianity's perverse core with Slavoj Žižek

Dionysios Skliris and Sotiris Mitralexis

This volume[1] explores aspects of Slavoj Žižek's work *on* Christian theology, the relevance of that work *for* Christian theology and his dialogue *with* Christian theologians. The assumption behind this volume is not that Žižek *does theology* as such – for this would require, well, faith – but that his insights on Christianity are of acute interest *for* theology, either in a straightforward or indirect and "perverse" way. For one might assume that an atheist, materialist, Marxist communist thinker cannot but be dismissive of Christianity – however, this would be gravely erroneous in a case as distinctive as Žižek's, who may indeed offer valid insights through treading the seemingly paradoxical territory of *atheist theology*. His reading of Christianity as expounded in his voluminous and on-going *oeuvre*, uniting elements of Lacanian psychoanalysis and Hegelian philosophy as well as modern and contemporary philosophical currents, has a rightful claim to originality. Far from being an outright rejection of Christian thought and intellectual heritage, Žižek's work can be seen as involving its perverse (or "decaffeinated") affirmation, arguably including elements of interest to Christian theology itself.

Žižek's interest in Christianity begins mainly with *The Ticklish Subject* (1999), in which he engages with the theology of Saint Paul. After that, he writes three books which have Christianity as their main subject, namely *The Fragile Absolute, or Why Is the Christian Legacy Worth Fighting for?* (2000), *On Belief* (2001) and *The Puppet and the Dwarf: The Perverse Core of Christianity* (2003). Christianity is also one of the important subjects in *The Parallax View* (2006), which recapitulates many of his main interests. Žižek is also the co-author of books on theology in which he has collaborated with noted theologians such as John Milbank of the Radical Orthodoxy movement – in *The Monstrosity of Christ: Paradox or Dialectic* (2009) and *Paul's New Moment: Continental Philosophy and the Future of Christian Theology* (2010), both edited by Creston Davis – as well as with Boris Gunjević (*God in Pain: Inversions of Apocalypse*, 2012).

Žižek's idiosyncratic approach to Christianity is such that he could be described as an "atheist Christian," in the sense that he does not believe in the existence of God, nor in the literal bodily Resurrection of Jesus Christ, yet he regards the "Christian experience" as extremely important. He further links Christianity with psychoanalysis and the communist idea as the three great traditions of emancipatory importance, which are more timely and relevant than ever precisely in their interconnection within our post-modern world. In order to understand Žižek's philosophy, we have to realize that in it there is a continuous passage from religion to psychoanalysis and to politics and back, with continuous correspondences between the three levels. His implicit claim is that everything that applies to religion applies in a certain similar way to psychology and to politics. To take a most important example to which we will return later, what Žižek perceives as the community of the Holy Spirit after the Resurrection of Christ can be illuminatingly likened, as will be shown in this volume, to certain psychoanalytic communities as Jacques Lacan conceived them, as well as to the political subject of communism, as Žižek himself perceives the true meaning of the term. Correspondingly, historical and institutional Christianity is perceived as a perverse form of Christianity (taking account of the psychoanalytic content of the term "perversion") in a similar sense in which Stalinism is a perverse form of communism, with psychoanalysis showing similar tendencies.

Slavoj Žižek was born in Ljubljana, Slovenia, in 1949, where he studied philosophy and sociology, completing his Ph.D. thesis on *The Theoretical and Practical Relevance of French Structuralism*. During his youth he participated in intellectual circles critical of the establishment and in magazines such as *Praxis*, *Tribuna* and *Problemi*, known for an alternative version of Marxism to the official one of the Yugoslav regime. In 1985, Žižek received a second Ph.D., in psychoanalysis, from *Université Paris VIII* under the supervision of the well-known psychoanalyst Jacques Allain-Miller. His international reputation began with the publication of *The Sublime Object of Ideology* in 1989, in which he analyzed the use of ideology, drawing on his experience of the establishment ideology in Tito's Yugoslavia. In the late 1980s, Slavoj Žižek took part in the struggle for Slovenia's democratization and even ran as the Liberal Democratic Party's candidate for the Slovenian presidency.

This first phase of Žižek's itinerary is characterized by the critique of "actually existing socialism's" totalitarian ideology and a certain proximity to liberalism, from which he has since distanced himself. Gradually, his critique became directed more against nationalism and, ultimately, its association with liberalism, despite the widespread common impression to the contrary. An early critique of the connection between nationalism and liberalism is already to be found in *Tarrying with the Negative* (1993). A turning point for Žižek was his philosophical encounter with Alain Badiou, with whom he came to share many philosophical themes, particularly on the theology of Paul the Apostle and Christianity in general, as well as on the need to conceive of the communist hypothesis anew, although in a way different from that encountered in "actually existing socialism," on the need for a re-interpretation of Lacan, and so on. The encounter with Badiou is located mainly in *The Ticklish Subject* (1999), where Žižek is in dialogue with Badiou's work *Saint Paul: The Foundation of Universalism*. In many ways, Žižek can be considered as a disciple of Badiou, since on these important issues the older Badiou will set an agenda and a terminology, with Žižek following and adding to the debate in a distinctive manner. Žižek's dialogue with his French colleague and comrade is, however, a critical one. Their great difference lies in the fact that Žižek insists on a dialectical perspective, following Hegel in a progress through contradictions where negativity plays the main role. Badiou, on the other hand, focuses on the notion of the *event*, i.e. of an occurrence that takes place in spite of the absence of its apparent preconditions, something which has a certain positivity. We could say, then, that in his interpretation of Christianity Badiou articulates a "theology of the Resurrection" or a "theology of Glory," while Žižek formulates a "theology of the Crucifixion." Badiou sees in the Apostle Paul the great visionary who began his journey through the vision of the resurrected Christ, "meeting" Him on the road to Damascus. The rest of Paul's life consisted in a faithfulness to this event, and in this sense "crucifixion" paradoxically follows the Resurrection as a "testimony" to the event. In Žižek's interpretation, on the contrary, "salvation" comes from the Crucifixion and the Resurrection, which is not understood literally, and is identical to the Pentecost and the coming of the Holy Spirit. We will return to this later in this volume.

Slavoj Žižek positions himself in the interpenetration of the multiple traditions to which he belongs. The two main ones are dialectical Marxist thinking and psychoanalysis. Dialectical Marxist thought, however, originates from German Idealism, which in turn is connected to modernity's general program, the latter having roots in a certain Christian tradition which also sometimes presents dialectical elements. In contemplating Žižek's intellectual lineage and heritage in a chronological sequence from the earliest to the most current, we would say that the thinkers who have defined him and constitute recurring reference points are the Apostle Paul from the period of the Christian *Urkirche*, Augustine of Hippo from the patristic period and German religious thinkers such as Meister Eckhart and Martin Luther, while he draws on John Calvin's understanding of absolute predestination. Beyond this, Descartes as the founder of the program of modernity, Kant, Schelling and Hegel from German Idealism, but also at the same time Kierkegaard, Feuerbach, Marx, Lenin and Althusser from the communist tradition, Freud and Lacan from psychoanalysis, Walter Benjamin, Hans Jonas, and Theodor W. Adorno from the great Jewish thinkers of the twentieth century, as well as Alain Badiou and Jacques Rancière from his contemporaries. Arguably, each of those thinkers has contributed a certain building block to the dialectical thinking of Slavoj Žižek, which, being dialectical, also constitutes a kind of recapitulation of the history of philosophy through an acutely original interpretative perspective. In this process, each previous element is interpreted by a later one. For example, the Apostle Paul's theology of the universality of love that goes beyond the Jewish Law is considered in the light of Martin Luther's Protestant emphasis on absolute individuality. Augustine's thought is contemplated in the light of its evolution in René Descartes' program of modernity, while in Meister Eckhart we can see a great German thinker, a precursor of German Idealism. Immanuel Kant, of course, is considered to be the philosopher of the Thing, from a viewpoint that is not only Hegelian, but also Lacanian, as we encounter in Lacan the distinction between the Real and the Symbolic somewhat as we encounter in Kant the distinction between the Thing (in-itself) and phenomena. German Idealism is considered in the light of its materialist interpretation. And Žižek's perhaps most crucial gesture is his reading of Hegel *through* Lacan, and vice versa, of Lacan *through* Hegel. It should also be noted that Žižek is strongly opposed to Levinas and to the interpretation of the Jewish tradition he represents, while he distances himself from Jacques Derrida and Judith Butler as far as their own combination of Judaism with elements of post-modern post-structuralist thought is concerned.

Let us consider an example of how Žižek is inspired by such sources. Žižek inherits from the theological tradition of German Idealism the question of what God was doing before the creation of the world. And he responds by resorting to Schelling in particular.[2] His answer is that, before the creation of the world, God *was becoming God*. We could thus say that before the creation of the world there was an abyss of primordial freedom, i.e. of an absolute freedom as an undifferentiated potentiality for everything and anything. The differentiation came about when God changed from not wanting anything, in the sense of anything *particular*, to wanting *nothing itself*. This latter object of volition signifies a kind of contraction in the triple sense of reduction, condensation and contracting a disease. The fact that God desires *a* nothing, *the* nothing entails that, suddenly, a zero is set next to God. This entails an emptying of God, a *kenosis*, a reduction of Him, so as to "fit" this zero, this nothing, next to Him. This emptying, however, is also a condensation of God in the sense that God is "transformed" into Being, or, as we could say, in the double meaning of the word contraction, God "contracts" Being as a disease, as Being can be considered to be a disease or even a reduction compared to the previous condition of absolute free will. From now on we will have a tug-of-war between the contraction and the expansion of Being, to which Žižek will give a name derived from Freudian psychoanalysis (as Lacan interprets Freud but even more as Žižek interprets Freud building on Lacan's intuitions): *drive*. The next stage is that in which God as Word, as *Logos*, creates the world. According to Žižek, this moment of creation *represses* the drive, which turns into the repressed past of the world. In this psychoanalytic reading, what the *Logos* represses is in essence the very founding act of creation. The *Logos* thus constitutes temporality, as the distinction between past and present emerges for the first time, with the past being the repressed drive and the present being the Logical creation.

However, in order to better understand this aspect of Žižek's thought, which draws from Lacan and Schelling, we have to also take into account a distinction between male and female that Lacan makes and which Žižek employs to its utmost potential.[3] What Žižek refers to as the male model is what he calls a "constitutive exception." This means that any symbolic system is based on the fact that the very moment of the symbolic system's creation violates the rules that govern it. This founding moment of the symbolic system is repressed as a kind of repressed exception that dictates the norm. We do possess, however, a dialectic concerning a totalizable symbolic system and its exception that constitutes it without belonging to it. In contrast to this, the female model signifies a "whole" that is *a priori* non-totalizable. Cosmogony, as Žižek describes it drawing from Schelling and Lacan, signifies a passage and transition from the female model to the male one. Prior to the advent of the Logos we have a female model, that is, a non-totalizable All. This female model "vanishes" in order for a world of the male model to emerge and thus becomes a "vanishing mediator." When we find ourselves in the ratiocentric world, we bear a repression of the founding moment of the symbolic system, which is categorized by Žižek as a *drive*. We could describe the same in Schelling's terms by claiming that God is trying to escape either from hell or from madness. This theogony–cosmogony resembles Neoplatonic theogonies-cosmogonies or even certain traditional Christian cosmogonies – but it has some key differences. First, we encounter here a process of God's own generation, a becoming within God himself, i.e. a process theology, which finds itself at a certain distance from traditional, orthodox theology. Second, temporality is not seen here as a reduction and degradation, as in Neoplatonism, but as a mode in which God Himself is becoming complete.

This leads us to a radical reconfiguration of temporality and history, which is consistent with modernity's program of configuring modern subjectivity and history as the *locus* of self-realization – not only of man, but of God Himself as well. Moreover, in contrast to Neoplatonism, where the main and primary division is between the One and Being–Nous, here the primary division is between Will–Freedom and Being. We have here, therefore, a voluntarist philosophy which accords to the importance of the will in the program of modernity in German Idealism. This process is also perceived as an emptying, a *kenosis* of God, in order for zero/nothing to emerge, out of which Being will arise. This is in contrast to traditional and orthodox Christian theology, where we do encounter the doctrine of *creatio ex nihilo*, yet the eternally Triune God remains an eternally absolute presence, and the creation of the world from nothing means that the world is contingent and that God exists independently of the world, which could have never existed. In the theogony–cosmogony, however, which Žižek refers to, God is initially an abyss of free will, followed by an emptying, a *kenosis* towards the emergence of nothing/zero and then the emergence of Being in opposition to nothing/zero, with God Himself being then self-realized through the creation of the world and within history, which emerges together with temporality.

Žižek develops this theogony–cosmogony, connecting it to the emergence of the subject and culture. The subject is constituted by the symbolic system.

And here we may remember Louis Althusser seeking to demonstrate how the subject is constituted precisely by the dominant symbolic discourse that, in a Godlike gesture, calls it forth to existence. The establishment of the Symbolic entails the repression of the Real in the Lacanian sense. The Real is at the same time what lies beyond the Symbolic, i.e. what cannot enter the symbolic order, something which the Symbolic cannot reach. The Real is also an inner core of the Symbolic that makes its appearance as a crack, a hole, an internal failure and subversion. What remains from the Real is the so-called *objet petit a*, according to the Lacanian terminology, which is an object, since it is external to the Symbolic and the subject that has been constituted as a subject by that Symbolic. And it is *small*, because it is that which is left from the repressed big Real. And it is "*a*" from "*autre*," as opposed to the Big Other. The *objet petit a* mobilizes the desire of the subject, which attempts to reach a Real that is simultaneously beyond the Symbolic but also in its inwardly subversive inner core. Since, however, the Real is perpetually beyond reach, desire operates permanently through substitutes. When a subject's desire is fulfilled, the subject understands that this is not what it wanted but a mere substitute. Thus, it has to desire something else, and this cycle takes place perpetually. Žižek juxtaposes the notion of desire operating through substitutions to the *drive*, which concerns the founding moment of the symbolic system and is repressed. The drive is more associated with the subject's fundamental fantasy. The fundamental fantasy defines the subject by being itself repressed and unconscious. It is a kind of founding act that constitutes the symbolic system by being itself its repressed exception. Žižek names this fundamental fantasy the "ultimate predestination" of the subject, reminding us of the term used by John Calvin and inspired by Augustine of Hippo. The paradox is that the fundamental fantasy may be a pre-conscious "absolute predestination" of the subject, but it is also the precondition for the exercise of the subject's freedom. It is, of course, distinguished from the primordial, abysmal freedom of the theogony before the subject's genesis. As a contributing factor to the constitution of the subject, however, the fundamental fantasy constitutes a freedom that is interwoven with what Žižek calls "absolute predestination" as it directs the subject to a horizon that has been chosen by it on a pre-conscious level, while subsequently the subject's freedom is being exercised in view of this horizon rather than in a vacuum.

It is worth examining how Žižek analyzes a variety of cultural traditions in relation to this process that constitutes the subject. He sees the Jewish tradition in relation to the Law. The Law forbids and thus, according to Žižek, creates the illusion that it is because of the Law that the Thing is inaccessible, while the Thing is inaccessible anyway. In this way, the Law mobilizes the desire, which is intensified by the prohibition dictated by the Law. This interconnection of Law and desire that Žižek formulates in Lacanian terms is also the psychoanalytic truth of the connection that the Apostle Paul makes between the Law and sin. The difference between the Jewish Law and law in general as we encounter it in other cultures, including pagan cultures like the Graeco–Roman one, is that Jewish Law excepts the Jews from the other nations and makes them special. It is a law that is neither utilitarian nor a social contract, but a law that constitutes an exceptional community. By extension, it does not have some features that law has in other systems as constitutive of a certain ideology, such as the obscene superego supplement, i.e. the categorical command to enjoy according to Lacan. The Jews are fully identified with their Law without the obscene superego supplement and without the false ideology we encounter in other ideological systems; their Law, however, exists in a dialectical relationship with the desire that it intensifies; hence, Judaism is in a sense a religion of desire.

When Žižek analyzes Judaism, the primary figure he focuses on is not Moses – as was the case with Freud – or David, but Job. Correspondingly, Christ is not so much a new Moses or a new David but rather a new Job. As we have seen, the relationship between Law and Thing is that the Law creates through its prohibitions the impression that it is the Law that makes the Thing prohibited and thus inaccessible, while the Thing is inaccessible anyway. Thus, the Law intensifies the desire and leaves it unfulfilled, in spite of the fact the desire would not be able to conquer the Thing regardless of the Law's prohibitions. In Žižek's theology, which is influenced here by Hans Jonas, God is weak. This would be the difference between Žižek and a properly Schellingian theogony. While the world of the Symbolic is created by the Word/Logos, and it is with this that we are incorporated in temporality, the Thing of religion that is repressed is rather the weakness of God or the absence of the divine Thing. This is what the story of Job implies. The story of Job comprises, according to Žižek, the first critique of ideology, since the theological reasons that the theologians invoke to account for the pain of Job are denounced by God Himself as false. Job is not, as in the cliché, the one who endures his misfortunes; on the contrary, he protests at any opportunity against these misfortunes, and God's answer, according to Žižek, is a void boasting that ultimately confirms his weakness. The crucial element for Žižek is that while Job perceives the Divine weakness, he is silent. Since then, according to Žižek, the attitude of the Jews consists in silence concerning the weakness of God. This is their secret and their apophaticism, which has made them into a community that has endured through the ages. And Christ is the new Job because He reveals the weakness of God where Job remained silent.

The truly important element for Žižek in this context is Christ's cry on the Cross: "My God, my God, why have you abandoned me?" (Mark 15:34; Matthew 27:46) – a central point which will be considered more fully later. For Žižek, the silence of God in the face of this question is the disclosure of God's absence. Therefore, according to Žižek, Christianity is the religion of revelation and disclosure, primarily in the sense that it reveals and discloses the non-existence of the divine Thing. And if in Job we had a relationship of man with God, where man honors the weakness of God in his silence, in Christ we have an internal dialectical evolution of God where the Son of God is in pain and is dying, and God is weak and incapable of saving Him. In this sense, Christianity is for Žižek the religion of exiting religion; it is the last religion, and Crucifixion, likewise, is not exactly a sacrifice, but it is the sacrifice of exiting all sacrifices, the sacrifice which abolishes the sacrificial logic in its very depth, the last sacrifice. Žižek is a theologian of the Cross; thus, for him, salvation is identified with the Crucifixion. We could say that the Crucifixion is equated in Žižek with the Revelation, the Resurrection, the Ascension and the Pentecost. Salvation is the revelation of God's non-existence, and the Resurrection is the coming of the Spirit, which is the interiorization of the sacrificed, which constitutes the community of the ones left behind, so that the Crucifixion coincides with the foundation of the Church at the Pentecost.

The community of the Holy Spirit, to which we shall return in greater detail shortly, is for Žižek a very special community. It is the community of those who are absolutely unique and special in the sense that it is the community of those who cannot belong to any community. This is because in this atheist theology, the revelation of the absence of the divine Thing on the Cross allows all those who desire ultimate freedom and responsibility to create each one's life for herself. The salvation offered on the Cross is defined by Žižek as "traversing the fantasy." With the revelation of the void in the place of the divine Thing, the Law is abolished because it can no longer render the Thing inaccessible to desire. Desire then no longer strives for the unattainable but can be invested in the wholly specific and particular. Desire turns into love. If desire in the pre-Christian world is an endless and perpetual hunt, Christian love denies this futile hunt and constitutes an insistence on the very specific and particular, an investment on the particular with an absolute value. This is the meaning of love for one's neighbor or even for one's enemy. The object of our desire is not the *perfect* or the *ideal*, so that we would constantly pursue substitutes of the Thing, abandoning the one for the other. When desire becomes love, the neighbor is the wholly contingent, any random person, whom we invest with the value of the divine Thing.

The moment of the Crucifixion, where the absence of the divine Thing is revealed, is a moment of vertiginous freedom. Žižek reformulates traditional theological visions in an arresting way via psychoanalysis. He considers the Crucifixion as the revelation of the absence of the divine Thing as a "traversing" of the fundamental fantasy, which "predestines" the subject. This means that the subject may be "re-pre-destined."[4] That is, if we consider the traditional doctrine of absolute predestination as it has been formulated e.g. from Calvin with St. Augustine as its precursor, then we could say in an original modification of their insights that this predestination is not final, but that thanks to the Crucifixion there is the possibility of a new "predestination." Thus, the theological notion of predestination is adopted by Žižek in the sense that freedom is not freedom of choice in the void but comes together with a pre-conscious fundamental fantasy. At the same time, Žižek thinks that this is a predestination that can be re-pre-destined *but not at will*, through a conscious choice. What is required for this is a "crucifixion" in the theological idiom, which, psychoanalytically, we may term deconstruction of the subject. For Žižek, the experience of "crucifixion" is not a velvety one; it is a symbolic death. "Resurrection" after "crucifixion" is for our atheist theologian not a literal physical resurrection, as in the traditional Christian faith. It is, however, a "rebirth" with the possibility of a new predestination in terms of our fundamental fantasy, which only arises when we have recovered our primordial and abysmal freedom at the Crucifixion, i.e. at becoming aware of the absence of the divine Thing. Rebirth is then identified with love, which is built on desire and orients it towards the absolutely specific, unique and particular object irrespective of its value – hence the love for the humble, the sinner or even the enemy.

The authentic community of love, which has emerged after the traversing of the fundamental fantasy and the vertiginous freedom of the Crucifixion as a community of the utterly unique ones that cannot belong to any community, can be likened to a particular community of psychoanalysts in the Lacanian sense or with an authentic communist collectivity. The important aspect in the community of psychoanalysts is that they themselves have passed through the stage of analysis, transfer and counter-transfer, and that is why they can be the *objet petit a* for their own analysands. We could say in a Christian idiom that this is a community where everyone is the "treasure" for his or her neighbor. The community among psychoanalysts is, according to Žižek's interpretation of Lacan, a community beyond the desire and towards the assumption of the drive. This satisfies Žižek's criteria for naming it a community of the Holy Spirit, that is, a community of the wholly unique, as it is a community based on unique relationships. Likewise, the communist community can be considered to have a similar relationship to capitalism as that of authentic Christianity to Judaism. Just as authentic Christianity is thought to be taking the momentum of the Jewish desire that is intensified by the Law and directing it towards love for the absolutely particular neighbor, so does the communist community assume the canalizing of desire that is a primary element of capitalism which works by substitution (i.e. by utilizing the desire of subjects and setting unattainable and constantly changing consumerist goals for them) and channels this momentum to real relationships with an emphasis on political particularity. And in the same way that we say that Christianity could not have existed if Judaism had not prepared its advent and preceded it, in a similar Marxist sense we could say that communism cannot exist unless capitalism prepares it in a dialectical manner. In both cases, love is built on a dialectical modification of desire. In certain cases, Žižek speaks of this communist community as if it is comprised by the ones that have been rejected by the capitalist world, by the ones who have no place in it. As a general observation, in Žižek the criterion of *exclusion* is an important criterion for asserting that we have here a real communist subject.

In all three cases, the emancipatory subject is by no means historical institutional Christianity or communism or, perhaps, any institutional community of psychoanalysts. On the contrary, historical institutional Christianity is analyzed by Žižek in terms of "perversion," and we could say that Stalinism and "actually existing socialism" (including non-Stalinist forms such as Titoism, to which young Žižek was opposed) follows institutional Christianity as a perverted version of communism. Historical institutional Christianity restores the Big Other of the Symbolic. This means that not only does historical Christianity fail to capture what Žižek considers to be the great message of emancipatory atheism in Christ's cry on the Cross, but it also builds a faith in a personal God, Who is indeed articulated with the wisdom of the Graeco–Roman world. We must, of course, observe that it would be too far from Žižek's logic to point out a certain particular moment after which the alienation of Christianity began, e.g. Pauline theology, or the Hellenization of Christianity, or Constantine the Great, or the Vatican, or the Crusades, or the Holy Inquisition and so on. On the contrary, according to Žižek's logic, alienation exists from the very beginning together with what is assumed as authenticity, and it is probably authenticity itself that is the exception or subtraction of an ever-existing alienation. On the other hand, we may also point out some elements that constitute the perverted core of historical institutional Christianity according to our atheist theologian. One of these is the coexistence of Christianity with the Graeco–Roman world: Christianity may have conquered the Graeco–Roman world, but ultimately it became united with it in a hybrid that retains the characteristics of the latter, such as cosmic order. Medieval Christian thinkers compose a Christianity with a certain particular cosmology where the position of man prevails in the cosmic and natural order, which constitutes a regression of Christianity to paganism. Here Žižek's critique of the Middle Ages (East and West) has certain Protestant elements, as does his theological thought in general. It is worth noting that while Žižek considers Christianity as a transcendence of Judaism, which necessarily leaves Judaism behind, at the same time he would assert that in order for a Christian to become an *authentic* Christian he or she has to be Judaized or re-Judaized, i.e. to abandon the cohabitation with paganism that was the historical fate of Christianity and to return to the Jewish roots, as some Protestant communities to some extent actually did.

The main core of historical Christianity's perversion is its sacrificial logic, which took the sacrifice of Christ on the Cross as another sacrifice among many sacrifices, repeating in its interpretation elements characteristic of paganism. Theories such as that Christ is offered as ransom to the devil for the redemption of a captive human race, or, on the contrary, to God the Father in order to satisfy His divine justice according to the teaching of Anselm of Canterbury, constitute a regression in a logic of sacrificial exchange, which is a symbolic system with a powerful divine Big Other and with all the features that such a system has, such as false ideology and the obscene superego supplement. One could even say that Christianity became the archetype of ideology with an obscene superego supplement, followed later by Stalinism as a perverted modification of communism with the same characteristics of sacrificial logic, and so on.

It is important to understand how a "perverse" core is to be defined. Certain fundamental psychoanalytic terms are interpreted by Žižek in relation to ideology and its Big Other. In this context, the "perverse" is the one who is identified with the (presumed) desire of the Big Other.[5] The "pervert" obeys the obscene superego supplement which is defined after Žižek's interpretation of Lacan with the categorical imperative "Enjoy!" The "pervert" draws an excessive pleasure from obedience to the orders of ideology as well as a certain shame, which is but the proof of having previously experienced an excessive enjoyment. Besides, what is characteristic of ideology is its "inherent transgressions," namely the fact that ideology leads to the psychological need for transgressions which are somehow tolerated by those who participate in it. In Christianity, the "pervert" is the one who follows the sadomasochism of the sacrificial interpretation of Christianity, which is turned into an ideological religion hiding its subjacent emancipatory content. In a similar way, a Stalinist ideologist is identified with the symbolic Big Other and draws excessive enjoyment from the obscene superego supplement by participating in the inherent transgressions of Stalinism.

Žižek belongs to a tradition of thinking which distinguishes emphatically between the institutional religion on the one hand and a deeper emancipatory meaning or ontological reality of Christianity on the other. The service that Žižek's view offers to Christians and atheists alike is in this context multiple. First, Žižek offers psychoanalytical intuitions on the "pervert" character of institutional Christianity and its evolution. It is then possible to develop an analysis of both Christianity and the cultures that have resulted from it. This is valuable for a Christian because it offers the possibility to distinguish between, on the one hand, some authentic elements and, on the other, its regression into paganism, the sacrificial logic, ideology and perversion. (Even though we would be more precise if we were to say that this is actually not a regression, but a novel hybrid reality.)

Second, Žižek enables us to see how Christianity is a symptom of wider cultural evolutions, both material and psychological. In this perspective, the atheist can witness in Christianity the archetype of ideological alienation, which mirrors evolutions in the material and psychological conditions. Third, and perhaps most distinctively, Žižek proposes Christ as an exit from ideological alienation. The event of Christ is thus more actual than ever in our ideological era. The theologian can find in Žižek's thought a version of Christ who is part of the solution and not of the problems of our post-modern world. Žižek thus offers a very distinctive Christological and theological vision. And, fourthly, this vision is linked to psychoanalytical and communist collectivities in a version of contemporary soteriology which combines both communitarianism and absolute individualism in a fascinating *coincidentia oppositorum*.

In Žižek's thought, Christ is placed in the very avant-garde of modernity's program. It is true that there have been in the past thinkers who have linked modern emancipatory currents of thought to Christianity, such as Christian existentialists, thinkers following Liberation theology, etc. However, what makes Slavoj Žižek unique is the fact that he links the particularly atheist emancipatory avant-garde of modernity with Christ; for example, he links atheist existentialism or communism, as well as the anti-ideological elements in psychoanalysis, with Christ. One could say that it is Slavoj Žižek who truly realizes the famous dictum of Fyodor Dostoevsky "If someone proved to me that Christ is outside the truth and that in reality the truth were outside of Christ, then I should prefer to remain with Christ rather than with the truth." What in Dostoevsky is only a hypothesis aiming to prove his love for Christ through a *regressio ad absurdum* becomes something meant quite literally by Žižek, even though the latter's version would rather be

> if someone proved to me that Christ is outside the existent God of theism and that in reality the existent God of theism were outside of Christ, then I should prefer to remain with Christ rather than with the existent God of theism.

Or even better:

> if Christ proved to me that the God of theism is outside truth and that in reality the truth were outside of the God of theism, then I should prefer to remain with Christ rather than with the God of theism.

Žižek thus puts Christ at the avant-garde of emancipatory atheism and shows in a very original way how one can be an atheist together with Christ. Žižek's version of the famous diction by Saint Paul, "I have become all things to all people so that by all possible means I might save some" (1 Corinthians 9:22) would be "to the atheists I have become an atheist, to win the atheists."

Christ thus becomes a liberator not only from every system of oppression, as is the case in Liberation theology, but from every system *as such*, from every ideology and from every quest for positivist knowledge, including the sort of positivist knowledge promoted by Christian theistic systems, such as for example certain forms of dogmatics or scholasticism. Thus, Christ is presented as the liberator from every dogmatism, including the dogmas about His own nature.

One could add that what Žižek realizes is a combination of the figure of Christ not only with existentialism – this was already performed by Christian existentialists – but with *properly atheist* existentialism. Žižek's Christ guarantees the absolute freedom of an absolutely singular individual – or of some version of subjectivity which would be even more singular than the individual – the absolute uniqueness and non-repeatability of such singularities, or even a sort of rebellion against the "heavens" and against any kind of metaphysical certainty. In a sense, Žižek's Christ also realizes the Nietzschean *Übermensch* not as a Superman, but as an "Overman" who has gone past man.[6] It could be said that such a Nietzschean "Overman" is in Žižek a complement of the Chalcedonian formula "fully God and fully man." In Žižek's interpretation, the divine element of Christ is the fact that he overcame man. What is more, Christ is an ally of man in his struggle against religious alienation as denounced by Ludwig Feuerbach, as well as against religion as an "opium of the people" criticized by Karl Marx. Žižek's Christ is thus present in all the emancipatory programs of modernity, especially in those which take place against religion or against the traditional God of theism. Žižek's Christ is the perpetual ally of man in his endeavor to be liberated from oppression, including the oppression he imposes upon himself in the guise of ideology and totalizing knowledge. Žižek links Christ with what is particularly human, namely the death drive as a quest for vertiginous freedom. The fact that Christ is the universal man means that he represents the drive as such, or the human excess that this drive entails. Chalcedonian Christology is reformulated in a radical way by Žižek. The faith in the full divine and human nature of Christ is seen by Žižek in relation to the Crucifixion. The Crucifixion entails a removal of the gap between God and man (human nature), which is an internal gap inside God. God is thus reconciled with Himself, and His catholicity (divine nature) is applied to humanity. Furthermore, the "community of the Spirit" – to which we shall return shortly – constitutes a Christological combination of the two most important programs of modernity, namely communitarianism and individualism, i.e. the emphasis on the liberation of the individual in its singularity or even solitude.

Okay – but can Slavoj Žižek be counted among the theologians?

No (i.e. not in the *strict* sense) – and it is precisely this that renders him exceedingly interesting from a theological point of view. One may assert that a theologian is, for all intents and purposes, someone who speaks and theorizes about God and religion, but arguably one of the truly *defining* characteristics of the theologian is that she *actually believes*, that she *has faith in God*. Žižek's engagement with theological topics presents us with all the characteristics of a theologian – a theoretical discussion about God, God's nature, the Christian religion, the Christian church, even a Christology and a Pneumatology[7] – yet he explicitly lacks the very defining characteristic of a theologian: *faith*. The totality of Žižek's engagement with Christianity rests on the premise that *God does not exist*. Fortunately, it is Žižek himself who has provided us through his writings with a terminology in order to describe someone that bears all the *external* characteristics of something, but certainly without having the *defining* characteristic thereof, the one characteristic that makes it what it is: *decaf*.[8] Slavoj Žižek is a decaffeinated theologian.

To respond to our titular question anew: *yes*, Slavoj Žižek can be counted among the theologians – as an *inverted* or, more accurately, *decaffeinated* version of a theologian. And one whose insights are in many ways, as we shall see, acutely interesting to full-caffeine theology – to a theology that, well, would assert the existence of the Christian God. For it may be the case that, so far as theology is concerned, Slavoj Žižek is, as it were, *on the outside looking in*; what he sees, however, might at times be more discerning and rich than what the intellectuals who are already "inside" are able to make out.

It is certainly the case that not everybody is convinced that such a dialogue would indeed make sense, i.e. that there is anything of actual theological significance in the dialogue between Christians and atheist theology such as Žižek's. To cite an example, one might recall John D. Caputo's review of the Milbank–Žižek dialogue as encapsulated in *The Monstrosity of Christ: Paradox or Dialectic*, where Žižek is portrayed as trying to create a Trojan horse in order to sack Christianity from the inside:

> Furthermore, we all know that Žižek can very well make his main case with no mention of Christ at all, that he can use the seminars of Lacan, the films of Alfred Hitchcock or the novels of Stephen King just as well. His whole point, as he says elsewhere, is subversive: to build a Trojan-horse theology, to slip the nose of a more radical materialism under the Pauline tent of theology in order to announce the death of God . . . For truth to tell, Žižek doesn't think there is a God himself who dies. Never was. The treatment is over when we realize that.[9]

Our concern with this critique lies in Caputo presenting the fact that Žižek does in no way whatsoever assert the existence of God or the divinity of Christ more or less as a concealed *secret* – a secret which at the precise moment it becomes revealed renders the whole treatment and discussion redundant. This, however, could not be farther from the truth: the explicit *starting point* of Žižek's engagement with Christian theology is that the vantage point of such an engagement consists in a conscientious atheism – something, of course, which is primarily declared *to the Christians*. In our understanding, no Christian theologian would look to Žižek on Christianity with precisely the same expectations of insights *from within* the faith with which she would approach a celebrated theological thinker: *one is never served decaf by mistake*. Of course, Caputo's position is much more nuanced than what we present here – but it remains the case that the thesis that Žižek attempts to "trick the Christian out" of her Christianity is indeed its core:

> "Christ" for [Žižek] is a nickname for a way to contract the void, and the Passion story is an allegory or Vorstellung of a philosophical point he can make in any number of ways. [Žižek] discusses Christian doctrines like the Trinity, the Incarnation and the Crucifixion the way an analyst talks with a patient who thinks there is a snake under his bed, trying patiently to heal the patient by going along with the patient's illusions until the patient is led to see the illusion. Žižek agrees with

Chesterton the way the analyst agrees with the patient, where the whole question is, how do we deal with this snake, as he is obviously quite large and growing larger with every day. Then at some precisely timed and strategic point, the analyst softly asks, "Do you think perhaps it is something else disturbing your sleep?"[10]

Rather than the treatment coming to a conclusion, it is in our opinion precisely when Žižek sets the frame of his *atheist* theology that the discussion with caffeinated theologians may take off. The question, then, is precisely *what* a dialogue *on this basis* may bring, and we hope that the present volume attests to the fact that it can prove to be quite an auspicious dialogue. In an indirect response to the question concerning the possible fruits of such a "Trojan horse" theology, allow us to digress and, adding Triadological insult to the theological injury, briefly present Slavoj Žižek's Christological and Pneumatological insights, along with taking a closer look at the influence of Alain Badiou on Žižek and at their creative engagement with the Apostle Paul as a symbol of *political* universalism.

Paul, Žižek, Badiou, the Holy Spirit and the Cross

If Alain Badiou can be described as an "atheist theologian," Slavoj Žižek self-identifies as an "atheist Christian" in an attempt to exhaust Hegelian dialectics. His rationale is that history in the Common Era progresses through contradictions and extensions, which according (not exclusively) to Žižek have been inaugurated by Christianity as a religion constituting an exit from religion. Painting with a broad brush, we would say that a (Western rather than Orthodox) Christian Triadology, in which the Son is juxtaposed to the Father and is sacrificed on the Cross while the Spirit is the loving link between them, is the archetype of the Hegelian dialectical position of thesis, antithesis and synthesis – or, more precisely, the *Aufhebung* of the *Aufhebung*.

But it would also be an archetype of Marxist dialectics, where the position of the sacrifice of the Son can be assumed by the revolution and the position of the community of the Holy Spirit can be assumed by the classless society.

In this Triadology, the Son and Christ is not the "Right Hand of the Most High," as many Christians like to remember it, but is instead as it were the "Left of the Most High," the "Revolutionary of God," and it is up to the Spirit to constitute universality.

Žižek's purpose is to demonstrate that the true dialectical materialist cannot but be the heir of Christian civilization, but also that the true Christian is one who through Christianity has transcended religion itself in the direction of dialectical materialism. In this reasoning, Žižek vigorously defends the Christian heritage and Paul in particular within a post-modern world of late capitalism that is turning to spirituality, alternative religions such as Zen and Buddhism and New Age syncretism – or regresses into an apophatic (deconstructionist) Judaism without the Incarnation of the Messiah.

In referring to dialectics, we refer to an understanding in which concepts are not static and self-defined but rather opposed to one another in a dynamic motion, in which a third sublates both of them at once and transforms them into a continuum at a higher level. Being, for example, cannot be defined *by itself*, but only in contrast to non-being, while both are sublated but also made complete in the *becoming*. In this, Žižek follows dialectical thinking to its most extreme paradoxes. What is particularly striking is that he contemplates the history of Judaism and Christianity, and Paul *par excellence*, with an acutely piercing and discerning psychoanalytic gaze and connects them to the modern realities of capitalism and communism as well as psychoanalysis itself – all these seen as generated from the Christian heritage through a historical dialectical itinerary.

It is Žižek's insistence on dialectics that opposes him, as noted earlier, to (his otherwise comrade, philosophically and otherwise) Alain Badiou, who paints an anti-dialectical portrait of Paul.[11] In theological terms, Badiou is a "theologian of the Resurrection," while Žižek a "theologian of the Crucifixion" – since dialectics emphasizes the inherent need for the Crucificial sacrifice for the advent of the Resurrection and the Pentecost of the Spirit. Despite his "heretical" interpretation of Christianity as a religion with a perverse core, Žižek is a valuable interlocutor for theologians, as he focuses on how Paul's Christianity is a way out of the "Judaism" of globalized capitalism in towards a new "communism" of love (one that would be different, of course, from "actually existing socialism").

In his analysis of Paul, Žižek follows a number of insights by Badiou and especially Agamben, who is more dialectical, and incorporates them into a kind of Hegelian dialectical process.[12] In Badiou we encounter the wholeness ("Greek"), the part and exception ("Jew"), and the subtraction (*soustraction*) of the universal from them both (the Christian fidelity to the *event*). In Agamben we encounter the triad of *whole*, *part* and *residue* as a non-non (the Christian: non-non-Greek and non-non-Jewish). Žižek reformulates this with the help of the Hegelian paradox of a *genus* that has only one species, whereas the residue that remains is the very universality of the *genus*. In a way, Žižek intends to maintain both a concept of universality along the lines of Badiou and a concept of residue along the lines of Agamben. Thus, we encounter a triad of *genus*, *species* and *residue* in which the latter ultimately assumes the nature of a universal genus.

This takes place within a dialectical movement. An initial universality is introduced. Its species may act as "the disgraceful," "the abhorrent." Žižek observes playfully that usually, when we refer to something as "special," this is because of its abhorrent nature – for example when we refer to "special measures" in state repression, or to "special conditions," and so on.

Ultimately, the residue forms an excess which helps the *genus* to reflectively find its own self within its species, in accordance with Hegelian dialectic. Following the (by now familiar) switch from Paul's time to ours, Žižek employs the conclusions of Michael Hardt and Antonio Negri, who analyzed the new order of globalized capitalism in terms of "empire" – precisely such as, as it happens, the Roman empire.[13] However, he also links those conclusions and tools to the thought of Ernesto Laclau and Jacques Rancière, according to whom the only truly democratic subject is the *residue*, i.e. that element of the Whole that does not have the particular characteristics that would grant it a place within the Whole, thus being temporary excluded.

By not being able to assume a certain ontic position, this residue becomes an ontological embodiment of universality. In other words, when each particular group asserts its particular interests, only the excluded are those who may embody universality. We may recall here the term *égaliberté* (liberty/liberté and equality/égalité together) of Etienne Balibar, which can only be embodied by the "non-existents," the "nobodies" such as the *liumang* (tramps) of modern feudal–capitalist China, who, by not participating in any existing class, "are displaced, and float freely, lacking work-and-residence, but also cultural or sexual, identity and registration."[14] It is with such a notion of reflective dialectical incarnation of universality within the residue that we can understand Paul's dictum: "God chose the lowly things of this world and the despised things – and the things that are not – to nullify the things that are" (1 Cor 1:28).

Žižek adds a dimension that is not stressed adequately in the two thinkers at hand, namely that this community of the non-existents is the community of the Holy Spirit. We will need to develop here Žižek's dialectical Triadology in its relevance to the capitalist context and psychoanalysis. If, according to Sigmund Freud, God the Father is the slain archaic father, for Žižek He is the absent Father who resembles the Thing of Lacanian psychoanalysis – that is, as we have said, that which remains unsymbolized and ineffable. We are here in the terrain of Judaism, which, with the terminology of Lacanian psychoanalysis, is based on the contrast of the Real and the Symbolic.

In referring to the "Symbolic," we are primarily referring to the Judaic Law, which, with the great detail of its provisions, is always lifting up obstacles and curtains in order to hide a unsymbolizable and uniconizable God such as the iconoclastic God of Judaism. St. Paul, however, in a spectacular psychoanalytic (*avant la lettre*) insight reveals that desire is caused by the Law (just like sin). Judaism is, therefore, the religion of desire, where the Symbolic, which in the form of the Law conceals an uniconizable God "behind a curtain," as it were, intensifies our desire indefinitely and establishes the subject itself as the desiring subject.

Thus, we arrive at the Žižekian interpretation of Pauline Christology,[15] a Christology that can be extended beyond Paul as well.[16] In Christian soteriology there are two primary ways of contemplating salvation. The first and more Eastern one consists in seeing it as divinization, as *theosis*. The second and more Western one is to see salvation as a path towards the perfect man. Žižek conjoins the two, however, in a rather "downward" direction. That is, according to Žižek, Christ is God *precisely in the sense that He embodies what is particularly human*: the excess in nature, that which is rejected from the natural world. We are situated here within a Hegelian Triadology, where everything that is the case in the relationship between God and man applies to the *interior* of God. The fact that Christ embodies the chasm between man and nature is identified with the chasm between God and man, but also between Father and Son. In contrast, however, with every individual human person, Christ fully embodies the rejected excess from nature that is humanity. It is for this reason that he is the human person *par excellence* (the *ecce homo* of Pontius Pilate) but also the "man without qualities" (the latter Christological title is derived from Robert Musil's homonymous novel, which reminds us of the dogmatic position – of a pending status within theology – that the human nature assumed by Christ is universal and "without properties"). This is why Christ is also the *Übermensch* in the Nietzschean sense of the term. Ultimately, Christianity is for Žižek the religion of revelation because Christ reveals the death of the divine Thing. This is particularly the case in the cry of God's abandonment on the Cross: "My God, my God, why have you forsaken me?"

The result is that Judaism is left behind as a religion based on desire seen as the dialectical contrast between Real (the uniconizable God the Father) and Symbolic (the Law) because, according to Žižek, of the revelation of the divine Thing's absence, which is defined by Žižek as the traversing of the fantasy. In Hegelian terms, Christ is the second part of a dialectical triad, a part that disappears (through the Crucifixion, but we would add to this the Ascension as well), so that the Spirit may enter the equation as the third term of the dialectical triad.

The Spirit is the constitution of the community of the "non-existents," the "non-beings" who have interiorized the sacrifice of Christ and have made the transition from the religion of the Law and desire to the religion of love.

What exactly does this mean? Alain Badiou underscores an absolute (non-dialectical) contrast between Law and love, as also do many Christian Orthodox theologians of the 1960s generation such as Christos Yannaras,[17] among others. Žižek, on the contrary, seems to contemplate love dialectically as opposed, of course, to the Law, yet in the sense that it results from an extreme absolutization and radicalization of the Law. For example, if the Law encourages you not to commit adultery, Christianity urges you not to commit adultery *even "in the heart."* Love is, as it were, a subversion of the Law by extending the Law to its most extreme consequences.

To this, however, the following should be added. The fading away of Judaism as a religion of the Law and desire (which are mutually supported by their antitheses) means that love has arrived as a focus on the absolutely particular that is the neighbor. In psychoanalytic terms, Judaism is based on the omnipotent desire which is metonymic, i.e. it flows infinitely from one object to another. Christianity, on the contrary, is founded on love as a drive (*Trieb*) that is addressed in a perpetually circular motion to a particular object.

Why Paul, then? Because today's globalized capitalism relies on a planetary predominance of desire as metonymy, according to which we are called to turn our attention to an endless hunt for shifting objects – commodities where this desire is invested. For capitalism, in a sense, sprang out of the quasi-neo-Judaizing roots of Protestantism. Today, Žižek is skeptical of neo-Judaizing theologies such as, for example, the deconstructionist philosophy of the (early) Jacques Derrida, which are compatible with capitalism rather than subversive of it. Against these, Pauline Christianity offers love as a non-negotiable focus on the absolutely particular neighbor. A love that is by definition violent, not so much because of its unwanted potential side effects, but in its very act of giving absolute value to the neighbor. In this sense, Žižek approaches Christian love as a kind of communism or socialism which, however, is not to be identified with "actually existing socialism." Rather than that, as we noted earlier, it is the community of the excluded who interiorize the sacrifice of Christ: the community of the Holy Spirit.

However, this is but one way to approach Žižek's atheist theology. What different routes could one take?

Theistic ways into an atheist theology

Among the potential strategies that could be employed in order to approach elements of Žižek's thought with theological relevance one can mention the following. (i) It is illuminating to examine the cases where Žižek's psychoanalytic analyses could serve in the direction of a fruitful cultural critique of institutional Christianity and Christian societies. This issue is important not only from a sociological point of view, but also for every Christian intellectual who would wish to take account of the cultural consequences of her religion, and Žižek offers a very interesting narrative. (ii) Religion can be plausibly understood as a symptom of dialectical material relations. The study of religion as such a symptom can thus offer insights not only into the deeper material relations of the society, but also into the symbolic which supports it. What is crucial is that a given religion provides a coherent narrative which could thus make explicit what is more difficult to discern at the level of material relations. Both atheists and theologians may thus be interested in how Žižek relates religious narratives or even dogmas to civilizational paradigms.

Furthermore, (iii) for a theologian Žižek's thought can be seen as of fundamental importance through the use it makes of its distinction between historical institutional Christianity on the one hand and the emancipatory message of Christ on the other. The latter leads to a quite distinctive soteriology, indeed a remarkably radical soteriological vision. A theologian could be interested in such a vision as an original interpretation of the traditional soteriological one, which is an interpretation that brings traditional soteriology into relation with the avant-garde of modernity, including psychoanalysis and Marxism but also existentialism, as well as some values of secular Enlightenment in general. (iv) Žižek's work is of special interest for someone concerned with apologetics and with the dialogue between the Christian religion and the sciences, since he has articulated his anthropology in an original dialogue both with religion and with scientific findings and theories such as quantum mechanics or the theory of evolution.

Apart from this, (v) what is urgently needed is a critical dialogue between theologians and Žižek's thought, putting the specific question of what could survive from Žižek's interpretation if one believes in the Resurrection of Christ and in the Holy Trinity as a Trinity of Persons coexisting in an eternal loving relation. The crucial question is whether the dialectical vision of Christianity that we find in thinkers such as Hegel and Žižek could be combined with a true faith in the Resurrection. Similarly, what could survive from the program of dialectical immanence, were one to believe in a transcendent God? Can the cry of the divine dereliction be read next to "Father, into your hands I command my spirit" (Luke 23:46)? The general sense of such questions would be whether faith in the actual Resurrection of Christ, in the eschatological bodily resurrection of humanity and in the eternal loving coexistence of the Persons of the Trinity, simply annuls Žižek's theory about Christianity as revealing an emancipatory message of dialectical immanence or whether something can be kept from these profound Žižekian insights, even if one is faithful. In this way, Žižek could be brought into dialogue with Christian thinkers who do believe in the Resurrection and endeavor to thematize it in their thought, even if in an apophatic manner. The latter possibility constitutes one of the main aims of our volume.

It is to be noted that the response of theologians to Žižek's thought has already lasted in time. One can mention representatives of the Radical Orthodoxy movement who have had a very fecund interaction with Slavoj Žižek. Graham Ward,[18] for example, thinks that a genuine theology can only be based on the notion of analogy, the latter being the correct response to a dialectics that leads to Hegelian immanence and Žižekian "Christian atheism." And we have already referred to the extensive Žižek–Milbank dialogue, so far including two books.[19] It will be helpful to pause at this point and see John Milbank's own response to the question why Žižek is relevant for theology proper in spite of his determinedly decaffeinated status:

You write of Slavoj Žižek, "In an important sense, he bears a theological witness." How can a self-described atheist bear a theological witness?

JOHN MILBANK: In Dostoevsky's novel *The Devils*, one character, Kirillov, speaks of both the necessity to believe in God as the reality of infinite goodness and the impossibility of doing so. His resolution of this dilemma is deliberate, meaningless suicide on the grounds that, in an atheistic world, he himself is now God, as possessor of a sovereign will, and that suicide is the highest demonstration of this will. Žižek tries to escape this dilemma in another way – by pointing to the figure of Christ, whom tradition has taken to be the incarnation of God in a single human life. Although, for Žižek, God is *only* present in incarnate guise and otherwise does not exist at all, he still insists that outside this Christian legacy we would not have had the sense of an absolute demand, exceeding all human law and custom. Indeed, the notion of incarnation sustains for Žižek the idea that this absolute demand, which orients our humanity, is more than human, even though it comes, he says, from "nowhere."

Against Žižek, you insist on the necessity of theism. What do you think are the prospects for a philosophical encounter with theology that doesn't assent to a transcendent deity?

JOHN MILBANK: I think that, in the end, the prospects are non-existent. Dostoevsky saw further than Žižek, because he dramatized the alternative existential stances in the face of nihilism, even a Christological nihilism. Kirillov tries self-assertion, but logically concludes that the only irrefutable act of "divine" self-assertion is self-slaughter. Stavorogin, in the same novel, adopts instead a malicious indifference, which he deploys seductively to derange the lives of others. But in the end, this leads to a suicide of mere despair. Žižek's Christ is merely a clown, the excreted everyman, the dross of the world. "The Good" is here reduced to the instance of that which exceeds reality, which finds no home. This places love beneath being, even if in a sense it is beyond being for Žižek, as the impossibility of realized desire. But at the end of *The Devils*, Dostoevsky suggests through the mouth of the dying Verkhovensky that love exceeds being in the sense that the real is orientated by the Good. Here, loving faith alone closes the circle of the ontological argument. The highest, which would include existence, must indeed exist. Without this idea of a perfect happiness for all of reality, which the most extreme misery cannot perturb, Dostoevsky contends that human beings lose their defining orientation. The final episodes of the novel try to depict scenes of disclosing recognition and forgiveness between people, which show how we can authentically participate in this infinite perfection and thereby transfigure the world.

Atheistic philosophy still finds itself caught in a theoretical version of the nihilistic *aporia* depicted by the 19th-century Russian novelist. Either, like Kirillov, it can assert human reason or freedom against the power of the void – but then this seems like self-vaunting wishful thinking; or else, like Stavrogin, it can deny the final reality of any human suppositions against the background of an indifferent nature. But in that case, the reality of reason itself is threatened. The atheistic logos will always lack either being or reason, without which there is no philosophy, no exercise of the love of wisdom.[20]

Of course, a *believing* theologian might engage in that most enriching dialogue with the atheist theology of Slavoj Žižek purely in order to understand, either *with the help of* Žižek's insights or *a contrario*, aspects and implications of her own tradition. One may not *necessarily* have the "ulterior motives" that John Milbank so succinctly, deliciously even, confesses to in that same interview:

Do you see your participation in this dialogue as evangelization? What do you hope to accomplish?

JOHN MILBANK: Yes. Victory.[21]

Žižek's dialogue with Boris Gunjević concerning Christianity, Judaism and Islam in *God in Pain: Inversions of Apocalypse* should certainly be mentioned here as well.[22] Other theological responses include the aforementioned John D. Caputo, among an ever-increasing number of scholars. Currently, at least two works present Žižek's relation to theology and study it, namely Frederick Depoortere's *Christ in Postmodern Philosophy*[23] and Adam Kotsko's doctoral thesis published as *Žižek and Theology*.[24] In light of all these we cannot but conclude that Žižek' dialogue with theology and theologians is a given, the only open question left being where this dialogue leads.

The world's most interesting heretic

To say that an atheist theologian such as Slavoj Žižek is, when considered from the perspective of historical orthodox Christianity, a "heretic" would be a redundant tautology which of itself brings little to the discussion. Such a proclamation, taken by itself, would be liable to give the impression that the one proclaiming it has not quite understood the context of the discussion and is at a certain dissonance with it, "not getting it," as one might say.

However, in Slavoj Žižek's case there are more, and more interesting, sides to considering him as a "heretic" – as a number of his intuitions and insights (from an external point of view as these might be) on the Christian God are based on premises that are readily identified in certain heresies of early Christianity, articulated at the time by people who did not, of course, consider themselves as atheist theologians, but whose confessions ended in their clash with the ecclesial community of the faithful and their exile from it. The fact that those same theological premises, particularly so far as the intra-Trinitarian relationships are concerned, appear in the twenty-first century in the work of atheist theologian Slavoj Žižek is, in our opinion, a particularly delicious coincidence or conjunction.

Anyone well-versed in the study of heresy (heresiology), which is also a favorite pastime of the Orthodox, can recognize in Žižek's thought a series of heresies of the early Church, which may be applied to Hegel as well. Sabellianism, theopassianism or patripassianism, supersessionism, epochalism, the heresy of the Son's Fatherhood (υιοπατορία), are only some of the names of interrelated Christian historical heresies with which one could compare this extreme form of dialectical thought.[25] (It is certainly the case, however, that other non-Žižekian forms of dialectical theology may be both orthodox and Orthodox.)

Our main point is that Žižekian thought is indirectly derived from forms of theology and Triadology in which it is not only the case that the divine Persons are contrasted (rather than just being related, as is the case with the Cappadocians), but also that the One disappears for the Other to come forth – as would be the case in the heresy of epochalism, in which history is divided into the ages and epochs of the Father, of the Son and of the Spirit. And also in the heretical doctrine of the Fatherhood of the Son (υἱοπατορία), where the sacrifice of the Son is inherently related to the death or disappearance of the Father (with the Žižekian addendum of the Son's death which is interiorized thanks to the Spirit).

To blame Žižek as a heretic is, of course, a futile enterprise, as one would be essentially preaching to the already converted, if not to the choir – no one is contesting Žižek's *un*orthodoxy. After all, it is he himself who has led dialectical thought to such a paradoxical form as to contend that only the heretic or even more so the *atheist* may embody today the truth of Christianity as a "Pauline materialism." In fact, he asserts that Paul himself is not only a new Moses, but also a "new Judas the Iscariot," namely a persecutor of the apostolic community who instead of committing suicide, repented and took the vacant position of Judas in order to "betray" the historical Jesus (of the micro-historical narrative) once more, so that through the interpretational "betrayal" the Christ of faith may emerge.

Furthermore, the fact that Žižek's conceptualization of the Trinity is readily recognized in a number of the heresies of the early Church should not, of course, render a Christian theologian unwilling to engage with the Lacanian heretic's thought, thinking that there is nothing of value therein – quite the contrary: the Christian should never forget that it is precisely in engagement with and contrast to "heresy," however defined, that the church's doctrinal formulations are actually articulated, that the church's testimony takes shape.

It is perhaps the case that a cultural relevance greater than that of heresiology, which Žižek himself would celebrate, lies in the observation that Žižek is born out of a Western Cross-centric mode of thinking, according to which the Incarnation of God the *Logos* is more or less identical to an "Indeathening," in which salvation emerges almost automatically as a result of the Crucifixion so that we do not have to wait for the Resurrection – and in which our salvation does not consist in being deified (*theosis*)[26] but in becoming "perfect" human beings (either in the sense of a moral superhuman or in the sense of a Nietzschean *Übermensch*, as is the case in Žižek). The question, then, of Paul's timeliness for the atheists of today seems to turn into a question of Žižek's timeliness for the Christians of today, and for Orthodox Christians at that. Our answer is that on the one hand he offers an acutely perceptive psychoanalytic probe into the history of a Christianity – mainly in its Western version – that is globalized today and is particularly relevant to the peoples of Southeast

Europe (let it be remembered that Žižek comes from Slovenia, the very border between East and West). Žižek is, therefore, a valuable interlocutor in the *a contrario* articulation of orthodox (and Orthodox) dialectical thought, such as the version based on Maximus the Confessor's triad of *logos–tropos–telos*. And, on the other hand, Žižek offers a very moving vision in our contemporary context: the vision of a community of the Holy Spirit comprised of the "non-beings," a community that breaks free from the perpetuation of capitalist desire, which circulates incessantly from one commodity to the other, in favor of a violent love for the concrete neighbor.

On the sublime object of this volume

To return to the contents of this book: following the present introductory chapter, the volume properly opens with Agon Hamza's "Žižek and the Dialectical Materialist Theory of Belief," which offers some crucial definitions relating to the subject of the volume. On the one hand, the chapter situates religion in terms of a philosophical tradition which has its roots in Hegel and Feuerbach, but also includes Marx and, arguably, Lacan, reaching up to Slavoj Žižek. On the other hand, it focuses on the importance given by the latter to the conception of a Christianity that is linked to dialectical materialism and to the claim that true dialectical materialism must pass through the Christian experience. Through these two questions of fundamental importance for our subject at hand, Agon Hamza endeavors to demonstrate why any thinker, i.e. not only Christian ones but also atheist ones, should take an interest in Christianity and in what the latter reveals. At a more specific level, the chapter points to the links between Christianity and dialectical materialism and responds to the question of why someone involved in the latter should also confront the issues raised by the Christian tradition.

A number of Agon Hamza's intuitions show the urgent character of this volume's endeavor. Feuerbach's fundamental insight was that religion is a redoubling of man's exteriorization in his creativity. In other words, man is externalized in his creations – such as his thoughts, dreams, imagination, feelings, beliefs, desires – and this exteriorization is redoubled by religion, which projects them to a transcendent realm. It is for this reason that Feuerbach's critique of religion aims at the comprehension of the particularly *human* character of human creativity. Karl Marx assumes this critique of religion as human alienation but focuses on the particularly material relations which are redoubled by religion. For Marx, it is capitalistic individual property that alienates man from the products of his labor, being aided in this by the state and the relevant social institutions. Religion then constitutes a redoubling of this particular capitalist state as well as of the associated capitalist society, and not just any kind of redoubling. Religion is, thus, the inverted consciousness of a world which is already inverted, since it is based on the worker's alienation. Religion can of course justify and confirm the social relations of power, but only because it mirrors them first. According to

Karl Marx, on the one hand, religion is a superstructure which is determined by material and social relations, which means that the alienation caused by religion is but a reflection of the alienation that already exists in these material and social relations. On the other hand, Hamza focuses on the particularly Marxist conception of religion as a redoubling, i.e. as a reflection or a mirroring of society. In examining this latter point, Hamza also valorizes some psychoanalytic intuitions.

When one sees oneself in the mirror, one does not only see oneself, but one also sees the world with oneself inside it. What the mirror offers is basically a coherent image of the world including ourselves in it. Hamza formulates this intuition dialectically as an absence of absence or an alienation of alienation offered by the mirror. When I see the world directly without a mirror, I myself am absent. But when I do see myself inside the world, as it is offered by the mirror, then the absence of myself in the direct view is lost and I thus acquire an excess of presence and coherence of myself. What such a Lacanian view seems to imply is that what appears in the mirror is not "less than me"; it is not a deficient copy of myself. On the contrary, it is "more than me"; it offers greater identity and coherence, as it grants me the possibility to witness myself from the outside.

This combination of Lacanian and Marxist intuitions leads to a very subtle analysis of religion. By being a mirror, a catoptric redoubling of social reality, religion offers consistency and coherence to this reality. Religion is a sort of mapping theory of the world. It allows the worker to see herself from the outside and thus dialectically "alienate her alienation." It is in this sense that religion constitutes, according to Marx, an encyclopedic compendium of the world. The redoubling of the world by religion offers to the "people" the possibility to "read" the relations which constitute its alienation. What in social reality is a *contradiction* (for example, the fact that the worker is not the owner of her products) becomes in religion an *opposition*, since religions are based on radical differences such as that between the Creator and the creature, and so on. Religion thus becomes a stage exposing the relations of social alienation to our gaze.

Hamza exposes the famous Marxist claim that religion is the "opium" of the people in its dual meaning, namely that opium is received by someone who is suffering and seeks a sort of anesthesia, but also a way out of reality in the realm of illusion. Hamza proposes, however, that we focus on the phrases which precede the claim where Marx also characterizes the suffering of religion as simultaneously an expression of real suffering and a protest against this suffering. The second part is, according to Hamza, a repetition of the experience of the world, which in some cases could even become a transcendence of the world, since the alienated man can conceive of his reflection in the mirror of religion as non-alienated. Hamza focuses on a sort of "epistemological" value of religion, as the latter can constitute a "theory of the world," offering man the possibility to see himself "from the outside" in a coherent narrative.

Whereas Feuerbach's critique consists in the fact that religion alienates man from the products of his creativity, in a Marxist perspective religion is rather the redoubling of a condition in which workers are already alienated by being deprived of the products of their labor. The critique of heaven becomes thus a critique of the earth; the critique of religion becomes a critique of the law and the critique of theology turns into a critique of politics. In all such cases, abstract relations replace concrete lacks of relation. One could equally add that religion as a redoubling makes visible a certain reification of abstract relations that takes place in capitalism. It is to be noted that Marx criticizes not religion in itself, but the social structure which is redoubled as religion. Religion is thus less an object of critique and more a model of comprehension which clarifies the social relations of alienation as well as the phenomenon of reification of abstract relations. For Hamza, the Marxist emphasis is not on how religion is an illusion which supports the capitalist system. On the contrary, it focuses more on how religion constitutes a stage where social relations become visible. It thus creates the possibility of interior critique to such relations.

And here is where the thought of Slavoj Žižek becomes exceedingly relevant. Žižek inherits a philosophical tradition in which immanence is the most crucial notion, and what is more, a version of *dialectical* immanence, i.e. an immanence which evolves through interior contradictions. What we should stress is that although a certain type of Christian religion could serve as a redoubling of relations of alienation and reification inside capitalism, Christianity can also show the exit out of this ideology. After demonstrating how religion is important as a mirror reflecting the relations which are developed in capitalism, a second, more crucial part, follows in which Christianity's dynamic can show the way out of such relations and their redoubling. The fundamental insight is here offered by Hegel, who stresses the significance of the divine dereliction in the Cross, i.e. the abandonment of Jesus by the Father. The theology of the Crucifixion leads Hegel to a "speculative Good Friday" which is tantamount to the "vanishing of the mediator." What "dies" on the Cross is the abstract character of the divine Being. If Christianity is the "religion of the Revelation," what is revealed is the abolition of the Divine Being in its abstract form. One could thus say that even if at a first level Judeo-Christian religion is mirroring the relations of the capitalist world, at a superior dialectical level this same structure of the theological mirror is "breaking" through the Christian emphasis on the Crucifixion and on the Sacrifice, by means of the latter being interpreted by Žižek as a dialectical abolition of the divine abstraction or rather as a revelation of the divine inexistence.

Judeo-Christianity presents two moments in dialectical tension: (i) a mirror which reproduces the alienation and reification of the world; and (ii) the possibility of disclosing this abstract conception of divine Being as abolishable, as the divine dereliction reveals. Žižek proceeds further than Hegel in that he insists on the material character of the abolishment of the abstract character of the divine Being. Whereas Hegel speaks of an objective Spirit that synthesizes the contradictions at a higher spiritual level, Žižek refers instead to the Spirit as the community of those who have interiorized sacrifice as the abolishment of the transcendent divine Thing. For Žižek, this community of interiorization of the abolishment of the divine abstraction can be not only an ecclesial community, a church, but also a community of heretics or even atheists. Such communities could nowadays include communities of communists, analysts, persons in love and so on. Žižek is the latest interpreter of a long tradition which includes Hegel, Feuerbach, Marx and Lacan, among many others, in that he sees Christianity as a religion of dialectical self-transcendence in the direction of atheist dialectical materialism. The crucial point is the (self-negating) belief in the sacrifice and the consequent "Spiritual" character of the communities that have interiorized this sacrifice. Agon Hamza's chapter demonstrates the basic point of this volume in a double sense: (i) religion is crucial because it is a mirror and a stage on which the relations of alienation and reification are repeated and reenacted in a more coherent and easily graspable way; the study of religion could thus prove fertile even for an atheist thinker. And (ii) what is offered by Žižek in particular is a dialectical comprehension according to which Christianity constitutes in its emancipatory core a possibility of exiting religious abstraction. The latter is achieved through the Crucifixion as divine dereliction and the community of the Spirit as an interiorization of the sacrifice. Žižek insists on a tradition of dialectical immanence in which Judeo-Christianity transcends divine abstraction from the inside in a way that nevertheless leads to atheist materialism. In the thought of Slavoj Žižek, the atheist will thus find the reasons for which it is Christianity itself which leads to the most authentic, heroic and profound form of atheism. Inversely, a believer will find in Žižek fascinating intuitions about the tensions within Christianity.

This volume thus properly begins with a chapter that touches upon the relation between the thought of Slavoj Žižek and Christianity in two crucial points: (i) the epistemological value of religion for whoever wishes to study our world in its social and material dimension, since religion offers a redoubling of this world as well as a reenactment of its relations with a greater coherence. This makes the thought of Slavoj Žižek especially relevant for an atheist. Further, (ii) in the context of a Hegelian–Marxist philosophical tradition of dialectical immanence, Christianity is not only a mirroring of social relations, but also a kind of emancipatory exiting from alienation and reification. However, by developing this subject from the point of view of dialectical immanence, Žižek insists that this emancipatory exit takes place from the inside and not from the outside. In other words, it is from the inside of the religion that one is saved from religion. This salvation from inside religion is achieved thanks to the two most important moments of Christianity as they are interpreted in a very distinctive way by Žižek. The first is the Crucifixion, i.e. the sacrifice of God in the person of Jesus Christ. And the second is the community of the Holy Spirit as an interiorization of the Crucified, and thus as a kind of Resurrection.

The volume aims to expose these two crucial moments of Christianity in the thought of Slavoj Žižek. The atheist will be able to witness in them an emancipatory exit from illusory ideology. But the faithful Christian will equally be able to observe an original interpretation of the two fundamental moments of Christian faith from the perspective of dialectical immanence. This exposition of Žižek's thought will not be a simple presentation, but rather a critical dialogue. Whereas Hamza's chapter touches upon Crucifixion and Resurrection from the point of view of an atheist thinker, in the continuation of the volume one may find chapters by Christian thinkers who engage critically with Žižek's dialectical materialist interpretation of the Crucifixion and the Resurrection. These chapters explore the fecundity of Žižek's proposal for an interpretation of Christianity in the context of dialectical immanence and its very distinctive contributions, but they also pose the question whether a genuinely theological interpretation could be combined with dialectical immanence as an absolute demand. Žižek's thought is thus compared to that of Christian thinkers such as Jean-Luc Marion, Emmanuel Falque, John Milbank, Thomas Altizer, Gabriel Vahanian, Gianni Vattimo and others, in order to examine different treatments of the same topics, and there is also a comparison with the Jewish thinker Emmanuel Levinas.

Some of the following chapters compare Žižek with thinkers who accept a communist or radical democratic stance, such as Alain Badiou and Jacques Rancière, whereas in one case there is a comparison with the psychoanalyst Jean-Claude Milner. Other chapters engage in a critical examination of Žižek's thought as part of a certain philosophical tradition which includes Georg Hegel, Ludwig Feuerbach, Karl Marx, Sigmund Freud and Jacques Lacan, but which also has Christian roots going back not only to modern thinkers such as Friedrich Schelling, Immanuel Kant or René Descartes, but also to more remote thinkers such as Martin Luther, Meister Eckhart, Thomas Aquinas or even Saint Paul. Such chapters place Slavoj Žižek in the context not only of the modern philosophical tradition of dialectical immanence, but also of Christian antecedents which sometimes present elements either of dialectics or of immanence, before these notions became a primary philosophical demand in the context of modern dialectical materialism.

Certain chapters, thus, critically inquire whether Slavoj Žižek has been a just interpreter of this long spiritual tradition. They point to some possible oversights in his interpretations or to the possibility of alternative interpretations of this same tradition. Last but not least, this volume includes a chapter that attempts a critical dialogue with Žižek's thought from the point of view of a Christian liberal thinker. For reasons of fullness, we have judged fit to include an exterior gaze on the tradition of dialectical materialism from a thinker who sees himself as belonging to the liberal tradition, namely Haralambos Ventis, who is nevertheless willing to converse with it, touching upon the same subjects of the Crucifixion and the Resurrection. The common ground between Christian liberals and Žižek is mainly the importance of the presence of Christianity in the public sphere in a post-modern world. In order to open and sustain a dialogue on the role of Christianity in the public square, it is vital to take account of the thought of different thinkers coming not only from the tradition of materialism, but also from that of liberalism, or supporting in general the ideals of the Enlightenment, as is the case, for example, with Jürgen Habermas.

The chapters in this volume contribute to the above questions in the following ways. A critical dialogue between the thought of Slavoj Žižek and a properly Christian belief in the bodily resurrection and in the eternal existence of the Trinity takes place in the chapter by Brian W. Becker, "From Psychoanalysis to Metamorphosis: The Lacanian Limits of Žižek's Theology," which undertakes a fruitful interdisciplinary dialogue with psychoanalysis. Becker starts by outlining Žižek's distinctive view that in the moment of the dereliction of Christ in the Cross, what dies is God as the Big Other, the One who pulls the strings of the historical drama. This could be seen as a "breaking" of the Symbolical in favor of the Real in the Lacanian sense of these terms. What is abolished is the sacrificial logic as a logic of exchange, in which *jouissance* is sacrificed in order to attain meaning. The Crucifixion is thus the last sacrifice, the sacrifice of exiting sacrifices and the sacrificial logic. The Resurrection which follows does not have a literal character of bodily resurrection but is rather the genuinely emancipated collectivity of the faithful without hierarchy or an ontological guarantee of symbolical meaning based on the Big Other.

Becker underscores the fact that Žižek indulges in a very serious study of finitude (or immanence, as we have preferred to term it). But he puts the question whether a genuine theology could be satisfied with finitude not only as a point of departure, but also as a *quasi* eschatological condition. He proposes to regard finitude both theologically and psychologically in the perspective of its transfiguration in the Resurrection of Christ. Becker is inspired by phenomenologists such as Emmanuel Falque and Jean-Luc Marion, maintaining, however, a dialogue with the key insights of Lacanian psychoanalysis. For Falque, finitude is philosophy's point of departure; it is the insurmountable horizon in which we confront suffering and mortality. Falque speaks of a primordial corporeal chaos which could be linked to a Nietzschean "unconscious of the body," i.e. an unconscious which is more immediately corporeal than Freud's psychological unconscious. In more Lacanian terms, this is the pre-symbolical flesh, the brute immediacy of the body, before it is inhabited by the signifiers of the Big Other. Falque speaks, just like Lacan, of a subject that is divided between raw corporeality and language, the primary difference being that in Falque this divide is in the version of oblivion and neglect, while in Lacan in that of the forced choice between either alienation or annihilation.

In Lacan, the primordial experience of finitude is tantamount to a forced dilemma between either meaning or the *jouissance* of the Thing. By choosing meaning, one is deprived of the *jouissance* and is alienated. By choosing being, one sacrifices meaning and is annihilated as a subject. This resembles a kind of "your money or your life" dilemma, in which if someone chooses her money she loses both and is thus forced to choose life. In the same way, one is forced to always choose meaning instead of being and thus alienation instead of annihilation, this forced choice being the drama of human freedom. This choice of the sacrifice of *jouissance* in order for someone to enter the symbolic realm is also known as "symbolic castration." Falque remarks that in psychoanalysis this dilemma is formulated precisely as one between alienation and death. The only way to choose Being or the Real is thus to die like Antigone in the Sophoclean drama. Becker does recognize the importance of psychoanalysis as a means to avoid an imaginary illusion of wholeness, as well as to be able to become subjects through assuming both our forced alienation and the unconscious desire that results after this alienation. However, he also formulates the question whether a genuine theology could go beyond this inherent division between being and meaning without envisaging a reconciliation between them.

Becker points out that Žižek's discourse on Christianity is integrated into the Lacanian forced dilemma. Thus, for Žižek, institutional Christianity promotes a perverted religion based on the logic of the masochistic sacrifice, in which the sacrifice continues to take place in order to produce meaning. Contrary to institutional Christianity, which constitutes a return of religion, the authentic message of Christ is the transcendence of the symbolic with the revelation of the inexistence of the Big Other. Christ's sacrifice is thus not the perpetuation of the sacrificial logic, but its abolition. Christ's sacrifice is the last sacrifice which abolishes all sacrifices. For Žižek, sacrifice consists in the concealment of the abyss of the Other's desire, of its lack and inconsistency. With His last sacrifice, Christ frees us from the sacrifices, since He reveals in His dereliction that the Big Other to whom the sacrifice is addressed does not exist. Becker remarks though that even if Christ's sacrifice is defined as the "last" sacrifice, it is still included in a certain definition of sacrifice and thus leaves us with nothing else than absolute absence and nothingness after its completion. The supposed emancipation is thus the one of a desperate man who has nothing to hope for. Becker's question is how one could conceive of the sacrifice in such a way that the Crucifixion would not be just one last sacrifice on the way to revealing inexistence.

One could remark that Christ does not extinguish His relation to the Father in the moment of the dereliction but rather intensifies it by saying "Father, into your hands I commend my Spirit" (Luke 23:46). From a theological point of view the dereliction does not entail the inexistence of God the Father, but the full reception of human psychology, contrary to the historical heresy of Apollinarianism. Christ receives even human ignorance, i.e. an ignorance about His future Resurrection. He thus assumes psychological and intellectual suffering together with the corporeal one. Modifying Žižek, one could say that Christ does not exceed the Symbolic towards the Real, but rather makes the Real speak through the Symbolic. One could speak of Christ's *lalangue*, in the Lacanian meaning of the term, as an excess of voice through which the unconscious Real enters speech. With His *lalangue*, Christ assumes man's existential and unconscious suffering. For Becker, this is not an abolition of the Symbolical God, but an opening of the way for the Symbolic, through transforming elements such as the Symbolic's inherent lack and alienation.

A theological exit from the sacrificial logic which would not itself be included in the same logic could be envisaged thanks to Jean-Luc Marion's notion of the gift. In the latter it is the Other who offers the gift, thus breaking any sacrificial logic of exchange. The one receiving the gift can repeat the act of gifting through a repetition of the gift which exits the sacrificial logic of exchange. If there is a lack on the human side, it is a lack due to the excess of the presence of God Who gives the gift. Marion's theory of the gift is different but also complementary to Falque's theory of finitude. God's gift includes the finitude assumed by Christ also comprising the unconscious.

Becker formulates more broadly the relation between psychoanalysis and theology. Psychoanalysis is included in the horizon of finitude and the sacrifice one must perform in order to become an (alienated) subject. Žižek might be right in following the Lacanian consideration of the forced choice. And any Christian should also admit that in the context of finitude it is impossible to evade the forced choice or to pretend that the latter does not exist. However, the theological outlet is not that of an exit from sacrifice into nothingness, but that of a transformation of both the real and the symbolical unconscious. And the latter transcends the realm of psychoanalysis. It happens in the Resurrection, which is not the admission of the Big Other's inexistence but God's gift, after which the sacrifice is turned into Eucharist, i.e. into a repetitive assumption of the gift and an offering of a gift back to the Giver. Brian Becker's chapter constitutes a theological response to Žižek's thought. A theologian cannot but take Resurrection literally as a salvation of both body and soul through transformation. In the latter, the Real is assumed and acquires a logical character by being referred to the Father, whereas the Symbolic is transformed from sacrifice into Eucharist.

The chapter by Chase Padusniak offers a second critical approach coming from a Christian thinker, but its primary concern is with Žižek's genealogy and his position in a certain spiritual tradition. It deals with theological actuality in the present, but only after drawing valuable elements from the past. Padusniak follows Milbank in maintaining that Žižek's thought is closer to Protestantism than to other versions of Christianity. This is only to be expected from a Hegelian thinker who considers that Catholicism is the negation of Orthodoxy and Protestantism the negation of Catholicism (and Žižek's own thought arguably is the negation of theist Protestantism). Padusniak focuses on the subject of the Resurrection as a community of the Holy Spirit. After the "death" of the abstracted God on the Cross, what remains is a community of persons who are all totally singular; a community of persons who have invested everything in concrete being, after having lost their faith in the institutions, in general norms, in the symbolic unification from above, and so on. One could wonder how persons who are thus absolutely singular could still constitute a community instead of taking each her own solitary road. But this is exactly the "miracle" and the work of the Holy Spirit. The sacrificed Messiah paves the way for persons who have but their complete uniqueness being deprived of any abstract or normative foundation. It is precisely the absence of God that binds together this paradoxical community. One could note that this notion of a community of totally singular and individualized persons is precisely the case in Protestant Christianity. The latter stresses the independent relation of each individual with Scripture but also the fact that the totality of these thoroughly individualized persons nevertheless constitutes a community. Žižek seems to be based on the historical experience of Protestantism, with the difference that in Žižek one finds an even more radical Protestantism that is ready to even negate theism, i.e. the eternal existence of the Big Other, for the sake of the most profound individualization.

By placing Žižek at the peak of a Protestant and mainly German tradition, Padusniak searches for his genealogy and traces it all the way back to the Middle Ages and Meister Eckhart. The discussion has two parts: the first concerns doing justice to the thought of the great German mystic, whereas the second engages the contemporary discussion on the thought of Emmanuel Levinas. In what concerns the latter, Padusniak emphasizes that Judaism does have an element of moral violence, since the goal of the Law is not to make social coexistence easier, but on the contrary to subtract the Jewish community from the pagan world. Violence is even greater in Christianity where we are summoned by the face of our neighbor. The neighbor of Christianity is not our double but the traumatic Thing, if one is allowed to use a Kantian expression interpreted along Lacanian lines. Žižek's difference from Lacan is that we should neither familiarize the neighbor nor use the notion of "face" in responding to the summons. Whereas Levinas insists on Otherness and on the notion of "face," the emphasis of Žižek lies on the third party, who is in some sense "faceless." The third introduces us to the domain of politics. In the latter, the particularly Christian love aims at someone who is without familiarized face, or who is even a "monster."

The first part of Padusniak's critique, written from the perspective of a Christian thinker, concerns doing justice to the thought of Meister Eckhart. In the latter we find a certain tension between the scholastic philosopher and the mystic, the intellectual master and the monk who belongs to a mendicant order. In his ontology, Meister Eckhart is based in the notion of analogy like Thomas Aquinas, in the sense that only the Absolute is Being proper, whereas other beings have being analogically. What is more interesting is that this ontology, although fundamentally analogical in character, includes some dialectical elements, in that it presents God as a negation of negation. The rationale is that each predicate constitutes a negation, since it situates a concrete element in a being by excluding other concrete elements. God's absolute unity and simplicity results only dialectically through the negation of the negation of predication, i.e. through transcending every predicate. At a more existential level, reaching this higher unicity and simplicity entails a dialectical return of the faithful to God as to a co-ground of her own being. For Padusniak, this notion of a co-ground is very close to what one could name, in a Žižekian fashion, "monstrosity," since it is an excess from humanity. It is true that in Meister Eckhart this excess bears the name of "peace" and not that of "monstrosity," but Padusniak argues that the former assumes the latter. The command "love your neighbor as yourself" (Mark 12:31) entails recognizing in the neighbor one's own monstrosity and excess. In a very counterintuitive interpretation, Meister Eckhart exalts Martha's crucial role over that of Mary, since Martha is the one who in a dialectical way transcends transcendence and thus returns to the world in order to engender love. In Žižek's terms, one could say that Martha returns to the concrete and invests it with absolute meaning.

More important for present purposes than historical justice to Meister Eckhart is the possibility that aspects of the medieval Christian tradition may prove fecund for contemporary political theology. For Padusniak, Meister Eckhart's notion of peace, which includes both the positivity of the plentitude of divine Being and the monstrosity of the neighbor, might be more satisfactory than a simple reference to the latter. A fuller Christian dialectic would include the detachment from the concrete (Mary), the elevation (*Aufhebung*) to the full unity of the Absolute, which we recognize as the co-ground of both ourselves and our neighbor – whom we love recognizing in her an excess of monstrosity similar to our own – and, finally, our return to concrete being, which we invest with absolute meaning (Martha). Thus, Padusniak's vision, based on Meister Eckhart, claims to represent a Christian worldview in a fuller way than that of the atheist thinker Slavoj Žižek. At certain points, this seems like an endeavor in Christian apologetics, attempting to adapt Žižek to the great syntheses of the Middle Ages. It might be true that the latter present elements of an inherent dialectic, which were made more explicit by Hegel, but one has to bear in mind that what is particularly interesting about Žižek is the way that he stresses the abolition of totality against any totalizing synthesis. In any case, Padusniak's chapter shows the position of a Christian thinker who draws inspiration from medieval Christian thought in order to articulate a fuller and particularly Christian political theology in the present.

The question of the community of the Holy Spirit is also engaged with in Gabriel Tupinambá's chapter, developing it in relation to psychoanalysis and Marxism. The issue here consists in the different ways available in order to compose a collectivity, and the examination of the Christian Spiritual community in relation to those ways. Whereas Marx wished for a synthesis between the theoretical catholicity of philosophy and the material catholicity of the proletariat, Lacan criticized universalism in general. Žižek's endeavor can be understood as a return to Hegel and to the latter's Christology, so that we could at the same time satisfy Marxist demands and respond to Lacan's critique. Žižek's turn to Christianity is not just theological but aims at a combination between Marxism and psychoanalysis.

In order to understand this project, Tupinambá turns to the psychoanalyst Jean-Claude Milner, who has written about three ways to compose a collectivity, corresponding broadly to the Lacanian triad of the Imaginary, the Symbolic and the Real. In the imaginary collectivity, individuals are united under a common property ascribed to them. The imaginary collectivity is thus based on the opposition between identity and otherness. The symbolic collectivity is constructed performatively: it is the interpellation by a signifier which of itself provokes the representation of some individuals with it, a very characteristic example being that of the insult. When people are called by an insulting name, what is crucial is not whether they have attributes that correspond to the insult, but the way they themselves react to it, how they try to evade it or what are the new questions that arise. A symbolic community is thus constructed in a performative way, in the sense that it does not previously exist but is performed through the interpellation itself. The symbolical collectivities are composed through suspicion and purification, since the subject is called to be performatively purified from what does not correspond to the signifier of the interpellation.

The third type of collectivity corresponds to the Lacanian Real. This is a "paradoxical" collectivity, according to Milner, which is founded on the singularity of each subject. The paradoxical collectivity is here provoked by the fact that each subject evades its name in an utterly unique way. A significant example comes from the domain of psychoanalysis, where the name "neurotic" shows exactly how different individuals evade being named in completely different ways. The paradoxical community shows how different subjects cannot be represented by their characteristic names and points to the Real of a desire. In Žižek's logic, one is truly universal only when one is singular in a radical way. This is a community that stands against any totalization, be it predicative or performative.

Tupinambá points out that Žižek is turned to a Christian Pneumatology inspired by Hegel in order to articulate the possibility of a community which would be close to Milner's "paradoxical community." In Hegel, the community of the Spirit is based precisely on the internal split and conflict inside self-consciousness. The community of the Spirit is then composed exactly by its opacity, by its lack of knowledge as to what unites it. This is a collectivity of those, whose failures to reach the universal idea constitute the only foundation for an indirect yet concrete existence of such an idea. Tupinambá observes that the paradoxical community is not beyond the symbolical one, but in between it as a non-coincidence with alienated social activity. In this sense, one could also conceive of the Kantian public sphere as a space in between social identities.

Žižek's program is thus a combination of Hegelian dialectic and Lacanian psychoanalysis. The Hegelian dialectic underlines the continuity between different moments in the evolution of an idea. Lacanian psychoanalysis rather points to the singularity in a dispersive and anti-universalist logic. What Žižek demonstrates through the notion of the community of the Spirit is not the passage from universality to absolute singularity, but rather the fact that we can have a new idea of catholicity that may even be different from or contradictory to the conventional notion of catholicity and which would be grounded on absolute singularity. The Marxist actuality of such a novel notion of catholicity could be very promising. It could entail the transcendence of an imaginary identification according to which we think of order only as a belonging to common properties of a precise social stratum. This new catholicity, to which Žižek refers as a "fragile absolute," enables a critique of the idealist form of imaginary universality of which historical Christianity has very often been the prey. At the same time, this new catholicity of the "fragile absolute" also critiques the Marxist and Lacanian tradition. It judges the Marxist tradition since its concrete universality has often taken place only inside the imaginary or symbolical realm in an essentialist way. And it critiques the Lacanian tradition, because its critique of universality has often been unproductive. Žižek's conception of the community of the Spirit deserves thus to be studied as a critical self-reflection of the three main traditions that he inherits, namely the Christian, the Marxist and the psychoanalytic.

In Haralambos Ventis' chapter we find a critical dialogue with Slavoj Žižek's thought from the point of view of a Christian liberal. The paper refers extensively to the liberal critique of both Christianity and Marxism, examines Žižek's responses to this critique and concludes with some questions from the point of view of someone who is friendly to the Christian tradition. In its first part, it develops positions by thinkers of liberal political constructivism against Christianity and Marxism. The main concern of thinkers included by Ventis in this current of thought, such as Richard Rorty and Cornelius Castoriadis, is that the eschatological visions of both Christianity and Marxism put a predetermined end in history and thus abolish autonomy, the dialogical emergence of freedom and the possibility of novelty. In the second part, Ventis presents communitarian thinkers who respond to liberal constructivism. William Desmond, for example, is concerned about the ontological minimalism and the phobia of liberal constructivists about eschatology; indeed, Terry Eagleton has even spoken of "holophobia." The communitarians show that a certain normativity is necessary for the emergence of the empirical subject, but also for its coherence and the avoidance of its total deconstruction. Ventis notes the return of ethics by Neo-Aristotelians, such as Alasdair MacIntyre, whereas thinkers like Paul Ricoeur have even put into question the division between ontology and deontology articulated by David Hume. Moderate communitarians such as Michael Sandel note that liberalism, especially neo-liberalism, tends to champion a narrow emphasis on freedom and the importance of private property, being thus deprived from any antidote to the excesses of the Markets. Ventis also draws our attention to the theories of thinkers who have traced an emancipatory potential in Christianity, such as Marcel Gauchet.

Ventis examines Žižek's thought in terms of a response to the dialogue between liberal constructivists and communitarians, noting how Žižek insists on the political significance of truth. It is to be noted that Žižek does follow the association between Christianity and Marxism identified by liberal constructivists, but with the twist that he celebrates this link. His view is that Christianity and Marxism should be allies supporting a politics of truth in a post-modern age, which is characterized by relativism and religious pluralism leading to a new kind of Gnosticism, as well as by other types of spiritualism which are entirely compatible with capitalism. Žižek insists on the emancipatory character of truth, echoing the saying of Christ, "then you will know the truth and the truth will set you free" (John 8:32). In approaching such truth, Žižek makes use of a combination of dialectics and psychoanalysis, in terms of which he diagnoses the existence of a suppressed truth inside contemporary capitalism, namely the absolute inequality that it provokes. The complete abolition of equality is the unconscious constitutive exception which haunts the ideological superstructure of pluralism, tolerance and other liberal values. It is to be noted that Žižek is also a fervent anti-populist. The populist is presented as someone for whom it is always the intruder to the system that is to be blamed for its shortcomings and never the system as such. In this sense, the populist helps to preserve the capitalist system, sharing this desire with the liberal, and being the contrary of the genuine emancipatory communist who wishes the subversion of the system, or, at least, a profound diagnosis of its problems. A related anti-populist stance of Žižek is his distrust of majorities.

Ventis concludes that the thinkers of the New Left might have good reason to claim that equality is the suppressed constitutive exception of capitalism, but they nevertheless underestimate other potentialities offered by liberal societies, such as personal self-realization and the right to personal otherness, the possibility of novelty, individual and social development and freedom of consciousness and speech as well as of sexual orientation. Such possibilities are not evident in the context of a communist system, and thinkers of the New Left should, according to Ventis, show whether they are compatible with their proper communist vision. It is of course important to recognize with Žižek the importance of the exteriority of truth, as well as of ontology, against any postmodern spiritualism, esotericism and pietism, which tend to be the natural allies of capitalism. However, a critical liberal reader would wish to find some principle of falsifiability in Žižek's thought, so as to avoid the totalitarianism that was the inherent characteristic of previous efforts to make a politics of truth. Ventis concludes his chapter with the reminder that the characteristic of genuine Christianity is eschatology rather than immanence, i.e. an eschatology after the end of history proper (even though eschatology should be seen as the completion of history rather than its abolition). Marxists who appropriate the Gospel sometimes tend to turn it into a sort of historical determinism, precisely because the demand of immanence annuls the post-historical eschatology, which is arguably Christianity's most salient feature.

Jack Louis Pappas is concerned to compare Žižek's and Badiou's interpretations of Saint Paul. What is essential for understanding Žižek's relation to Christianity is the fact that the Slovenian thinker regards Judeo-Christianity as the only religious tradition that rejects the idea of justice as an adaptation to the cosmic order. The Christian God presents an absolute otherness both to the cosmic order that He has Himself created and to the Law that He has Himself given. Consequently, Christianity's fundamental particularity lies in the fact that the Christian God is the only one who has sacrificed Himself in the person of His Son, i.e. precisely what did *not* happen in the case of Isaac.

The God of the Christians is neither the omnipotent God of the natural order, as in paganism, nor the external mediator, as in the great monotheistic traditions. He is the God who through His sacrifice and death puts on the shoulders of men the terrible burden of freedom and responsibility. The death of God paves the way for the death of man, the way for his transformation and rebirth. The importance of Christianity lies thus in its exceptionality. Christ constitutes the absolute exception, the innocent who is punished by the Law, the God who becomes man and so on. He thus valorizes something that was condemned by paganism, namely the division from the world, an act in which love constitutes a violent individualization of man, subverting the cosmic balance. Christian catholicity is thus not an abstract catholicity of assimilation, but on the contrary a catholicity that sacrifices itself in favor of the particular.

This means, however, that the particular is not the self-existent subjective identity of individualism, but an off-center point of focus of a new catholicity which is based on love for those who are on the margin of the cosmic order. In this, Žižek is very close to Alain Badiou's notion of *subtraction*. Jack Pappas puts the two thinkers in their historical context, namely the collapse of socialist regimes and what Francis Fukuyama has named (in a not particularly successful attempt at prophesy) "The End of History." According to Pappas, this could be seen as a sort of "realized eschatology" of the liberal consensus. What is valuable in the notions of both "subtraction" by Alain Badiou and "community of the Spirit" by Slavoj Žižek is that they transcend identitarian communities, such as the ethnic, racial or tribal, which are sometimes proposed as a false form of resistance to capitalism. The two thinkers trace an emancipatory alternative both to abstract internationalism and to the particularism of closed communities.

In Pappas' paper, one can also find some profound remarks on the relation between the notion of "forced choice" that we find in Žižek and that of the *Entschlossenheit* (anticipatory resoluteness) that we find in Martin Heidegger, i.e. the revelation of the finite horizon of the agent which forces her to discern the conditions of her response. Žižek interprets in these terms a whole theological line of reasoning about the so-called absolute predestination found in Augustine of Hippo, theologians of early Protestantism such as John Calvin, in Jansenism etc., partially having roots in the Apostle Paul himself. This is an original interpretation of the text of Saint Paul, according to which Truth is an event which constitutes the subject as an agent. This is a theory of "I choose because I am chosen," in which freedom and grace are intertwined. In this sense, both Badiou and Žižek present some elements of "anti-philosophy," which brings them close to the "anti-philosophical" stance of Saint Paul. They are, however, quite remote from the voluntarist individualism of fideism, which is founded on the individual's decision to believe. Belief is rather a fidelity to the event, according to Badiou, or an interiorization of God's sacrifice in the Spirit, according to Žižek.

The chapters by Haralambos Ventis and Jack Pappas both start by sketching aspects of the contemporary politico–cultural scene, focusing on questions at once philosophico–theological and political, but that by Pappas does so by also engaging with some of the sources of Žižek's thinking, St. Paul of course but especially Badiou's St. Paul. In the following, eighth, chapter, Sinan Richards interrogates a further crucial source in the work of Friedrich Schelling. This exploration takes further a key concern of the present volume, that of tracing the Christian genealogy of Žižek's thought, echoing the comparable endeavor of Padusniak to relate it to that of Meister Eckhart. Žižek does not only draw from Christian predecessors, but he reads them anew, through the lens of Lacanian psychoanalysis. He thus presents us with novel "updated" versions of Christian thinkers, which incorporate Lacanian intuitions. This procedure is particularly apparent in Žižek's reading of Hegel. Sinan Richards, however, shows us how something similar is performed in the case of F. W. J. Schelling. Žižek finds in Schelling a great thinker of immanence, who tried to distance himself from the dualism of both Kant (understanding and reason) and Fichte (ego and non-ego). Being inspired by Baruch Spinoza, Schelling sets out to re-establish a philosophy of immanence, according to which the structure of spirit is not separate from the structure of nature. Schelling's point of departure is the universe in its entirety and not just self-consciousness as in Fichte. In Schelling's view, nature evolves dialectically through polarities and not through a mechanism of causal chains. The fundamental questions of his philosophy are the emergence of finitude from infinity, freedom and the problem of evil as an indispensable condition for human freedom. In his response, Schelling contemplates a God who is reproduced in His image, the latter acquiring self-dependence as a form of freedom. When God checks His image, however, He is performing this from the perspective of His image and thus falls from being God and from being the Absolute. Creation and fall are thus conflated in Schelling's thought. What is more, the creation and the fall are linked to God becoming sort of a subject Himself, since they entail an internal split in God Himself. This means that God is Himself emptied and divided between His ground, on the one hand, and His ecstatic existence on the other. The latter means that God "contracts" Being, as if contracting a disease, and is Himself alienated.

For man, on the contrary, salvation entails an examination of his beginnings in order to transcend the fall. But Schelling thinks that the true origin is the "beginning before the beginning." The latter is both unconscious and theological, since it constitutes the divine "ground" of the world, or, rather, God as the ground before His ecstatic existence. Žižek follows Schelling in this consideration of God as both "ground" and "existence" in the world. In what concerns the former, one could say that Žižek interprets Schelling's God through the Lacanian notion of the Real. God founds the world and continues to exist as suppressed inside it. What is equally important is the consideration of a God who is "historicized," who not only enters history but becomes history Himself. Žižek draws this idea from Schelling, but he also celebrates it, whereas in the German philosopher God's historicization has rather the character of a tragedy. God as the Real inside history entails that the historical world is not a totalizable whole. In this sense, Schelling's romantic idealism leads us to think from the side of the "night," in contrast to the tendency of Enlightenment to regard subjectivity precisely as "light."

This, indeed, is a theology which stands in total opposition to that of René Descartes. In contrast to Descartes, Schelling writes about a subject that is not herself the master of her thoughts but presupposes some form of unconscious. This version of human subjectivity is in agreement with the Lacanian intuition that God can play with the surface of the world and can lie in total opposition to Descartes' notion of God's absolute reliability. In Lacan, the lie is a necessary implication of speech. Žižek interprets in this way the theology of both the Trinity and the economy of salvation. The production of matter results from an internal split in God, which resembles a differentiation between Father and Son. The teaching on the Incarnation of the Son has to be considered in relation to the dogma of the creation of matter out of nothing. The Son is incarnated, becomes matter, because He also becomes temporality and history. But the difference between Father and Son lies mainly in that God the Father is tantamount to an unconscious that retains the cruelty and the arbitrariness of the origin of the world precisely by being unconscious. On the contrary, God the Son is the God who is "historicized" and thus suffers His own arbitrariness, violence and cruelty. What is more, He is precisely the God of the revelation of this primordial cruelty and arbitrariness.

It is in this point that Žižek proceeds further than Schelling by insisting on drawing conclusions which would be too blasphemous for the German philosopher, as well as by pointing out that it is God Himself in the person of Jesus Christ who makes this revelation in a blasphemous way. The way in which Žižek reads Schelling is characteristic of a more general way Žižek uses some of his sources. He takes a Christian thinker and rethinks him through Jacques Lacan, who is usually performing a deconstruction of theological narratives. Žižek then presents a novel version of that Christian thinker, which is radicalized and even goes against the explicit intentions of this same Christian thinker by revealing conclusions that the Christian thinker would probably wish to honor with silence. What is more, in Žižek's view it is Christianity itself and the Christ in particular who draws all the blasphemous conclusions which were honored with silence by pre-Christian monotheism. In this sense, Žižek's blasphemous interpretation of his Christian predecessors could arguably be viewed as an *imitatio Christi*. Bold hermeneutics is thus a "Christological" work and interpreters who reveal the hidden blasphemous consequences of the thought of their predecessors are but imitators of Christ.

Following Sinan Richards' examination of Schelling as a prime source of Žižek's thought, the last two chapters of this volume (prior to Slavoj Žižek's Afterword), by Bruce J. Krajewski and Mike Grimshaw respectively, refocus in different ways on this volume's central questions: a critique of Žižek is offered by Krajewski, and a more sympathetic speculative inquiry into "Christian atheism" by Grimshaw. In the ninth chapter, we find a critical dialogue between Bruce Krajewski and Slavoj Žižek in a series of questions relating mainly to the subject of universalism. Krajewski remarks that the universalism sought by theologians such as Milbank or Žižek is very different from the abstract universalism of equality sought by communism. Krajewksi's paper is a serious engagement with the dialectical way of thinking. Krajewski accepts Žižek's observation that modern atheism is conditioned by Christianity, since it constitutes a dialectical negation of the latter that is answering to questions posed for the first time by Christians. In this sense, Krajewski's paper answers to the fundamental question of this volume by pointing out that the relation between Slavoj Žižek and Christianity is crucial even for an atheist, since the Slovenian philosopher exposes a dialectical understanding according to which modern atheism is inconceivable apart from Christianity. A dialectical comprehension of religion is thus important for the atheist as a profound endeavor of self-consciousness. However, Krajewski's discussion is not limited to endorsing and elaborating on this. He proceeds in a critical dialogue with Žižek by employing this notion of dialectics in order to cast some doubts on Žižek's own narrative. Krajewski remarks that Christianity's emphasis on hierarchy is itself a dialectical negation of anti-hierarchical polytheism. The origins of Christianity are thus not outside dialectics but constitute themselves a dialectical response to the previous polytheistic universe. Krajewski continues, however, by asking whether Christian universalism is satisfactory for contemporary communists. For the latter, universalism is linked to a demand for thorough egalitarianism. On the contrary, in the Christian vision, catholicity coexists with hierarchy. This is evident in the fact that in Christianity we find hierarchical institutions or a distinction between the external official religion and the internal religion of the mysteries. We also find, however, a radical gap between heaven and hell pointing to a fundamental inequality in Christianity's' eschatological vision.

It is to be noted that in Žižek's thought we do find antidotes against such objections, a fact that makes Krajewski's objections all the more valuable in highlighting the Slovenian philosopher's distinctive perspective on Christianity. Žižek does not celebrate the hierarchical structure of the church that we find in Catholicism or Orthodoxy. The community of the Holy Spirit that he expounds in his works is precisely the community of the singulars, a vision that radicalizes certain anti-hierarchical tendencies of Protestantism, going beyond even them. Krajewski's objections, nevertheless, point to some important issues. For example, how could one interpret the violent opposition between heaven and hell in Christian theology by taking into account Žižek's intuitions? Žižek is of course an "atheist Christian" not believing in an eschatological state *post mortem*; his only eschatological vision concerns the immanent community of the Holy Spirit as a sort of paradise inside history. It would be fruitful, however, to pose the question of how one could reinterpret the Christian vision of heaven and hell aided by Žižek's dialectical thinking.

At some points Krajewski implies that dialectics do have their own inherent limits. It usually shows the negativity of the existent, without being always capable of showing a positive alternative with practical value. In this context, Krajewski considers negatively certain consequences of Žižek's engagement in contemporary political issues, such as his support of Donald Trump in the context of "accelerationist" politics, namely the idea that a possible aggravation of the capitalist condition might pave the way for envisaging other alternatives. He is equally critical of what he perceives as Žižek's inadequacy to propose a specific communist alternative that would include individual liberties. Krajewski formulates such objections through a creative reading of G. K. Chesterton, who is a positive source of inspiration for Žižek himself. Krajewksi's originality lies in the fact that, at certain times, he turns Chesterton against Žižek himself. For example, he combines the figure of the Reverend Father Brown with the motif of the Lacanian detective, but also with a reading of Agatha Christie's work *Murder at the Vicarage*. What he seems to imply is that the gesture of the absence of the divine Thing's revelation, performed by Christ according to Žižek, might be repeated revealing the absence of many more things than Žižek himself would be ready to admit. In general, Krajewski's chapter makes a challenging use of Žižek's dialectical thought in a way that subverts certain conclusions that Žižek himself would like to draw.

In the tenth chapter, Mike Grimshaw examines *The Puppet and the Dwarf* in relation to the thought of great theologians of the "death of God" such as Thomas Altizer, Gabriel Vahanian and Gianni Vattimo. Žižek maintains that contemporary man should pass through the "Christian experience," in the sense of an assumption of temporality. In Christianity, it is God Himself Who becomes temporal and dies. Žižek would add that in Christianity, it is God Himself who becomes an atheist. What is crucial about the Crucifixion is precisely the fact that God does not intervene in order to save the Messiah. God is thus revealed to be definitively thrown into temporality and mortality. Grimshaw notes that after the experience of the "revolutionary" Good Friday, the experience of the morning of Holy Saturday is as if nothing has changed. The change has occurred only within the very small circle of the disciples who have gone through the death of the Big Other, an act of teleological and ontological violence.

On this reading, Christ's Crucifixion is the death not only of God but also of man, and Grimshaw seeks to encourage Žižek to take this with full seriousness, to become a theologian not only of the death of God but also of the death of man, in the sense that there is a double subtraction from both divinity and humanity. Here, he suggests, Žižek has as yet been insufficiently radical. The separated, divided man dies and what is subtracted is the concrete universal of the new community. After the death of God, there is no longer a gap between God and man, but rather a gap inside humanity itself. We are thus invited to an atheist *imitatio Christi* which consists in ourselves bringing "a sword to the earth" (Matthew 10:34). The day of Holy Saturday is the day in which everything seems to be the same, even though in reality everything has changed. It is just like the day after the revolution. There are those who have nostalgia for the *ancien régime*, while others seek a "Stalinist Christianity." The experience of Holy Saturday is crucial, because it is neither the event of the revelation in the Cross (Good Friday), nor the moment of the Resurrection as a confirmation of eternity. It is rather the opening of the possibility for a novel humanity that insists on the revelation of the Crucifixion without expecting the Resurrection. However, the true meaning of the death of God is, according to Žižek, that what is left is *deficiency*, a necessary deficiency of the world, which is however tantamount to a call for universal love. This universal love is now materialist and immanent in character. For Grimshaw, Christian atheism is the Lacanian Real, dialectical materialism being its Symbolic. In this context, the Crucifixion is a revolution from which results the new, Godless humanity. Grimshaw's chapter is written from the perspective of someone who identifies with Žižek in that he is simultaneously an atheist and a Christian, since Christianity is for him precisely the religion of the exit from religion, i.e. the religion of atheism. Christianity is in this case the name for the politics of revolutionary emancipation. Or, after Walter Benjamin's imagery, Christianity is, after all, the dwarf that moves the puppet of dialectical historical materialism.

Our volume concludes with Slavoj Žižek's own Afterword, "The Antinomies That Keep Christianity Alive" – a treatment of the Book of Job via Pope Francis, Martin Luther and (against) the primarily Eastern Orthodox teaching on deification, *theosis*.

On the scandalous possibility of caffeine

The Afterword of this volume belongs to Slavoj Žižek, who so graciously agreed to participate in this project by contributing his "The Antinomies That Keep Christianity Alive." However, since we are here dealing with Žižek and/on Christianity and theology, another implicit "afterword" looms large on the wider horizon of this book: a fundamental and logically sacrilegious

What if? That is, *what if* the emergence of the Christian Church and its itinerary in history is not merely a (however singular) social, philosophical or religious phenomenon of (however lofty) importance, out of which valuable reflections can be elaborated – *what if* we were to entertain the perpetually scandalous idea that the Christian Church is indeed what it professes, i.e. the historical body of God, the ineffable uncreated creator, incarnated, crucified and resurrected out of manic love for his creature? *What if* it is truly and literally the case that "the Son of God became man so that we might become God"[27] – against which, as found in the works of St Maximus the Confessor, Slavoj Žižek protests in his Afterword? *What if* this madness were indeed true, rendering all "*meta-*" analyses deliciously redundant? *What if* caffeine prevails?

The editors subscribe to the perversion that such a scandalous redundancy should be hoped for. After all, even if the reader does not find this volume *deifying*, then at least she may find it *edifying*.

Notes

1 With this opportunity we would like to warmly thank the series editors of the *Transcending Boundaries in Philosophy and Theology* series, Martin Warner and Kevin Vanhoozer, as well as Joshua Wells, our editor at Routledge: without their help and support, this volume would not have materialized. Martin Warner's generous assistance and helpful remarks in particular are of exceptional importance during the preparation of this book's material; we extend our most sincere gratitude.
2 On a comparison between Žižek and Schelling on this matter, see Adam Kotsko's *Žižek and Theology* (London: T&T Clark, 2008), 51–5. Since the present chapter is of an introductory character to a volume that studies particular aspects of Žižek's engagement with Christianity in the chapters that follow, we have opted for approaching and commenting on Žižek's work as a whole rather than focusing on particular passages of relevance to our inquiry here.
3 Kotsko, *Žižek and Theology*, 46–51.
4 Ibid., 65–9.
5 Ibid., 62.
6 See Frederick Depoortere's analysis in *Christ in Postmodern Philosophy: Gianni Vattimo, René Girard, and Slavoj Žižek* (London: T&T Clark, 2008), 121.
7 The reader wishing to take a closer look at Žižek's views on the Holy Spirit beyond our analysis of Žižek's core idea of the role of the Holy Spirit as the community of those that have interiorized Christ's sacrifice could consult Slavoj Žižek's *The Parallax View*. Short Circuits (Cambridge, MA: MIT Press, 2006), 80, 99; *The Puppet and the Dwarf: The Perverse Core of Christianity* (Cambridge, MA: MIT Press, 2003), 9–10, 130; pages 28–9, 32, 61, 148, 281–3, 291–5 from Slavoj Žižek and John Milbank's chapters in *The Monstrosity of Christ: Paradox or Dialectic?*, ed. Creston Davis (Cambridge, MA: MIT Press, 2009), as well as pages 55, 104, 172 from Slavoj Žižek and Boris Gunjević's chapters in *God in Pain: Inversions of Apocalypse* (New York: Seven Stories Press, 2012).
8 See, for example, Slavoj Žižek's "Passion in the Era of Decaffeinated Belief," in *Religion and Political Thought*, ed. Michael Hoelzl and Graham Ward (London & New York: Continuum, 2006), 237–42.
9 John D. Caputo, Review of *The Monstrosity of Christ: Paradox or Dialectic?*, by Slavoj Žižek and John Milbank, ed. Creston Davis. *Notre Dame Philosophical*

Reviews 2009.09.33, September 30, 2009. Retrieved March 14, 2018 from https://ndpr.nd.edu/news/the-monstrosity-of-christ-paradox-or-dialectic/.
10 Caputo, Review of *The Monstrosity of Christ*.
11 See Alain Badiou, *Saint Paul: The Foundation of Universalism*, trans. Ray Brassier (Stanford, CA: Stanford University Press, 2003).
12 Žižek, *The Puppet and the Dwarf*, 108–12, 129–33.
13 See Michael Hardt and Antonio Negri, *Empire* (Cambridge, MA: Harvard University Press, 2000).
14 Žižek, *The Puppet and the Dwarf*, 64–5.
15 Ibid., 80–2.
16 See also Slavoj Žižek's, *The Fragile Absolute: Or Why Is the Christian Legacy Worth Fighting For?* (New York: Verso Books, 2008) and *On Belief* (New York: Routledge, 2001).
17 Christos Yannaras, *The Freedom of Morality*, trans. Elizabeth Briere (Crestwood, NY: St. Vladimir's Seminary Press, 1984), first published in Greek in 1970.
18 Graham Ward's engagement with Žižek's thought begins in his *Cities of God* (London: Routledge, 2000), *passim*.
19 Žižek and Milbank, *The Monstrosity of Christ*, as well as John Milbank, Slavoj Žižek and Creston Davis, *Paul's New Moment: Continental Philosophy and the Future of Christian Theology* (Grand Rapids, MI: Brazos, 2010).
20 John Milbank, "Orthodox Paradox: An Interview with John Milbank," interview by Nathan Schneider, March 17, 2010. Retrieved March 17, 2018 from https://tif.ssrc.org/2010/03/17/orthodox-paradox-an-interview-with-john-milbank/.
21 Ibid.
22 Žižek and Gunjević, *God in Pain*.
23 Depoortere, *Christ in Postmodern Philosophy*, particularly 92–142.
24 An exhaustive account on *what* can be found *where* as far as Žižek's engagement with Christianity in his labyrinthoid corpus is concerned will not be provided in our chapter, as this can be largely found in Kotso's aforementioned *Žižek and Theology*, particularly in pages 1–3, 71–128, as well as 129–154 on theological responses to Žižek up to the book's publication date. The present book operates on the assumption that *Žižek and Theology* marks territory already explored, thus providing both takes on issues *beyond* that book and *alternative* readings to the ones there offered.
25 See the acutely accurate critique of Frederiek Depoortere in *Christ in Postmodern Philosophy*, 139–41.
26 Something which Žižek conveniently asserts in the Afterword to the present volume, where he criticizes the notion of *theosis*.
27 St. Athanasius, *De incarnatione* 54.3, Patrologia Graeca 25:192B.

Bibliography

Badiou, Alain. *Saint Paul: The Foundation of Universalism*. Translated by Ray Brassier. Stanford, CA: Stanford University Press, 2003.

Caputo, John D. Review of *The Monstrosity of Christ: Paradox or Dialectic?*. By Slavoj Žižek and John Milbank. Edited by Creston Davis. *Notre Dame Philosophical Reviews* 2009.09.33, 30 September 2009. Retrieved March 14, 2018 from https://ndpr.nd.edu/news/the-monstrosity-of-christ-paradox-or-dialectic/.

Depoortere, Frederick. *Christ in Postmodern Philosophy: Gianni Vattimo, René Girard, and Slavoj Žižek*. London: T&T Clark, 2008.

Hardt, Michael and Antonio Negri. *Empire*. Cambridge, MA: Harvard University Press, 2000.

Kotsko, Adam. *Žižek and Theology*. London: T&T Clark, 2008.
Milbank, John. "Orthodox Paradox: An Interview with John Milbank." Interview by Nathan Schneider, March 17, 2010. Retrieved March 17, 2018 from https://tif.ssrc.org/2010/03/17/orthodox-paradox-an-interview-with-john-milbank/.
Milbank, John, Slavoj Žižek and Creston Davis. *Paul's New Moment: Continental Philosophy and the Future of Christian Theology*. Grand Rapids, MI: Brazos, 2010.
Ward, Graham. *Cities of God*. London: Routledge, 2000.
Yannaras, Christos. *The Freedom of Morality*. Translated by Elizabeth Briere. Crestwood, NY: St. Vladimir's Seminary Press, 1984.
Žižek, Slavoj. *The Fragile Absolute: Or, Why Is the Christian Legacy Worth Fighting For?* London: Verso Books, 2008.
———. *The Neighbor: Three Inquiries in Political Theology*. Religion and Postmodernism. Chicago, IL: University of Chicago Press, 2005.
———. *The Parallax View*. Short Circuits. Cambridge, MA: MIT Press, 2006.
———. "Passion in the Era of Decaffeinated Belief." In *Religion and Political Thought*, edited by Michael Hoelzl and Graham Ward, 237–42. London & New York: Continuum, 2006.
———. *The Puppet and the Dwarf: The Perverse Core of Christianity*. Cambridge, MA: MIT Press, 2003.
———. *On Belief*. Thinking in Action. London: Routledge, 2001.
———. *The Sublime Object of Ideology*. London: Verso Books, 1989.
———. *Tarrying with the Negative: Kant, Hegel, and the Critique of Ideology*. Post-Contemporary Interventions. Durham, NC: Duke University Press, 1993.
———. *The Ticklish Subject: The Absent Centre of Political Ontology*. Wo Es War. London: Verso Books, 2000.
Žižek, Slavoj and Boris Gunjević. *God in Pain: Inversions of Apocalypse*. New York: Seven Stories Press, 2012.
Žižek, Slavoj and John Milbank. *The Monstrosity of Christ: Paradox or Dialectic?* Edited by Creston Davis. Cambridge, MA: MIT Press, 2009.

2 Žižek and the dialectical materialist theory of belief

Agon Hamza

There is always a certain difficulty, not to say confusion, when a materialist philosopher, that is to say an atheist, writes about religion. Rousseau warned us about this long ago when he said that one excuses oneself for being a philosopher by accusing the other of being religious.[1] This difficulty becomes even more complicated when, from the position of what Lenin called a "fighting materialist," one has to struggle against the "return" of religious fundamentalism in all its forms: from Christian, Muslim, Jewish, up to new forms of spiritualism (which masks itself as a-religious), to New Age Buddhism, and so on. Against this, many unexpected alliances can emerge alongside what Slavoj Žižek calls "new age obscurantism." Here, we Marxists should unashamedly join forces with "true" religious people against the madness of fundamentalism and spiritualism.

So, where are we today? In our epoch, religion is becoming an omnipotent force. The happy era of the decline of belief, which resulted in the "permissive societies," is clearly coming to an end. The historical materialist analysis is receding, operating with obscure terms which rarely give phenomena their true names. The left is in one of its most impotent positions for a very long time.

Why is obscurantism requiring us to move towards true religion? The reason why the left seems to fall into such an impotent position when confronted with contemporary obscurantism is that, unlike the previous relation between religion and the secular world, it is the former that currently follows from the latter. That is, fundamentalism is incomprehensible if not seen as a response to secular Western values. This is why countering fundamentalism with already existing democratic and liberal values does nothing more than reinforce the very thing one is fighting against, insofar as obscurantism was produced as a reaction to the West. True secular thinking, Enlightenment at its best, was not a movement against religion but an extraction of religion's rational kernel, a subversion of true spirituality in the name of its continuation. This is why today, in order to fight fundamentalism, we should not look for an ally in democratic and liberal values, which themselves carry a good dose of idealist spirituality – as the "non-religious religiosity" which Westerners can attest to – but rather return to the original gesture of the Enlightenment and find a subversive alliance with true and unabashed religiosity, which for centuries was the sole seat of universal and generic thinking. Therefore, the return of the theological dimension in the "post-secular" world is of structural necessity.

Žižek designated the role of religion in our era as *critical* or *therapeutic*. It is easy to account for the latter: in such cases, religion helps individuals to function in a society, gives them a higher cause than the "daily pleasures," fills up their lives with a divine meaning. The former is more complicated, as it tries to articulate the popular discontents with the present order (in which, if we follow this path, religion takes up a heretical role).[2]

The aim of the present chapter is to try and clarify how religion is always the other of philosophy, science and politics. But, perhaps it is precisely because religion was always thought of as the other that the above-mentioned fields are now incapable of finding a materialist alliance with religion to fight the very *other of religion*, which is fundamentalism and New Age spiritualism.

This is the point of departure from which we can think of the philosophical and political consequences of Žižek's engagement with religion, and more precisely with Christianity. Let us begin by asking the obvious question: why does Žižek need religion, or more precisely Christianity, in his philosophical project?

Žižek is both a Marxist and an atheist; therefore, at first sight, his engagement with theology and thus the call for "defending the Christian legacy" cannot but appear odd and oxymoronic. For somebody who is a self-proclaimed "fighting atheist" to have four books on Christianity and at the same time devote a crucial role to Christianity in his work for over a decade cannot but puzzle even his most consistent and faithful followers. It is not surprising that one would be tempted to evoke Mannoni's formula *je sais bien, mais quand-même* to designate his position. I know very well Žižek is an atheist, *but nevertheless . . .* – or: Žižek knows perfectly well there is no God, *but nevertheless . . .* This can be pushed furthermore to another level: Žižek knows (that Christianity is the religion of atheism), *but nonetheless* (he treats it as a religion). One can easily conclude that Žižek's "atheist Christianity" is a euphemism for the "barred" belief: that is, the claim that Žižek is not courageous enough to make the "final" step into reconciling the form of Christianity (which he embraces) and the actual content of the religion. But is this really the case?

The foundation of irreligious criticism

Marxism has always had a particularly complicated relationship with religion.[3] Marx's famous quotation identifying religion as "the opium of the people" is usually taken as a sign that religion numbs the critical sense, justifying historically determined social injustices through transcendental means. The full quotation, however, is much more interesting than this:

> The foundation of irreligious criticism is: Man makes religion, religion does not make man. Religion is, indeed, the self-consciousness and self-esteem

of man who has either not yet won through to himself, or has already lost himself again. But man is no abstract being squatting outside the world. Man is the world of man – state, society. This state and this society produce religion, which is an inverted consciousness of the world, because they are an inverted world. Religion is the general theory of this world, its encyclopedic compendium, its logic in popular form, its spiritual *point d'honneur*, its enthusiasm, its moral sanction, its solemn complement, and its universal basis of consolation and justification. It is the fantastic realization of the human essence since the human essence has not acquired any true reality. The struggle against religion is, therefore, indirectly the struggle against that world whose spiritual aroma is religion.

Religious suffering is, at one and the same time, the expression of real suffering and a protest against real suffering. Religion is the sigh of the oppressed creature, the heart of a heartless world, and the soul of soulless conditions. It is the opium of the people.[4]

Let us analyze it in detail. The first paragraph sets out the well-known Feuerbachian argument against the illusion of absolute transcendence. Feuerbach promoted the famous "promethean" thesis that religion is essentially a form of self-estrangement of human creative powers from itself, an estrangement which, effacing its own origins, then confronts man as an alien force. As he writes in the concluding section of *The Essence of Christianity*:

We have shown that the substance and object of religion is altogether human; we have shown that divine wisdom is human wisdom; that the secret of theology is anthropology; that the absolute mind is the so-called finite subjective mind. But religion is not conscious that its elements are human; on the contrary, it places itself in opposition to the human, or at least it does not admit that its elements are human. The necessary turning-point of history is therefore the open confession, that the consciousness of God is nothing else than the consciousness of the species; that man can and should raise himself only above the limits of his individuality, and not above the laws, the positive essential conditions of his species; that there is no other essence which man can think, dream of, imagine, feel, believe in, wish for, love and adore as the absolute, than the essence of human nature itself.[5]

Feuerbach's argument comprises two movements: first there is an exteriorization of man in his creations – his thoughts, dreams, imagination, feelings, beliefs and desires live on outside of us – but then there is still a redoubling of this exteriorization – for the marks of having been created are not kept by the creation, which therefore "places itself in opposition to the human." The critique of religion does not seek to undo its content, but rather to make it "admit that its elements are human," thus completing the circle: religion makes man, but man made religion and, therefore, man made man. And just as the self-estrangement of the human species in the form of religion leaves no trace of its origin – and is all the more effective for it – so does the suspension of this alienation leave no alien markings in the alienated creations as they are finally recognized as the historically produced essence of humanity.

It is worth noting that Feuerbach is not suggesting that by overcoming the illusion of absolute transcendence every man comes to recognize himself in the products of mankind, but rather that the domain which transcends us individually now itself appears as the historical product of the human species – it is a wholly natural and localized transcendence. In other words, this product of mankind's spiritual efforts remains beyond the grasp of any given individual, but this does not mean that it is an absolute or metaphysically transcendent beyond, but rather the transcendence of the human species over each of us – a generic transcendence, which exceeds us personally without thereby constituting an autonomous or fully separate realm.

In the paragraph of *A Contribution to the Critique of Hegel's Philosophy of Right*, Marx takes up this critical model – mediated, of course, by his own critique of Feuerbach. In his famous theses from 1845, he would state his supplementary "turn of the screw" in terms of a move from the abstract idea of the human genre – based on the passive fact that men naturally belong to the same genre – to the concrete existence of the species in concrete individuals,[6] who transform it through labor. Thus, the "generic being" [*Gattungswesen*] of man is no longer understood, as by Feuerbach, as an abstract point of view which, transcending individuals, nonetheless connects them together in a historically changing social whole, but rather as a situated dimension of human activity itself, an effective potency that realizes itself in man's concrete transformative relation to nature. As we change nature through labor, we also change our own species' determinations. For Marx, man is a generic being because he "makes his life activity itself the object of his will and of his consciousness":[7] insofar as we actively transform nature in accordance with our free will, we also transform our own human nature, since we are part of nature, and thereby concretely change ourselves – not as one individual separate from others, but as a species.

What takes place here is not so much a transformation of the model of critique proposed by Feuerbach but a displacement of its point of incidence from the abstract to the concrete, a shift that does bring about some important alterations to the previous model. By hypothesizing a natural or contemplative link between the individual man and his species, Feuerbach did not have to analyze the historicity of this very bond, that is, the way "'religious sentiment' is itself a social product"[8] and therefore did not tackle the question of why and how "the secular basis detaches itself from itself and establishes itself as an independent realm in the clouds."[9] The critique of religion still remains for Marx the critique of man's self-estrangement from the standpoint of man's generic capacity, but once it is aimed at the social production of the concrete existence of men, this critical standpoint has the additional task of explaining the detachment of the other world through the "cleavages and self-contradictions within this secular basis." That is, the very activity of self-estrangement which constitutes religion as an autonomous and opposite realm to that of human action must itself be explained as a social human activity.

So, when we read the above quotation from *A Contribution to the Critique of Hegel's Philosophy of Right*, we can recognize there, first of all, Marx's use of the Feuerbachian critique of self-estrangement. Such is the sense of statements such as "man makes religion, religion does not make man." But the affirmation that the social world conditions and determines the otherworldly nature of religion is not explained here by an innate or ahistorical religious tendency of mankind as such, but by the social conflicts of really existing societies: "this state and this society produce religion, which is an inverted consciousness of the world, because they are an inverted world." In capitalist societies, it is the "inversive" character of the institution of private property, through which the worker confronts the products of his labor as "something alien, as a power independent of the producer,"[10] which conditions the "inverted consciousness of the world" which emerges with it.

But it is at this point – having understood that it is the alienated social relations in this world which redouble themselves in the alienated world of religion – that Marx's critique goes into a strange praise of its object: "religion is the general theory of this world, its encyclopedic compendium, its logic in popular form" as well as "its spiritual *point d'honneur*, its enthusiasm, its moral sanction, its solemn complement and its universal basis for consolation and justification." The second part of this praise has a clearer critical sense underlying it, insofar as the inverted world of religion, mirroring the inverted social relations of domination, justifies and sanctions them by giving them a transcendental foundation. But what about the first part, in which religion is presented as a "theory," a "compendium" and a popular "logic" of the world?

Here we must point out one intricate aspect of Marx's presentation of the redoubling or mirroring of the secular in the religious world. We have already mentioned that Marx's "correction" of the Feuerbachian critical model involved not hypothesizing the alienating relation which connects man to God, but rather affirming that this relation is in fact a social and historically determined relation, which is *then* redoubled as the relation between man and God: first man becomes estranged from other men, and only then this estrangement assumes the features of an alienation from human nature into the supernatural. But we must take a closer look at how this redoubling in fact takes place for Marx, because it involves a very particular sort of repetition.

When we look in the mirror, we see ourselves *plus* something we cannot see without the reflective surface: we see the world *with us in it*. Another way of putting it is that we see the world "without our absence" – that is, without that blind spot which marks our indelible immersion in it. The famous figure of "the double," once popular in fantastic literature, and which Freud and Lacan later associated with the anguishing experience of the uncanny,[11] concerns precisely this "missing absence": what if the reflected image were suddenly to start moving while I remained in the same position? The anguishing effect of the double – of someone other than me who is nonetheless me – is not that he is a poor copy of me who fools other people into believing in his authenticity. The problem is that the double is effectively *more me than myself*: the blind spot from which I gaze at the mirror, this *absent* standpoint which at the same time marks my embedding in the world and divides me from it, is *absent* in the double: as I gaze at him, *I see myself fully embedded in the world* – more so than myself (insofar as I include this absent standpoint from which I see the double). My being in the world is marked by an alienation from this grasping at once my own being, as I am deprived from the capacity of seeing myself "from the outside," but the double is constituted through the *alienation of this alienation*, the embedding of my image in the image of the world in a fit more perfect than the one I experience within my own skin. And we find this same operation – through which an alienation is first marked as the presence of an absence, and then, through a redoubling, becomes a more fully constituted being – in the way Marx conceives the shift from social to religious alienation.

This comparison allows us to highlight that, in the passage from the precarious status of concrete men, alienated from their social production process and its results, to the redoubling of this alienation into a religious sphere, this social condition is not made invisible, but rather *made even more visible*. Religion portrays man's relation to God in the same alienated terms in which man relates to other men in this world, but precisely because of the very form of this redoubling, the repetition of this content *adds consistency to it* – that is, adds something that is missing in social reality, namely, the visibility of the worker to himself. Insofar as the social relations of production necessary for the very existence of men alienate the producers from themselves – an alienation which is marked by a loss or recognition – the mirroring of this alienation in a religious realm, just like in the case of the double, includes something in this "fantastic" picture that is missing in reality, namely, the absent or negative standpoint from which the worker experiences the estrangement from his own production. While in reality the alienated ones are deprived of what transcends them, in the transcendent world the alienated and the alienating force are both featured as parts of the same realm. Something missing in reality is featured in religion, which is why, from the standpoint of "the fantastic reality of heaven," man relates back to his concrete being as "the mere appearance of himself, the non-man [*Unmensch*]"[12] – just as how, when confronted with my double, it is I, with my alienated immersion in the world, who seems to have all the telling signs of a bad, unauthentic copy.

However, this process of redoubling does not only qualify religion as the "universal basis for consolation and justification" by creating a standpoint from which the precariousness of the world becomes the index of its own illusory and vacuous essence, but also insofar as the redoubling "positivizes" this imperfect or lacking dimension of the world, it creates a *mapping* relation between the social and the otherworldly realms. It is this mapping, through which two sets of the same "logic" are correlated, which leads Marx to also refer to religion as a "theory of the world." Here, the fact that the secular is constituted as the inessential and the religious as the essential poles of this correlation is secondary to the fact that a correlation between the two is established. It is from the perspective of this bijective relation – conditioned by the inversive character of repetition – that religion can be understood as an "encyclopedic compendium" of the secular world. This is not so much a point about the general model of critique based on the critique of religion – the "foundation of irreligious criticism" – as an entry point to approach religion itself as a *model* of social relations.

At stake here is the meaning of Marx's characterization of religion as this world's "logic in popular form [*populärer Form*]." Rather than the trivial suggestion that religion has popular appeal because it promises us life after death, or tells us that we have eternal souls, Marx is affirming something about the *form* in which the logic of the world is expressed in religion: somehow, this redoubled map of our social relations, due to its very redoubling, manages to make these same alienated relations *legible for everyone*. While in the "secular basis" the form of alienation entails "cleavages and self-contradictions" in the worker – since *he is and is not* the producer of his products – in the duplicated world of religion the creator and the creation are transcendentally opposed to each other: a self-contradiction *is pictured as an opposition*, in a formal shift which not only preserves but rather makes the content *more consistent*. As we previously mentioned, this makes alienation *more* rather than less visible for the alienated worker himself – at the cost of separating him from his own condition, yes: but isn't this separation between thinker and what is thought a characteristic of theory in general?

This question leads us, finally, to the last part of this passage from Marx:

> Religious suffering is, at one and the same time, the expression of real suffering and a protest against real suffering. Religion is the sigh of the oppressed creature, the heart of a heartless world, and the soul of soulless conditions. It is the opium of the people.[13]

Usually this statement is read backwards, starting from our understanding of the last metaphor and backtracking towards the problem of suffering. Opiates make suffering bearable, therefore religion is a form of coping with our real suffering – and since drugs make suffering bearable by providing us with an escape, religion must do the same, numbing us from our pain. But, as we have seen, this reading does not capture the way religion in fact *stages* our alienating social relations for us to see. Rather than explain the meaning of "religious suffering" through the opium metaphor, we should rather begin from the perplexing definition of this suffering as being "at one and the same time the *expression* [...] and a *protest* against real suffering" in order to arrive at what aspect of the metaphor is really being highlighted.

This dual character of religious suffering – being *the same* as real suffering, that is, its expression, while being *the opposite* of it, a protest against it – is clearly conditioned by the operation which we have been tracking here, and which Marx considers constitutive of religious consciousness. The inversive redoubling of negative alienation in this world into a positive marking of another world does *express* one's precarious condition while at the same time being its very opposite: a repetition – on the one hand, our production confronts us as an alien power, on the other, God confronts us as an alien power – but an *overcoming* nonetheless – since, from the standpoint of this transcendental power of God, we see ourselves as non-alienated men. What is at first enigmatic, however, is that the structure of religious suffering is presented here in the same terms as the structure of a "general theory of the world." But how can suffering, insofar as it both expresses and opposes itself to the world, be structured as a theory?

The mist-enveloped regions of the religious world

Marx's writings also have a complicated relation to politics itself. Even though "scansions" like the one proposed by Louis Althusser – dividing the "humanist" from the "scientific" phases in his work – are surely useful, none of these proposals substitute the historical scansions which confronted Marx throughout his life: a first "event," when in 1842 he found himself "in the embarrassing position of having to discuss what is known as material interests"[14] regarding the case of forest thefts and the division of landed property; the failure, in 1848, of the so-called Springtime of the Peoples and the subsequent proclamation of Louis Bonaparte as emperor; the 1857 financial crisis – arguably the first worldwide economic crisis – with its social and political effects in Britain; and the emergence of the Paris Commune in 1871.

Each of these events brought about important changes to Marx's thinking. The "young Hegelianism" of his student years was shattered in 1842 by the intrusion of the problem of survival, of men's need to produce their own means of subsistence – a question which oriented Marx's early critique of private property and his take on man's universality as a concrete consequence of our transformative relation to nature in general and our own nature in particular. A whole view on work, humanity and the future of the poor was constructed upon this first critique of private property. But Marx's writings on the limits of right and the state were later confronted by the failure of the 1848 revolutions – and, especially, by the emergence of a new emperor through the very democratic means supposed to bring the working class's interests into direct conflict with the bourgeoisie's. The critique of political economy acquired a new place in the following years of Marx's studies: rather than focusing on the relation between civil society and the state, we see a shift towards the infra-structure of civil society itself, in the problem of value and commodity production. This is the time of Marx's deepened critical studies of the classical economists, leading him to a first presentation of the theory of surplus value and a renewal of his political theory. But nothing in the works of classical bourgeois economists could have anticipated the paradoxical fact that a crisis in the very economic structure responsible for exploitation and inequality could serve to reinforce, rather than destroy, its functioning. This was, however, what the 1857 economic crisis brought to view. In order to respond to it, Marx had to devise a new entry point into his critique of political economy – one in which the "limits" of capital functioned as internal rather than external ones, a shift with deep consequences for the understanding of value, production, international relations and the role of the state. It was surely this new view of the global dimension of capitalism which made Marx at first irresponsive to the outbreaks of the communes in 1871 – since these confronted the global panorama of Marx's work with local political resistance. But if Marx was surely not going to drop his analysis of the globalized economic network of capitalism, the new sequence of political struggles in the 1870s did nonetheless pose the question of the "timelines" of capitalist development: was industrialization truly a necessary step in the passage from the communal properties of feudal life to a post-capitalist egalitarian society? In these years, even though Marx was not to publish any other works, he furthered his understanding of non-capitalist social formations – a study emblematically exemplified by his correspondence in 1881 with the Russian revolutionary Vera Zasulitch.

Each of these different sequences in Marx's thinking brought about important changes in his conceptual framework. But our interest in this section is just to highlight the different roles that his interlocution with Hegel took on throughout these shifts, as they point to the insistence of a precise problem at the heart of Marx's critique of capitalism.

As we analyzed in some detail in the previous section, at early stages of his work, Marx linked the critique of capitalism to the critique of religion – in a double sense. First of all, following Feuerbach, the critique of religion meant the undoing of mystifications which naturalized social relations of domination, that is, which made the "inverted world" brought about by capitalist property relations consonant with our consciousness. But it also meant, against Feuerbach, a critical outlook on social relations in capitalism attentive to how these same relations produce and reproduce these mystifications in the first place. It is this second aspect of "irreligious criticism" which structures the series of displacements with which Marx understands the "research program" of 1842–1851:

> It is, therefore, the task of history, once the other-world of truth has vanished, to establish the truth of this world. It is the immediate task of philosophy, which is in the service of history, to unmask self-estrangement in its unholy forms once the holy form of human self-estrangement has been unmasked. Thus, the criticism of Heaven turns into the criticism of Earth, the criticism of religion into the criticism of law, and the criticism of theology into the criticism of politics.[15]

If Feuerbach came to Marx's aid in order to undo "the other-world of truth," it is the ensuing "criticism of Earth" which truly characterizes Marx's own thinking. But, as we have also seen, the way Marx approaches the problem of "self-estrangement in its unholy forms" appears as an *extension of*, rather than as a break with, the critique of religion. So, when one shifts "the criticism of religion" into the criticism of law and property relations – the basis for the worker's alienation from his productions – and the "criticism of theology" into the criticism of political representation – the basis for the worker's invisibility as an orienting force of society – these displacements still take the form or model of the original Feuerbachian critique of self-estrangement. That is, they still take the form of a denouncing of the way *abstract* relations in fact stand for *concrete* non-relations – property rights ensure the worker's expropriation, political representation ensures his political impotence.

The movement from the abstract to the concrete – from the ideal to the real, from the divine to the human – was the principal dynamic of the Marxian model of critique while its objects were the "criticism of law" and the "criticism of politics," in sum, while it focused on the relation between labor and property, or civil society and the state.

However, when we juxtapose the way religion functions as a negative of critique in this theoretical sequence to the way it re-emerges in Marx's most well-known work, and more specifically, the most-well known chapter of that work, the section "The Fetishism of Commodities and the Secret Thereof" from the first volume of *Capital*, a crucial shift seems to have taken place. Here, Marx is no longer discussing how the products of labor appear as an alien power, acquiring an essential *difference* from their producers, a proprietary difference, but rather how products of labor become *equivalent* to each other – and ultimately to the producers themselves – the equivalence between commodities. In order to explain this impossible homogeneity between concretely distinct products and processes of production, Marx makes use, first, of an analogy with physics:

> The mysterious character of the commodity-form consists therefore simply in the fact that the commodity reflects the social characteristics of men's own labor as objective characteristics of the products of labor themselves, as the socio-natural properties of these things. Hence it also reflects the social relation of the producers to the sum total of labor as a social relation between objects, a relation which exists apart from and outside the producers. Through this substitution, the products of labor become commodities, sensuous things which are at the same time suprasensible or social. In the same way, the impression made by a thing on the optic nerve is perceived not as a subjective excitation of that nerve but as the objective form of a thing outside the eye. In the act of seeing, of course, light is really transmitted from one thing, the external object, to another thing, the eye. It is a physical relation between physical things. As against this, the commodity form, and the value-relation

of the products of labor within which it appears, have absolutely no connection with the physical nature of the commodity and the material [*dinglich*] relations arising out of this. It is nothing but the definite social relation between men themselves which assumes here, for them, the fantastic form of a relation between things.[16]

The problem Marx is trying to render legible is a central one. If we take the standpoint of what is concrete taking place at the production process – if we enter a factory and see what we find there – nowhere are the social relations which truly condition this process visible: we don't find inequality anywhere, no social relations appear, but rather equally self-serving individuals, putting their private properties to use – be this one's own labor force, or previously bought means of productions, such as machines, etc. But from the standpoint of property we cannot even find the reason why the capitalist would prefer to invest his money into other property – laborers, rent, machinery, etc. – if the end product would be worth the sum of the money he spent. So, the very reason of being of the factory is not visible, and so is not the reason why this process begets more money than the money invested in it. It is only from the standpoint of the exchange of products – that is, from the products of labor taken as commodities – that the social relations at stake in the very production process become themselves legible. It is only by considering labor as a commodity – therefore not only something a laborer possesses, but something which, like any other commodity, is consumed in accordance to its use value and exchanged for the cost of its reproduction – that the social relation between workers, their distinction from those who buy the labor-commodity, the production of surplus value, etc., are expressed. In other words, if we take the standpoint of the "relation between people," between concrete individuals, social relations are effectively invisible – substituted by property relations, which are immediate and equal, and therefore explain nothing of the production process itself – while if we take the standpoint of "relation between things," between commodities, the social relations between people are suddenly expressed – at the cost of making concrete individuals "invisible." Marx (2007) must explain, therefore, the logic of process through which social relations acquire "qualities [that] are at the same time perceptible and imperceptible by the senses."

He turns to physics here, proposing an analogy with light. We see things lit because light hits our eyes, but even though the "being" of the thing seen depends on a relation between the eye and the thing, that is, of light hitting the thing and then our eyes, we confront these things as separate from us, "not as the subjective excitation of our optic nerve, but as the objective form of something outside the eye itself." The analogy is therefore: social relations appear as social things outside the subjects of this relation just as the relation between eye and what is seen appears as an objective thing outside the eye. But at this point Marx points out the limit of the analogy: in the case of the eye, "there is a physical relation between physical things," that is: the eye, the thing been seen and the light hitting both the eye and the object are all materially homogeneous – all the elements in this process are physical. "But it is different with commodities." Why? Because the relation at stake here is heterogenous to the things it relates: "the existence of the things qua commodities [. . .] [has] absolutely no connection with their physical properties." In the case of light, we can deduce properties about light by analyzing the objects it relates: because light in fact interacts with objects, being part of the same material world as they are, at a truly infinitesimal level, it can be seen that it exerts force over the objects it hits or produces heat or excites the optic nerve. On the other hand, the exchange relations between commodities "do not contain an atom of use value"[17] – that is, they are *indifferent* to the concrete and material substratum of the things being related. Nothing about value can be deduced by looking at what is concretely put into relation through value relations – however, it is only from the standpoint of these relations that the social relations between concrete people and things becomes visible. So, while there is "a definite social relation between men" this relation assumes for them "the fantastic form of a relation between things." The term that is not captured by the physical metaphor is "fantastic": it implies that information is *lost* when we only accept the existence of material and concrete things and people – it is not a mere perceptible distortion, like a transcendental illusion which structures our visual field, but "concretely" plays no part in the behavior of light and sight. The "fantastic" aspect of this process concerns the fact that, if we try to move from the distortion back to the "concrete" process, *we also lose the causal enchainment which truly structures these concrete components*. At this point, Marx makes a novel use of religion, clearly distinct from the critical model based on Feuerbach:

> In order, therefore, to find an analogy we must take flight into the misty realm of religion. There the products of the human brain appear as autonomous figures endowed with a life of their own, which enter into relations both with each other and with the human race. So it is in the world of commodities with the products of men's hands. I call this the fetishism which attaches itself to the products of labor as soon as they are produced as commodities, and is therefore inseparable from the production of commodities.[18]

The "mist-enveloped regions" of religion are called upon here not as a model of what is to be criticized, but rather as a model of how social relations truly function in capitalism – as a fantastic domain which effectively transcends us, to the point that, without assuming the existence of this transcendental or supernatural standpoint, the legibility of concrete and localized social relations themselves is compromised. Considering how central the critique of religion was to the constitution of Marx's own critical stance, it is worth pondering the fact that Marx here claims that, in order to account for the reality of the value form we "must have recourse" to religion. What exactly is the status of this necessity?

There seems to be a strange enlargement of the scope of materialism in the passage from Feuerbach to early Marx, and then to the standpoint of *Capital*. At first, Feuerbach proposed that a materialist position would recognize that the religious form operates an *illusory alienation* through which our own productions appear to us as autonomous or otherworldly – which is why the spiritual overcoming of this illusion would reveal that the human species itself is the source and site of our self-transcendence. Marx then claimed that this relation of alienation is not an illusion, but rather a redoubling of a very real form of social alienation, through which workers are materially deprived of the products of their labor – alienation is not the essential religious phenomena, for it is conditioned by the social reality of alienation; the essential dimension of religion would rather be *the illusory separation* that this alienated sphere then acquires in regards to real social life. Finally, with the shift from property relations to the problematic of value, this separation itself is recognized as part of the social world, since the logic of value *is materially separated from its own material substratum*. What is then proper to religion as a form? It is true that Marx does refer in *Capital* many times to capitalism or aspects of it as religious-like, for example in the third volume, when he writes:

> It is the great merit of classical economics to have dissolved this false appearance and deception, this autonomization and ossification of the different social elements of wealth vis-a-vis one another, this personification of things and reification of the relations of production, this religion of everyday life.[19]

But to say that the way social wealth is falsely hidden from us in capitalism under the illusory "personification of things and conversion of production relations into entities" makes it the "religion of everyday life" is not to criticize religion, but rather to critique capitalism in its religion-like features. It is hard to miss that an inversion has taken place here: it is not religion that is being attacked for aiding the reproduction of a veiled social structure, but rather this social structure which is being represented as a religion. And so, once again, religion appears not as the object of critique, but as a model of the world.

Some authors, most notably Walter Benjamin, define this new relation between social structure and religion as a direct identity: capitalism *is a religion*.[20] That is, the reason why Marx would *need* to resort to a reference to the "mist-enveloped regions" of religious phenomena in order to account for the social form of a commodity-producing society is because this society is nothing but a "pure religious cult"[21] – there is therefore no modeling of social relations through religious ones: in capitalism these two would be one and the same thing. Productive as this reading may be – and it does allow us to move beyond the paradigm which treats religion as the realm of ineffective illusions – it does not account for one main difference between religion and capitalism: that capitalist social relations are somehow *clarified* by being exposed as religious, while religious life gains nothing when compared to religion itself. This is the point we have previously touched upon, when we analyzed the ambivalent status of the redoubling of social alienation into transcendental alienation: if capitalism is *immediately* a religion, then why are capitalist social relations passive of being redoubled – and through this process, made *more visible – as otherworldly relations?*

What is missing for capitalism to truly be a religion (and not merely function as a religion) is precisely the capacity to serve as the model of something else, to function as a mediation that can be handled as such. Unlike religion, when capitalism becomes the model of something other than itself – say, of human interactions outside the productive sphere, which can be thought of in terms of investments, risk, property relations, etc. – it is in fact already in the process of encompassing what it represents into itself, perpetually moving back towards being the thing in need of representation.

This brings us back to Marx's analysis of the commodity form in the first chapter of *Capital*. If the recourse to religion as a model of sociality was not necessary because capitalism is itself a religion, then what accounts for this new position of religious phenomena in Marx's critical apparatus? Precisely the fact that religion has the *form of a model*: when materialism needed a model for alienation, religion offered one, though social alienation is itself a materialist category, when materialism needed a model for the autonomization of abstractions, religion also served as a double, though the value form is in fact a real abstraction, a historically constituted domain which nonetheless transcends those who support it.

We come thus to the conclusion that, behind the program of an "irreligious criticism," modeled after the critique of religion and theology, there lies not an unveiling of religion's role in the constitution and maintenance of capitalism (though nothing prevents such a social analysis of its religious institutions) but rather the slow recognition that religion offers itself as a stage capable of making capitalist relations visible, a form capable of *signifying* these social relations, and therefore a condition for criticizing them.

Žižek and Christianity

We come, thus, to the perplexing situation of recognizing in religion a condition for the critique of ideology and ideological mystifications. But how could it be that the critique of beliefs necessarily passes through belief itself? This is precisely the thesis argued by Žižek. The premise of *The Puppet and the Dwarf* (and of his entire "Christian materialist" project) is the following:

> What we are getting today is a kind of "suspended" belief, a belief that can thrive only as not fully (publicly) admitted, as a private obscene

> secret. Against this attitude, one should insist even more emphatically that the "vulgar" question "Do you really believe or not?" matters – more than ever, perhaps. My claim here is not merely that I am a materialist through and through, and that the subversive kernel of Christianity is accessible also to a materialist approach; my thesis is much stronger: this kernel is accessible only to a materialist approach – and vice versa: to become a true dialectical materialist, one should go through the Christian experience.[22]

The structure of this proposal is deceptively simple, for in fact it proposes two contradictory movements: to produce a materialist reading of Christianity – that is, to produce a materialist theory of belief that doesn't coincide with its immediate notion – and to reform dialectical materialism itself through the consideration of Christianity – that is, to demonstrate that the Christian religious experience poses a challenge to materialism that calls for its reinvention. Taken together, these are seemingly circular tasks, and therefore impossible: how can we produce a materialist reading of Christianity if this reading itself is supposed to change what we mean by "materialist," and therefore affect the way we read Christianity to begin with?

The way of out this circularity was already well-known to Hegel, a philosopher who was troubled by the question of foundations and beginnings in all matters speculative. For Hegel, there is a twist in this circular relation between rational thinking and the religious experience, an asymmetry that is in fact what characterizes Christianity to begin with, namely, the way Christianity stages the limit of belief within its own faith. The title of "revealed" religion is merited for Christianity not because it reveals "a" religious truth, but rather because it stages the truth of religion *as such*, showing us that the suspension of belief has the structure of a belief – a "barren belief," so to speak. This is why, already in his *Faith and Knowledge*, Hegel proposes a strange continuity between the "Historical Good Friday" – the death of God within Christian faith – and the "Speculative Good Friday" – the doing away with God in rational thinking:

> But the pure concept or infinity as the abyss of nothingness in which all being is engulfed, must signify the infinite grief [of the finite] purely as a moment of the supreme Idea, and no more than a moment. Formerly, the infinite grief only existed historically in the formative process of culture. It existed as the feeling that "God Himself is dead," upon which the religion of more recent times rests; the same feeling that Pascal expressed in so to speak sheerly empirical form: "la nature est telle qu'elle marque partout un Dieu perdu et dans l'homme et hors de l'homme" [Nature is such that it signifies everywhere a lost God both within and outside man]. By marking this feeling as a moment of the supreme Idea, the pure concept must give philosophical existence to what used to be either the moral precept that we must sacrifice the

empirical being (*Wesen*), or the concept of formal abstraction [e.g., the categorical imperative]. Thereby it must re-establish for philosophy the Idea of absolute freedom and along with it the absolute Passion, the speculative Good Friday in place of the historic Good Friday. Good Friday must be speculatively re-established in the whole truth and harshness of its God-forsakenness. Since the [more] serene, less well grounded and more individual style of the dogmatic philosophies and of the natural religions must vanish, the highest totality can and must achieve its resurrection solely from this harsh consciousness of loss, encompassing everything and ascending in all its earnestness and out of its deepest ground to the most serene freedom of its shape.[23]

So, Hegel provides us an entry point into the Žižekian encounter between materialism and religion: while the religious or idealist undertones of materialism cannot be directly accessed by materialism itself, the materialist core of the religious experience is itself thematized within Christianity and, in particular, in the special role the death of God takes in it. We could venture that the death of God is the point in which the two sides of a circle cross, as in a Möebius band, and the materialist kernel of religion motivates a reformed dialectical materialism, in which the other side of this same "twist" can now be found, since it is a materialism which can now account for the general theory of barren beliefs, that is, for the effective structure of belief's separation from the believer in general.

Therefore, in his return to Hegel, Žižek is also recuperating a view of religion which in fact recognizes within Marxism an "underlying current" that was already dormant in it, namely, the understanding that the space of representation – of the discourse which models the world – is itself inconsistent and passes over into that which it models. This, in fact, is one of Hegel's most important ideas in the *Phenomenology of Spirit*, and the true turning point of the passage between Christianity and speculative thinking. Hegel is essentially a superficial thinker: all his philosophy is dedicated to emptying out the "beyond" of any substance, doing away with all essentialist dualisms – or, as mentioned in the above quotation, a thinker who tries to carry out the task of accepting "the whole truth and harshness" of the world's "God-forsakenness." But if this is the case, then Hegel cannot criticize mystifications from the standpoint of the de-mystified, or representations from the standpoint of the underlying reality. He has himself willingly thrown away the philosopher's main tool of critique and therefore should accept the title that has been given to him by most of his commentators – Marx included – of being a great idealist, committed to the all-encompassing surface of ideas. But this understanding of Hegel leaves out the other side of his gesture, for the emptying out of the world's "depth" is correlate with the recognition that its superficiality is "bent" or "twisted": it contains sites where what is becomes its own negation. And so, another way out of religious thinking opens up: not "beyond," "beside" or "behind" it, but through its own immanent inconsistency, the site where representation undermines itself, becoming its other. For Hegel, this is precisely what happens with the passion of Christ – and in a double sense – since it is both the first religious experience of the inner limit of religion *and* the first non-religious thinking of the existence of such contradictory sites within representation in general. The Passion therefore does not only locate the point where representation touches on its other – were this its limit, Christianity would be an ode to the "unrepresentable" – but it also empties out the substance of this otherness by rendering it co-extensive with rational thinking:

> in the Christian Revelation, no one comes towards us, nothing comes out of this manifestation, it does not *show* anything. Nothing, except that now the relations "referring/referent," "signifier/signified" do not have a continuation. God does not *become* manifest: he *is*, side by side, *für sich seiende Manifestation*. What is unveiled, if one still wants to use this term, is only that there was the necessity of appearing in Him, in the very strict sense of being-for-an-Other, the impossibility of being totally "Him" in the case of remaining solely "in Himself" [. . .] On the other hand, if one no longer imagines God as an objectifiable content, one also does not incur on the risk of splitting him between His *essence* and his *appearance*, His *before* and His *after*.[24]

Returning to Žižek's materialist theory of religion, we can now understand why he explicitly says: "since Hegel was the philosopher of Christianity, it is no wonder that a Hegelian approach to Christ's death brings out a radical emancipatory potential."[25] At the beginning of his *The Fear of Four Words*, after quoting Chesterton at length, Žižek puts forward the axiom of his Hegelian reading of Christianity:

> The axiom of this essay is that there is only one philosophy which thought the implications of the four words ["He Was Made Man"] through to the end: Hegel's idealism – which is why almost all philosophers are also no less frightened of Hegel's idealism.[26]

In his Seminar VII, Lacan opposes the thesis of the "death of God," arguing that God was dead from the very beginning, but only in Christianity is he self-aware of that. He refers to Hegel when he speaks about a "certain atheistic message in Christianity itself." But, which God dies and what are the consequences? Žižek argues that God has to die twice: in Judaism "in itself," whereas in Christianity God dies "for itself." And this is the true atheistic dimension of

> Christianity as the "religion of atheism": God cannot be directly negated, it is the subsequent erasure of the individual that sets the Holy Spirit free from its embodiments, that sublates God into a virtual fiction sustained only by the collective of believers.[27]

It is at this point that the relevance of a "return to Hegel" makes itself felt, because, from the standpoint of his Hegelian-inspired Marxist theory of belief, the critique of belief does *not* take the form of an increasing passivity or a retreat from those practices that are structured by beliefs – rather, the critique of the belief in God *has the form of a collective practice*. It is the immediate, passive engagement with reality which appears, from Žižek's standpoint, as the idealist – secretively social – commitment to fantasies, ideals and mystifications, while the active, collective engagement with practices that are explicitly mediated by abstractions, emptying out the substance of these mediations, has the potential to produce true critical effects. Rather than turn from religion to "social practice," as the orthodox Marxist analysis suggests, Žižek's Marxism transposes the full Hegelian passage between religion and speculative thinking into the relation between religious practice and materialism: just as Reason generalizes and radicalizes the "infinite grief" of the "historical Good Friday" by emptying out every "beyond" of its substance, so would materialism preserve and radicalize religious collective practice by emptying out every belief of its substantial mediator.

In the *Phenomenology of Spirit*, Hegel writes:

> The death of the Mediator [that is, Christ] is the death not only of his natural aspect or of his particular being-for-self, not only of the already dead husk stripped of its essential Being, but also of the *abstraction of the divine Being*. For the Mediator, in so far as his death has not yet completed the reconciliation, is the one-sidedness which takes as *essential* Being the simple element of thought in contrast to actuality: this one-sided extreme of the Self does not as yet have equal worth with essential Being; this it first has as Spirit. The death of this picture-thought contains, therefore, at the same time the death of the *abstraction of the divine Being* which is not posited as Self.[28]

However, in the *Philosophy of History*, he gives a slightly distinct presentation:

> The followers of Christ, united in this sense and living in the spiritual life, form a community which is the Kingdom of God. "Where two or three are gathered together in my name," (that is, in the determination of that which I am) – says Christ – "there am I in the midst of them." The community is the real and present life in the Spirit of Christ.[29]

The conclusion to be drawn from this is that God emerges only through his loss (the dialectic of supposing and presupposing that Hegel relies on) and this loss is fully consummated in the Holy Spirit.[30] The Holy Spirit is kept alive only through the interaction of the individuals; it is a virtual Substance (which should not be confused with Hegel's "objective spirit" *qua* virtual substance) which exists when the people recognize themselves in it (the Communist Party, psychoanalytic institutions/societies, amorous couples, et cetera). In short, this is the most radical form of atheism: one doesn't proclaim the inexistence of God, but it is God himself who proclaims it himself, makes us believe in his inexistence. It is in this point that the truly materialist dimension of Christianity emerges, a materialism which is concerned with the form of the life of the collectivities.

This Hegelian–Žižekian view of religion as a self-sublating process, out of which atheism is born, allows us to imagine a different sort of critique of fundamentalisms – one that doesn't attack fundamentalism by referring back to the "fundaments" or "foundations" (*Grund*), since that is exactly what fundamentalisms already do. Instead, Hegel provides us with an alternative form of critique, one which seeks in the rational kernel of religious thinking an ally against mystification and obscurantism in both religious and secular forms.

Notes

1. Jean-Jacques Rousseau, *Julie, or the New Heloise* (New York: University Press of New England, 1997), 568.
2. Slavoj Žižek, *The Puppet and the Dwarf: The Perverse Core of Christianity* (Cambridge: MIT Press, 2003), 3.
3. We have opted for the vague and indeterminate sense of the term "religion" insofar as Marx himself adopts such a conceptual stance. It is our wager that even if the term clearly stands for a generalization of the particular forms of Christian religion in Marx's time, this generalization ends up producing a singular Marxian theory of the "elementary forms of religious life."
4. Marx, Karl, *A Contribution to the Critique of Hegel's Philosophy of Right*. Retrieved from www.marxists.org/archive/marx/works/1843/critique-hpr/intro.htm.
5. Ludwig Feuerbach, *The Essence of Christianity* (New York: Dover, 2008), 221–2.
6. Karl Marx, "Theses on Feuerbach," in *The Communist Manifesto and Other Writings* (New York: Barnes & Noble Classics, 2005), 180.
7. See the chapter on *Estranged Labor* in Karl Marx, *Economic and Philosophical Manuscripts 1844* (New York: Dover, 2007), 75.
8. Marx, *Theses on Feuerbach*, §6, 180.
9. Ibid., §4.
10. Marx, *Economic and Philosophical Manuscripts*, 69.
11. Sigmund Freud, *The Uncanny* (London: Penguin Books, 2003).
12. Marx, *A Contribution to the Critique of Hegel's Philosophy of Right*.
13. Ibid.
14. Karl Marx, *Preface to the Contribution to the Critique of Political Economy*. Retrieved from www.marxists.org/archive/marx/works/1859/critique-pol-economy/preface.htm.
15. Marx, *A Contribution to the Critique of Hegel's Philosophy of Right*.
16. Karl Marx, *Capital*, vol. 1 (London: Penguin Books, 1976), 164–5.
17. Ibid., 128.
18. Ibid., 165.
19. Karl Marx, *Capital*, vol. 3 (London: Penguin Books, 1991), 969.
20. In his famous "fragment 74," Benjamin writes: "one can behold in capitalism a religion, that is to say, capitalism essentially serves to satisfy the same worries, anguish and disquiet formerly answered by so-called religion." See Walter Benjamin, "Capitalism as Religion," in *Selected Writings* (Cambridge, MA: Harvard University Press, 1966), 259.

21 Ibid.
22 Žižek, *The Puppet and the Dwarf*, 6.
23 G.W.F. Hegel, *Faith and Knowledge* (New York: State University of New York Press, 1977), 190–1.
24 Gérard Lebrun, *La patience du concept: essai sur le discours hégélien* (Paris: Gallimard, 1972), 39, my translation.
25 Slavoj Žižek, *Less Than Nothing: Hegel and the Shadow of Dialectical Materialism* (London: Verso Books, 2012), 6.
26 Slavoj Žižek and John Milbank, *The Monstrosity of Christ: Paradox or Dialectic?* (Cambridge, MA: MIT Press, 2009), 26.
27 Slavoj Žižek, *Absolute Recoil: Towards a New Foundation of Dialectical Materialism* (London: Verso Books, 2014), 261–2.
28 G.W.F. Hegel, *Phenomenology of Spirit* (Oxford: Oxford University Press, 1977), 476.
29 G.W.F. Hegel, *Philosophy of History* (New York: Dover, 1991), 328.
30 Žižek, *Absolute Recoil*, 261.

Bibliography

Benjamin, Walter. "Capitalism as Religion." In *Selected Writings, Vol. 1: 1913–26*, edited by Marcus Bullock and Michael W. Jennings, 288–91. Cambridge, MA: Harvard University Press, 1966.

Feuerbach, Ludwig. *The Essence of Christianity*. New York: Dover, 2008.

Freud, Sigmund. *The Uncanny*. Translated by David McLintock. London: Penguin Books, 2003.

Hegel, G.W.F. *Faith and Knowledge*. Translated by H.S. Harris and Walter Cerf. New York: State University of New York Press, 1977.

———. *Phenomenology of Spirit*. Translated by A.V. Miller. Oxford: Oxford University Press, 1977.

———. *Philosophy of History*. Translated by James Sibree. New York: Dover, 1991.

Lebrun, Gérard. *La patience du concept: Essai sur le discours hégélien*. Paris: Gallimard, 1972.

Marx, Karl. *Capital*. Translated by Ben Fowkes, vol. 1. London: Penguin Books, 1976.

———. *Capital*. Translated by David Fernbach, vol. 3. London: Penguin Books, 1991.

———. *Capital: A Critique of Political Economy–The Process of Capitalist Production*, vol I, part I. New York: Cosimo Classics, 2007.

———. *A Contribution to the Critique of Hegel's Philosophy of Right*. Retrieved from www.marxists.org/archive/marx/works/1843/critique-hpr/intro.htm.

———. "Estranged Labor." In *Economic and Philosophical Manuscripts 1844*. New York: Dover, 2007.

———. *Preface to the Contribution to the Critique of Political Economy*. Retrieved from www.marxists.org/archive/marx/works/1859/critique-pol-economy/preface.htm.

———. "Theses on Feuerbach." In *The Communist Manifesto and Other Writings*. New York: Barnes & Noble Classics, 2005.Rousseau, Jean-Jacques. *Julie, or the New Heloise*. Translated and annotated by Philip Stewart and Jean Vaché. New York: University Press of New England, 1997.

Žižek, Slavoj. *Absolute Recoil: Towards a New Foundation of Dialectical Materialism*. London: Verso Books, 2014.
———. *Less Than Nothing: Hegel and the Shadow of Dialectical Materialism*. London: Verso Books, 2012.
———. *The Puppet and the Dwarf: The Perverse Core of Christianity*. Cambridge, MA: MIT Press, 2003.
Žižek, Slavoj and John Milbank. *The Monstrosity of Christ: Paradox or Dialectic?* Edited by Creston Davis. Cambridge, MA: MIT Press, 2009.

3 From psychoanalysis to metamorphosis
The Lacanian limits of Žižek's theology

Brian W. Becker

For Slavoj Žižek, when Christ on the Cross makes his cry of dereliction ("Father, why have you forsaken me?"[1]) God becomes an atheist, and what dies on the Cross is God as transcendent Big Other, the one who "pulls the strings behind the stage and teleologically justifies (guarantees the meaning of) all our earthly vicissitudes."[2] Though the Hegelian influence is evident, this formulation of Christ's sacrifice also follows along a path carved out by psychoanalyst Jacques Lacan, whose notion of the vel of alienation[3] situates the subject within a tragically inescapable forced (vel) choice emerging out of the antagonistic registers of the real (being) and symbolic (meaning). Žižek interprets Christ as breaking out of the symbolic in favor of the real, resulting in the end to the sacrificial logic that produces meaning in exchange for *jouissance*.

Psychoanalysis provides significant contributions to our understanding of human subjectivity in its unique examination of finitude. Though we could turn to St. Augustine as breaking ground for what psychoanalysis will ultimately claim for itself, Sigmund Freud and his distinguished innovator, Jacques Lacan, reveal in new ways the degrees and modalities to which I am a question to myself (*Mihi quaestio factus sum*). Their contributions offer penetrating insights into what it means to be *truly* and *all too* human. Yet, when applied to theology, psychoanalysis runs up against its own limits. From Freud to Lacan, and now Žižek, Christianity is consistently interpreted within *the limits of psychoanalysis alone*, leading to this chapter's central concerns: can the psychoanalytic contribution to finitude inform theology without reducing theology to its limits? And can theology, in turn, demonstrate how this specifically psychoanalytic finitude is transformed through the Incarnation, death and Resurrection of Christ?

The interdisciplinary methodology of Emmanuel Falque offers a model for engaging psychoanalysis and theology that can assist in addressing these questions. His approach emphasizes finitude as the starting point of thought for believer and non-believer alike. For this reason, philosophy can make legitimate contributions to theology. Yet, philosophy runs up against the limit of its own limit when confronted with the bodily Resurrection of Christ, and it is at this point where, according to Falque, finitude undergoes a metamorphosis carried out by the Holy Spirit.[4] What applies to philosophy also applies to psychoanalysis and, as such, the first part of this chapter explores the distinctively psychoanalytic contribution to finitude in the context of Falque's work, focusing on 1) the Lacanian real, 2) the tragedy of the forced choice, and 3) Žižek's use of these Lacanian concepts, and their embedded notion of sacrifice, for developing his Christology. The second part of this chapter will argue that the metamorphosis of finitude includes not only our animality and inner chaos (Falque) but also those limits and conflicts (i.e. the forced choice) that produce psychological subjectivity. The consequence of this analysis is not to reinterpret theology within the limits of psychoanalysis (notwithstanding its insights into the humanity of Christ as well as of the Christian) but rather to bring psychoanalysis to its limit, showing that the tragic implications of the forced choice do not have to be the last word but an overture to the transformation that awaits in Christ's Resurrection.

The finitude of the unconscious

Finitude for Falque serves as a starting point for philosophy. It is the unsurpassable, blocked horizon whereby we encounter the burden of suffering and mortality. Not to be confused with the finite, Falque presents finitude as a positivity rather than merely a domain of deficit or sin. Finitude serves as a critical point of contact between philosophy and theology and demands that "we have the courage to loiter with all those who are our contemporaries, within the blocked horizon that comes from the simple fact of existing."[5] Although in referring to "contemporaries" Falque appears to address philosophers, this invitation for engagement should not exclude other disciplines. Herein psychoanalysis can impact this conversation for it provides conceptually significant contributions to the analysis of finitude.

Before proceeding with the content of that claim, a concern must be addressed regarding disciplinary boundaries. By suggesting convergences between philosophy and psychoanalysis on the question of finitude, are we not in danger of disciplines treading on each other's territory? The question itself assumes certain dogmatic divisions that are a by-product of historical and political forces, motivating a rage for specialization and professionalization. Rather than accept such artificial boundaries, I consider psychoanalysis to be intimately connected to philosophy, directed toward a regional domain of phenomenality.[6] To use a taxonomic metaphor, the *species* of finitude addressed by psychoanalysis participates in the wider *genus* examined by philosophy. This formulation will help us consider the contribution of the psychoanalytic unconscious to finitude and its relationship to the analysis of the unconscious bodily chaos as developed by Falque. Though not equivalent, they share notable family resemblances worthy of further investigation.

The finitude of the Lacanian real

Falque's notion of a primordial chaos addresses a dimension of human finitude concerning our bodies, which are "subject to decay ([and] putrefaction)."[7]

Falque, in *The Wedding Feast of the Lamb*, writes that "chaos remains as a fissure, or gap, in the abyss of all existence,"[8] that

> goes deep down in our emotions as well as into our drives and into our physiological and instinctive bodies . . . It starts as a kind of bottomless descent into our own animality . . . it ensures that our embodiment, or our drives, reach into what we live without ever being able to signify what it is that we live.[9]

It is an anonymous corporality, unable to formulate itself, that "overflows, without ever being received or transformed into consciousness,"[10] and upon which humankind is constructed. Drawing on Nietzsche, it is the unconscious of the body.[11]

Falque distinguishes this bodily unconscious from the Freudian one, indicating that the bodily unconscious is not psychological, "goes far beyond"[12] and "is not attached to . . . or simply enclosed"[13] in the mind, and reducing it to that would be "tantamount to forgetting its somatic roots."[14] Despite the id being "somewhere in direct contact with somatic processes"[15] as Freud indicates, the unconscious is "*not* the [Nietzschean] Body,"[16] as the id is ultimately subsumed in Freud's speculative theory of the drives, reducing it to representational concepts drawn from biology and evolution. As Michel Henry, in *The Genealogy of Psychoanalysis*, writes, "[t]he unconscious, originally representation's other, now contains representations. The aberrant concept of an 'unconscious representation' is born."[17]

Have we then run afoul in pursing points of convergence between psychoanalysis and Falque's notion of bodily chaos? Indeed not, for we find stronger convergences with the Lacanian real on three points: (i) an unrepresentable bodily dimension, (ii) a departure from the lived experience of the flesh, and (iii) a discordant relation to language.[18]

(i) Lacan discusses the real in terms of its pre-and post-symbolic expressions. In the pre-symbolic, it serves as an undifferentiated, unsymbolizable dimension of bodily existence, a frightening state of fragmentation that "Hieronymus Bosch fixed for all time in painting."[19] It is "the plentitude of the pre-Symbolic flesh, the brute, raw immediacy of the body prior to its being colonized and overwritten by the signifiers of the big Other."[20] In a manner that resembles Falque's articulation of the bodily unconscious, the real is an "obscene mass of raw, putrefied flesh, palpitating slime . . . 'the disgusting substance of life' and the 'ugliness' of *jouissance*."[21]

Upon entering language, the real feeds parasitically off the symbolic order, finding expression as "an insubstantial, ephemeral nothingness, a fleeting non-presence haunting the constituted field of reality and rendering it 'not whole'."[22] Through the symbolic, the real shifts from a source of unmediated bodily excess to a lack and "surplus effect of representation," the "bodily consequence of the insufficiency of the symbolic law."[23] Impossible to "com[e] to terms with" and "formulate," the Lacanian real appears to reflect much of the criteria for what Falque names the *limited phenomenon*.[24]

(ii) The real and the bodily unconscious both depart from the phenomenological notion of flesh that, from a Lacanian perspective, speaks to "the tendency of philosophy to succumb to the temptations of Imaginary closure"[25] and, from Falque's perspective, tends toward an "over-spiritualized lived experience."[26] Falque argues that the notion of an organic, active flesh (*Fleisch*) provides a missing dimension of bodily experience not found in the objectified, extended body (*Körper*) nor the living, passive flesh (*Leib*). The living flesh leaves out the "organicity" of the body in its raw animality with its forceful and chaotic passions and drives. Possibly converging with this is the Lacanian real. It resists psychosomatic unity as well and does not constitute a lived experience in the phenomenological sense but, rather, through the symbolic, is expressed as a disorienting crack, absence and impossibility resistant to meaning. Attempts to formulate psychological life in terms of a unified lived-body (*Leib*)

> risks resulting in a conflict free model of subjectivity . . . [that] threatens unjustifiably to downplay the various ways in which the body becomes a burdensome problem, something violently dis-identified with by the "I."[27]

Instead, the Lacanian subject consists of a radical division within itself. The mind and body are "negatively related" in an "oppositional discord" whereby the subject [*Je*] emerges through an "immanent genesis" of corporality that is, nonetheless, in "antagonistic opposition to this primordial material *Grund*."[28] If the living flesh has a place in Lacanian psychoanalysis, it may be located in Lacan's notion of the imaginary bodily ego *(moi)* that he developed through, in part, his reliance on Merleau-Ponty's early phenomenology.[29] Though a psychological development necessary for the ensuing emergence of the subject, this fanciful image of bodily unity later obscures a fundamental division within subjectivity between the symbolic and real.

(iii) This antagonism between symbolic and real finds a parallel in Falque's analysis of what he calls a "non-*signifying* chaos" that is not "able to *signify* what it is that we live."[30] Though not addressed as a full-fledged conflict, we find a tension between language and the body at several points in Falque's texts. He notes that the possession of language "comes after"[31] the arrival of organic flesh, resulting in our animality being "quickly forgotten and denied."[32] This forgetting is "more fundamental than the neglect of being"[33] and produces a loss or at least avoidance of the self's immediacy to itself. The distinction Falque makes between the raw [*crue*] voice and speech offers yet another example of this tension between body and language, one that will become highly relevant in the second section of this chapter.[34]

In sum, recalling the distinction made between philosophy and psychoanalysis as one of scope rather than complete separation, the real and bodily chaos are not equivalent but rather intimately connected, with Falque's notion offering a broader conception of embodiment. The unconscious real is the child of this bodily unconscious, emerging out of it as, in Hesiod's *Theogony*, Erebus and Nyx, darkness and night, are born of Chaos. The Lacanian real forms a regional domain of finitude that participates in the wider, philosophical notion of a bodily unconscious. As the material drives come into contact with and are structured by language, a divided subject emerges. Falque and Lacan appear to diverge on the nature of this divide, however. Whereas Falque describes one's relation to this inner chaos, following the acquisition of language, in terms of neglect, forgetting and avoidance, for Lacan this division produces a forced choice that tragically leads to either alienation or annihilation.

The tragedy of the forced choice

The very heart of psychoanalysis consists of the subject's confrontation with the finitude of the forced choice, or vel of alienation, between what Lacan somewhat problematically calls meaning and being.[35] In choosing meaning one gives up the *jouissance* of *das Ding*, becoming a lacking being (*manque-à-être*). One enters a state of deprivation, an *aphanisis* of the subject. If being is chosen, one sacrifices meaning and plunges into a state of subjective destitution and annihilation. Lacan presents the forced choice as follows: "*Your money or your life!* If I choose the money [being], I lose both. If I choose life [meaning], I have life without the money, namely, a life deprived of something."[36] Inevitably, meaning is chosen, however. One is not only forced to choose, but the choice itself is forced, resulting in an alienated subjectivity plagued by perpetual lack. The alienated subject, Lacan states, "emerges in the field of the Other, to be in a large part of its field, eclipsed by the disappearance of being, induced by the very function of the signifier."[37] While the ego [*moi*] experiences itself as independent and the owner of its thoughts and desires, the subject [*Je*] of the unconscious is born of the Other, and "overflow[s] with *other people's desires*."[38] The subject unavoidably must navigate the treacherous waters of this mysterious and alienating desire. Forgoing the *jouissance* of the real to become an alienated subject is the necessary sacrifice (i.e. symbolic castration) for achieving a meaningful existence, establishing what Lacan calls "the tragic sense of life."[39]

If alienation is inevitable, how is it possible to *choose* the real? Following the assumption of language in childhood, the only path forward here is through the symbolic itself, with its holes and cracks. When one does not cede on desire but rather pursues it ceaselessly, the subject no longer works within its conventional network of signifiers. Lacan's interpretation of Antigone exemplifies this path.[40] She pursues desire by rejecting Creon's (symbolic) order not to bury Polyneices, a decision that ultimately leads to her death. Her "no" to Creon serves as the ultimate transgressive ethical act whereby she assumes her own unalienated desire and pursues it "beyond social limits," free from "conventional signifiers."[41] This makes Antigone a tragic hero.

Whether it is the path toward alienation or annihilation, psychoanalysis leaves us with tragedy, which Freud concludes from as early as *Studies in Hysteria* (1895) to as late as *Analysis Terminable and Interminable* (1937) and from which Lacan does not alleviate us.[42] However, this claim is not meant as a criticism. The principal strength of psychoanalysis is its leading us to the edge of what is possible within the field of psychological finitude, to shift melancholy to mourning (Freud) or to traverse fantasy by not ceding on one's desire and thus preserve lack (Lacan). To avoid this tragic dimension of human existence is to escape into the imaginary that besets the dominant humanistic forms of psychology today. Psychoanalysis helps navigate the neurotic consequence of choosing meaning and the subsequent lack that results, minimizing the distorting influence of the imaginary and assuming greater responsibility for unconscious desire through a process of subjectivization. Yet, it does not allow for any kind of reconciliation between being and meaning and certainly does not allow for it, in Falque's words, "to be metamorphosed joyously."[43] Alienation or annihilation – this is our lot within the finitude of psychological existence.

The forced choice of Žižek's Christ

Žižek's theology is developed in terms of this psychoanalytic condition of finitude. Christ either gives up the symbolic by revealing the non-existence of the Big Other (Žižek's interpretation) or promotes a perverse religion that perpetuates masochistic alienation in its reaffirmation of the Big Other (his view of institutional Christianity). Thus, his theology does not avoid the tragic forced choice that determines the conditions of possibility for each subject.

Žižek's approach to Christianity presupposes a certain interpretation of sacrifice that reinforces this forced choice and prevents him from affirming the paradox of the Incarnation. In fact, sacrifice has been an implicit dimension of the forced choice all along. This is "the price to be paid for meaning."[44] Sacrifice as symbolic castration is the necessary mechanism by which our psychic finitude expresses itself. Žižek describes two ways in which this perverse sacrifice manifests. First, the subject sacrifices itself as a means of disavowing the impotence and lack of the Big Other, as when a child (or perhaps White House official) willingly forgoes their own *jouissance* in order to protect the honor of an abusive parent (or a narcissistic president). Second, the subject feigns symbolic castration by disavowing the *jouissance* it already possesses in order to prevent the Big Other's prohibition of it, as when we manufacture an appearance of laboring to keep the Other from demanding more of our time. In one situation the subject covers over the lack of the

Other and, in the other, covers over the lack of lack within itself. Both are attempts to appease the Big Other, thereby preserving meaning. Žižek writes

> sacrifice is a "gift of reconciliation" to the Other, destined to appease its desire. Sacrifice conceals the abyss of the Other's desire, more precisely: it conceals the Other's lack, [and] inconsistency . . . Sacrifice is a guarantee that the Other exists.[45]

In *The Wizard of Oz*, the citizens of Oz, to maintain the social order, preserve the big secret that in fact there is no wizard. At the same time, those who approach this supposed great wizard, such as the Tinman, Lion, Scarecrow and Dorothy, all proclaim that they lack something they had all along. The subject resists revealing the lacking Other to the point of engaging in these perverse sacrifices. We are not only forced into alienation, but also unconsciously preserve it at all costs, thereby forming the basis for our individual and collective neuroses.

Responding to Jean-Luc Marion's essay on sacrifice, Žižek argues that perverse sacrifice is "immanent to sacrifice-as-exchange."[46] In becoming a subject, i.e. undergoing symbolic castration, we unwittingly erect a master signifier that can guarantee the meaning (value) of all subsequent economic transactions, whereby, as Marion describes,

> the sacrifice (sacrificing agent) abandons a good (by dispossession, of exposure or destruction), so that the supposedly superior other (divine or mortal) will accept it, and in so doing, enter into a contractual relation and by contract, return a good (real or symbolic).[47]

This kind of exchange can only take place if an Other exists who makes sacrifice meaningful by guaranteeing the value of this exchange. The purpose of symbolic castration is to establish the existence of this Big Other.

This understanding of sacrifice is certainly contradictory to the very meaning of sacrifice, leading to an *aporia* in which, as Derrida demonstrates, the conditions of the possibility of sacrifice are the conditions of its impossibility.[48] Marion attempts to resolve this *aporia* through the logic of the gift that brackets those conditions. Žižek diverges from Marion's approach and instead formulates a way out of sacrifice altogether through his unconventional interpretation of Christianity. In a manner analogous to Antigone, he argues that Christ makes "a sacrifice *for* the real"[49] in a transgressive ethical act whereby Christ proclaims, through his cry of abandonment, that "God is dead, that there is no big Other"[50] to appease. The curtain has been lifted to reveal the lack of the Big Other: there is no all-powerful wizard. Christ "breaks with sacrificial logic because what dies is the very guarantor of such a system."[51]

Although showing a way out of the *aporia*, Žižek's theology preserves and presupposes the basic logic of sacrifice. As the Catholic theologian and scholar of Lacan and Žižek, Marcus Pound, argues, "[Žižek's] entire theoretical apparatus is predicated upon such a sacrificial system . . . Žižek remains locked into the very system he is critical of."[52] In the second part, I explore Falque's alternative, showing that, in fact, while Christ does experience dereliction at the height of his suffering, this need not lead to the conclusion that the Father abandons him but, on the contrary, points to the humanity that Christ assumes. A metamorphosis is not enacted through escaping these conditions of finitude and leaping into transcendence. Rather, it is enacted in and through Christ fully assuming the finitude of humanity. And if indeed Christ is *fully* human, as he is fully divine, he also *fully* assumes that regional domain of finitude revealed by psychoanalysis. We must then affirm, against the heresy of Apollinarianism, that Christ possesses a fully human mind and, as such, assumes our psychological finitude as much as our existential finitude in order to accomplish our salvation in it. As Falque writes, "God arrives at the *totality* of humankind precisely in order to metamorphose humanity."[53] That Christ enters into psychological suffering as well, rather than debasing the divinity of Christ, reveals ever more the extent of Christ's salvific action, offering hope to those suffering from intractable psychological maladies. The metamorphosis of psychoanalysis, should there be one, will thus entail a conversion from cathartic tragedy that turns "hysterical misery into common unhappiness"[54] into a theological hope for "the peace of God that surpasses all understanding" (Philippians 4:7).

Metamorphosis of the unconscious

The previous section addressed two dimensions of finitude: (i) the bodily real as the primordial ground of subjectivity, and (ii) the forced choice that emerges out of the antagonistic relation between the real and symbolic. This forced choice leads the subject to confront either (i) the sacrificial logic of exchange that produces alienation or (ii) the loss of any transcendent guarantee of meaning, thereby producing subjective annihilation. This section examines what implications a fully Christian metamorphosis would have for these dimensions of finitude. *Specifically, do the Incarnation, death and Resurrection have any bearing on psychoanalysis?* Without being exhaustive in the numerous paths to explore here, two possibilities are considered concerning the metamorphosis of the real and symbolic as they address the forced choice.

Metamorphosis of the real

Falque, in *Le passeur de Gethsémani* (§37), affirms Christ's experience of existential meaninglessness on the Cross. Yet, he argues, responding chiefly to Jürgen Moltmann's theology, that there is no basis in scripture for concluding this entails the death of God, for

> the Father does not cease to be Father for his Son but on the contrary becomes even more so, first in the cry itself directed toward his God in

the "*my god, my god*, why have you abandoned me?" (Mark 15:34) ... and finally in Christ's last words on the cross "*Father*, into your hands I commend my spirit" (Luke 23:46).[55]

For Falque, Christ's cry of dereliction signals not the death of the Father whom he still addresses, but rather his assumption of the fullness of human finitude as the dread and anxiety before death. What Žižek does not consider, and what Falque establishes, is that the fullness of the Incarnation requires this, for the "weight" of death is proportional to the "glory" of the Resurrection.[56]

Christ assumes not only existential human suffering but also reaches down into that regional domain of suffering that comes with being a psychological subject. A dimension of this suffering includes Christ, in his humanity, assuming the condition of not-knowing, i.e. a lack of cognitive understanding concerning the Resurrection:[57] a place where the signifier fails. In arriving at the failure of the symbolic, Christ confronts the trauma of the unconscious real. Yet, *contra* Wittgenstein, "whereof [he] cannot speak," he does not remain silent. Crying out to God in the midst of his suffering, Christ persists in a kind of speech. The very fact that Christ speaks at all in his moment of abandonment suggests something other than the death of God. Lacan, in his seminar *The Sinthome*, writes that "in spite of everything, the fact of saying aims to be heard."[58] To claim, as Žižek does, that Christ announces the death of God in his cry of abandonment is to miss the point of speech itself, which is to be received. In his cry of abandonment, Christ does not forego the symbolic order altogether, but rather discloses the real of the voice within it. "Christ's point," Pound writes, "is not to exit the symbolic into the real, but rather manifest the real in the symbolic."[59] This assumption of the traumatic real within the midst of persisting signifiers is accomplished in Christ's lamentation, whereby the immanence of speech itself is revealed.

This is no ordinary discourse. Speech recedes into the background as the voice emerges from its invisible recesses. In his seminar *The Sinthome*, Lacan offers the neologism *lalangue* to describe a function of language whereby the real breaks through ordinary speech. *Lalangue* is the language of the unconscious real associated with a surplus of the voice, communicating something over and beyond speech. Falque's analysis of the voice in *Crossing the Rubicon* offers something analogous within the broader context of existential finitude. Here the voice expresses something irreducible to speech that is directed toward our animality. To become "aphonal" to the brute, raw voice of Christ in his cry of agony, Falque argues, is to "lose what it signified originally – not only the interrogation of the meaning (why?!) but the tearing of the body,"[60] a tearing that, in psychoanalysis, can be articulated as an encounter with the traumatic real.

The metamorphosis takes place in *passing* this suffering voice on to the Father. Falque maintains that this *passing* consists of existential suffering. However, the *passing* of the traumatic real should not be excluded here. The metamorphosis of the real transpires in the *lalangue* of Christ whereby the suffering voice that cries out to a distant God ("*my God, my God* (Ἐλωῐ

Ἐλωΐ) why have you abandoned me?"; Mark 15:34) is passed on through a paternal intimacy ("*Father* (Πάτερ), into your hands, I commend my spirit": Luke 23:46). This linguistic shift to the personal term "Father" is no superfluous variation of speech but rather represents a transformation in humanity's relationship with the Other. Notably, Žižek takes the liberty to simultaneously ignore Luke 23:46 and to reinterpret Christ's words in Mark 15:34 as "*Father*, why have you forsaken me?," which serves his purpose of demonstrating the death of the symbolic father. Yet, close adherence to Christ's words in scripture suggests that if any God truly and permanently dies it is the God of the real rather than of the symbolic. Such an impersonal God, John Manoussakis argues in *The Ethics of Time*, is "an encounter with the divine without incarnation and without relation"; it is "without temporal mediation (history) and without the mediation of the face of the Other (intersubjectivity)."[61] In contrast, Christ reveals to us a very different kind of God, one that is a compassionate father with a face temporally revealed through the icon of Christ whose lamentation completes what the Incarnation inaugurated: God assumes our humanity from birth (incarnation) all the way to the suffering of death (crucifixion) and thereby transforms both (resurrection).

This raises another difficulty concerning the alienation and lack produced through the symbolic order. If the metamorphosis of the real transpires in the passing of Christ's traumatic suffering to the Father and what dies is the God of the real rather than the real God (Manoussakis), then is there not a corresponding metamorphosis of the symbolic that transforms alienation and lack? We have already seen the beginnings of this in the shift of Christ's language from the impersonal to the personal. As it is impossible, in actuality, to separate the real and symbolic, it is not surprising that a transformation in one leads to a transformation in the other. Yet, the analysis above does not exhaust the possibilities and, in what follows, we shall explore a metamorphosis that begins with the symbolic and its economic logic of sacrifice.

Metamorphosis of the symbolic

Psychoanalysis teaches us that behind a veneer of civility lies the hostile nature of human relationships. This hostility begins with one's parents, whose desire is unconsciously appropriated at the cost of *jouissance*, which subsequently becomes the mode of relating to God as the Big Other. The analysis above revealed that in fact Christ does not leave the symbolic but rather manifests the traumatic real within it, which he passes on to his Father. For there to be meaning without alienation requires a corresponding metamorphosis of the perverse sacrificial system whereby one enters the symbolic order.

In the first section, I indicated that Žižek preserves the basic logic of economic sacrifice. In doing so, he obscures the distinctively Christian contribution of the primacy of the gift. If perverse sacrifice is immanent to the logic of economic exchange that produces alienation, then perhaps the logic of the gift offers a counter possibility to Žižek's proposal whereby sacrifice is not exited but transformed. Marion's analysis of the gift offers a resource for considering this transformation. Admittedly, appropriating Marion's work on the gift in this context runs the risk of contradiction as the gift is usually thought within the horizon of unconditioned givenness, whereas Falque's project begins within the conditions of finitude. To move forward requires, for a moment, bracketing the larger phenomenological project of givenness to consider Marion's trenchant analysis of the gift principally as a theological concept that finds its origin in Christ, thus reading his more recent essays on the gift and sacrifice in light of his earlier theological text *Dieu sans l'être*.[62] Doing so provides the possibility of considering the transition from economy to gift as a metamorphosis that has far-reaching implications for the hostile sociality, rivalry and scarcity that ground our alienated subjectivity.

To be in relationship with the Other, according to Lacan, I inevitably become, through symbolic castration, a *manque-à-être*. Lack is a precondition of subjectivity and an essential dimension of human finitude that most singularly defines the subject. According to Marion, "I can exchange what I possess, but not the lack that possesses my heart."[63] The metamorphosis of the symbolic will not rid us of lack but changes the meaning of sacrifice that produces this lack. Christ's metamorphosis of the economic logic of sacrifice into the logic of the gift produces a kind of lack that is, in Pound's words,

> a product of the plenitude of God's truth; it is not that there is not enough, it is that there is too much! And herein is the difference between the respective goals of analysis and worship: in the former one must be reconciled to an ontological lack; in the latter lack is a sign of God's excessive love in which we share.[64]

In this economy, the signifier points to a *lack* due to absence, whereas the signifier under the logic of the gift *lacks* proportionality to the excess of the gift itself. Thus, lack undergoes a metamorphosis corresponding to the transformation of sacrifice from economy to gift.

This transformation also brings about a change in the relation with the Other, for relations under the gift are not defined by obligations and contracts, and the act of sacrifice does not signify destruction, dispossession, or transfer. Rather, sacrifice becomes a matter of repetition and recognition. Repetition because the act of sacrifice, Marion writes, "makes a gift by taking from among gifts already given in order to re-give it . . . to make a gift by reversing the first gift toward the one who gives it."[65] This repetition opens up the possibility of a non-alienating meaning because repetition recognizes the origin of the gift. An alienating economic sacrifice, as Karl Marx demonstrates regarding labor and commodities, permanently separates the gift from its origin through a logic of ownership. And whereas becoming an alienated subject commands a loss of being, becoming a gifted subject renews being, for, as with meaning, it originates from an exteriority. Interpellation does not stop at the symbolic (meaning) but goes all the way down to the real (being) and, as such, even being is given. It is, as Eric Santner writes, an "'interpellation' beyond ideological interpellation."[66] This reconciles me to the divine Other who, rather than a source of oppression, is revealed as the origin of my creation, a creation that in full abandonment (through the *imitatio Christi*) repeats itself as gift, thereby reconciling one's being to its non-originary origin. This transformed sacrifice gives more than it loses, for it repeats the lack I always already am by recognizing and reconciling myself to the origin of the gift that I always already am not.

Christ does not break from sacrifice, nor does his sacrifice conceal the abyss of the Other's desire; rather, he transforms the relation with the Other from one of master–slave (alienation) to one of friendship whereby the desire of the Other is no longer a source of mysterious terror. As Christ, in John 15:15, proclaims:

> I no longer call you servants, because a servant does not know his master's business.
> Instead, I have called you friends, *for everything that I learned from my Father I have made known to you.*

This is not a cognitive knowledge but the most important knowledge of all: the desire of the Other. The question of the Other's desire, which we grope blindly to satisfy, has been revealed through Christ who, by assuming the unconscious, offers a theological hope for the transformation of our psychic suffering born out of a perverse sacrificial system. Yet, this revelation of God's desire does not undo his otherness nor does it subdue desire or lack in the subject; it rather reveals a kenotic lack within the Trinity, making possible a non-alienating "*communion* of Desire at the very heart of otherness,"[67] exemplified in the fifteenth century icon of the Holy Trinity by Andrei Rublev. Lack is portrayed here in the space that opens up between the three persons of the Trinity, welcoming the ontological lack constitutive of human subjectivity. It is a communion of lacks that does not alienate but reconciles being and meaning, the real and symbolic, producing the joy of metamorphosis that exceeds even *jouissance*.

Conclusion: "crossing the Rubicon"

In speaking of theology's contribution to psychoanalysis, we must not forget psychoanalysis's contribution to theology. Psychoanalysis speaks to the horizon of finitude vis-à-vis our access to ourselves and the compromises we are forced into in order to preserve a fragile and alienated subjectivity. Herein, religion is easily co-opted into a perverse source of that alienation.[68] To ignore the bodily *or* psychic unconscious would be tantamount to taking flight into what Falque identifies as "angelism," and, for Lacan, is an imaginary suturing of lack. While believers cannot accept that the subversive kernel of Christianity is *only* accessible through the Lacanian forced choice as Žižek proposes, they are well-served not to flee from it, as doing so obfuscates the ways in which neurotic subjectivity is positioned relative to the Big Other of ideology and its perversion of Christianity.[69] The pervasive filtering of faith through politics and economics among believers today, notably in the United States, is sufficient to warrant such a concern.

Yet, as this paper has attempted to demonstrate, this is not a one way "*crossing of the Rubicon.*"[70] Theology offers the possibility for this psychoanalytic limit to undergo a metamorphosis. Rather than reading Christ's sacrifice reduced to this finitude as Žižek appears to do, Falque offers a model for how his sacrifice inaugurates a metamorphosis of the real and symbolic unconscious and, as such, surpasses and transforms the distinctively psychoanalytic limit, affirming not only the "more we theologize, the better we philosophize"[71] but also the better we psychoanalyze.

Notes

1 For an analysis of Žižek's problematic insertion of the word "father" in this passage, see Marcus Pound, *Žižek: A (Very) Critical Introduction* (Grand Rapids, MI: William B. Eerdmans Publishing Co., 2008), 49.
2 Slavoj Žižek, "The Fear of Four Words: A Modest Plea for the Hegelian Reading of Christianity," in *The Monstrosity of Christ: Paradox or Dialectic*, ed. Creston Davis (Cambridge, MA: MIT Press, 2009), 57.
3 I will refer to the vel of alienation as "the forced choice" throughout the rest of this chapter.
4 Notably, Žižek's analysis excludes the bodily resurrection and instead interprets resurrection as the Holy Spirit, which is none other than the emancipatory collective of believers outside of hierarchy and with no ontological guarantee of meaning in the Big Other.
5 Emmanuel Falque, *The Metamorphosis of Finitude: An Essay on Birth and Resurrection*, trans. George Hughes (New York: Fordham University Press, 2004/2012), 17.
6 In this regard, I diverge here from Freud and Lacan and follow a path paved by Ludwig Binswanger, whose *Daseinsanalysis* represents a focused use of Heidegger's thought while at the same time broadening its application to domains that Heidegger did not intend. See Ludwig Binswanger, *Being-in-the-World*, trans. Jacob Needlemann (New York: Harper & Row Publishers, 1963/1967).
7 Emmanuel Falque, *The Wedding Feast of the Lamb: Eros, the Body, and the Eucharist*, trans. George Hughes (New York: Fordham University Press, 2011/2016), 100.
8 Ibid., 16.
9 Ibid., 26.
10 Ibid., 22.
11 Ibid., 107.
12 Ibid.

13 Ibid., 72.
14 Ibid., 108.
15 Sigmund Freud, *New Introductory Lectures on Psycho-Analysis*, trans. J. Strachey (New York, NY: W. W. Norton & Company, 1933/1965), 91.
16 Paul-Laurent Assoun's, *Freud and Nietzsche*, trans. Richard L. Collier Jr. (New York: Continuum, 1980/2000), 117. I would not go as far as Assoun to claim that the body "does not have a status for Freud," but rather that its sense must be teased out from the implicit assumptions concerning the embedded in Freud's thought, assumptions that do not conform to the bodily terminology at his disposal. See Brian W. Becker, "Flight from the Flesh: Freud's Id and Ego as Saturated Phenomena," in *Breached Horizons: The Work of Jean-Luc Marion*, ed. Rachel Bath, Antonio Calcagno, Kathryn Lawson and Steve Lofts (Lanham, MD: Rowman & Littlefield, forthcoming). In this chapter, I explore a phenomenological approach to the Freudian id through Marion's examination of the flesh as saturated phenomenon.
17 Michel Henry, *The Genealogy of Psychoanalysis*, trans. D. Brick (Stanford, CA: Stanford University Press, 1985/1993), 298. The same has been argued concerning another dimension of finitude in Freud, the death drive. See Roger Frie, "On the Nature and Meaning of Human Finitude," *The American Journal of Psychoanalysis* 73, no. 2 (2013): 158–72.
18 This is a thesis originally developed by Babich, who writes "that Nietzsche's concept of nature . . . is a notion corresponding to the value of the register of the Real for Lacan." And: "The Dionysian understanding of the nature of the world as terrifying reflects the rigor of the Real." Babette Babich, "On the Order of the Real: Nietzsche and Lacan," *Articles and Chapters in Academic Book Collections* 13 (1996): 55, 58.
19 Jacques Lacan, *Écrits*, trans. Bruce Fink (New York, NY: W. W. Norton & Company, 1949/2006), 78.
20 Adrian Johnston, *Žižek's Ontology: A Transcendental Materialist Theory of Subjectivity* (Evanston, IL: Northwestern University Press, 2008), 147.
21 Ibid., 24.
22 Ibid. Where does the Freudian id fall within Lacan's notion of the real? Lacan writes that "[libido], as its name indicates can only be a participant in the hole . . ." The id and its erotic drive participates in the real just as I've suggested the real participates in our bodily chaos. Jacques Lacan, *The Seminar of Jacques Lacan, Book XXIII: The Sinthome, 1975–1976*, trans. A.R. Price (Malden, MA: Polity Press, 2005/2016), 29.
23 Charles Shepherdson, "A Pound of Flesh: Lacan's Reading of 'The Visible and the Invisible'." *Diacritics* 27, no. 4 (1997): 73n9.
24 Falque, *Wedding Feast*, 22.
25 Tom Eyers, *Lacan and the Concept of the "Real"* (New York: Palgrave Macmillan, 2012), 123.
26 Falque, *Wedding Feast*, 41.
27 Johnston, *Žižek's Ontology*, 53.
28 Ibid., 57.
29 "In effect he [Merleau-Ponty] hangs on to the notion of totality, of unitary functioning, he always presupposes a given unity accessible to what in the end will be an instantaneous, theoretical, contemplative apprehension . . . . one can no longer assert, as Merleau-Ponty would like to, the primacy of consciousness. Consciousness . . . plays, without him realizing it, the function . . . of the dialectic of the ego." Jacques Lacan, *The Seminar of Jacques Lacan, Book II: The Ego in Freud's Theory and in the Technique of Psychoanalysis, 1954–1955*, ed. Jacques-Alain Miller, trans. Sylvana Tomaselli (New York & London: W.W. Norton & Company, 1978/1991), 78.
30 Falque, *Wedding Feast*, 26 [italics added].

31 Ibid., 93.
32 Ibid., 89.
33 Ibid., 43.
34 Emmanuel Falque, *Crossing the Rubicon: The Borderlands of Philosophy and Theology*, trans. Reuben Shank (New York: Fordham University Press, 2013/2016).
35 Lacan ambiguously calls this a forced choice between meaning and being, "terms that I [Lacan] do not propose without some reluctance." Jacques Lacan, *The Seminar of Jacques Lacan, Book XI: The Four Fundamental Concepts of Psychoanalysis*, ed. Jacques-Alain Miller, trans. Alan Sheridan (New York & London: W.W. Norton & Company, 1973/1998), 246. Lacan's usage of the term "being" here, while seeming to connote something ontological, conforms to neither traditional nor Heideggerian uses. Although I will often use the term "meaning" to refer to the symbolic, it is more accurate to say that meaning entails the intersection of the symbolic and imaginary.
36 Lacan, *Four Fundamental Concepts of Psychoanalysis*, 212.
37 Ibid., 211.
38 Bruce Fink, *The Lacanian Subject: Between Language and Jouissance* (Princeton, NJ: Princeton University Press, 1995), 9.
39 Jacques Lacan, *The Seminar of Jacques Lacan, Book VII: The Ethics of Psychoanalysis 1959–1960*, ed. Jacques-Alain Miller, trans. Dennis Potter (New York: W.W. Norton & Company, 1986/1997), 313.
40 Lacan, *Ethics of Psychoanalysis*, 243–87.
41 Mari Ruti, *The Singularity of Being: Lacan and the Immortal Within* (New York: Fordham University Press, 2012), 71. This interpretation is a matter of some debate among Lacanian scholars, with some (e.g. Žižek, Ruti, and Zupancic) arguing for an "ethics of the real," whereas others such as Marc de Kesel reject this approach and interpret Lacan as rendering impossible and nonsensical any plunge into the real.
42 As Freud famously wrote: "But you will see for yourself that much has been gained if we succeed in turning your hysterical misery into common unhappiness. Having restored your inner life, you will be better able to arm yourself against that unhappiness." Sigmund Freud and Josef Breuer, *Studies in Hysteria*, trans. Nicola Luckhurst (New York: Penguin Group, 1895/2004), 306. Lacan echoes Freud: "There is in Aristotle a discipline of happiness . . . . . Please note that one finds nothing similar in psychoanalysis." Lacan, *Ethics of Psychoanalysis*, 292–3.
43 Falque, *Wedding Feast*, 112.
44 Slavoj Žižek, *God in Pain: Inversions of Apocalypse* (New York: Seven Stories Press, 2012), 52.
45 Slavoj Žižek, *Enjoy Your Symptom!: Jacques Lacan in Hollywood and Out* (New York: Routledge, 2001), 56.
46 Žižek, *God in Pain*, 52.
47 Jean-Luc Marion, *The Reason of the Gift*, trans. Stephen E. Lewis (Charlottesville, VA: University of Virginia Press, 2011), 74–5.
48 See Jacques Derrida, *Given Time: I. Counterfeit Money*, trans. Peggy Kamuf (Chicago, IL: University of Chicago Press, 1991/1992); *The Gift of Death*, trans. David Wills (Chicago, IL: University of Chicago Press, 1992/1995).
49 Žižek, *God in Pain*, 55 [italics added].
50 Ibid.
51 Pound, *Žižek*, 19.
52 Ibid., 41.
53 Falque, *Wedding Feast*, 94.
54 Freud and Breuer, *Studies in Hysteria*, 306.
55 "le Père ne cesse pas de demeurer Père pour son Fils, mais au contraire le devient plus encore: d'abord dans le cri lancé vers son Dieu – c'est-à-dire celui du

Fils – dans le 'mon Dieu, mon Dieu pourquoi m'as-tu abandonné?'" (Mc 15, 34); . . . et enfin dans la dernière parole du Christ en croix: "Père, entre tes mains je remets mon esprit (Lc 23, 46)." Emmanuel Falque, "Le Passeur de Gethsémani," in *Triduum Philosophique* (Paris: Les Éditions du Cerf., 1999/2015), §37 [my translation].

56 Emmanuel Falque, "Suffering Death," trans. Christina M. Gschwandtner, in *The Role of Death in Life: A Multidisciplinary Examination of the Relationship between Life and Death*, ed. John Behr and Connor Cunningham (Eugene, OR: Wipf & Stock Publishers, 2015), 47.

57 Falque writes: "The distinction between the two natures in the person of Christ makes it possible to bring about a division between his divine nature's complete vision of the resurrection and his human nature's absolute ignorance of the afterlife . . . One can speak with Hans Urs von Balthasar of the 'certainty of faith,' rather than of strict 'intellectual knowledge,' in regard to the consciousness of the resurrection in Christ's person." Falque, "Suffering Death," 49.

58 Lacan, *The Sinthome*, 110.

59 Marcus Pound, *Theology, Psychoanalysis, and Trauma* (London: SCM Press, 2007), 114.

60 Falque, *Crossing the Rubicon*, 64.

61 John Panteleimon Manoussakis, *The Ethics of Time: A Phenomenology and Hermeneutics of Change* (New York: Bloomsbury, 2016), 126.

62 This raises the rather recalcitrant issue concerning the possibility of the gift "outside the actuality of Revelation given as such." For Falque, "[t]he theologization of givenness" provides its "power" and "true sense." Emmanuel Falque, "Larvatus pro Deo," trans. Robyn Horner, in *Counter-Experiences: Reading Jean-Luc Marion*, ed. Kevin Hart (Notre Dame, IN: University of Notre Dame Press, 2007), 195. I would not go as far as Falque as I believe Marion has rigorously established the philosophical legitimacy of the concept of the gift reduced to givenness that has a "power" and "sense" independent of its theological context. However, Marion's analysis of the gift, even in his later writings, can also be appropriated for theological purposes without necessarily resorting to givenness itself, particularly when, rather than starting from the thing itself, we begin, as Falque does, with the finitude of the believer. Rather than opposing views, Marion and Falque offer different but complementary starting points. Falque suggests as much when, concerning the differences between his concept of the limited phenomenon and Marion's saturated phenomenon, he writes: "In reality, these two approaches [Marion's and Falque's] are not opposed: they signal two different, even complementary, ways to consider the rupture and the opening; that is, the absoluteness of revelation but also the possibility of transformation." Falque, *Crossing the Rubicon*, 145.

63 Jean-Luc Marion, *The Erotic Phenomenon*, trans. Stephen E. Lewis (Chicago, IL: University of Chicago Press, 2003/2007), 108.

64 Pound, *Theology, Psychoanalysis, and Trauma*, 169.

65 Jean-Luc Marion, *The Reason of the Gift*, 83. This notion of repetition offers a counter to the repetition compulsion.

66 Eric Santner, "Miracles Happen: Benjamin, Rosenzweig, and the Matter of the Neighbor," in *The Neighbor: Three Inquiries in Political Theology*, by Slavoj Žižek, Eric L. Santner and Kenneth Reinhard (Chicago, IL: University of Chicago, 2013), 131.

67 John D. Zizioulas, *Communion & Otherness* (New York: T&T Clark, 2006), 51. In a footnote, Zizioulas indicates that Lacan's understanding of desire and otherness "differs fundamentally" from the Greek Fathers (51n112). However, following Falque's philosophical approach, this is not a difference of mutual exclusion but one that emerges through a metamorphosis of desire.

68 "psychoanalysis involves the function rather than the truth of religious belief." Merold Westphal, *Suspicion & Faith: The Religious Uses of Modern Atheism* (New York: Fordham University Press, 1998), 56.
69 See Slavoj Žižek, *The Puppet and the Dwarf: The Perverse Core of Christianity* (Cambridge, MA: MIT Press, 2003).
70 See Falque, *Crossing the Rubicon*. Falque uses the metaphor of "crossing the Rubicon" to communicate how philosophy and theology can cross each other's boundaries and influence each other while preserving their legitimate differences. To extend this metaphor, I would place psychoanalysis as an allotment along the river bank where philosophy resides.
71 Emmanuel Falque, *God, the Flesh, and the Other: From Irenaeus to Duns Scotus*, trans. William Christian Hackett (Evanston, IL: Northwestern University Press, 2008/2015), 16.

Bibliography

Assoun, Paul-Laurent. *Freud and Nietzsche*. Translated by Richard L. Collier Jr. New York: Continuum, 1980/2000.
Babich, Babette. "On the Order of the Real: Nietzsche and Lacan." *Articles and Chapters in Academic Book Collections* 13 (1996): 43–68.
Becker, Brian. "Flight from the Flesh: Freud's Id and Ego as Saturated Phenomena." In *Breached Horizons: The Work of Jean-Luc Marion*, edited by Rachel Bath, Antonio Calcagno, Kathryn Lawson and Steve Lofts. Lanham, MD: Rowman & Littlefield, forthcoming.
Binswanger, Ludwig. *Being-in-the-World*. Translated by Jacob Needleman. New York: Harper & Row Publishers, 1963/1967.
Derrida, Jacques. *The Gift of Death*. Translated by David Wills. Chicago, IL: University of Chicago Press, 1995.
———. *Given Time: I. Counterfeit Money*. Translated by Peggy Kamuf. Chicago, IL: University of Chicago Press, 1992.
Eyers, Tom. *Lacan and the Concept of the "Real."* New York: Palgrave Macmillan, 2012.
Falque, Emmanuel. *Crossing the Rubicon: The Borderlands of Philosophy and Theology*. Translated by Reuben Shank. New York: Fordham University Press, 2013/2016.
———. *God, the Flesh, and the Other: From Irenaeus to Duns Scotus*. Translated by William Christian Hackett. Evanston, IL: Northwestern University Press, 2008/2015.
———. "Larvatus pro Deo." Translated by Robyn Horner. In *Counter-Experiences: Reading Jean-Luc Marion*, edited by Kevin Hart, 181–99. Notre Dame, IN: University of Notre Dame Press, 2007.
———. *The Metamorphosis of Finitude: An Essay on Birth and Resurrection*. Translated by George Hughes. New York: Fordham University Press, 2004/2012.
———. "Le Passeur de Gethsémani." In *Triduum Philosophique*. Paris: Les Éditions du Cerf, 1999/2015.
———. "Suffering Death." Translated by Christina M. Gschwandtner. In *The Role of Death in Life: A Multidisciplinary Examination of the Relationship Between Life and Death*, edited by John Behr and Connor Cunningham, 45–55. Eugene, OR: Wipf and Stock Publishers, 2015.
———. *The Wedding Feast of the Lamb: Eros, the Body, and the Eucharist*. Translated by George Hughes. New York: Fordham University Press, 2011/2016.

Fink, Bruce. *The Lacanian Subject: Between Language and Jouissance*. Princeton, NJ: Princeton University Press, 1995.

Freud, Sigmund. *New Introductory Lectures on Psycho-Analysis*. Translated by J. Strachey. New York: W.W. Norton & Company, 1933/1965.

Freud, Sigmund and Josef Breuer. *Studies in Hysteria*. Translated by Nicola Luckhurst. New York: Penguin Group, 1895/2004.

Frie, Roger. "On the Nature and Meaning of Human Finitude." *The American Journal of Psychoanalysis* 73, no. 2 (2013): 158–72.

Henry, Michel. *The Genealogy of Psychoanalysis*. Translated by D. Brick. Stanford, CA: Stanford University Press, 1985/1993.

Johnston, Adrian. *Žižek's Ontology: A Transcendental Materialist Theory of Subjectivity*. Evanston, IL: Northwestern University Press, 2008.

Lacan, Jacques. *Écrits*. Translated by Bruce Fink. New York: W.W. Norton & Company, 1949/2006.

———. *The Seminar of Jacques Lacan, Book II: The Ego in Freud's Theory and in the Technique of Psychoanalysis, 1954–1955*. Edited by Jacques-Alain Miller. Translated by Sylvana Tomaseilli. New York & London: W.W. Norton & Company, 1978/1991.

———. *The Seminar of Jacques Lacan, Book VII, The Ethics of Psychoanalysis 1959–1960*. Edited by Jacques-Alain Miller. Translated by Dennis Potter. New York: W.W. Norton & Company, 1986/1997.

———. *The Seminar of Jacques Lacan, Book XI: The Four Fundamental Concepts of Psychoanalysis*. Edited by Jacques-Alain Miller. Translated by Alan Sheridan. New York & London: W.W. Norton & Company, 1973/1998.

———. *The Seminar of Jacques Lacan, Book XXIII: The Sinthome, 1975–1976*. Edited by Jacques-Alain Miller. Translated by A. R. Price. Malden, MA: Polity Press, 2005/2016.

Manoussakis, John Panteleimon. *The Ethics of Time: A Phenomenology and Hermeneutics of Change*. New York: Bloomsbury, 2016.

Marion, Jean-Luc. *The Erotic Phenomenon*. Translated by Stephen E. Lewis. Chicago, IL: University of Chicago Press, 2003/2007.

———. *The Reason of the Gift*. Translated by Stephen E. Lewis. Charlottesville, VA: University of Virginia Press, 2011.

Pound, Marcus. *Theology, Psychoanalysis, and Trauma*. London: SCM Press, 2007.

———. *Žižek: A (very) Critical Introduction*. Grand Rapids, MI: William B. Eerdmans Publishing Co., 2008.

Ruti, Mari. *The Singularity of Being: Lacan and the Immortal Within*. New York: Fordham University Press, 2012.

Santner, Eric. "Miracles Happen: Benjamin, Rosenzweig, and the Matter of the Neighbor." In *The Neighbor: Three Inquiries in Political Theology*, by Slavoj Žižek, Eric L. Santner and Kenneth Reinhard, 76–133. Chicago, IL: University of Chicago, 2013.

Shepherdson, Charles. "A Pound of Flesh: Lacan's Reading of 'The Visible and the Invisible'." *Diacritics* 27, no. 4 (1997): 70–86.

Westphal, Merold. *Suspicion & Faith: The Religious Uses of Modern Atheism*. New York: Fordham University Press, 1998.

Žižek, Slavoj. *Enjoy Your Symptom: Jacques Lacan in Hollywood and Out*. New York: Routledge, 2001.

———. "The Fear of Four Words: A Modest Plea for the Hegelian Reading of Christianity." In *The Monstrosity of Christ: Paradox or Dialectic*, by Slavoj Žižek and John Milbank. Edited by Creston Davis, 24–109. Cambridge, MA: MIT Press, 2009.

———. *The Puppet and the Dwarf: The Perverse Core of Christianity*. Cambridge, MA: MIT Press, 2003.

Žižek, Slavoj and Boris Gunjević. *God in Pain: Inversions of Apocalypse*. New York: Seven Stories Press, 2012.

Zizioulas, John D. *Communion & Otherness*. New York: T&T Clark, 2006.

4 "No wonder, then, that love itself disappears"[1]

Neighbor-love in Žižek and Meister Eckhart

Chase Padusniak

What has Meister Eckhart to do with Slavoj Žižek? One was a fourteenth-century German scholastic theologian and mystic, the other is a Slovenian Marxist, atheist and self-identified "materialist theologian."[2] *Prima facie*, very little. In *The Monstrosity of Christ*, for example, Žižek devotes only ten – largely dismissive – pages to the medieval master.[3] And yet, digging beneath their superficial differences, the worthiness of a comparison begins to emerge.

In one of his responses to Žižek in their shared volume, John Milbank notes his interlocutor's Protestantizing reading of history, a Hegelian narrative driving with the force and violence of dialectical logic, which itself has a tendency to erase or otherwise efface the Catholic-medieval vein of Christian thought:

> But here one can point to an interesting *symptom* in Žižek's writings. Basically, he endorses a Whiggish, Protestant metanarrative. Christianity gradually, if dialectically, posits its own covertly presupposed radicalism. Protestantism negates the Catholic negation of (Eastern) Orthodoxy, Hegel is the fully-fledged Protestant consummation of Christian metaphysical logic.[4]

In other words, like Milbank, we might pause on Žižek's reading of Eckhart and thereby recuperate something of the medieval Christian embedded within the relentless logic of his "Whiggish, Protestant metanarrative."[5] Unlike Milbank, however, we might note how Eckhart's views (those of a distinctly medieval personalism) *complement* Žižek's notion of "the neighbor," a topic largely absent from *The Monstrosity of Christ* but of particular interest in other works.[6] In doing so, Žižek's "ethical violence" of the neighbor might find its supplement – even fulfillment – in a de-Protestantized Eckhart, a theologian not merely of the abyssal Godhead but also of works, of the problematic realization of the justice–love paradox in time, that is, in Eckhart the ethicist.

In setting forth this reading, we must pay attention to Eckhart *qua* paradoxical man: the Thomist and Neoplatonist, the scholastic and Dominican prior–vicar.[7] Žižek himself glosses over the multifaceted Eckhart, whose thought, especially as manifested in his Latin works, directly concerns itself with ontological questions, that is, with *existential* questions, which themselves undergird his ethics. In missing this dimension, in only painting Eckhart as unable to cope with the radical insight of Christ's humanity, Žižek ignores the topic of love in Eckhart; hence, he believes it to be absent entirely.[8] The "materialist theologian" thus passes over fecund ground for theorizing love – something he believes to be present only alongside cruelty. The need for this reevaluation of neighbor-love is made all the more necessary by the escalating tensions lurking beneath the discomfort – the discomfort with excess – felt by so many, especially in Europe.[9] A rejuvenated political theology thus might emerge from a reversal, a backtracking, that is, through the revenge of the medieval on Žižek's ethical violence.[10]

Who is my neighbor?

To begin to understand how Eckhart might play a role, however, we must investigate what precisely Žižek means by the neighbor – a concept central, in his view, to the Judeo-Christian tradition and a worthy cause for which to fight, even after the theistic kernel has been dislodged from Christianity.[11]

In *The Neighbor*, Žižek frames his argument as a corrective to an age of tolerance, which finds expression not through the negativity of censorship, but rather through the positive condition of permissiveness: "This radical stance is more than ever needed today, in our era of oversensitivity for 'harassment' by the Other, when every ethical pressure is experienced as a false front for the violence of power."[12] Taking Judith Butler as his primary target, he sees tolerance as symptomatic of an age tortured by its own belief in self-knowledge. We live, he argues, in times when the directive to know oneself has become the condition for all possible relations with the Other; the very opacity of self-fragmentation, limitation and thrownness – make possible what, in a Nietzschean turn, he calls an "ethics of finitude [. . .] making a virtue out of our very weakness."[13] This stance in all its empowerment of limit, its potency to challenge norms through self-assertion, is to be opposed, to be corrected, by a properly dialectical reconfiguration of the neighbor *qua* traumatic–traumatized Other.

Acknowledging our lack of self-transparency, he instead designates the Jewish law – the Decalogue – as the case study *par excellence* in what is missed by the contemporary regime of tolerance. Imposed on people thrown into an opaque background filled with opaque selves, the Biblical Law does not lay its stress on coming to terms with the world-self problematic organically. For Žižek, rather, the Decalogue is violence; it is laid over the flux in which we find ourselves in an attempt to make bearable an otherwise burdensome life:

> The pronouncement of the Decalogue is *ethical violence at its purest*. The Judeo-Christian tradition is thus to be strictly opposed to the New

Age Gnostic problematic of self-fulfillment, and the cause of this need for a violent imposition of the Law is that *the very terrain covered by the Law is that of an even more fundamental violence, that of encountering a neighbor:* far from brutally disturbing a preceding harmonious social interaction, the imposition of the Law endeavors to introduce a minimum of regulation onto a stressful "impossible" relationship.[14]

We thus have an axis constituted by self-realization and traumatic encounter. The Jewish breakthrough is the recognition that one does not solve the problem of opacity by gesturing at self-knowledge; instead, the Law acknowledges the primacy – and the difficulty – of encounter. In doing so, it places stress on making such a meeting possible. In essence, it embraces this opacity, for it is, from a Hegelian point of view, the very condition for the possibility of freedom.[15] Žižek summarizes the point:

> When the Old Testament enjoins you to love and respect your neighbor, this does not refer to your imaginary *semblance*/double, but to the neighbor qua traumatic Thing [...] The core of this presence, of course, is the Other's desire, an enigma not only for us, but also for the Other itself.[16]

A question, however, remains: what can be done with this tradition *politically*? As a representative of a major and influential tradition, Žižek turns to Levinas, whose ethics is both rooted in the Jewish Law and, as far as he is concerned, woefully misguided in its principles; his teaching fails to account for the fullness of ethical violence demanded by the traumatic encounter with the neighbor. For Levinas, ethical life emerges out of familiarity. One domesticates some Other, and thus establishes a familiar world – a familiar Other – only to have to face an absolutely distinct call, a separation from the particular and known world. Shattering the comfort of the particular realm (Peter Sloterdijk's "Sphere"), this radical call introduces responsibility: "I enter the domain of justice and universal laws when I renounce my small world and its possessions and offer to see things from the standpoint of the Other."[17] What must be kept in mind is that this is not some particular event to be recalled, but the constitution of subjectivity itself. The movement from familiarity to responsibility "always already happens, in a past which never was present."[18]

In order to ground this responsibility, Levinas invokes the irreducibility of the human face, which Žižek takes to be precisely the wrong move; such a gesture attempts to rein in the abyss of the Other, to domesticate the central insight of the Jewish tradition *qua* ethical imposition. The neighbor in the Levinasian sense becomes not too human, but instead not human enough – his inner turmoil, the opacity of each self, is forgotten: "at a more radical level, the abyss/void of the Other [is lost]: the human face 'gentrifies' the terrifying thing that is the ultimate reality of our neighbor."[19] As the argument goes, Otherness is sublated into Sameness, common humanity overtakes the trauma of the encounter; yet, excess must define this other, an excess of humanity to the point of monstrosity. Since each individual human subject is himself dispersed against a fragmented backdrop and fails to achieve full self-transparency, humanity is itself, at least in part, defined by opacity. To recognize that the Other exists in this same state is to recognize his inhumanity (in the Kantian sense of infinite judgment, not negative judgment).[20] In fact, Žižek insists that the Jewish Law must not flee the monstrosity of the Other; it must stay true to its own insight and – contra Levinas – mobilize itself most especially when confronted with the inhumanity of the face:

> What if the Levinasian face is yet another defense against this monstrous dimension of subjectivity? And what if the Jewish Law is to be conceived as strictly correlative to this inhuman neighbor? In other words, what if the ultimate function of the Law is not to enable us to forget the neighbor, to retain our proximity to the neighbor, but, on the contrary, to keep the neighbor at a proper distance, to serve as a kind of protective wall against the monstrosity of the neighbor? In short, *the* temptation to be resisted here is the ethical "gentrification" of the neighbor, the reduction of the radically ambiguous monstrosity of the Neighbor–Thing into an Other as the abyssal point from which the call of ethical responsibility emanates?[21]

What hinges on this difference is precisely *politics*, the possibility of an ethics commensurable with the political sphere. For Levinas, the primordial call of the Other's face suggests an entirely unequal relationship. Reciprocity has no meaning here; only sacrifice and duty, the irresistible summons to serve, have any place. This responsibility is contrasted with the equity of justice – that is, of politics – a sphere interested not in the absolute call–response dynamic, but instead in symmetry. Žižek, however, asks, "is this solution not all too neat? That is to say, is such a notion not already 'postpolitical' [. . .] excluding precisely the dimension of what Carl Schmitt called political theology?"[22] In terms of the Christian legacy, he finds this separation particularly offensive, because it ignores the Holy Spirit, what is, in Žižek's reading of Christianity, the substance-community of believers, whose actions are necessarily political insofar as they are "reborn" as organized activity following the death of Christ.

It is this Incarnation-centered reading of Christian praxis that now concerns us; it holds the key to the proper overcoming of Levinasian ethics, that is, to a renewed "political theology" of the neighbor. As he states again and again, Christianity hinges precisely on taking seriously Christ's Incarnation (he faults Eckhart for failing to do just this).[23] Insofar as the Messiah's intervention stands for the negativity of subjectivity, the Holy Spirit arises (in almost radical *Filioque*-logic) from the self-alienating action of God's death on the Cross:[24]

> Incarnation is the birth of Christ, and after his death, there is neither Father nor Son but "only" the Holy Spirit, the spiritual substance of the religious community. Only in this sense is the Holy Spirit the "synthesis" of Father and Son, of Substance and Subject: Christ stands for the gap of negativity, for subjective singularity and in the Holy Spirit the substance is "reborn" as the virtual community of singular subjects, persisting only in and through their activity.[25]

Here, his Hegelian Protestantizing shines through as he locates the final subdivision of the triad Orthodoxy–Catholicism–Protestantism in the alienated singularity (and yet community!) of Protestant believers.[26] As such, Christ did come to bring the sword and not peace. In these terms, the Christian mission consists in establishing a community of believers who radically reconstitute the existing order of relations; hence, Žižek cites Luke 14:26 as the distilled essence of Christian socio-political thought:

> Does this not recall Christ's scandalous words from Luke ("if anyone comes to me and does not hate his father and his mother, his wife and children, his brothers and sisters – yes even his own life – he cannot be my disciple.")[27]

What, however, is the relationship between the neighbor and the community of the Holy Spirit? The answer is – though not in a cliché manner – love. Žižek argues that revolutionary justice means love, though love made comprehensible in a gesture of separation, or, as he puts it in *The Fragile Absolute*: "Christianity *is* the miraculous Event that disturbs the balance of the One-All; it *is* the violent intrusion of Difference that precisely *throws the balanced circuit of the universe off the rails.*"[28] In his view, this is where Levinas really misses the mark. By designating the face as always the face of another, he misses the always already omnipresent faceless Third. No person is immediately, or at first, a commanding visage; rather, the primordial encounter is that with the monster, the Third. The neighbor mired in his own excess may be loved in his own monstrosity precisely through the Christian act of separation, of the recognition of the faceless-ness of this Third:

> The neighbor is not displayed through a face; it is, as we have seen, in his or her fundamental dimension a *faceless* monster. It is *here* that one has to remain faithful to the Jewish legacy: in order to arrive at the "neighbor" we have to love, we must pass through the "dead" letter of the Law, which cleanses the neighbor of all imaginary lure, of the "inner wealth of a person" displayed through his or her face, reducing him or her to a *pure subject*.[29]

Christian separation, reconstituting community and thus acting in a spirit of love on behalf of the properly Other, is the proper response to the neighbor.

This is ethical violence, that is to say, this is the violent gesture of separation (from existing social relations and community) aimed at constituting a new socio-political relationship in which (at least in theistic Christian terms) love drives service even to those most inhuman, or otherwise most ignored.

He ends his analysis of the neighbor by arguing that the Christian God of love and the Jewish God of excessive cruelty are the obverse of one another and therefore not to be opposed.[30] Justice and love find reconciliation in this delicate balance. Still, his reading here necessarily falls victim to his Protestant metanarrative, which fails to account for how love may be just in spite, and not as the obverse, of cruelty.[31] Here, Eckhart is a helpful corrective, arguing that one may exist without the other. But first, we must develop an understanding of what Žižek misses in Eckhart's theology in order to offer a proper supplement to his (otherwise elegantly analyzed) concept of the neighbor.

Esse and Eckhart

Žižek's misapprehension of Eckhart (and thus his limited use of his work) is rooted primarily in his lack of attention to the German master's vital focus on lived experience. It is ironic that, although a Marxist, he misses the material conditions surrounding Eckhart: his tireless efforts on behalf of a mendicant order along with his dedication to the art of preaching. To compound the irony, Žižek primarily pays attention (seemingly drawing on the work of Reiner Schürmann) to Eckhart's vernacular works, hardly mentioning his great accomplishments *qua* medieval scholastic.[32] Attentiveness to these dimensions of his thought shows the inadequacy of Žižek's reading. More importantly, it indicates just where Žižek and a rehabilitated Eckhart might cross paths: the neighbor.

By way of overview, we ought to recognize that Meister Eckhart truly did move through life as both a *lesemeister* and a *lebemeister*; his work cannot be reduced to, nor fully understood by a study of, his speculative – and yet always pastoral – sermons.[33] His order was founded to be active, that is, to preach – its full title being the *Ordo Praedicatorum* (the Order of Preachers). Likely studying for a time under the aging Albertus Magnus, Eckhart excelled as a student and eventually found himself first at the prestigious University of Paris and then back in Germany, serving as the prior of the Dominican house at Erfurt as well the vicar for the Order's Thuringian province.[34] In these pastoral positions, he produced *Die rede der unterscheidunge* (*The Talks of Instruction*), which are modeled on works by John Cassian; their primary focus is Dominican novices and their need to learn obedience, self-denial and the value of work – both internal and external.[35] Deprived of his job as vicar, he was left with the more pastoral of the two roles and, considering his ascendency within the Order, seems to have prospered.[36]

Not long afterwards, we find him back at Paris, no longer as a student, but now as a *magister actu regens*, that is, now as an active teacher, only to find him back at a pastoral post (the provincial for the newly formed northern portion of the now split Teutonian Province of the Order) soon afterwards.[37] During these years, he produced the *Paradisus anime intelligentis* (*The Paradise of the Intelligent Soul*), a collection of sermons in the vernacular, but testifying to his Latinate erudition.[38] And, never failing to remain active, in 1307 he was entrusted with the reformation of the Order's houses in Bohemia; soon after, he was elected the Thuringian provincial, though the general chapter thwarted the attempt.[39] As if all of this were not enough, Eckhart would eventually return to Paris to teach (this twice-in-a-lifetime appointment is a distinction he shares with his fellow student of Albertus Magnus – Aquinas) and from there live out his days in Strasbourg and Cologne, preaching in both places and solidifying his reputation as a popular spiritual guide.[40] It is likely during this final period of his life that he produced *The Book of Divine Comfort* – a work of Boethian consolation – and continued to exert an influence on popular lay spiritual groups like the Beguines.[41] Eckhart himself rather nicely summarizes the dual role he played during his own life:

> And some will say that such teaching should not be uttered or written to the unlearned. To this I reply: if one may not teach the unlearned, then no one can teach or write. For we teach the unlearned so that from being unlearned they may become learned.[42]

In other words, Eckhart saw himself as a learned man, but a learned man devoted to the dissemination of learning; moreover, this dissemination was to take place not only through vernacular writings but also through his various appointments and duties – his work with people.

While this brief introduction to his life and works indicates the complicated nature of his character, it does not bear direct witness to the primary dimension of his corpus missed by Žižek, namely his scholastic ontology, which lays the framework for best understanding the *ethical* dimensions of his thought. Here the work of Robert Dobie is particularly helpful, as he emphatically argues for the centrality of Eckhart's repeated dictum: "Esse est Deus" (Being is God).[43] Further, his stance is that even – and perhaps especially – in his scholarly writings, Eckhart's approach is "always grounded in the lived concrete experience of the existing individual."[44] Specifically, this ontological dimension finds manifestation in his analysis of the *transcendentalia* (transcendentals): being, goodness, truth and so forth.

Eckhart's argument for God as being rests on his investigation of these transcendentals. For example, in his *Prologus generalis in opus tripartitum*, he writes:

> First we should by no means imagine or think of universal terms like existence, unity, truth and wisdom, goodness and so on, after the manner and nature of accidents. Accidents receive existence in and through

their subject and through its change. Moreover they are posterior to the subject and take on existence by inhering [in] it [. . .] The case is completely different with the general terms mentioned above. Existence itself, and the terms convertible with it, are not added to things as though posterior to them; on the contrary they are prior to every aspect of things.[45]

The *transcendentalia* are not accidents, and this is integral to his scheme. Being is prior to all accidents, and yet being may only come from other being – "to be" thus precedes all else, or, as he comments:

> It is not the nature of existence itself to be something or from something or through something; neither is it added or joined to anything. On the contrary, it precedes and comes before everything. So the existence of things is immediately from the first and universal cause of things. All things exist from existence itself, and through it and in it, for what is different from existence is not or is nothing.[46]

The consequence of this argument is that nothing (in the sense of no entity) is truly good; only the Absolute – being itself – is good (or wise and so forth). Thus, entities themselves "are" only analogically. To illustrate this point, Eckhart speaks of a wreath on a tavern door.[47] It signifies that wine may be found within but contains no wine itself. In the same way, creatures may point to existence, may offer up the possibility to understand that things exist, but themselves can only be said to exist analogically, as signs pointing to that which truly "is."[48] Distinguishing between *per se esse* (being through itself) and *ab alio esse* (being from another), Eckhart demonstrates that God is the Absolute which truly may be said to exist. Using Aristotelian terms, he suggests that one entity may only enact an *alteratio* (alteration) on another. Fire may burn wood, but its very being presupposes the being of wood (which allows it to burn); this is mere *alteratio*. In other words, these entities receive their being from another – God.[49]

Eckhart sees evidence of this truth in the inadequacy of language. Relevant here are two types of medieval logical statements: propositions *secundum adiacens* and propositions *tertium adiacens*. When we say "x is" we typically mean "x is this," a connection of subject and predicate enacted by the copula "is" – a proposition *tertium adiacens*. Actually saying "x is" would be a proposition *secundum adiacens*, in which an absolute statement would be made with existence itself predicated. Put otherwise, the former sort of statement signifies a connection, the latter an unchanging fact of being.[50] In *tertium adiacens* statements, we are thus merely stating a quality and its relationship to some entity; nothing is actually being said about existence. In fact, one is able to articulate such a proposition whether or not the entity and the quality actually exist at all. In Eckhart's view, *secundum adiacens* propositions (those made of existence itself and not merely designating a relationship) may only be said of the Absolute, which, as he has argued, is God. Thus, Eckhart writes:

> We must speak and judge differently of being and this being, similarly of the one and this one, of the true and this truth, of the good and this good. When something is called being, one, true, good, each of these is a predicate of a proposition and it lies second to the subject. But when something is called this being, this one, this true, this good (for example, a man or a stone or the like), then "this" and "this" are the predicate of the proposition, and the general terms just mentioned (for example "being") are not predicates, nor do they lie second to the subject, but they connect the predicate with the subject. For instance, when I say "this man or stone," I do not predicate existence but I predicate man or stone or something of the kind ... When I say "a rose is red," I do not assert or affirm that a rose exists, nor that redness exists, but only the natural connection of the two terms. So "existence" or "is" is not a subject or a predicate, but a third term besides them: it is the copula of the predicate with the subject.[51]

Even, Eckhart, of course, is forced to use a *tertium adiacens* proposition: "Esse est Deus," because of the limits of human language, but what he means is "God is." In other words, the only predicate that can be used formally or substantively of the verb "to be" is God, and so every proposition *tertium adiacens* is actually a reference to God, who is the only proper predicate of the copula "is." Dobie summarizes the insight well:

> What Eckhart wants to say is that the existential import of the copula "is" mostly gets lost in our ordinary discourse about finite beings. The meaning of "is" becomes abstracted into that of a binding agent and loses its existential reference.[52]

In developing this linguistic argument, Eckhart reveals that God is the ultimate negation of the negation, precisely because of his unity. Every predication is a denial of one-ness, because it places a "this" alongside being. One must negate this difference in order to return to the plenitude of being itself:

> Absolutely nothing of entity, then, can be denied to being or existence itself. It follows that nothing can be denied to the being itself which is God except the negation of the negation of all existence. This is why unity, which is the negation of negation, is most closely related to being.[53]

The ultimate human act is thus the denial of difference; in anachronistic terms, we might say that the true introduction of Christian difference for Eckhart – the true act of violence – is the imposition of peace through the negation of the negation found in every particularly existing entity. He spells this out more fully in a vernacular sermon:

"No wonder, then, that love itself disappears" 95

A master says: "One is a negation of negation." If I say God is good, that adds something. One is the negation of the negation and a denial of the denial. What does *one* mean? One means that to which nothing is added. The Soul receives the Godhead as it is purified in itself, with nothing added, with nothing thought. *One* is a negation of the negation. All creatures have a negation in themselves: one negates by not being the other. An angel negates by not being another.[54]

Very significant here is that we see the word "gotheit" (Godhead), which is the nakedness of God's very essence, in which God and man are at one in their co-ground.[55] Žižek calls this "the 'desert' of the divine nature."[56] The "retreat" (that is, the doubling of the negation) here is precisely what Žižek sees as the fatal flaw in Eckhart's schema. To him, there is no love here, no encounter with the monstrosity of Christ, which could even hope to produce an ethical response rooted in Pauline agape. With the theoretical framework we have established – that is, having explored the basics of Eckhart's ontological thought – we are ready to problematize Žižek's assumptions.

Gotheit, Isticheit and the neighbor

How is it, then, that a person enacts the *negatio negationis* (negation of the negation) and returns to the naked plenitude of the Godhead? The answers are *Abgeschiedenheit* (letting be) and *Gelassenheit* (detachment).[57] It is in this way that one becomes "ein juncvrouwe, diu ein wîp ist." (a virgin who is a wife).[58] One empties oneself in order to become a perfect mirror, in which God may reflect Himself and thus bear fruit (have the Son born in the soul) – just as a virgin who is a wife is both "pure" and "fruitful." So far, this depiction sounds very much like Žižek's version of Eckhart, a mystic obsessed with negativity, who cannot deal with actual material conditions. This sounds true until we recall that the return to the Godhead (the *Durchbruch*, or "breakthrough") is understood as a return to the co-ground with the Godhead, which is the abyss behind God *qua* person. As Eckhart painstakingly argues in his Latin works, God is being. Thus, the Kantian infinite judgment of God – Godhead – is the truth of being, the abyss in which all things find their co-ground. A human being reaches this truth by creating a perfect mirror for the same within oneself through detachment. In other words, a person achieves the truth of existence by recognizing his own inhumanity (again, in the Kantian sense of infinite judgment), that is, his own excess. This excess is precisely what Žižek argues that Levinas misses – the monstrosity both within oneself and inhering in others.

The difference, one might argue, is that for Eckhart this excess is not monstrosity *per se*, but actually peace – a true, lived version of the abyssal truth of existence. What is key here, however, is that this realization does not remove the monstrosity of the Other. In fact, it assumes it. A person seeks detachment precisely because of the difficulty in loving one's neighbor, because living for others, accepting the regulation of the traumatic relationship to the Other, is hard. To this point, Eckhart contends that loving others as much as oneself is made possible precisely by this process. The truth of excess – inhumanity – is within us all; *Gelassenheit* provides a way of mediating this problem through a recognition of universal, essential similarity (even if covered over by accidental difference). For Eckhart, love depends upon what the Slovenian Marxist calls monstrosity.[59] And is this not the basis for community – for the Holy Spirit so beloved by Žižek? Still, there is Žižek's concern that Eckhart's solution is too Zen after the manner of D.T. Suzuki, that it uses peace/non-violence to defraud us into violence.[60] The German master, however, evades this charge as well.

In identifying Isticheit (is-ness) with the active role of loving and caring for others, Eckhart demonstrates that cruelty (or any form of violence) need not accompany love in the way Žižek argues; instead, the traumatic encounter with the neighbor can be accepted in its trauma and endured precisely because one has become a virgin who is a wife (one might say, has managed to pass through cruelty to universal love, has emerged from the recognition of essential inhumanity to complete care for one's neighbor).[61] In his reading of the Mary and Martha pericope, the mystic holds up *Martha* as the greater figure (a major break with tradition), because she knows the love and joy of contemplating God, of being still and silent, but has not allowed this joy to hold her back.[62] Instead, she has reemerged into the world – with all its pain and inconvenience – precisely because she recognizes the call to act that arises from detachment:

> But Martha stood there in her essence, and hence she said, "Lord, bid her get up", as if to say "Lord, I do not like her sitting there just for joy. I want her to learn life and possess it in essence: bid her arise that she may be perfect".[63]

Martha moves beyond joy, beyond complacency and into the difficult terrain of living love through detachment. And, in fact, she seeks the same for her sister, encouraging her to stand up and be filled with the Spirit in works. Here, then, we see interpersonal activity, testifying that the communal (even political dimension), which is not obvious in Eckhart's works, is not absent either. Martha's peace, however, is not without challenge; it does not lead to the dissipation of all pain:

> Now our good people imagine they can reach a point where sensible things do not affect the senses. That cannot be: that a disagreeable noise should be as pleasant to my ear as the sweet tones of a lyre is something I shall never attain to.[64]

As he continues, Eckhart does clarify that one may find joy (in doing God's will) in the painful difficulties of lived existence, yet, again, these pains can never fully be destroyed or overcome. The detached person – the one who knows his own identical "is-ness" with God, and who therefore can live *without why* – actualizes love (the universal) in particular circumstances.[65] He, however, cannot be said to decide between justice and love, to prize one over another, that is, to enact, as Žižek would have it, both cruelty and love;[66] instead, by embracing the abyss of the Godhead, such a person both accepts the neighbor *qua* traumatic thing and meets such a realization with joy and love. In other words, Eckhart's ethics, as Žižek himself almost recognizes, allow for peace "*in* and *of* this flux itself."[67]

Understood in these terms, then, Eckhart may be said to offer the fulfillment of – or at least a supplement to – Žižek's reading of the neighbor, an issue with clear relevance today. Moreover, this re-reading provides precisely a sort of political theology, what Žižek feared was missing in Levinas and clearly glossed over in his reading of Eckhart. And can we not learn from this political theology? There is ample room for the recognition of the monstrous difficulty of maintaining relationships with others, specifically those faceless ones "out there" with whom we seem to share so little. Yet, recognizing monstrosity does not preclude love, a love reached paradoxically through detachment. Eckhart provides the contemporary theorist with a way of addressing this problematic: a deeply medieval approach to an undeniably modern situation. And yet, in spite of the distance in time, it is precisely the mystic's thought that makes a purer form of love possible in dealing with the Other, that reinvigorates the Christianity in Žižek's atheistic concept. In other words, the reintroduction of the purity of love signifies here, then, as Milbank hints, the revenge of the medieval (and thus perhaps the Christian) on Žižek.

Notes

1 Slavoj Žižek, "The Fear of Four Words: A Modest Plea for the Hegelian Reading of Christianity," in *The Monstrosity of Christ*, ed. Creston Davis (Cambridge: MIT Press, 2009), 40: "But is the Incarnation not precisely Christ's descent among creatures, his birth as part of the 'nothingness' submitted to corruption? No wonder, then, that love itself disappears here."
2 Creston Davis, "Introduction: Holy Saturday or Resurrection Sunday? Staging an Unlikely Debate," in *The Monstrosity of Christ*, ed. Creston Davis (Cambridge: MIT Press, 2009), 17.
3 Žižek, "The Fear of Four Words," 33–43.
4 John Milbank, "The Double Glory, or Paradox Versus Dialectics: On Not Quite Agreeing with Slavoj Žižek," in *The Monstrosity of Christ*, ed. Creston Davis (Cambridge: MIT Press, 2009), 112.
5 For a recent attempt to recognize the medieval roots of Hegelian dialectic, see Andrew Cole, *The Birth of Theory* (Chicago, IL: University of Chicago Press, 2014). For a volume demanding that we re-theorize the modern through the lens of the medieval, see Andrew Cole and D. Vance Smith, eds., *The Legitimacy of the Middle Ages: On the Unwritten History of Theory* (Durham, NC: Duke University Press, 2010).
6 See Slavoj Žižek, "Neighbors and Other Monsters: A Plea for Ethical Violence," in *The Neighbor: Three Inquiries in Political Theology* (Chicago, IL: University of Chicago Press, 2005) as well as Slavoj Žižek, *Against the Double*

Blackmail: Refugees, Terror and Other Troubles with the Neighbours (New York: Melville House, 2016).
7 For more information on Eckhart the Thomist, see Benedict M. Ashley, "Three Strands in the Thought of Eckhart, the Scholastic Theologian," *The Thomist: A Speculative Quarterly Review of Theology and Philosophy* 42, no. 2 (1978). For the Neoplatonic elements in his thought, see Richard Woods, "Meister Eckhart and the Neoplatonic Heritage: The Thinker's Way to God," *The Thomist: A Speculative Quarterly Review of Theology and Philosophy* 54, no. 4 (1990). For an overview of his life (including his teaching and pastoral duties), see Bernard McGinn, *The Mystical Thought of Meister Eckhart: The Man from Whom God Hid Nothing* (New York: Crossroad, 2001). Cf. Kurt Flasch, *Meister Eckhart: Philosopher of Christianity*, trans. Anne Schindel and Aaron Vanides (New Haven: Yale University Press, 2015) as well as Frank Tobin, *Meister Eckhart: Thought and Language* (Philadelphia: University of Pennsylvania Press, 1986). For a distinctly non-constructivist approach, cf. Robert K.C. Forman, *Meister Eckhart, Mystic as Theologian: An Experiment in Methodology* (Rockport: Element, 1991).
8 Žižek, "Fear of Four Words," 40.
9 See Žižek, *Refugees, Terror, and Other Troubles*.
10 For a more traditional, "Protestant" reading of Eckhart, see Donata Schoeller, *Gottesgeburt und Selbstbewußtsein: Denken der Einheit bei Meister Eckhart und G.W.F. Hegel* (Hildesheim: Bernward Verlag, 1992). After quoting William James on the commonality to be found between Hegel and the mystics, Schoeller writes, "Meister Eckhart wäre mit dieser von Hegel sich gesetzten denkerischen" Aufgabe" sicherlich sehr einverstanden gewesen" (19). In English: "Meister Eckhart would very surely agree with this self-set, intellectual 'task' from Hegel." My translation. Cf. Stephan Grotz, *Negation des Absoluten: Meister Eckhart, Cusanus, Hegel* (Hamburg: Felix Meiner Verlag, 2009).
11 See Milbank, "Double Glory" for the contention that Žižek's Hegelian Christianity is far from orthodox. My argument here might help make Milbank's case while preserving and reinvigorating the insights reached by Žižek through his investigation into the neighbor within the Judeo-Christian tradition.
12 Žižek, "Neighbors and Other Monsters," 134.
13 Ibid., 137.
14 Ibid., 140. Emphasis original.
15 Ibid., 142.
16 Ibid., 140–1. Emphasis original.
17 Ibid., 145.
18 Ibid., 144.
19 Ibid., 146.
20 Ibid., 158.
21 Ibid., 163. Emphasis original.
22 Ibid., 149.
23 Žižek, "Fear of Four Words," 40.
24 "What is sublated in the move from the Son to Holy Spirit is thus God himself: after the Crucifixion, the death of God incarnate, the universal God returns as a Spirit of the community of believers, i.e., he is the one who passes from being a transcendent substantial Reality to a virtual/ideal entity which exists only as the 'presupposition' of acting individuals." Ibid., 61.
25 Ibid., 33.
26 Ibid., 29. He makes the same point suggestively (though he does not explore its implications in full) in Žižek, "Neighbors and Other Monsters," 187.
27 Ibid., 186. To a similar end, Žižek quotes 2 Corinthians 5:16–17 in Slavoj Žižek, *The Fragile Absolute: Or Why Is the Christian Legacy Worth Fighting for?* (New York: Verso Books, 2000), 127.

"No wonder, then, that love itself disappears" 99

28 Ibid., 121. Emphasis original.
29 Žižek, "Neighbors and Other Monsters," 185. Emphasis original.
30 "That is also why it is wrong to oppose the Christian god of Love to the Jewish god of cruel justice: excessive cruelty is the necessary obverse of Christian Love. And, again, the relationship between these two is one of parallax." Ibid., 189. In characteristic Žižek style, he introduces this point with a Johnny Cash song, "The Man Comes Around."
31 As I will argue below, love is the necessary response to the recognition of true Otherness. Cruelty and love are not obverses (as Žižek thinks must be the case, at least on his reading of Calvin via Johnny Cash); rather, love, in its fullest sense, is an overcoming of cruelty, not merely its parallax.
32 For more information on Schürmann's approach, see Eckhart von Hochheim, *Wandering Joy: Meister Eckhart's Mystical Philosophy*, trans. Reiner Schürmann (Great Barrington: Lindisfarne, 2001).
33 McGinn, *Mystical Thought*, 1.
34 Tobin, *Thought and Language*, 5–6.
35 McGinn, *Mystical Thought*, 4.
36 Forman, *Mystic as Theologian*, 46.
37 For details, see McGinn, *Mystical Thought*, 4 as well as Tobin, *Thought and Language*, 6.
38 McGinn, *Mystical Thought*, 5.
39 Tobin, *Thought and Language*, 7.
40 Ibid., 8.
41 For *The Book of Divine Comfort*, see McGinn, *Mystical Thought*, 12. For his influence on the Beguines, see Kurt Ruh, "Meister Eckhart und Die Spiritualität der Beguinen," *Perspektiven der Philosophie* 8, no. 1 (1982).
42 "Ouch sol man sprechen, daz man sôgetâne lêre niht ensol sprechen noch schrîben ungelêrten. Dar zuo spriche ich: ensol man niht lêren ungelêrte liute, sô enwirt niemer gelêret, sô enmac nieman lêren noch schriben. Wan dar umbe lêret man die ungelêrten, daz sie werden von ungelêret gelêret." The original text is quoted in McGinn, *Mystical Thought*, 191, n. 81. The translation is from Eckhart von Hochheim, "The Book of Divine Comfort," in *Meister Eckhart: Sermons & Treatises*, ed. and trans. Maurice O'Conell Walshe, vol. 3 (Shaftesbury: Element Books, 1990), 101.
43 For Dobie's work most germane to my point here, see Robert Dobie, "Meister Eckhart's 'Ontological Philosophy of Religion'," *The Journal of Religion* 82, no. 4 (2002). For an example of Eckhart's use of the phrase in question, see Eckhart von Hochheim, "Prologus generalis in opus tripartitum," in *Die lateinischen Werke*, ed. and trans. Konrad Weiss, vol. 1 (Stuttgart: W. Kohlhammer Verlag, 1964), 156.
44 Dobie, "Ontological Philosophy of Religion," 565.
45 "Primum est quod de terminus generalibus puta esse, unitate, veritate, sapientia, bonitate et similibus nequaquam est imaginandum vel iudicandum secundum modum et naturam accidentium, quae accipiunt esse in subiecto et per subiectum et per ipsius transmutationem et sunt posterior ipso et inhaerendo esse accipiunt [. . .] Secus autem omnino se habet de praemissis generalibus. Non enim ipsum esse et quae cum ipso convertibiliter idem sunt, superveniunt rebus tamquam posteriora, sed sunt priora omnibus in rebus." The Latin is from Hochheim, "Prologus generalis," 152–3. The translation is from Dobie, "Ontological Philosophy of Religion," 568–9.
46 "Ipsum enim esse non accipit quod sit in aliquot nec ab aliquot nec per aliquid, nec advenit nec supervenit alicui, sed praevenit et prius est omnium. Propter quod esse omnium est immediate a causa prima et a causa universali omnium. Ab ipso igitur esse 'et per ipsum et in ipso sunt omnia', ipsum non ab alio. Quod enim aliud est ab esse, non est aut nihil est." The Latin is from Hochheim, "Prologus

generalis," 153. The translation is from Dobie, "Ontological Philosophy of Religion," 569. Dobie's translation omits the quotation marks found in the Latin text.
47 Note also Eckhart's penchant for deeply material metaphors, another sign that he was far from a practitioner of "pure" apophatic mysticism. He clearly took the power of everyday images seriously.
48 The example comes from Eckhart von Hochheim, "Sermones et lectiones super Ecclesiastici," in *Die lateinischen Werke*, ed. and trans. Josef Koch, vol. 2 (Stuttgart: W. Kohlhammer Verlag, 1954), 281. For analysis of the image, see Dobie, "Ontological Philosophy of Religion," 571.
49 For Eckhart's argument for God's existence as being, see Hochheim, "Prologus generalis," 156–7. For Dobie's analysis, see Dobie, "Ontological Philosophy of Religion," 571.
50 For a discussion of this idea, see ibid., 575ff.
51 "Secundum est quod aliter loquendum est et iudicandum de ente et aliter de ente hoc, similiter de uno et de uno hoc, de vero et de vero hoc, de bono et de bono hoc. Cum enim dicitur aliquid ens, unum, verum, bonum, tunc haec singula sunt praedicta propositionis et sunt secundum adiacens. Cum vero dicitur aliquid ens hoc, unum hoc, verum hoc, aut bonum hoc, puta homo vel lapis et huiusmodi tunc li 'hoc et hoc' sunt praedicatum propositionis, et praemissa communia, puta esse, non sunt praedicta nec secundum adiacens, sed sunt copula praedicati cum subiecto. Verbi gratia cum dico: 'hoc est homo vel lapis', non praedico esse, sed praedico hominem vel lapidem aut huiusmodi aliquid [. . .] Sic cum dico rosam esse rubeam, non dico nec praedico rosam esse, nec rubedinem esse, sed solam cohaerentiam naturalem terminorum. Unde li 'esse' vel 'est' non est subiectum nec praedicatum, sed tertium extra haec, puta copula praedicati cum subiecto." The Latin text is from Eckhart von Hochheim, "Tabula prologorum in opus tripartitum," in *Die lateinischen Werke*, ed. and trans. Konrad Weiss, vol. 1. (Stuttgart: W. Kohlhammer Verlag, 1964), 131–2. The translation is from Dobie, "Ontological Philosophy of Religion," 574.
52 Ibid., 575.
53 "Nihil ergo entitatis universaliter negari potest ipsi enti sive ipsi esse. Propter hoc de ipso ente, deo, nihil negari potest nisi negatio[ne] negationis omnis esse. Hinc est quod unum, utpote negationis negatio, immediatissime se habet ad ens." The Latin text is from Eckhart von Hochheim, "Prologus in opus propositionum," in *Die lateinischen Werke*, ed. and trans. Konrad Weiss, vol. 1. (Stuttgart: W. Kohlhammer Verlag, 1964), 175–6. The translation is from Dobie, "Ontological Philosophy of Religion," 576–7.
54 "Ein meister sprichet: ein ist ein versagen des versagennes. Spriche ich, got ist guot, daz leget etwas zuo. Ein ist ein versagen des versagennes und ein verlougen des verlougennes. Waz meinet ein? Daz meinet ein, dem niht zuogeleget enist. Diu sêle nimet die gotheit, als si in ir geliutert ist, dâ niht zuogeleget enist, dâ niht benâht enist. Ein ist ein versagen des versagennes. Alle crêatûren hânt ein versagen an in selben; einiu versaget, daz si diu ander niht ensî. Ein engel versagt, daz er ein ander niht ensî." The Middle High German comes from Eckhart von Hochheim, "Predigt 21," in *Die deutschen Werke*, ed. and trans. Josef Quint, vol. 1 (Stuttgart: W. Kohlhammer Verlag, 1958), 361–3. The translation is from Eckhart von Hochheim, "Sermon Ninety Seven," in *Meister Eckhart: Sermons & Treatises*, ed. and trans. Maurice O'Conell Walshe, vol. 2 (Shaftesbury: Element Books, 1987), 339.
55 For a direct treatment of this question by Eckhart, see Eckhart von Hochheim, "Predigt 59," in *Die deutschen Werke*, ed. and trans. Josef Quint, vol. 2 (Stuttgart: W. Kohlhammer Verlag, 1971). For a translation of this sermon, see Eckhart von Hochheim, "Sermon Seventy One," in *Meister Eckhart: Sermons &*

"No wonder, then, that love itself disappears" 101

  Treatises, ed. and trans. Maurice O'Conell Walshe, vol. 2 (Shaftesbury: Element Books, 1987).
56 Žižek, "Fear of Four Words," 41, in the same discussion where our title quotation appears. It is also the Kantian infinite judgment of God, as Žižek says at ibid., 33–4.
57 For an analysis of these ideas in Eckhart, see John D. Caputo, "Fundamental Themes in Meister Eckhart's Mysticism," *The Thomist: A Speculative Quarterly Review of Theology and Philosophy* 42, no. 2 (1978). I have used the Modern German terms here, following Caputo.
58 For Eckhart's explanation of this idea, see Eckhart von Hochheim, "Predigt 2," in *Die deutschen Werke*, ed. and trans. Josef Quint, vol. 1 (Stuttgart: W. Kohlhammer Verlag, 1958). For a translation of this text, see Eckhart von Hochheim, "Sermon Eight," in *Meister Eckhart: Sermons & Treatises*, ed. and trans. Maurice O'Conell Walshe, vol. 1 (Shaftesbury: Element Books, 1987).
59 For a thorough presentation of this argument, see Eckhart von Hochheim, "Predigt 30," in *Die deutschen Werke*, ed. and trans. Josef Quint, vol. 2 (Stuttgart: W. Kohlhammer Verlag, 1971). For a translation, see Eckhart von Hochheim, "Sermon Eighteen," in *Meister Eckhart: Treatises & Sermons*, ed. and trans. Maurice O'Conell Walshe, vol. 1 (Shaftesbury: Element Books, 1987).
60 Žižek implies this concern about Eckhart in Žižek, "Fear of Four Words," 40. The general statement about Buddhist ethics occurs in Žižek, "Neighbors and Other Monsters," 186. To pursue his reference to Suzuki, see D.T. Suzuki, *Mysticism: Christian and Buddhist* (New York: Routledge, 2002).
61 On "Isticheit," see Eckhart von Hochheim, "Predigt 83," in *Die deutschen Werke*, ed. and trans. Josef Quint, vol. 3 (Stuttgart: W. Kohlhammer Verlag, 1976). For a translation, see Eckhart von Hochheim, "Sermon Ninety Six," in *Meister Eckhart: Sermons & Treatises*, ed. and trans. Maurice O'Conell Walshe, vol. 2 (Shaftesbury: Element Books, 1987).
62 As an aside, one might note how the grace-works dynamic of Eckhart's Martha contrasts with the Calvinism of Žižek's God.
63 "Aber Marthâ stuont sô weselîche, dâ von sprach si: 'herre, heiz sie ûfstân!', als ob si spræche: herre, ich wöllte gerne, daz si dâ niht ensæze durch lust; ich wöllte, daz si lernete leben, daz si weselîche besæze. 'Heiz sie ûfstân', daz si durnehte werde'." For the Middle High German text, see Eckhart von Hochheim, "Predigt 86," in *Die deutschen Werke*, ed. and trans. Josef Quint, vol. 3 (Stuttgart: W. Kohlhammer Verlag, 1976), 491. For the translation, see Eckhart von Hochheim, Sermon Nine," in *Meister Eckhart: Sermons & Treatises*, ed. and trans. M.O'C. Walshe, vol. 1 (Shaftesbury: Element Books, 1987), 88.
64 "Nû wænent unser guoten liute erkriegen, daz gegenwürticheit sinnelîcher dinge den sinnen niht ensî. Des engât in niht zuo. Daz ein pînlich gedœne mînen ôren als lustic sî als ein süezez seitenspil, daz erkriege ich niemer." The Middle High German text is from Hochheim, "Predigt 86," 491. The translation is from Hochheim, "Sermon Nine," 88.
65 Recall that Eckhart was deeply influenced by Neoplatonism and Thomism.
66 For Eckhart's response to the universal-particular problem, see Milbank, "Double Glory," 186.
67 Žižek, "Fear of Four Words," 39. Further, it should not surprise us that Eckhart's notion of temporality is more complex than Žižek anticipates – finding a middle ground between extreme medieval positions. For more information, see Niklaus Largier, "Time and Temporality in the 'German Dominican School': Outlines of a Philosophical Debate between Nicolaus of Strasbourg, Dietrich of Freiberg, Eckhart of Hoheim, and Ioannes Tauler," in *The Medieval Concept of Time: Studies on the Scholastic Debate and Its Reception in Early Modern Philosophy*, ed. Pasquale Porro (Leiden: Brill, 2001).

Bibliography

Ashley, Benedict M. "Three Strands in the Thought of Eckhart, the Scholastic Theologian." *The Thomist: A Speculative Quarterly Review of Theology and Philosophy* 42, no. 2 (1978): 226–39.

Caputo, John D. "Fundamental Themes in Meister Eckhart's Mysticism." *The Thomist: A Speculative Quarterly Review of Theology and Philosophy* 42, no. 2 (1978): 197–225.

Cole, Andrew. *The Birth of Theory*. Chicago, IL: University of Chicago Press, 2014.

Cole, Andrew and D. Vance Smith, eds. *The Legitimacy of the Middle Ages: On the Unwritten History of Theory*. Durham, NC: Duke University Press, 2010.

Davis, Creston. "Introduction: Holy Saturday or Resurrection Sunday? Staging an Unlikely Debate." In *The Monstrosity of Christ: Paradox or Dialectic*, edited by Creston Davis, 2–23. Cambridge: MIT Press, 2009.

Dobie, Robert. "Meister Eckhart's 'Ontological Philosophy of Religion'." *The Journal of Religion* 82, no. 4 (2002): 563–85.

Hochheim, Eckhart von. "The Book of Divine Comfort." In *Meister Eckhart: Sermons & Treatises*, edited and translated by Maurice O'Connell Walshe, vol. 3, 61–104. Shaftesbury: Element Books, 1990.

———. "Predigt 2." In *Die deutschen Werke*, edited and translated by Josef Quint, vol. 1, 21–45. Stuttgart: W. Kohlhammer Verlag, 1958.

———. "Predigt 21." In *Die deutschen Werke*, edited and translated by Josef Quint, vol. 1, 353–70. Stuttgart: W. Kohlhammer Verlag, 1958.

———. "Predigt 30." In *Die deutschen Werke*, edited and translated by Josef Quint, vol. 2, 90–109. Stuttgart: W. Kohlhammer Verlag, 1971.

———. "Predigt 59." In *Die deutschen Werke*, edited and translated by Josef Quint, vol. 2, 619–36. Stuttgart: W. Kohlhammer Verlag, 1971.

———. "Predigt 71." In *Die deutschen Werke*, edited and translated by Josef Quint, vol. 3, 204–31. Stuttgart: W. Kohlhammer Verlag, 1976.

———. "Predigt 83." In *Die deutschen Werke*, edited and translated by Josef Quint, vol. 3, 434–49. Stuttgart: W. Kohlhammer Verlag, 1976.

———. "Predigt 86." In *Die deutschen Werke*, edited and translated by Josef Quint, vol. 3, 472–503. Stuttgart: W. Kohlhammer Verlag, 1976.

———. "Prologus generalis in opus tripartitum." In *Die lateinischen Werke*, edited and translated by Konrad Weiss, vol. 1, 148–65. Stuttgart: W. Kohlhammer Verlag, 1964.

———. "Prologus in opus propositionum." In *Die lateinischen Werke*, edited and translated by Konrad Weiss, vol. 1, 166–82. Stuttgart: W. Kohlhammer Verlag, 1964.

———. "Sermon Eight." In *Meister Eckhart: Sermons & Treatises*, edited and translated by Maurice O'Connell Walshe, vol. 1, 71–8. Shaftesbury: Element Books, 1987.

———. "Sermon Eighteen." In *Meister Eckhart: Sermons & Treatises*, edited and translated by Maurice O'Connell Walshe, vol. 1, 147–52. Shaftesbury: Element Books, 1987.

———. "Sermon Nine." In *Meister Eckhart: Sermons & Treatises*, edited and translated by Maurice O'Connell Walshe, vol. 1, 79–90. Shaftesbury: Element Books, 1987.

———. "Sermon Ninety Six." In *Meister Eckhart: Sermons & Treatises*, edited and translated by Maurice O'Connell Walshe, vol. 2, 331–6. Shaftesbury: Element Books, 1987.

———. "Sermon Ninety Seven." In *Meister Eckhart: Sermons & Treatises*, edited and translated by Maurice O'Connell Walshe, vol. 2, 337–42. Shaftesbury: Element Books, 1987.

———. "Sermones et Lectiones super Ecclesiastici." In *Die lateinischen Werke*, edited and translated by Josef Koch, vol. 2, 231–300. Stuttgart: W. Kohlhammer Verlag, 1992.

———. "Tabula prologorum in opus tripartitum." In *Die lateinischen Werke*, edited and translated by Konrad Weiss, vol. 1, 127–32. Stuttgart: W. Kohlhammer Verlag, 1964.

———. *Wandering Joy: Meister Eckhart's Mystical Philosophy*. Translated by Reiner Schürmann. Great Barrington: Lindisfarne Books, 2001.

Flasch, Kurt. *Meister Eckhart: Philosopher of Christianity*. Translated by Anne Schindel and Aaron Vanides. New Haven: Yale University Press, 2015.

Forman, Robert K.C. *Meister Eckhart, Mystic as Theologian: An Experiment in Methodology*. Rockport: Element, 1991.

Grotz, Stephan. *Negation des Absoluten: Meister Eckhart, Cusanus, Hegel*. Hamburg: Felix Meiner Verlag, 2009.

Largier, Niklaus. "Time and Temporality in the 'German Dominican School': Outlines of a Philosophical Debate between Nicolaus of Strasbourg, Dietrich of Freiberg, Eckhart of Hoheim, and Ioannes Tauler." In *The Medieval Concept of Time: Studies on the Scholastic Debate and Its Reception in Early Modern Philosophy*, edited by Pasquale Porro, 221–53. Leiden: Brill, 2001.

McGinn, Bernard. *The Mystical Thought of Meister Eckhart: The Man from Whom God Hid Nothing*. New York: Crossroad, 2001.

Milbank, John. "The Double Glory, or Paradox Versus Dialectics: On Not Quite Agreeing with Slavoj Žižek." In *The Monstrosity of Christ: Paradox or Dialectic*, edited by Creston Davis, 110–233. Cambridge: MIT Press, 2009.

Ruh, Kurt. "Meister Eckhart und die Spiritualität der Beginen." *Perspektiven der Philosophie* 8, no. 1 (1982): 323–34.

Schoeller, Donata. *Gottesgeburt und Selbstbewußtsein: Denken der Einheit bei Meister Eckhart und G.W.F Hegel*. Hildesheim: Bernward Verlag, 1992.

Suzuki, D.T. *Mysticism: Christian and Buddhist*. New York: Routledge, 2002.

Tobin, Frank. *Meister Eckhart: Thought and Language*. Philadelphia: University of Pennsylvania Press, 1986.

Woods, Richard. "Meister Eckhart and the Neoplatonic Heritage: The Thinker's Way to God." *The Thomist: A Speculative Quarterly Review of Theology and Philosophy* 54, no. 4 (1990): 609–39.

Žižek, Slavoj. *Against the Double Blackmail: Refugees, Terror and Other Troubles with the Neighbours*. New York: Melville House, 2016.

———. "The Fear of Four Words: A Modest Plea for the Hegelian Reading of Christianity." In *The Monstrosity of Christ: Paradox or Dialectic*, edited by Creston Davis, 24–109. Cambridge: MIT Press, 2009.

———. *The Fragile Absolute: Or, Why Is the Christian Legacy Worth Fighting For?* New York: Verso Books, 2000.

———. "Neighbors and Other Monsters: A Plea for Ethical Violence." In *The Neighbor: Three Inquiries in Political Theology*, 134–90. Chicago, IL: University of Chicago Press, 2005.

5 Concrete universality
Only that which is non-all is for all

Gabriel Tupinambá

Marx famously imagined that the proletarian revolution would somehow combine the universality of the working class and the universality of philosophy: "philosophy cannot realize itself without the transcendence [*Aufhebung*] of the proletariat, and the proletariat cannot transcend itself without the realization [*Verwirklichung*] of philosophy."[1] The overcoming of the particular and the abstract theory of the universal is achieved through the overcoming of a society in need of such a formal redoubling. One of the greatest challenges to such an imagined political destiny came not, however, from philosophy or Marxism – even if the two do keep an "enigmatic" relation until this day – but rather from psychoanalysis. That is, not from the already troubling articulation of two different logics of universality, but from the critique of universality as such, epitomized by Jacques Lacan's theory of the "pastout" – the "non-all" – as the logic of singularity. But does psychoanalysis truly bring to an end any hope for a politics of universalism? It is from the standpoint of this question that Slavoj Žižek's return to Hegel should be read – and, in particular, his return to the Hegelian Christology: as the search for a logic of collectivity in which the failure of the universal gives rise to a new, and singular, form of universality. But could we really find within Hegel's philosophy of Christianity the means to articulate the *dispersive* quality of the singular back into some form of collective logic?

In his book *Les noms indistincts*,[2] Jean-Claude Milner discusses the deployment of the Lacanian triad of the Real, Symbolic and Imaginary as three structuring logics of assembling multiplicities, a task which is of great use to us, preparing the ground for our discussion of the Žižekian logic of collectivity. Let us therefore schematically reconstruct Milner's theory of the three classes.

In the chapter *Les rassemblements*, Milner first distinguishes between the imaginary and the symbolic classes. The first is conceptualized as a logic of grouping in which individual elements are brought together under the heading of a common property which can be attributed to them. For example: the class of individuals brought together by a certain recognizable trace in them – their age, race, etc. – simultaneously constitutes the set of that which does not have that trace. Just as it establishes an opposition between the Same – the common property – and the Other – the negation of the property – the imaginary class also requires the reference to a hierarchy of properties and elements:

> The property subsists, thus, in reality, independently from the statement of a judgement: in other words, the property is definable and can, in its turn, become subjected to a judgement of attribution, which analyses it. From this results an hierarchy of the individual x to the property, of the property to the property of the property, etc. In the same movement, we obtain thus the metalanguages and the types.[3]

The symbolic class, on the other hand, is organized by a radically distinct principle. In it, the collective logic is structured in such a way that the very uttering of the name convenes the subjects to be represented by that signifier:

> there are those [multiplicities] whose principles share nothing with those of a representable property, but everything with the signifier which names them as a multiplicity. These, therefore, cannot pre-exist the utterance of the signifier itself; the property is reduced to the denomination that we make and the subject only receives it in the very instant in which the link is spoken. In this way, if we want to speak of a class, we should add that it only groups in an incessantly moving way, always affected by the statements that are spoken.[4]

The symbolic class has an intrinsically performative dimension, and in a double sense: not only the grouping "cannot pre-exist the utterance of the signifier," but it is the subject's own recognition that the signifier represents something of her that includes her in the multiplicity gathered by the name. The example of the insult, which was developed in great detail by Milner in one of his works on linguistics,[5] is particularly clear because it is precisely the subject's active engagement with the signifier that makes the insult so humiliating: the crucial operation is not that the name matches or not an attribute of the individual, but that the subject herself answers to the invitation to bear that name through the very process of trying to "escape" signification – something is signified by the very mismatch between the predicate and the predicated. The insult also allows us to recognize that the uttering of the name not only convenes the multiplicity, but that the symbolic multiplicity is conditioned by this enigmatic place of utterance – in the case of the insult, a place marked by the question "why did you call me that?" or "what does the word name in me?"

In this sense, the place of utterance of this binding signifier remains both inside and outside the class it founds. If, on the one hand, the symbolic class is organized around the convening of the subject by the utterance of a name – that is, through the split which invites the subject to recognize something of herself in the statement – on the other hand, the unassignable dimension of the utterance itself never allows the subject to be fully represented by the name, the enigma of its utterance gets in the way of its own effects. Milner exemplifies this other side of the symbolic performativity with the role of *suspicion* in certain collectives and, in clear resonance with the superegoic inversion of the Kantian imperative, shows how the more universal the calling which brings together a symbolic class, the more terrifying are the effects of not being fully represented by this universal, sometimes through different processes of *purification*, attempts to violently reduce the subject to the name which convened her, leaving nothing lacking or in excess to it.

After describing the imaginary and the symbolic classes, Milner moves on to construct a real multiplicity – what he calls a *paradoxical class*.[6] Contrary to the symbolic logic of assemblage, in which we have seen oscillation between the signifier always partially representing the subject and simultaneously never fully representing her, the paradoxical class is founded not by the two sides of the name, but by the singularity of each subject. This means that the paradoxical class is organized by the very thing which disperses its elements, the singular way each subject escapes being totally convened by the name. As Milner writes:

> the very instance which makes them resemble and mix with each other is what disjuncts them; this very thing which disjuncts them is what makes them refer to each other, though they do not resemble nor connect to each other.[7]

The paradoxical class is thus not formed as an imaginary consistent group, nor exclusively through the symbolic principle of identification. As examples of such a real multiplicity, Milner refers to the subjective structures conceptualized by psychoanalysis. Take the case of the name "neurotic": the judgment that an individual is neurotic is neither verified by the reciprocity between property and element – for there is no particularly "neurotic" behavior in and of itself – nor by the partial representation which convenes the subject – we do not become neurotic by accepting to be called this way. The only possible verification of neurosis is the *neurotic way in which the subject escapes any naming*. In the paradoxical class, "the predicate aims only at a subjectivity and this can only come *from the subject*"[8] – that is, comes from the failure of a previous predicate to fully capture the subject.

This is why Milner emphasizes that the crucial trait of this structure is that the "class that is aimed at by these names is not evoked by them":[9] the name of the paradoxical class does not represent the subject but marks the way each subject is never fully represented by its emblems. It marks, therefore, the singular or the real of a desire. The paradoxical class is, thus, "paradoxical" because even though it distinguishes a logic of naming, a way through which names can be assigned to subjects, it does not form any discernible collectivity, any totalization of elements, predicative or performative.

Even though the logic of the paradoxical class seems to take us to the contradictory limit of universality, pointing towards a dispersive dynamic in which one partakes of a given naming by detaching oneself from any common ground with the others, it nonetheless bears striking resemblance to the way Hegel conceptualizes the incarnation of the Holy Spirit, after Christ's death on the Cross, in the form of a community.

Hegel concludes the chapter on religion in the *Phenomenology of Spirit* with the elaboration of the movement through which the Spirit makes itself present as the community of believers. The shift from the section on the *Revealed Religion* to that of *Absolute Knowing*, which closes the book, is first presented by Hegel as the shift from a *future* to a *present* reconciliation, which is essentially a change in the role of the religious Word: first, a medium to mobilize the absence of a world still to come – an afterlife, for example – but, in a second moment, transformed into an end in itself, the material and immanent basis of a community of people which share nothing in common.

Hegel accounts for this transformation by providing us with a theory of names which, like Milner's and Lacan's, thinks the contradiction at the fringe of universality. He begins by describing how absolute Spirit becomes actual for self-consciousness when the absence of a future godly Love that would be capable of reconciling Good and Evil is itself grasped as something present today: neither Good nor Evil are superseded, but something emerges from their split or conflict, a promise made into an object: that Thing which will bring about a solution to the conflict, an absolute. This inversion between objectifying the conflicting poles of Good and Evil to focusing on this unknowable future "makes the object in itself into a spiritual essence."[10] In short: the more substance that is given to the Thing absent in the community, the more substance the community itself acquires. In this way, the promise of a future conciliation between the universal and the particular – the Good and Evil – which splits self-consciousness and the present existence of one's consciousness come together, the former actualized in the latter:

> This reconciliation of consciousness with self-consciousness is thereby shown to have been brought about from two sides; at one time in the religious spirit and once again in consciousness itself as such. They are distinguished from each other in that the former is this reconciliation in the form of *being-in-itself*, the latter in the form *being-for-itself*. [. . .] that unification wraps up this series of shapes of spirit, for within it spirit reaches the point where it knows itself not merely as it is *in itself*, that is, in terms of tis absolute *content*, and not merely as it is *for itself* in terms of its contentless form, that is, in terms of the aspect of self-consciousness.[11]

The essential movement, which brings Hegel's thinking closer to Lacan's, concerns the passage from the community of believers which is held together by its Other – the godly Love currently absent – to the emptying out of this external, albeit purely symbolic reference. What takes place here is, for Hegel, an inversion between the conscious and the self-conscious aspects of reconciliation: rather than organizing the community around the *knowledge* that god's love is universal, that is, its conscious anticipation, Hegel recognizes the incarnation of the Holy Spirit in the community of believers in the universality of every self-consciousness's conflict. Self-consciousness' schism, first divided between Good and Evil, then made thinkable by the promise of its overcoming in an Other's love, is now conceived as the very principle of the community. The dialectics here, from clear partition, to mediating otherness, to contradiction, come close to the triad of imaginary, symbolic and paradoxical classes. This self-consciousness "in the unity with its self-emptying"[12] is both the figure of self-consciousness known as Absolute Knowing – the subject who, relinquishing her self-sufficiency[13], "is Spirit knowing itself in the shape of Spirit"[14] – and the coming forth of "pure universality of knowledge."[15] The Hegelian passage from the symbolic class to the paradoxical class is accomplished in the guise of the passage from representational thought to speculative Reason – that is, the activity of the Concept:

> What in religion was *content*, that is, the form of representing an *other*, is here the *self's own activity*. The concept makes it binding that the content is that of the self's own activity – For this concept is, as we see, the knowledge of the self's activity within itself as all essentiality and all existence, the knowledge of *this subject* as *substance* and of the substance as this knowledge of its activity.[16]

We find here the tying together of Absolute Knowing – "the knowledge of *this subject* as *substance*" – with Spirit – "the substance as this knowledge of its activity." In sum: there where the singular subject does not recognize herself – where something of substance remains caught up in the subject, impeding its self-transparency – that is where Spirit as community of believers comes to be, its lack of knowledge of what binds it together having become the very marking of its consistency.

With the Hegelian community of believers as our main example of the functioning of the paradoxical class, let us now return to Milner's account of the shift between symbolic and paradoxical classes and attempt to elaborate in more precise terms the relation between the "for all" and the "non-all" in terms of the distinction between Kant and Hegel.

In fact, it is in this very passage from symbolic to real multiplicity – in which we are required to conceive of the limit of the logic of representation – that Milner turns to Kant's "transnational universality":

> What is also cast aside [from the paradoxical class] is the symbolic ethics, that is, the formal universality, and the demand that all maxims should be valid only insofar as they are valid as a law of the Universe. For it is, on the contrary, the evanescence of every Universe that would be the sign of desire, at a blank [*blanc*] instant, in which the evidence allies itself to the contentment, as long as the good encounter takes place. Maybe the Cartesian terms are more appropriate than others to

spell the unavoidable assertion of anticipated certainty. We would say, willingly, that Kant should let this one pass, he who so strongly incites the symbolic ethics, if we did not also know that his language sometimes is necessary and the only one capable of creating a truth effect.[17]

Kant's definition of the public space already traverses the imaginary "place of circumstances and conjunctures"[18] towards the truly singular inscription of each subject in the universal, beyond one's particularities and identifications. By cutting across the imaginary dimension of social identities, the Kantian formal universality also substitutes the oppositional configuration of norms, institutions and groups for a duality inherent to the very space it founds. The Milnerian paradoxical class, on the other hand, takes place at the "evanescence of all Universe," that is, it is structured *from the standpoint* of what is in excess to the name: it does not answer to the demand that is addressed to us to say "the true about the truth," but it takes place there where truth itself speaks.

It is crucial to note, however, that even though Kantian ethics is rooted in the absent core of the symbolic, through which every universal declaration *names something* of the subject,[19] Milner's shift towards the paradoxical class – rooted in how every emblem necessarily *misses* something of the subject in a singular way – does *not* consist in simply dismissing the Kantian position:

> For, in the game of homonymies, sometimes it is necessary to make the signifiers serve themselves of an ethics which prevents the subject from entangling itself to another ethics. That is why we see that the vocabulary of the symbolic ethics, serving the dis-incarnation of the Universe, ends up splitting from the realist ethics the real ethics – for it prevents the subject, on the pretext of not giving in, from being content in always preferring his stubbornness.[20]

Milner affirms that Kantian conception of the public use of Reason *does* open up the space for a real multiplicity by separating "from the realist ethics the real ethics," but also that, since this scission can only be accomplished on account of the exceptional character of the ethical call, the price to pay for the "dis-incarnation of the Universe" is that the constitutive impossibility of pure desire, the very emptiness at the origin of the law, is always threatened by its own reversal, the superegoic injunction. Indeed, if we follow Alenka Zupančič's detailed account of Kant's ethical thought in *The Ethics of the Real*, it is not hard to see that it is precisely the remainder of this scission between Real and reality which, endowing the Absolute with its own pathological force, returns to disrupt the Kantian "symbolic ethics" from within and to give it its truly radical underpinning.[21]

From a Hegelian standpoint, we could say that Kant's conception the public use of Reason is actually thought from the perspective of the

Understanding: the ethical call inviting us to partake in the universal requires the impossible to function in the guise of an *exception*. It stands for the absolute condition for which we would sacrifice of "the 'all' of what one is ready to sacrifice."[22] That is: the fantasy of *reducing oneself to the pure signifier that represents us* – the purity of "duty for duty's sake" – remains operative, even if only as an absolute and unobtainable reference, supporting "the distinction between the 'performative' level of social authority, and the level of free thinking where performativity is suspended," mentioned by Žižek (2009). Therefore, the shift from symbolic to paradoxical class can be understood as the passage from the formal, abstract universality to the logic of universality at stake in the Hegelian concept of Reason.

Just as Gerard Lebrun described the Hegelian concept as something which is "not tailored in the measure of our knowledge"[23] – for Actuality "inhabits" it from within – Alenka Zupančič also resorts to the same expression to designate how this shift to a real ethics gives rise to "a body which is not made in the measure of the infinite."[24] Finally, we cannot but hear in this incommensurability between the body and the infinite the echo of psychoanalysis' paradoxical typology of the subject, used above by Milner as an example of a paradoxical class.

Indeed, this reference to a fundamental *inadequacy* should not seem strange to the reader, as for Žižek Christ's monstrosity stands for the inscription in the world of an absolute "*Unangemessenheit*," around which the dialectical reversal of failed reflection into reflective failure[25] revolves. As we have also mentioned, Hegel places a fundamental division between Christ and the community of believers gathered in the Holy Spirit: while Christ had to die, after Christ we must accomplish this history *in ourselves* in order to exist as Spirit, or to become a child of God, a citizen of his kingdom – we are "inhabited" *in life* by an incommensurable excess that is proper of infinity.

The task of thinking the relation between Kantian philosophy and Christianity was already at the core of Hegel's early writings, such as *The Positivity of the Christian Religion* and *The Spirit of Christianity and Its Fate*,[26] where the Kantian "invisible church"[27] of Reason was conceived the product of the philosophical overcoming of the positive and alienating dimension of Christian Church.[28] However, in *The Phenomenology of Spirit*, as we have seen, the passage from the Revealed Religion to Absolute Knowledge is no longer conceived as the shift from positive to negative representation of the law – this passage is now understood as constitutive of the Jewish Spirit itself[29] – but precisely as the parallaxian shift through which the inadequacy of representational thought itself, incarnated in the figure of Christ, *falls into knowledge*, radically subverting the very core of Reason:

> What belongs to the element of representational thought, namely, that absolute spirit represents the nature of spirit in its existence as *an individual spirit* or, rather, as a particular spirit, is therefore shifted here into self-consciousness itself, into the knowledge that sustains itself in its

> *otherness*. This self-consciousness thus does not therefore actually *die* in the way that the *particular* is represented to have *actually* died; rather, its particularity dies away within its universality, which is to say, in its *knowledge*, which is the essence reconciling itself with itself.[30]

In fact, Hegel explicitly presents the constitution of self-consciousness qua Absolute Knowing as an infinite judgment, in which the "I" is placed in an incommensurable relation with the communal Thing:

> The thing is I: In fact, in this infinite judgement, the thing is sublated. The thing is nothing in itself; it only has meaning in relationships, only *by virtue of the I* and *its relation* to the I. – In fact, this moment emerged for consciousness in pure insight and Enlightenment. Things are purely and simply *useful* and are merely to be considered in terms of their utility. – The *culturally matured* self-consciousness, which traversed the world of self-alienated spirit, has by way of its self-emptying created the thing as itself. It thus still retains itself within the thing, and it knows the thing to have no self-sufficiency, that is, it knows that the thing is *essentially* merely *being for others*.[31]

Absolute Knowing is only formed when it "retains itself within the thing" – Spirit as the Real of the community, the "as if" which, in the social field "is the thing itself"[32] – and, on the other hand, the community itself is only formed because self-consciousness' impurity reveals its utility in "being for others." Following this passage, we propose that a Hegelian reading of the Kantian conception of the public use of Reason, thought of against the background of the dialectical move from religion to philosophy, could be condensed in the following speculative proposition: "collectivity is Reason."[33]

Substituting the coordinate or subordinate conjunction of the two terms for the paradoxical tension of their very incommensurability, this formulation relies on the very excess of each term over itself in order to constitute a relation between the two. Reason's universality endows the collective with its truly public dimension – for we dwell in the Holy Spirit when, parasitized as we are by infinity, we must account for that in us which is not tailored in our own measure "within its universality, which is to say, in its knowledge" – and the collectivity serves as the only true ground of Reason – for Reason can only be thoroughly distinguished from Understanding when the community disrupts from within the very formal universality of the symbolic class, which remains dependent on the logic of representation, always haunted by its superegoic inversion. In sum, there is only community where the inconsistency of the social field itself speaks and does so *in a rational way – and there is only Reason where the subject tarries with the inadequacy of enjoyment to the body in terms of the inadequacy of the Concept to knowledge. A psychoanalyst might recognize here a certain fundamental operation of the mechanism of the passe.*

This, however, also means that we should not think the paradoxical class as being *beyond* the symbolic one: one of the most important consequences of thinking Kant's notion of the public use of Reason from the Hegelian standpoint is that the "beyond" is no longer to be understood in the sense of a transcendental term regulating from without the social space, but as that which is "in between,"[34] as the very non-coincidence at play in one's alienated social activity. As Žižek puts it "one is truly universal only when radically singular, in the *interstices* of communal identities."[35]

We can also understand this shift, from a beyond to an in-between, as the distinction between two attitudes of knowledge towards the communal – the Kantian "dare to . . ." and the Lacanian "you may. . . ." In the case of the *Sapere Aude*, the public use of Reason redefines the relation between the public and the private, but the principle of transmission, the empty core of the law, does not affect knowledge itself – it does not change what knowledge is permitted and prohibited to know. In the case of the Lacanian *Scilicet*, the principle of transmission is itself caught up in what is transmitted, opening up the space for the articulation of truth and knowledge. Žižek makes this point very clear in *For they know not what they do*:

> We can see, now, how far Lacanian psychoanalysis is from the pluralist–pragmatic "liberalism" of the Rortyan kind: Lacan's final lesson is not relativity and plurality of truths but the hard, traumatic fact that in every concrete constellation *truth is bound to emerge* in some contingent detail. In other words, although truth is context-dependent – although there is no truth in general, but always the truth *of* some situation – there is none the less in every plural field a particular point which articulates its truth and as such *cannot* be relativized; in this precise sense, truth is always *One* . . . . We even lack an appropriate term for this "X" [which is neither prescribed, nor prohibited, nor permitted, but contingent], for the strange status of what is "not prescribed," "facultative," and yet not simply "permitted" – like, for example, the emergence of some hitherto forbidden knowledge in the psychoanalytic cure which holds up to ridicule the Prohibition, lays bare its hidden mechanism, without thereby changing into a neutral "permissiveness." The difference between the two pertains to the different relationships towards the universal Order: "permissiveness" is warranted by it, whereas this guarantee lacks in the case of "you may . . ." which Lacan designates as *Scilicet*: you may know (the truth about your desire) – if you take the risk upon yourself. This *Scilicet* is perhaps the ultimate recourse of the critical thought.[36]

Our wager is that this crucial dimension is precisely what is at stake in the rational core of Hegel's account of the community of believers:

> The movement of propelling forward the form of its self-knowledge is the work which spirit accomplishes as *actual history*. The religious

> community, insofar as it is initially the substance of absolute spirit, is
> the brutish consciousness which, the deeper its inner spirit is, both has
> an existence all the more harsh and barbaric and its dull and expressionless self an even more difficult labor in dealing with its essence,
> that is, with the alien content of its consciousness. *Not until it has
> abandoned the hope of sublating that way of being alien in an external,
> i.e., alien, manner and because the sublated alien manner is itself the
> return into self-consciousness, does that consciousness in itself turn to
> itself, turn to its own world and present time, and discover that world
> to be its own property.* When it has done this, it will have taken the first
> step to climb down from the *intellectual world*, or, to a greater degree,
> to spiritualize the abstract element of the intellectual world with the
> actual self.[37]

There is an essentially "brutish consciousness" at play in the collectivity organized by a negative condition, but it is only *in it* and *through it* that we can recognize ourselves in the "alien content" which in vain we attempt to sublate. Hegel clearly relates this second step to the passage of Understanding – the "abstract element of the intellectual world" – to its spiritualization, in its descent to the "actual self," that is, to Reason.

The crucial point in Hegel's description of the collective is, thus, the properly dialectical step through which the public space is constituted not as a domain beyond the social, but *between* the social identities. Rather than a dialectical "overcoming" of the formal universality, the paradoxical class introduces a further split into it, adding to the logic of imaginary opposition and the twofold logic of the symbolic ethics a third division, that of the parallax Real: the impossible beyond the symbolic being *supplemented* by the impossible inherent to Reason itself.

We should be able to recognize in the conjunction of the Kantian public use of Reason and of the Christian community of believers *not* the mere substitution of the symbolic universality for the paradoxical class – a position which seems to have been adopted by Milner himself later on – but the affirmation that *the real multiplicity is nothing but the parallaxian shift itself*. A "parallaxian" class, so to speak: the collective of those whose failures to live up to a universal idea form the only basis for this idea's indirect – but concrete – existence.

As we have seen, the Hegelian account of the constitution of the community of believers presents a dialectical version of Milner's "nodal" theory of the three forms of grouping – with one essential distinction. Dialectics is a grammar that highlights the underlying continuity between its moments, forcing us to rethink the conceptual form of a certain idea when the movement of its realization seems to rather undo its relevance. The logic of singularity seems, when considered on its own, a dispersive or anti-universal logic. But when it is temporally conceived, that is, as a moment of a dialectical movement, it is not a matter of stating that we have passed from the universal to the singular, but rather that we moved towards a new concept of universality, even if it contradicts our own criteria of what universality should look like.

Žižek's return to Hegelian Christology, and in particular to Hegel's theory of the Holy Spirit, constructs a possible bridge between the Marxist praise of concrete universality and the Lacanian critique of predicative generalization, but at the cost of engaging in a complicated polemic. This logical connection allows us to develop important tools for Marxist theory and practice: for instance, a theory of universality that is not hindered by singularity might help us to overcome the dualism which can only think class formations by presupposing common properties to a certain social strata. But, on the other hand, it also requires us to reevaluate the Christian legacy and its reception by the Marxist and psychoanalytic traditions. That is, if Žižek's take on Christianity reveals religion's capacity to model a critique of idealist universality, then the recuperation of Hegel's Christology also entails a critique of Marx and Lacan from the standpoint of the Christian "fragile absolute": if there is such a thing as a real universality, the historical and material existence of which is conditioned by our failure to be "positively" universal, then what are the ideological commitments in both Marx and Lacan which prevent these thinkers – both close readers of Hegel – from assuming this essential Hegelian insight?

Notes

1. Karl Marx, *Marx's Critique of Hegel's Philosophy of Right* (London: Oxford Press, 1970), 32.
2. Jean-Claude Milner, *Les noms indistincts* (Paris: Editions Verdier, 2007).
3. Ibid., 98.
4. Ibid., 99–100. My translation, as with all quotes from Milner.
5. Jean-Claude Milner, *De la syntaxe à l'interprétation* (Paris: Seuil, 1978).
6. Milner, *Les noms indistincts*, 107.
7. Ibid., 109.
8. Ibid., 110–11.
9. Ibid., 112.
10. G.W.F. Hegel, *Phenomenology of Spirit* (Oxford: Oxford University Press, 1979), §788.
11. Ibid., §794.
12. Ibid., §795.
13. Ibid., §797.
14. Ibid., §798.
15. Ibid., §796.
16. Ibid., §797.
17. Milner, *Les noms indistincts*, 113.
18. Ibid., 112.
19. Ibid., 99–100.
20. Ibid., 113.
21. See, for example, the subchapter "The Unconditional" in Alenka Zupančič, *Ethics of The Real: Kant, Lacan* (London: Verso Books, 2000), 53–61.
22. Ibid., 257.

23 Gérard Lebrun, *La patience du concept: essai sur le discours hégélien* (Paris: Gallimard, 1972), 350–1.
24 Zupančič, *Ethics of The Real*, 258.
25 Slavoj Žižek, *For They Know Not What They Do: Enjoyment as a Political Factor* (London: Verso Books, 2008), 85.
26 G.W.F. Hegel, *Early Theological Writings* (Philadelphia: University of Pennsylvania Press, 1971).
27 Immanuel Kant, *Religion and Rational Theology* (Cambridge: Cambridge University Press, 2001), 179.
28 Hegel, *Early Theological Writings*, 100.
29 Slavoj Žižek, "Is It Still Possible to Be a Hegelian Today?," in *The Speculative Turn: Continental Materialism and Realism*, ed. Levi Bryant, Nick Srnicek and Graham Harman (Melbourne: re.press, 2011), 218.
30 Hegel, *Phenomenology of Spirit*, §785.
31 Ibid., §791.
32 Slavoj Žižek, *Living in the End Times* (London: Verso Books, 2010), 285.
33 This statement could itself be understood as a Žižekian version of Rancière's "equality and intelligence are synonymous terms," Jacques Rancière, *The Ignorant Schoolmaster: Five Lessons in Intellectual Emancipation* (Stanford, CA: Stanford University Press, 1991), 73. Hopefully this argument helps in shedding some light as to why it is an essential element of Žižekian philosophy to engage with so-called "pop culture," especially with examples which do not present any "sublime splendor," but are "not made in the measure of the infinite which inhabits [them]."
34 Alain Badiou, *Court traité d'ontologie transitoire* (Paris: Seuil, 1998), 64; See also Alenka Zupančič, *The Shortest Shadow: Nietzsche's Philosophy of the Two* (Cambridge, MA: MIT Press, 2003), 87.
35 Slavoj Žižek and John Milbank, *The Monstrosity of Christ: Paradox or Dialectic?* (Cambridge, MA: MIT Press, 2009), 295.
36 Ibid., 196–7.
37 Hegel, *Phenomenology of Spirit*, §803.

Bibliography

Badiou, Alain. *Court traité d'ontologie transitoire*. Paris: Seuil, 1998.
Bryant, Levi, Nick Srnicek and Graham Harman, eds. *The Speculative Turn: Continental Materialism and Realism*. Melbourne: re.press, 2011.
Hegel, G.W.F. *Early Theological Writings*. Philadelphia: University of Pennsylvania Press, 1971.
———. *Phenomenology of Spirit*. Oxford: Oxford University Press, 1979.
Kant, Immanuel. *Religion and Rational Theology*. Cambridge: Cambridge University Press, 2001.
Lebrun, Gérard. *La patience du concept: Essai sur le discours hégélien*. Paris: Gallimard, 1972.
Marx, Karl. *Marx's Critique of Hegel's Philosophy of Right*. London: Oxford Press, 1970.
Milner, Jean-Claude. *De la syntaxe à l'interprétation*. Paris: Seuil, 1978.
———. *Les noms indistincts*. Paris: Editions Verdier, 2007.
Rancière, Jacques. *The Ignorant Schoolmaster: Five Lessons in Intellectual Emancipation*. Stanford, CA: Stanford University Press, 1991.
Žižek, Slavoj. *For They Know Not What They Do: Enjoyment as a Political Factor*. London: Verso Books, 2008.

Žižek, Slavoj. "Dialectical Clarity versus the Misty Conceit of Paradox", in *The Monstrosity of Christ: Paradox or Dialectic?*, edited by Creston Davis, 234–306. Cambridge, MA: MIT Press, 2009.

———. *Living in the End Times*. London: Verso Books, 2010.

Žižek, Slavoj and John Milbank. *The Monstrosity of Christ: Paradox or Dialectic?* Edited by Creston Davis. Cambridge, MA: MIT Press, 2009.

Zupančič, Alenka. *The Shortest Shadow: Nietzsche's Philosophy of the Two*. Cambridge, MA: MIT Press, 2003.

6 Pacifist pluralism versus militant truth
Christianity at the service of revolution in the work of Slavoj Žižek

Haralambos Ventis

Introduction

Notwithstanding their legendary differences, Marxism and Christianity share a common denominator regarding the question of the Truth: both purport to offer a privileged, "behind-the-scenes," as it were, account of ultimate reality, either in regards to the direction of history and the role of the economy as regulator of human culture and social relations, or in the form of "getting it right" concerning the being of God as purveyor of life and meaning in a heartless universe. Both entail an eschatology with emancipatory promises for humankind and are equally criticized on account of it by liberal thought: Marxism is reproached for the determinism of its eschatological vision, for its unmitigated confidence in the so-called iron laws of history and the consequent stigmatization of those refusing to comply with the revealed direction of history, as "bourgeois enemies of the people." Similarly, Christianity gets a black eye for calling "sinners" all those who stray from the one, exclusive path of salvation prescribed once and for all by Scripture and the Church – the slightest diversion is often condemned as sin and, at worst, as "heresy."

The insistence of both worldviews on making categorical truth-claims has been repeatedly linked to intolerance and fanaticism, on the premise that monotheism's reductive insistence on one, single Truth at the expense of rival alternatives enslaves the mind, whereas pluralism sets it free – and Marxism has been aptly described as a form of monotheism, in the sense of comprising a static set of infallible doctrines, immune from external criticism and unsusceptible to reconsideration, much like a secular counterpart to the three major monotheistic faiths.[1] Raising as it does the charge of *heteronomy* as the premier damage caused by monotheism, liberal atheism hones to a finer edge the classic critiques of religion, memorably raised by Modernity's masters of suspicion: for example, as an intrinsically irrational phenomenon, spawned by intellectual weakness (as Bertrand Russell would have it); as constituting nothing more than the "opium of the people," in Karl Marx's oft-quoted phrase; or "humanity's Oedipal complex" and perishing illusion, according to Sigmund Freud; as being the projection of human subjectivity into heaven, in Ludwig Feuerbach's account of the origins of religion, or as likewise being a crude "Platonism for the masses," as Friedrich Nietzsche once wrote, with plain scorn for Christianity in particular.

At a moment in history when the politics of Truth were widely dismissed as "totalitarian," thanks to the combined might of epistemological minimalism[2] and a post-structuralist aversion to "grand narratives" (which naturally slammed the grandiose truth-claims of both Marxism and Christianity, among those of other belief systems), Slavoj Žižek, along with Alain Badiou (and to a certain extent, Giorgio Agamben), launched a counter-attack to liberal pluralism,[3] affirming Christianity's claim to truth as a paramount virtue, not a vice. Before we examine the possible soundness and worth of the said defense, let us review the intellectual background of Liberalism's reservations towards inflated truth-claims and their rigid ethical spin-offs, usually amounting to exclusivist accounts of the common Good laden with matching eschatologies.

Some major highlights before the emergence of Slavoj Žižek's Christian–Marxist apologetics: the theoretical paradigm of liberal political constructivism[4]

In general, what modern, liberal critics of religion appear to worry about mostly is the loss of *autonomy*, personal as well as social, that metaphysical, all-encompassing underpinnings of ethics and politics may incur. The philosophical ideal of *autonomy* has been at the heart of liberalism since the movement's inception, but its value has been considerably amplified in recent years in the works of several influential philosophers, mostly Kantian in philosophical outlook, such as John Rawls, Jürgen Habermas, Thomas Scanlon, Alain Renault and Christine Korsgaard, to name but a few, as well as Cornelius Castoriadis (albeit from a non-Kantian intellectual lineage). What these Kantian liberals share is a pronounced sensitivity against the peril of comprehensive worldviews, religious or not, infiltrating public dialogue and from there making their way into public policies and legislature. Their concern has been aptly referred to in recent Greek scholarship as "the fear of Platonism,"[5] if by "Platonism" is denoted any set of transcendent metaphysical premises with normative moral and political implications. Succinctly put, their views (subtle differences among them notwithstanding) converge in promoting a "procedural" kind of ethics devoid or innocent of metaphysical foundations. Habermas, in many ways a leading figure on this side of the debate, has been persistently vocal about the futility and pointlessness, as he sees it, of searching for ontological underpinnings to ethics, insisting as he does (along with Richard Rorty, at least in that respect) that after Hegel and especially in the aftermath of the so-called linguistic turn, philosophy has irrevocably entered a post-metaphysical stage.[6]

But epistemology aside, Kantian "constructivism" is chiefly driven by an ethical consideration: it is upheld out of fear that any non-constructivist, i.e. a "realist" approach to ethics would reinstate the long deceased "is–ought" merger, thereby reintroducing "non-falsifiable" and hence non-negotiable (i.e. "dogmatic" and arbitrary) moral preconceptions, such as the "revealed truths" of religion, which in turn would inevitably lead to the tyranny of "uniquely correct" answers to social and political problems, as Thomas Scanlon suggests.[7] The feared outcome, then, is that given its immutable metaphysical foundations, moral realism would almost certainly hinder all social progress and development by not allowing, or at least by discouraging, innovation and any reconsideration of established norms and values, along with the freedom to create alternative models of social organization in the direction of a progressively less exclusivist society. In other words, should so-called final truths begin to inform public policies once again, the possibility of attaining an open-ended, forward-looking society would suffer a terrible setback, after years of slow and painstaking progress in civil liberties.

One such champion of the modernist notion of autonomy is Cornelius Castoriadis. Castoriadis, formerly of a socialist persuasion, is famous for his astute analyses of ancient Athenian democracy, whose self-instituting model of government he utilized in a lifelong intellectual effort to oppose the inherent totalitarianism of theocratic as well as communist regimes. As an adamant upholder of what the present writer calls the "metaphysics of finitude," my rather idiosyncratic neologism for the perspective of austere ontological immanentism, Castoriadis shares some considerable ground (although none in terms of objectives) with his near-contemporary Panagiotis Kondylis:[8] both writers, intellectual giants who flourished in France and Germany, respectively, preached a credo of radical[9] empiricism that staunchly denied an existence to non-physical entities, with an eye especially to debunking the inflated status of transcendent worldviews, ideals and values as nothing but human fabrications. Convinced as both had been that every form of discourse, no matter how institutionally or religiously polished, could be tracked down to finite origins, they urged a renewed acquaintance with classical Greek wisdom for instruction on reconciliation with human mortality as the surest block to the claims of self-serving prophets and holy warriors of all stripes supposedly conveying the voice of God, History, Reason or Being.

The very title of Castoriadis' philosophical masterwork, *The Imaginary Institution of Society*,[10] encapsulates his lifelong thesis that all social and historical phenomena, as human constructs, owe their emergence to the unceasing and utterly indeterminate activity of the imagination. By giving ontological pre-eminence to the imagination over reason as the foremost human attribute, Castoriadis does not dispense with western rationalism, although he does break with those espousing a thick rationalist line of thought that sees history propelled chiefly by reason. To be sure, Castoriadis praises Kant for his re-discovery of the role of the imagination as a device deeply instrumental in world-making; at the same time, however, he regrets the Kantian consolidation of the imagination to a transcendental mechanism that fatally restricts the free-flowing creativity of the human mind. Castoriadis' interjection of the imagination as the chief hermeneutic key for uncovering the buried origins of religion was thus intended to expose the latter's humble beginnings as lying nowhere save in the minds of leading figures and social groups: this was the first, crucial step in his broader aim to assist society in acquiring the self-transparency required for its eventual autonomy. For, the genuinely autonomous society, as he pictures it, is precisely one which is conscious of itself as a self-accomplished, artificial entity free from the grip of extra-societal (particularly religious) underpinnings obscuring its real, unglamorous origins.

Unfortunately, however, the attainment of self-transparency (as Castoriadis indicated) proves to be a very rare historical occurrence, something of a scandal even, if and when it ever occurs, given the strong resistance it meets from the established authorities and institutions, whose endurance and self-propagation clearly rest on their sanctified image as divinely sanctioned. A false consciousness, reminiscent of the Marxist concept of the "superstructure," is thus created by the authorities to shield social institutions from probing enquiries into their genesis by portraying them as holy, necessary and universal. It is the business of philosophy, then, as the *par excellence* critical activity, to pierce the veil of extra-societal projections by setting in motion a process of de-divinization which, as Richard Rorty puts it, "would have no room for the notion that there are non-human forces to which human beings should be responsible," a process culminating "in our no longer being able to see any use for the notion that finite, mortal, contingently existing human beings might derive the meanings of their lives from anything except other finite, mortal, contingently existing human beings."[11] On the view suggested by Castoriadis, accordingly,

> The making of democracy negates all transcendent sources of meaning, at least in the public sphere, but ideally, I should add, if democracy is to be complete, for the individual as well . . . for a democratic polity, as I have said, is unthinkable apart from the actual autonomy of its particular members, namely without each person's capacity to freely ascribe their own meaning in life. Needless to say, all this presupposes a philosophical position . . . admitting that there actually exists no *intrinsic* meaning in the universe, say in the form of a veiled treasure awaiting to be extracted, whether from nature or History or our inner life; that it is none other but ourselves who are the true makers of meaning and value, creating it and then planting it on the bottomless abyss, and in that sense that it is also ourselves who give shape to chaos with our thoughts and deeds, apart from extrinsic guarantees to lean upon.[12]

Political autonomy, therefore, in the form that it was attained in fifth-century Athens, correlates in Castoriadis' view with the abrogation of religion and metaphysics at least from the public sphere, thanks to a happy convergence of philosophical skepticism, materialism and (consequent upon these) relativism at that time and place. "Skepticism and doubt," writes Castoriadis, "comprise the common root of democracy and philosophy alike,"[13] a skepticism unmistakably mirrored in the subversive Greek dichotomy of *law* versus *nature*,[14] and decisively instrumental in the ostracism of messianism from the public arena of the Athenian *agora*:

> The very notion of a historical guarantor, like the related ideas of a Messiah or the possibility of an otherworldly escapism [from history] are completely alien to the Greeks. [The Greek mind rests on] the conviction, instead, that whatever is possible [and desirable] to occur will occur here. Anything that cannot be realized here simply cannot concern us [human beings]: it takes place elsewhere, either in the domain of the gods or at the bottom of the abyss (chaos). What is truly significant for us happens here, depends upon us, and will be carried out by us and no one else. Neither God, nor historical determinism shall bring it about . . . It is up to us human mortals to accomplish it – should Fate and circumstances allow so – else it will never happen.[15]

The communitarian flipside to constructivism and its exaltation of autonomy: the response of the neo-Aristotelians

As we shall see, Žižek begs to differ with Castoriadis' strategy, inasmuch as he keenly enlists Christianity as a vital ally to his emancipatory project. On the other hand, theorists of the communitarian persuasion have launched a more direct, head-on attack on the celebrated ideal of a *totally* self-legislating, autonomous subject, whose rise mandates the obliteration of religious spirituality from the individual conscience. For example, writers like William Desmond have repeatedly taken issue with the patronizing one-sidedness of the cult of autonomy, whose ontological minimalism and fear of eschatology (the "nominalist" cultural attitude descried by Marxist literary theorist Terry Eagleton as *holophobia*),[16] may foster a high degree of relativism, raising the twin fears of social anomie and nihilism. Not only that: when absolutized, autonomy is now feared by many as being apt to lead not to Kant's (and Castoriadis') noble ideal of the self-governed moral agent, but to the Nietzschean "overman." In Desmond's words,

> If each is self-legislating, what of the other? Do I legislate for the other? Does the other legislate for me? Does not the *pluralizing* of self-legislation create serious difficulties to holding on to the notion of *self*-legislation as the primary model of moral freedom? . . . We are only projecting ourselves [as God] then. We project ourselves, we recover ourselves, by dissolving God back into ourselves, and thus we become truly self-legislating. We start as morally righteous Kantians and end as self-glorifying Nietzscheans beyond good and evil, ourselves the source of the moral law.[17]

Charles Taylor, a leading communitarian theorist, voices the same concern in his study on Hegel, namely that the prospect of an unrestrained autonomy ignoring even the partial human embeddedness in communal and cultural values is only bound to result, over the long run, in the naked exaltation of the "will to power."[18] In a later work, Taylor likewise bemoans the Nietzschean one-sidedness tainting recent deconstructionist attempts to extol authenticity as amoralism of creativity, and to promote it thusly at the expense of the social and communal "horizons of significance," as Taylor calls them.[19] As a genuine communitarian, Taylor is nervous about the so-called deontological priority of the *right* over the *good* traditionally espoused by liberals and designed as a Kantian counter-attack against utilitarianism. And while Taylor finds this priority "highly justified in its anti-utilitarian thrust," he nevertheless worries that "it can also be used to downgrade not just the homogeneous good of desire-fulfilment central to utilitarian theory but also any conception of the good, including the qualitative distinctions underlying our moral views."[20] Not surprisingly, Taylor complains as well about John Rawls' "veil of ignorance" method of ensuring the impartiality of distributing rights and goods in society (a thought experiment intended to blind political parties as to the identities of the recipients of these goods, expounded in *A Theory of Justice*): to ensure the kind of benevolent ignorance proposed by Rawls, we must develop a notion of justice starting only with a "thin theory of the good," which roughly corresponds to what Taylor calls weakly valued goods, a suggestion that he claims to find incoherent.[21]

These and similar voices of resistance to the glorification of autonomy as upheld by Kantian constructivists come from the camp of the so-called neo-Aristotelians, most notably Alasdair MacIntyre,[22] Martha Nussbaum[23] and Charles Larmore,[24] who largely overlap with communitarian thinkers (Larmore identifies himself explicitly as such) in assigning priority to communal notions of the Good as opposed to rights and pluralism. Neo-Aristotelians maintain that philosophy should by no means shy away from drawing general normative values capable of creating a sense of communal belonging under the guiding narrative of a tradition. A big driving motive for this group of theorists is the fear of anomie and relativism, chiefly moral but epistemological as well, that they believe is intrinsic to Kantian constructivism.

For communitarians and neo-Aristotelians, it is Plato (or a revised Platonism, at any rate), and especially Aristotle, but certainly not Kant, who serves as an inspiration. For despite Kant's deep preoccupation with ethics and the catholically normative character of his celebrated categorical imperative, Kantian moral philosophy is still perceived by the communitarian camp as fostering an individualism of sorts,[25] chiefly by upholding the non-negotiable value of personal autonomy and by thusly seeing individual persons as ends in themselves, even at the cost of the community and the common Good. Plato, on the other hand, is appreciated as being more conducive to a communitarian ethic, given the predilection in his *Republic* for what is general and communal, i.e. for the *polis*, over the individual citizen. Communitarian Charles Larmore, for example, sides explicitly with Plato over Kant in his philosophical exchange with Alain Renaut, describing his position as a "mild Platonism": this standpoint is carefully nuanced as acknowledging the existence of a self-standing, independent set of normative values, which are discovered rather than created by us.[26] In what looks like a condensed summary of the neo-Aristotelians' agenda, Larmore expresses his deep dissatisfaction with Renaut's vision of personal autonomy, which he accuses of ultimately being incompatible with, and even deleterious to, the acts of thinking and reasoning themselves![27]

What are the reasons that prompt Larmore to pronounce such a harsh judgment against personal autonomy? Succinctly speaking, he argues that in principle there can be no context-free, wholly abstract form of reasoning apart from the benefit of an established pool of knowledge, tradition and wisdom, a social reservoir forged cumulatively by a community or a number of interacting communities. For, in contemplating any problem or question, Larmore explains, we always rely on past knowledge, even when we see fit to react against the very premises and the conclusions reached by that antecedent, inherited social context. In what seems like an intellectual loan from Wittgenstein's insights regarding the social genesis and function of language (as is well known, Wittgenstein rejected the sheerest possibility of there ever being meaningful "private" languages), Larmore points attention to the individual's inescapably communal manner of growth into a thinking subject. The philosophical ideal of a completely autonomous person is an impossibility according to Larmore, because (and this is fully shared by communitarian theorist Charles Taylor) it would be more reminiscent of a case of autism, as opposed to the "fleshed out," truly human subject; for, J. J. Rousseau's ideas to the contrary, human personhood is reared and nourished not in isolation, but within a community sharing some fundamental moral norms and assumptions – even if these are in constant flux and progressively replaced by new ones.

For Larmore, in other words, as for Taylor, the self is socially constituted, without necessarily being deprived of the freedom of self-determination, which the Kantians are so worried about. In his own words,

> Normativity is more than a hermeneutic instrument that may help us explain one's behavior. It is constitutive of one's individual perspective. Normativity actually constitutes the bedrock, out of which the self, the empirical subject, emerges. Even in our tiniest thought, we find ourselves deeply engaged.[28]

Hence, apart from the nurturing environment of a communally sanctioned normativity, the self is dramatically robbed of its unity and coherence; in time, selfhood runs the risk of being shattered to a myriad of unconnected splinter fragments, the dispersion of which is feared as eventually incurring the long-term disintegration of the social fabric and, worse, as signaling the end of humanism,[29] as novelist William Golding dramatically depicts in *Lord of the Flies* and (from an entirely different perspective) as Michel Foucault sardonically states in the concluding sentence of his celebrated monograph, *The Order of Things: An Archaeology of the Human Sciences*.[30]

The most compelling philosophical enunciation of the interpersonal, social comprisal of the self, in this writer's opinion, comes from French hermeneuticist Paul Ricoeur, who made creative use of linguistic philosophy (in particular, Austin's insights in *How to Do Things With Words*) to reinstate the self's integrity as an active agent who speaks language instead of being spoken by it ("it is not statements that refer to something but the speakers themselves who refer in this way"),[31] and whose speaking requires listeners, so that "utterance equals interlocution."[32] All this, for the purpose of stipulating from the outset "that the selfhood of oneself implies otherness to such an intimate degree that one cannot be thought of without the other, that instead one passes into the other, as we might say in Hegelian terms."[33]

This thesis bears certain political implications, which overlap with Larmore's and Taylor's conclusions: As Ricoeur explicitly states,

> living well [as Aristotle, hero of most communitarians and adherents of social teleologies, held] is not limited to interpersonal relations but extends to the life of *institutions* . . . By "institution," we are to understand here the structure of living together as this belongs to a historical community – people, nation, region and so forth – a structure irreducible to interpersonal relations and yet bound up with these in a remarkable sense . . . what fundamentally characterizes the idea of an institution is *the bond of common mores and not that of constraining rules*. In this, we are carried back to the *ethos* from which ethics takes its name.[34]

Quite predictably for a Continental neo-Aristotelian, Ricoeur rejects the Humean is/ought disjunction[35] and draws an interesting demarcation between *ethics*, on the one hand, and *morality*, on the other. Between the two, he prioritizes the former as consorting with the Aristotelian teleological tradition, a much-needed, broader and unifying normative horizon than mere morality, which he assigns to the line of Kantian deontology as a narrowly instrumental enactment of ethics.

How is this all related to selfhood and, ultimately, to political life? Succinctly put, Ricoeur asserts a direct link between teleology and ethical practice, which is assumed to have social repercussions from the very outset:

> practices, we observe following MacIntyre, are cooperative activities whose constitutive rules are established socially; the standards of excellence that correspond to them on the level of this or that practice *originate much further back than the solitary practitioner* . . . if one asks by what right the self is declared to be worthy of esteem, it must be answered that it is not principally by reason of its accomplishments but fundamentally by reason of its capacities. To understand the term "capacity" correctly, we must return to Merleau-Ponty's "I can" and extend it from the

physical to the ethical level. I am that being who can evaluate his actions and, in assessing the goals of some of them to be good, is capable of evaluating himself and of judging himself to be good . . . The question is then *whether the mediation of the other is not required along the route from capacity to realization*. The question is in no way rhetorical. *On it as Charles Taylor has maintained, depends the fate of political theory*. In this way, many philosophies of natural law *presuppose a subject, complete and already fully endowed with rights, before entering into society*. It results that this subject's participation in community life is in principle contingent and revocable, and that the individual – since this is how the person has to be called under this hypothesis – is correct in expecting from the state the protection of rights constituted outside of him or her, without bearing any intrinsic obligation to participate in the burdens related to perfecting the social bond. This hypothesis of a subject of law, constituted prior to any societal bond, can be refuted only by striking at its roots. Now the root is the failure to recognize the *mediating* role of others between capacities and realization.[36]

Now, alongside such speculative reasons for advocating virtue ethics and the social constitution of human subjectivity, the return of more communal visions of the public good has been largely facilitated by the on-going global fiscal crisis, which has prompted leftist and Christian intellectuals to voice what many now consider a much-needed "prophetic" criticism of neo-liberal excesses, such as the replacement of democratic politics by the self-serving Markets. A good case in point is the defense of the public good versus a neo-liberal bloated emphasis on individualism, penned by Michael Sandel in his *What Money Can't Buy: The Moral Limits of Markets*[37] (and relayed by Michael Ignatieff in a book review of the same work):

> The ultimate good in a liberal state is liberty. But Sandel thinks that liberty is not enough for life in a liberal order. A liberal political order should be more ambitious. It should aim at "soulcraft," or the shaping of a citizen's character. It should promote the virtues of honor, respect and sacrifice, and wean people away from private selfishness, and make them more devoted to the public good. Without these civic virtues, the liberal republic will lack the community spirit to maintain a healthy democracy. As he once observed, "The public philosophy by which we live cannot secure the liberty it promises because it cannot inspire the sense of community and civic engagement that liberty requires."
>
> By prizing only the value of liberty and hence of private property, Sandel has argued, liberalism disarmed itself in the battle against the power of money. The liberal state has allowed market principles to shape public debate and mold private consciousness, leaving a public world in which (as Oscar Wilde said) too many of us know the price of everything and the value of nothing. So Sandel is trying to force open

a space for a discourse on civic virtue that he believes has been abandoned by both left and right.[38]

As described, Sandel is more subtly communitarian than his quoted peers and in fact stands closer to the republican side of liberalism: for, he leaves the "common good" only vaguely stated as a civic virtue countering individualism, greed, consumerism and selfishness, without positively defining it in metaphysical terms or attaching it to a communal teleology detrimental to the individual's rights and interests. Furthermore, Sandel displays a more realistic grasp of social affairs than most full-blooded liberals appear to be capable of or would care to: he is attentive to such deleterious first-world problems as compulsive consumerism, the overblown fetish of property, an ever-growing inequality and greed, whose excess corrodes the civic conscience from within and creates passive, withdrawn and politically disinclined consumers – joined in apathy by the long-term unemployed and destitute who live below the poverty line and have massively lost interest and trust in mainstream politics, often falling prey to populist rhetoric and the demagoguery of the far right.

Parallel developments in the study of religion also helped re-establish the intellectual dignity and worth of theological discourse, as a contributor to civic alertness and emancipation, an image of it far removed from its stereotypical caricature as an incorrigibly reactionary body of thought. Two landmark works, deeply instrumental in this recent re-appreciation of the intellectual and cultural contribution of the Christian faith to the definitive shape of the Western world (alongside other contributing factors, such as ancient Greek democracy and Roman Law), are Jacques Le Goff's *The Birth of Europe*[39] and Marcel Gauchet's *The Disenchantment of the World*.[40] Le Goff's and Gauchet's surprising thesis (pursued from very different angles, with all due cautious attention to historical fortuity and indeterminism) is that Modernity and the emergence of secularism, far from being inimical to or incompatible with Biblical monotheism, have been largely precipitated by certain motifs drawn and enlarged from the Christian Scriptures. By shedding fresh light on the emancipating and radical aspects of Christ's ministry and message, Gauchet in particular set the scene for the subsequent emergence of positive appraisals of Christianity by a cluster of influential secular intellectuals and philosophers, who have gone a long way toward further unfolding the liberating spirit of the Gospel. These include, among others, Alain Badiou, Gianni Vattimo, Giorgio Agamben and Slavoj Žižek. Gauchet's statement, theologically echoed by Jürgen Moltmann,[41] may be hard to accept at face value, given the long period of religious bloodshed in Europe and the persistently pre-modern, conservative proclivities of institutional Christendom; nevertheless, the combined thrust of Gauchet's and Le Goff's scholarship has compellingly highlighted the unappreciated dynamic undercurrents of Christianity that uphold the dignity of humanity.

Christianity and the New Left, as epitomized in the corpus of Slavoj Žižek

Such has been the intellectual scene around the time that neo-Marxist scholarship began paying court to Christianity, in a nutshell. One way of appreciating Slavoj Žižek's particular contribution to the ensuing scholarship is by seeing him as responding rather vehemently to the anti-eschatological trumpets of liberals such as Richard Rorty. Among liberal theorists, Rorty has done an impressive job of warning readers to steer clear of every possible version of teleology, but particularly from the Christian and Marxist versions of it. In their stead he proposes the adoption of a pragmatist, fluid and typically constructivist view of the truth, as a matter of contingency, which is dialogically created and not discovered. This is his proposed model for ensuring the free revision of political institutions and social mores in accordance with new needs, against the unexamined flow of received wisdom. As Rorty relates,

> Failed prophesies often make invaluable inspirational reading. Consider two examples: the New Testament and the Communist Manifesto. Both were intended by their authors as predictions of what was going to happen – predictions based on superior knowledge of the forces which determine human history. Both sets of predictions have, so far, been ludicrous flops. Both claims to knowledge have become objects of ridicule . . . [still] the inspirational value of the New Testament and the Communist Manifesto is not diminished by the fact that many millions of people were enslaved, tortured or starved to death by sincere, morally earnest people who recited passages from one or the other text in order to justify their deeds. Memories of the dungeons of the Inquisition and the interrogation rooms of the KGB, of the ruthless greed and arrogance of the Christian clergy and of the Communist nomenklatura, should indeed make us reluctant to hand over power to people who claim to know what God, or History, wants.[42]

What is the bottom line of these ruminations? "To sum up," Rorty concludes,

> it is best, when reading both the Communist Manifesto and the New Testament, to ignore prophets who claim to be the authorized interpreters of one or the other text. When reading the texts themselves, we should skip lightly past the predictions, and concentrate on the expressions of hope.[43]

When Rorty published his indictment of eschatology, the time seemed ripe for its widespread endorsement among political philosophers with liberal proclivities as one of the most hard-earned lessons bequeathed to us from the twentieth century. Memories of the fall of communism were still fresh, and the Western world was still enjoying what is now known to have been the last vestiges of a prosperity that lent credence to the neo-liberal identification of the open society with the open market – eschatology was less and less tolerated as a historically debunked relic, irrevocably correlated with socio-political rigidity and paternalism, if not with outright oppression.

In the meantime, however, for reasons already stated, it became increasingly understood that the automatic reduction of all forms of eschatology to determinism was rather too simplistic and unfair, at least in the absolute manner pursued by ultra-liberal writers like Rorty, etc. It also became clear (and this is fundamental for getting to the gist of Žižek's flirtation with Christianity) that Rorty's pragmatist "hope" (i.e. his anti-eschatological vision of the open society) came with a dramatic attenuation of the robustness of the notion of Truth, a perspectivism that renders Christianity and Marxism totally helpless. For, their respective visions and promises of deliverance depend on a set of maximalist truth-claims, not on any sort of anemic pluralism celebrated for its own sake, as Rorty, Habermas and the liberal constructivists would prefer. This post-modern exaltation of tolerant but harmless pluralism is exactly what Žižek reacted against when he reaffirmed the worth of Marxist soteriology (now aided by psychoanalysis, particularly of the Lacanian sort) as a valuable critical tool for assailing the establishment.

Against the liberal notion of a politics which would have been but a series of "pragmatic, procedural interventions" and nothing more (in essence, "a politics without politics" as the art of mere expert administration enacted by technocrats),[44] Žižek categorically opts for "the politics of Truth."[45] This latter concept is, in turn, dismissed offhand by Liberalism as "totalitarian" because of its vulgar reductionism, i.e. its promise to furnish a full explanation of the world along the lines of Marxist economics. For, as already mentioned, the standard liberal/constructivist warning against total (metaphysically privileged) accounts of reality is that assigning an exclusivist, non-varying value or concept of the Good to politics, as Žižek wants to do in pursuit of a Leninist blueprint,[46] turns societies into monophonic, static and above all centrally organized bodies, fully controlled from the level of the economy down to the private lives of citizens. Yet, this is precisely what Žižek's strong sense of realism translates to, by his own admission: it is envisaged as

> a political project that would undermine the totality of the global liberal-capitalist world order and, furthermore, a project that would unabashedly assert itself as acting on behalf of truth, as intervening in the present global situation from the standpoint of its repressed truth.[47]

On closer examination, the "repressed truth," which Žižek is anxious to bring to the surface, concerns the *structured* social inequality nowadays harshly plaguing Western societies, much as it has afflicted the developing countries all along. He bluntly asserts that the current widening disparity between haves and have-nots (in the form of a rapid emaciation of the formerly stout Western middle class) is the natural outcome of a globalized capitalism serving an economic oligarchy – a body of plutocrats with a vested interest in concealing this very fact from the public eye, through a smokescreen of "rights" and "pluralism." In his eagerness to expose the scam of liberal rhetoric, Žižek is bent on reviving the religious fervor of Marxism's prophetic belief in the emancipatory direction of historical progression, counter to its trendy dismissal by such far-flung iconoclasts as Rorty and George Steiner:[48] what these saw pejoratively as a secularized version of Judeo-Christian messianism, Žižek unreservedly praises as a virtue, merrily acknowledging the eschatological common ground between Scripture and *The Communist Manifesto*. The following heartfelt passage is illustrative of Žižek's agenda:

> Against the old liberal slander which draws on the parallel between the Christian and Marxist "Messianic" notion of history as the process of the final deliverance of the faithful (the notorious "Communist-parties-are-secularized-religious-sects" theme), should one not emphasize how this holds only for ossified "dogmatic" Marxism, not for its authentic liberating kernel? Following Alain Badiou's path-breaking book on Saint Paul, our premise here is exactly the opposite one: instead of adopting such a defensive stance, allowing the enemy to define the terrain of the struggle, what one should do is to reverse the strategy by *fully endorsing what one is accused of*: yes, there is, a direct lineage from Christianity to Marxism; yes, Christianity and Marxism *should* fight on the same side of the barricade against the onslaught of new spiritualisms – the authentic Christian legacy is much too precious to be left to the fundamentalist freaks.[49]

Also, as opposed to Rorty's sternly dogmatic atheism, if such it may be called, which blinded him to the Christian Gospel's blurred but real contribution to the advancement of personal and social emancipation (however marred this contribution may have been by the flaws of institutional Christianity), Žižek attempts to resuscitate the messianic denominator common to both Christianity and Marxism – minus its twisted perversion in the hands of the Bolsheviks and fundamentalists of all sorts. Like French author Frédéric Lenoir, who more recently penned a poignant book unfolding the radical message of Christ,[50] Žižek managed to discern and decipher the liberating aspects of Christ's ministry and kerygma: not least among those, are the stern condemnation of the Pharisees' typolatry (love of the letter as opposed to substance) and hypocritical attachment to religious "externals," as well as Christ's injunction to His followers for a radical break from the established social, racial, ethnic and moral order favored by the status quo and the powers that be, as a prerequisite for becoming a Christian. As Žižek elegantly indicates,

> The very core of pagan Wisdom lies in its insight into this cosmic balance of hierarchically ordered Principles . . . Perhaps the most elaborated

case of such a cosmic order is the Ancient Hindu cosmology, applied first to the social order, in the guise of the caste system . . . Christianity [on the other hand] (and, in its own way, Buddhism) introduced into this global balanced cosmic Order a principle that is totally foreign to it, a principle which, measured by the standards of pagan cosmology, cannot but appear as a monstrous distortion . . . "If anyone come to me and does not hate his father and his mother, his wife and children, his brothers and sisters – yes, even his own life – he cannot be my disciple" (*Lk* 14:26). Here, of course, we are *not* dealing with a simple brutal hatred demanded by a cruel and jealous God: family relations stand here metaphorically for the entire socio-symbolical network, for any particularly ethnic "substance" that determines our place in the global Order of Things. The "hatred" enjoined by Christ is not, therefore, a kind of pseudo-dialectical opposite to love, but a direct expression of what Saint Paul, in Corinthians 1: 13, with unsurpassable power, describes as agape . . . it is love itself that enjoins us to "unplug" from the organic community into which we were born – or, as Paul puts it, for a Christian there are neither men nor women, neither Jews nor Greeks . . . We can see here how thoroughly heterogeneous is the Christian stance to that of pagan wisdom: Christianity asserts as the highest act precisely what pagan wisdom condemns as the source of Evil: the gesture of *separation*, of drawing the line, of clinging to an element that disturbs the balance of All . . . [Christianity] *is* the violent intrusion of Difference that precisely *throws the balanced circuit of the universe off the rails* . . . As every true Christian knows, love is the *work* of love – the hard and arduous work of repeated "uncoupling" in which, again and again, we have to disengage ourselves from the inertia that constraints us to identify with the particular order we were born into . . . it is this Christian heritage of "uncoupling" that is threatened by today's "fundamentalisms," especially when they proclaim themselves Christian. Does not Fascism ultimately involve the return to the pagan mores which, rejecting the love of one's enemy, cultivate full identification with one's own ethnic community?[51]

Here, Žižek presses home to us a valuable insight also elaborately raised by Orthodox theologian Thanassis Papathanassiou:

The dominant logic of the ancient world [i.e. one's inescapable rootedness in his or her land of birth] is thoroughly overturned by the God of the Old Testament. The relationship between Yahweh and Abraham does not come from a domestic or national, but from a *personal* agreement, which, thanks to the choice given to humans by God, liberates the human race from its enslavement to the local deities, customs and tradition. The LORD had said to Abraham, "Go from your country, your people and your father's household to the land I will show you" . . . The basic innovation introduced by Christianity was the belief that the individual can place the question of the truth against everything, even against the faith of his or her fathers. This means that human persons do not automatically receive the meaning of life alongside all the other features that come with birth (such as gender, family, homeland, culture, etc.), but need to puzzle themselves seriously in order to find it. They must themselves decide, that is, to whom they shall give their consent and heart. The whole process is strongly reminiscent of the jeopardy of leaving the safety and comfort of one's parental home.[52]

Papathanassiou juxtaposes the new freedom of selfhood instituted by Judeo-Christianity against pre-Christian, mostly pagan forms of identity-acquiring based on loyalty to one's tribe and land, wherein detachment from the inherited superego was as difficult as was the injunction to love foreigners, those falling outside one's native turf. For Žižek, likewise, all forms of paganism, ancient as well as modern (from ahistorical New Age "spirituality" down to the unsocial entrenchment in multicultural politics and the private pursuits dictated by the Markets), enslave followers to the tyranny of tightly sealed monologues that give the false impression of freedom of opinion, while actually entrapping them to the homogeneity of class, culture, nation and shared tastes. These modern fetters are harder to shake off, because they are idols in disguise and so pass largely unseen, all the while pretending to give adherents the illusion of choice.

The new cult of Oriental religions, in particular, functions in Žižek's assessment as a convenient ideological handmaid to the established world order: unbeknownst to their adherents, these spiritual fads lend support to unrestrained, relentless capitalism and the tyranny of the Markets, and only help solidify the malaise of political apathy. How so? By cultivating an exaggerated mode of inwardness, a self-absorbed subjectivity detached from broader social affairs, in a manner reminiscent of modern marketing techniques creating compulsive, self-preoccupied customers through an inflated promotion of artificial needs. Also (particularly in the case of Hinduism and Buddhism), by making the world appear as an illusion, or at best as something that can be toyed with, with no serious consequences.[53] As long as the concept of verity is relativized to myriad splintered, *self-contained* truths, while "grand narratives" critical of history are obsessively repudiated as hopelessly totalitarian, one's perception of reality runs the risk of losing sight of the "hard facts" that force us to tell right from wrong, discern injustice and protest it as such. From Žižek's perspective, the menacing prospect of social immutability is not thwarted by any naïve recourse to the fluid but powerless rhetoric of *non-representationalism*, *anti-foundationalism* and pragmatist or post-structural semantics, as Rorty thought. Social stagnation can only be countered, rather, through a traumatic yet eye-opening contact with the Real, as Lacan intended the term, which can be greatly aided by the alertness and critical tools drawn from a faith tradition capable of exposing the socio-political institutions (and their ideological superstructure) that solidify and perpetuate inequality and injustice.

Hence, a stronger, more radical idiom is required to point attention to real as opposed to fake forms of emancipation, and for Žižek Christianity is an irreplaceable ally in that direction. Ernst Bloch would concur: in his landmark work, *Atheism in Christianity*, he contends that from cover to cover, Scripture is a long, progressive narrative of human emancipation from an assortment of different forms of oppression: Abraham is asked by God to leave his home town (essentially, to escape the tyranny of stifling sameness) and open himself up to the freshness of an undetermined future, to what is alien and unknown while en route to a new dwelling place; the Jewish people's 40-year wandering in the desert signifies a sense of freedom not only from their bondage to Egypt but from the slavery and dependence to a single, given land; the Prophets react strongly against the pompous authority and spiritual oppression inflicted by the high priests; Job surpasses everyone else by going so far as to challenge the justice and moral superiority of God Himself! And in the New Testament, Christ drives the merchants away from his Father's temple in a fit of rage, and strongly condemns the shallow, legalist and inhuman piety of the Pharisees, only to end up being crucified by the political and religious establishment, which he finally overpowers with His Resurrection – a victory that entitles Christ to instill new hope to His disciples by telling them "Take courage, for I have conquered the world" (John 16:33).

As Peter Thompson aptly indicates in his introduction to Bloch's book, "what the Christian and the communist share in the end is a belief in something as yet impossible, unimaginable and unworkable. What they also share is the desire to reach the place where it will be imaginable."[54] And in Bloch's own words,

> over and against all this [humanly instituted suffering] stand sentiments no other religious book contains: suffering that will suffer no longer; buoyant expectation of Exodus and restoration transformation . . . Piety here, from first to last, belongs to the restless alone; and the particular brand of Utopian loyalty which keeps him restless is the only thing that is, in the long run, deep.[55]

Žižek, as already indicated, concurs. "Christianity and Marxism," as we noted above, "should fight on the same side of the barricade against the onslaught of new spiritualisms – the authentic Christian legacy is much too precious to be left to the fundamentalist freaks."[56] It is as part of this ambitious project that he vehemently seeks to undermine the "tired" liberal refrain insisting that "the era of big explanations is over," that "we need 'weak thought,' opposed to all foundationalism" and other similar tag-lines building up to the conclusion that "in politics too, we should no longer aim at all-explaining systems and global emancipatory projects . . . [as well as] grand solutions."[57] Against such a timid, small-scale "political nominalism" amounting to mere *doxa* (the "atonal world" of liberal and post-modern compromise with the establishment castigated by Badiou), Žižek counter-suggests the robustness of Marxist and Christian Truth, best arrived at through a "Leap of Faith"[58] – an intellectual feat reminiscent of Søren Kierkegaard's famous spiritual recommendation of the same name. Counter to the conceptual (and, by extension, the political) nihilism wrought by the triumph of fluid rhetoric and limitless "dissemination" versus the merest hint of solid meaning, Žižek wishes to resurrect the long discarded "Master Signifier," a grand narrative capable of "tonalizing" the world by giving it a center (better yet, a *spine*) once again.[59] Hence,

> this book [like Žižek's overall project] is unashamedly committed to the "Messianic" standpoint of the struggle for human emancipation. No wonder, then, that to the partisans of the "postmodern" *doxa* the list of lost Causes defended here must appear as a horror show of their worst nightmares embodied, a depository of the ghosts of the past they put all their energies into exorcising: Heidegger's politics as the extreme case of a philosopher seduced by totalitarian politics; revolutionary terror from Robespierre to Mao; Stalinism; the dictatorship of the proletariat . . . [Nevertheless] the true aim of the defense of lost causes is not to defend Stalinist terror, and so on, as such, but to render problematic the all-too-easy liberal-democratic alternative . . . The argument is thus that, while these phenomena were, each in its own way, a historical failure and monstrosity (Stalinism was a nightmare which caused perhaps even more human suffering than fascism; the attempts to enforce the "dictatorship of the proletariat" produced a ridiculous travesty of a regime in which precisely the proletariat was reduced to silence, and so on), *this is not the whole truth*: there was in each of them a redemptive moment which gets lost in the liberal-democratic rejection – and it is crucial to isolate this moment.[60]

As has become obvious from the foregoing analysis, Žižek to some degree aligns with the communitarian camp of the political debate we have sketched in opposing "liberal individualism"; not, however, on national or cultural lines, but in the name of economic egalitarianism and class solidarity.[61] How would liberal thought, in turn, assess Žižek's crusade? Doubtlessly, as something along the lines of a misguided pursuit akin to chasing windmills. The very title of one of his books, *In Defense of Lost Causes*[62] (emblematic as it is of his overall agenda), clearly shows that Žižek is well aware of the scorn that liberal theorists and post-structural advocates of philosophical minimalism have heaped upon "grand narratives" with radical aspirations. In his efforts to revive what has been dead and well lost according to liberals,

Žižek is much subtler than his critics often assume. Central to the liberal objections is that all we have in Western societies is a plurality of antagonisms in the forms of sexism, cultural intolerance, discrimination, religious fundamentalism, etc., but not class struggle as *the* fundamental antagonism, as Marxism, old and new, has assumed ("one of the standard topics of post-Marxism," he concedes, "is that, today, the working class is *no longer* the 'pre-destined' revolutionary subject, that contemporary emancipatory struggles are plural, with no particular agent who can claim to occupy a privileged place)."[63] In other words, the open society has several enemies but not a single overriding one, and anyone, like Žižek, who ignores this basic fact must resort to intellectual populism to give a semblance of credence to his/her "diagnosis." Žižek provocatively defies these charges by spitting them back to senders as "ultra-conservative," the opposite of what they are sold as. For, at the core of his vision, as already mentioned, lies the conviction that programmatic pluralism and its philosophical consort, a pragmatist or multicultural conception of Truth (resulting in a sort of "pure" politics, "decontaminated" from the economy),[64] strips us of the much-needed sense of idealism and purpose that we need in order to improve life conditions and envision a better world – one rescued from the uncritical perpetuation of existing economic/political institutions deceivingly pushed as "necessary" and "self-evident" as well as from the litany of the Market, long upheld as an omnipotent deity.

At a deeper level, Žižek retorts by acknowledging the pernicious, corroding effect of populism for politics just as anxiously as liberals and moderate theorists do, but begs to differ from these in the role that he assigns to it:

> Populism is [indeed] ultimately always sustained by ordinary people's frustrated exasperation, by a cry of "I don't know what's going on, I just know I've had enough of it! It can't go on! It must stop!" – an impatient outburst, a refusal to understand, exasperation at complexity, and the ensuing conviction that there must be somebody responsible for all the mess, which is why an agent who is behind the scenes and explains it all is required.[65]

"In other words," Žižek further explains,

> for a populist, the cause of trouble is ultimately *never the system as such*, but the intruder, who corrupted it (financial manipulation, not capitalists as such, etc.); not a fatal flaw inscribed into the structure as such, but an element that does not play its part within the structure properly.[66]

What Žižek is at pains to drive home to his readership here is that populism isn't instigated by radical revolutionaries like himself, who allegedly swell people's expectations by promising utopian, militant emancipation (as apologists of the global Order and the status quo routinely wail); it is created rather by the opposite camp as a means of diverting people's attention from the inherent injustices of the system itself, whose legitimacy is strengthened in the public's conscience by the construction of handy scapegoats such as Jews, immigrants, homosexuals, etc., all negatively pinpointed as subversive conspirators, deleterious to social harmony and justice:. Further,

> For a Marxist, on the contrary (as for a Freudian) the pathological (the deviant misbehaviour of some elements) is the symptom of the normal, an indicator of what is wrong in the very structure that is threatened with "pathological" outbursts: for Marx, economic crises are the key to understanding the "normal" functioning of capitalism; for Freud, pathological phenomena such as hysterical outbursts provide the key to the constitution (and hidden antagonisms that sustain the functioning) of a "normal" subject.[67]

In view of this cunningly crafted disorientation of the masses intended to cover up the true antagonism, the one between the people versus capitalism and not amongst themselves, Žižek insists that we train our minds to look with suspicion past the beguiling, reassuring superstructure erected by the Markets. His exhortation further stipulates it is worth retaining the benevolent determination of past revolutionaries like Robespierre, Mao and the Bolsheviks, despite the risks of falling into the same round of violence, for eventually we do learn from previous mistakes and are therefore bound to become wiser over the long run.

Historically, of course, the long record of human atrocities bears witness to the opposite of Žižek's optimism, if there's any value to Thucydides' timeless warning about the stability of human nature and its negative perennial attributes, incorrigibility and greed. Soberly speaking, it is doubtful whether people ever learn enough from history to the point of mending their ways. This rueful insight should not be invoked to foil protest against injustices of any sort, but it should give us some skeptical pause against incitements like Žižek's to take up arms and risk trading the just State (our Western legal civilization) for radical outbursts driven by unaccountable messianic zeal, which almost always results in endless terror. Anxious to get the ball rolling, Žižek rejects Karl Kautsky's defense of multi-party democracy, his conception of the victory of socialism as the parliamentary victory of the Social-Democratic Party and his warning that one should not risk the revolution too early, without a democratic legitimization from the majority of the population. Instead, Žižek sides with Leon Trotsky, who despite his opposition to Stalinism held that "the role of emancipatory forces is not to passively 'reflect' the opinion of the majority, but to instigate the working classes to mobilize their forces and thus to *create* a new majority."[68] But revolutionary violence aside, even non-liberal readers of Žižek's engrossing prose may take issue with his adamant correlation of real progress with economic equality alone, including many who are alert to the injustices incurred by the current fiscal crisis, like the present writer. To be sure, economic egalitarianism implies further forms of equality irreducible to money and property per se, such as equal standing before the law as well as the respectful treatment of the least members of society by the authorities. Nevertheless, by his own admission, Žižek, like Badiou, singles out economic inequality as the sole, premier problem facing the world today, to the detriment of other valuable and worthwhile human causes like personal fulfillment, diversity and otherness (counter to any pressure for homogeneity), innovation, individual and social development, freedom of conscience and speech, digression from established or received beliefs and a host of other essential human rights, which must be sidestepped, ignored, crushed or at best given a backseat to Žižek's chief drive: the attainment of a classless society, the only one capable of setting life on the right course, once and for all.

Assuming the feasibility of such a tall order in a momentary suspension of disbelief, we should still question its desirability; because yielding to a centralized, top-down financial management of human affairs (in essence, to the command of self-appointed sages who seek to improve the world *once and for all*) is tantamount to having one's life managed down to the slightest detail – this and worse are in store for the hapless individuals who surrender their freedoms on the promise of imposed happiness from "above," supposedly enforced "for their own good." This point is persistently missed by most leftists and hard-line communitarians,[69] inattentive to Karl Popper's wise indication, that

> the attempt to make heaven on earth invariably produces hell. It leads to intolerance. It leads to religious wars, and to the saving of souls through the Inquisition. And it is, I believe, based on a complete misunderstanding of our moral duties. It is our duty to help those who need our help; but it cannot be our duty to make others happy, since . . . it would only too often mean intruding on the privacy of those towards whom we have such amiable intentions.[70]

Be that as it may, it can hardly be disputed that Christianity, while irreducible to social welfare programs, still cares deeply about social and political injustices and therefore ought to protest inequities of all stripes unfailingly. "Blessed are those who hunger and thirst for righteousness, for they shall be satisfied" (Matthew 5:6). Christianity, for all its sins and errors, has in fact produced powerful manifestos promoting justice, racial equality and liberation from oppression of all sorts. One would only need bring to mind the corpuses of Jürgen Moltmann and Dietrich Bonhoeffer (to cite but two cases), both of which broaden the horizons of Christian theology beyond conventional thought and have vigorously denounced social, economic, and political forms of oppression in the loudest terms. Serious theologians, throughout the twentieth century, have in fact explicitly called for the structural change of political institutions that inflict and prolong suffering and injustice; their protest can be echoed in the words of Dominican priest and scholar Edward Schillebeeckx, who proclaimed that "human freedom . . . is physically directed outwards and can only become fully conscious of itself when it encounters free people within structures that make freedom possible,"[71] to which he added that "the Christian may be committed to the task of bringing salvation to the whole of society in the form of better and more just structures for all men,"[72] and that the Church, as a whole, "must never forget that, in imitation of Jesus, it is seeking freedom not so much for itself as for others."[73] Roman Catholic Liberation theology is probably the most outspoken instance of modern Christian protest, an awakening force shedding light on on-going forms of suffering, structured and perpetuated by powerful economic interests, regimes and institutions. It is no exaggeration to say that

> no study of political theology today can ignore liberation theology, which promises the liberation – spiritual as well as social/political/cultural – of all humans and peoples. This theological trend appeared in an early form in Latin America among progressive Catholics as early as the 1950s and achieved definitive form in 1971 with the publication of the book by the Peruvian Dominican Gustavo Gutiérrez: *Teología de la liberación*, which was followed by the publication in 1976 of Leonardo Boff's work *Teologia do Cativeiro e da Libertação*. If the urgent need to struggle against poverty and exploitation was the first and foremost fundamental impetus behind the emergence of this trend, its theological tenets were no less important. These tenets can be summarized as the position that political action and revolutionary activity against the unjust structures and mechanisms of the capitalistic system – which, in certain cases, such as in the case of the Columbian priest Camilo Torres, who was an associate of Che Guevara, can include armed violence – are not only an extension and update of the long Christian tradition of solidarity with the poor. They actually spring from the very core of the Christian faith and its Gospel, which denounces and combats every form of injustice and exploitation, and every form of alienation, subjugation and institutionalized sin. Because sin, as Gustavo Gutiérrez reminds us, is not only, or even primarily, an individual affair, but is evident in oppressive structures, in the exploitation of humans by humans, in the domination and slavery of peoples, races and social classes. [It appears as] the fundamental alienation, the root of injustice and exploitation . . . Sin demands a radical liberation, which in turn necessarily implies a political liberation . . . The radical liberation is the gift which Christ offers us.[74]

These are strong, bold words, challenging not only received authority but also the presumptuous contempt with which the Christian faith is treated by the atheist quarter of autonomy seekers, who see it merely as a bastion of passive heteronomy and alienation, a reactionary legitimizer of the status quo.[75] Bearing this in mind, Žižek (like Terry Eagleton[76] and David McLellan,[77] both Roman Catholics) rightly sees Christianity as a potent ally to systematic efforts aiming at a global emancipation from the prevailing hegemony of Capital and its ideological mechanisms.

But how exactly does Žižek understand Christianity in the first place? The question is crucial, because this faith comes in a remarkable assortment of forms and shapes. So which one of these does the Slovenian philosopher find most helpful to his emancipating agenda? If we take *The Puppet and the Dwarf* to be his most complete statement on the subject, his is a social version of the Christian Gospel, devoid of institutional and sacramental elements. The real essence of Christianity, according to Žižek, lies in its liberating message, while the Sacramental, dogmatic, liturgical and soteriological dimensions belong to the redundant and expendable shell, precisely to what must be overridden in order for the subversive Gospel narrative to emerge and shine. *Mutatis mutandis*, this verdict is not far from the supposed core of Christianity pinpointed by one of the leaders of Protestant "liberal theology," Adolf Harnack,[78] a century or so prior to Žižek: here as well, the essence of Christianity concerns history and not metaphysics, the latter (an unfortunate side effect from the Gospel's encounter with Greek philosophy) serving solely as the pretext for the emergence and maintenance of a privileged priesthood that Christ himself took pains to undermine, amidst His overall agenda of reversing religious, political and social hierarchies along with their oppressive power structures. Badiou certainly concurs, having explicitly remarked that "so far as we are concerned it is rigorously impossible to believe in the resurrection of the crucified."[79]

This reductive construal of Christianity as a fleshless ideology and a mere message of good intentions is rapidly gaining momentum among secular intellectuals troubled by the rising phenomenon of religious fanaticism and intolerance, which is habitually attributed to the exclusivist, non-negotiable nature of doctrines; hence a "spiritualized," doctrinally free version of Christianity as a declaration of universal love and brotherhood conducive to dialogue and peaceful coexistence, as Nikos Mouzelis among others advocates,[80] with just enough criticism of the new World Order, is far preferable to the arcane, primitive faith mired by otherworldly and supernatural promises. As already mentioned, however, Žižek (unlike Mouzelis) is at the opposite end of interpretation from pacifist portrayals of Christ, preferring rather the Lord who "has come not to bring peace, but a sword" (Matthew 10:34). In that sense, Žižek is more loyal to Christ's declaration, "I am the way, and the truth, and the life. No one comes to the Father except through me" (John 14:6). In the meantime, mainstream Christians (Orthodox, Catholics, etc.) who (ideally) find the truth about Christ's personhood just as liberating as His earthly ministry and preaching, thereby also investing in truth, still prefer to abstain from violence in adherence to Luke 9:55, where Christ sharply rebukes zealots that are too eager to correct the world through bloodshed: "You do not know what kind of spirit you are of." Far from forfeiting protest against injustice or being a compromise with bourgeois complacency (a "see no evil, hear no evil" attitude of reactionary submission to the status quo), this Christian reluctance to pick up arms and force the Kingdom of Heaven on earth actually comports with the Biblical notion of spiritual authority, whose only form of violence occurs within the soul against one's own vices.

Here, Martin Luther seems to the present writer a wiser (and surprisingly modern) guide than Žižek in matters of civil disobedience and protest, as is indicated by his clash with the zealotism displayed by the more radical quarters of the Reformation, and in particular as regards his skirmish with Thomas Müntzer.[81] Müntzer's messianic mission, as he saw it, consisted in instigating the revolution of peasants for the overthrow of the oppressive landlord rule. In Müntzer's mind, the revolt exceeded political parameters, affixed as it was to a broader picture aiming at the historical establishment of God's kingdom on earth, even by force if necessary. So determined was Müntzer to see his dream materialize that he would not even scruple at murder, and that in the name of the Gospel. In his famous "Princes' Sermon," a classic text for all apocalyptic magisterial Reformers, Müntzer preached the following:

> Do not, therefore, allow the evil-doers, who turn us away from God, to continue living, [Deut. 13] for a godless man has no right to live if he is hindering the pious . . . I suspect, though, that our scholars will reprove me at this point by referring to the clemency of Christ, which they drag in to cover their hypocrisy . . . But if they [meaning "spineless" scholars like Luther] do not carry it out the sword will be taken from them . . . For the godless have no right to live, unless by the sufferance of the elect.[82]

What was Luther's reaction to statements like Müntzer's? Convinced as he was that Müntzer's preaching would ultimately beget violence, Luther hastened to counter it with his July 1524 *Letter to the Princes of Saxony Concerning the Rebellious Spirit*. There, by appealing to Romans 13:4, Luther draws a bold and surprisingly modern, for his day, divide between secular and religious authorities, setting up proper limits to both. Overall, the Lutheran text clearly demonstrates the courageous intellectual maturity demanded of critical looks at one's own faith, against the current of self-appointed propagandists too deeply absorbed in their beliefs to discern faith's excesses or the broader social good apart from sectarian (cultural or religious) interests:

> Let them [Müntzer and the radical Reformers] preach as confidently and boldly as they are able and against whomever they wish . . . But when they want to do more than fight with the Word, and begin to

> destroy and use force, then your Graces must intervene, whether it be ourselves or they who are guilty, and banish them from the country. You can say, "We are willing to endure and permit you to fight with the Word, in order that true doctrine may prevail." But don't use your fist, for that is our business, else get yourselves out of the country. For we who are engaged in the ministry of the Word are not allowed to use force.[83]

Even as a pre-modern thinker, Luther vehemently resisted the subordination of the State to Church authority,[84] privy as he was to the fact that an unholy alliance of that sort twists the nature of both partners: for, as history amply shows, even in mildly theocratic regimes, the State frequently uses religion to lull citizens into submission, while the Churches progressively compromise the Gospel in exchange for state benefits and, worse than that, are subject to institutional corrosion. The popularity of both theocratic regimes and militant action in the name of Christ among well-meaning but naïve believers feeds on the confusion of spiritual and state authorities and must be resisted in the name of the Gospel. With this in mind, the Reformer sketches a realistic scenario of the nightmarish results to be expected from the sanguine ignorance of those pushing for the creation of "Christian regimes," an oxymoron not altogether unappealing in our more "enlightened" days, as well:

> If anyone attempted to rule the world by the gospel and to abolish all temporal law and sword on the plea that all are baptized and Christian . . . what would he be doing? He would be loosing the ropes and chains of the savage wild beasts and letting them bite and mangle everyone, meanwhile insisting that they were harmless, tame and gentle creatures . . . Just so would the wicked under the name of Christianity abuse evangelical freedom, carry on their rascality, and insist that they were Christians subject neither to law nor sword, as some are already raving and ranting.[85]

Conclusion

Slavoj Žižek is a fascinating polymath who has breathed valuable fresh air into Continental philosophy and has likewise done much to highlight the subtle emancipatory relevance of the Christian faith for every age, ours especially. His revolutionary gospel comes with a caveat: only the truth emancipates, but it is suppressed by the hegemony of the ideological superstructure concocted by society's base, i.e. the sum total of its productive relationships. Thus, in the interests of deliverance from bondage, we simply cannot afford to forfeit the binary divide of truth versus deception, notwithstanding the lure of iconoclastic theories promulgating various forms of all-encompassing, kaleidoscopic contextualism (e.g. fluid Rortyan pragmatism or deconstructionist repudiations of "transcendental signifieds"). For despite their own

Pacifist pluralism versus militant truth 141

liberating intentions, these destabilizing projects nihilate meaning and sever all ties with extra-linguistic reality. Žižek's stipulation is a valid one, strongly sanctioned by Christ Himself ("You will know the truth, and the truth will set you free," John 8:32) and echoed by more rigorous neo-pragmatists than Rorty, such as Robert Cummings Neville. Against the still somewhat trendy post-modern dictum that "truth" (especially of the grander sort) is a hopeless and totalitarian illusion, which had better surrender to interpretation, Neville dedicated an entire monograph to defend the exact opposite:

> The outcome of the imperial triumph of interpretation is that reality cannot measure our claims to truth. The only measure seems to consist in what survives future interpretation . . . reality [according to this line of thought, chiefly championed by Rorty] can be dismissed as the stuff mind was falsely thought to mirror, and culture's quest for truth is simply an on-going conversation, hopefully edifying. *Of course* culture's quest for truth is a conversation, or many conversations. But is not their worth measured by the reality of their topic? And in a deeper sense, does not reality measure the appropriateness of the topics? These are not quite rhetorical questions, since Rorty might be right about the implications of truth seeking an interpretation. If he is, however, the consequences are sad indeed. The cultural conversation, measured by its own future assessments, is only a language game of elite Western culture, with no worth except that found in its own enjoyment.[86]

Žižek would certainly concur with the above pronouncement, that truth is by no means a disposable notion, interpretation and all. Be that as it may, we would be remiss if we failed to indicate that his understanding of truth is deeply ideological, not one grounded in nature, science or anything similarly objective and falsifiable; subscribing as it does to the Marxist–Leninist worldview, his truth requires a leap of faith for its espousal, just as its Christian counterpart does – with the exception that Christianity situates itself unashamedly in the realm of metaphysics and does not share the reductionisms of classical Marxism, such as historical determinism or its exhaustive, absolutized materialism.[87] Acknowledging this does not in the least undermine the perceptive insights of Žižek's critique of the current state of global economy and its unchallenged hegemony; nor does it deny the thoughtful, heartfelt bridges he has been toiling to build with politically alert Christians. Žižek deserves further applause, too, for designating the ontological character of the Christian notion of truth, whose *externality*[88] sets it apart from the socially harmless quietism of inner piety – in contrast to both Gnostic esotericism and Buddhism's negative view of physical reality and the self as illusions. In our post-Soviet world, however, critical readers would demand more caution and more attention to falsifiability and past error from any fresh effort to reinstate Marxism or any strong leftist variant in the public consciousness.

Critics of his ideas may, moreover, suggest that emancipation is a richer, multidimensional concept encompassing a wider array of meanings than mere economic equality, however important the latter may be for human well-being; civil liberty means several things at once, such as the freedoms of self-determination, of conscience, thought and expression, of sexual identity as well as freedom from persecution of any sort. Without totally disregarding them, Žižek appears to be oblivious to these forms of freedom, often dismissing them as parasitic spin-offs of conservative neo-liberal "pluralism" that distract well-meaning but naïve people from the real enemy, i.e. the capitalist new World Order. At worst, he seems willing to sacrifice these "lesser" freedoms until people are freed from the grand oppression of capitalism. In that regard, Žižek's communitarian ethos, while far more open-minded and inclusive than traditionalist collectivisms based on national/racial bonds, still falls short of the breadth and inclusiveness of the open society with its ceaselessly expanding and self-correcting propensity. History shows that while poverty, wide income disparity and economic exploitation are real problems in developed countries that must be dealt with, the cost of centralized, collectivist regimes is nevertheless too high a price to pay if the aforementioned freedoms must be suppressed, as indeed they have been in the cruelest manner in Soviet regimes where the State designed not just the economy but people's very lives. Thatcher-type individualism is not the ideal counter-model to collectivism, but it is worth keeping in mind that democratic institutions are, at the end of the day, the only available and largely effective recourse for the least of us.

If these critical remarks hold any water, Žižek may be a more conservative thinker than he may realize or even care to admit. Be that as it may, theologically speaking, what is valuable in his thesis must be acknowledged: Christians ought to be vigilant and vocal about socio-political injustices of all sorts and it is a sorry historical fact that they have often flagrantly refrained from exercising this duty. Leftist appropriators of the Gospel, on the other hand, ought as well to be mindful of the intrinsic incongruence between Judeo-Christian eschatology and historical determinism, Marxist or other; just as they must realize that while attempts to improve society and the world are part and parcel of Christian ethics, the Kingdom of Heaven cannot be forcefully established on earth – not without creating hell.

Notes

1 See Richard Rorty, "Failed Prophecies, Glorious Hopes," in *Philosophy and Social Hope* (London: Penguin Books, 1999).
2 Philosophers of a nominalist bent have also striven to push, one way or another, for a move away from *robust* (i.e. grand ontological) theories of truth, simply because they find such theories untenably dogmatic and, in the last analysis, superfluous or pointless. These are known as *deflationist* philosophers (with Richard Rorty, Donald Davidson, Paul Horwich and Hartry Field among the most pre-eminent representatives of this trend), maintaining a minimalist conception of the

truth reminiscent of Occam's razor, by denying that there is an issue of the nature of truth in general. In other words, deflationists deny that "there is, in fact, any real project of discovering what truth is," that there is anything to say about the truth in general, other than uttering simple empirical statements of fact. See the "Introduction," in *Truth*, ed. Simon Blackburn and Keith Simmons (Oxford: Oxford University Press, 1999), 2. More elaborately put, "deflationism" is the view that "truth is not a 'real' property or a 'robust' or metaphysically interesting property, or even that 'is true' is not a predicate at all. At their most flamboyant, deflationists have maintained that the concept of truth is 'redundant', or that talk in terms of truth is purely 'formal', so that the forms of words in which we say that something is true merely represent 'devices' with various logical purposes. The details of how to formulate a general deflationism matter . . . [b]ut all such views agree that a general enquiry into the nature of truth as an abstract property is wrongheaded" (ibid., 3. In his contribution to this volume, "Deflationist Views of Meaning and Content," Hartry Field calls the perspective opposite to deflationism *inflationism*: *Truth*, 355). Hard-line nominalists that they are, deflationists scoff at attempts such as those of traditional metaphysics and religion to arrive at an outside view – God's-eye view – of the world and/or entities supposedly getting between words and the world. For a critique of deflationism, see Anil Gupta, "A Critique of Deflationism," in *Truth*, ed. Simon Blackburn and Keith Simmons (Oxford: Oxford University Press, 1999), 282–307. Most interestingly, Thomas Nagel has critiqued the neo-nominalist perspectives that have spawned deflationism as amounting to a new kind of idealism, by conflating what is known with how it is known, i.e. with its human conditions of knowing. See Thomas Nagel, *The View from Nowhere* (Oxford: Oxford University Press, 1989). Personally, I share Nagel's criticism as well as the one offered by Michele Marsonet in "Linguistic Idealism in Analytic Philosophy of the Twentieth Century," in *Current Issues in Idealism*, ed. Paul Coates and Daniel D. Hutto (Bristol, England: Thoemmes Press, 1996), 83–118.

3 It should be pointed out that liberals are pluralists but not necessarily *relativists*. For example, John Rawls' Political Liberalism stands altogether outside the entire problematic of the nature of truth, in contrast to "metaphysical liberals" such as Richard Rorty and Cornelius Castoriadis, or left-wing theorists like Chantal Mouffe, who make relativism and atheism a prerequisite for the exercise of democratic politics (notwithstanding Rorty's vehement denial that he is a relativist in any sense of the term). As Rawls says, "my aim is only to stress that the ideal of public reason does not often lead to general agreement of views, nor should it. Citizens learn and profit from conflict and argument, and when their arguments follow public reason, they instruct and deepen society's public culture." See John Rawls, *Political Liberalism, With a New Introduction and a Reply to Habermas* (New York: Columbia University Press, 1996), lvii. True to this programmatic statement, Rawls persistently proclaimed his intention to leave religious doctrines intact, i.e., not to subject them to any intellectual or philosophical criticism whatsoever: "Central to the idea of public reason is that it neither criticizes nor attacks any comprehensive doctrine, religious or non-religious, except insofar as that doctrine is incompatible with the essentials of public reason and a democratic polity." See John Rawls, "The Idea of Public Reason Revisited," *The University of Chicago Law Review* 64, no. 3 (Summer 1997): 766.

4 Here I would like to express my heartfelt gratitude to Prof. Stelios Virvidakis for much that is related in this section of my paper regarding liberal political constructivism. See his excellent Afterword to Golfo Maggini's *Ο Χάμπερμας και οι Νεοαριστοτελικοί: Η Ηθική του Διαλόγου στον Γιούργκεν Χάμπερμας και η Πρόκληση του Νεοαριστοτελισμού* (Athens: Patakis, 2006), 343–74.

5 Pavlos Sourlas, "Philosophy and Democracy: The fear of Platonism in Rawls and Habermas," *Isopoliteia* 4 (2000): 29–97.

6 As shown in the emblematic title of Jürgen Habermas, *Das Nachmetaphysiches Denken. Philosophische Aufsätze* (Frankfurt am Main: Suhrkamp, 1988). For an excellent rejoinder to Habermas' constructivism, resisting the latter's attempt to strip ethics of all ontological foundations, see Hilary Putnam, "Values and Norms," in *The Collapse of the Fact-Value Distinction and Other Essays* (Cambridge, MA: Harvard University Press, 2002), 11–134; also, Putnam, *Ethics without Ontology* (Cambridge, MA: Harvard University Press, 2004). Putnam, it should be noted, recommends moderation in ethical matters, much as previous works of his bespoke of a similar moderation in epistemology, e.g. his *Realism with a Human Face* (Cambridge, MA: Harvard University Press, 1990).
7 T.M. Scanlon, "Metaphysics and Morals," *Proceedings and Addresses of the American Philosophical Association* 77 (2003): 10.
8 Kondylis' brilliance consists in disclosing the deep metaphysical undercurrents of Enlightenment rationalism. In a famous retort to critics challenging his ontological dismissal of values (fiercer than Nietzsche's in its consistent disapproval of flagrantly self-serving alternatives to humanistic or Christian values, like the notorious "overman," as intolerably didactic), Kondylis puts all kinds of ideals to the test of a radical empiricism intended to show their vacuity: "When we claim that humankind and the world at large are devoid of intrinsic meaning, we mean that whatever meaning these are perceived at times to possess is always an *ascribed* meaning. Also, that there is no other known agency capable of producing and attributing meaning than individual human beings: for it was certainly humans, not stones or fish, that proclaimed their like to be made in the image and likeness of God; similarly, none other than human beings, as opposed to trees or birds, were responsible for the Declaration of Man's Rights . . . And I shall hold firmly to this view until the day it is empirically proven to me that someone or something other than humans grants meaning and value to things, as surely testable as the length and weight of an object." Panagiotis Kondylis, *Μελαγχολία και πολεμική: δοκίμια και μελετήματα/Melancholy and Polemics: Essays and Studies* (Athens: Themelio, 2002), 142, 155.
9 I should explain that by calling it "radical" I am only stressing the unmitigated *physicalism* of their empiricism, not to be confused with David Hume's counterpart, which may be called radical in the different sense of denying necessary connections in experience.
10 Cornelius Castoriadis, *L' Institution imaginaire de la societe* (Paris: Seuil, 1975), in Greek *Η φαντασιακή θέσμιση της κοινωνίας*, Athens, Ράππας, 1981, 2002. For Castoriadis' superb analyses of the Aristotelian and Kantian uses of the imagination, see *Domaines de l' homme* (1986), in Greek *Χώροι του ανθρώπου*, Athens, Ύψιλον, 1995, 233–74.
11 Richard Rorty, "The Contingency of Community," in *Contingency, Irony, and Solidarity* (Cambridge: Cambridge University Press, 1998), 45.
12 Cornelius Castoriadis, *Ανθρωπολογία, πολιτική, φιλοσοφία/ Anthropology, Politics, Philosophy* (Athens: Ypsilon, 2001), 76–7. Cf. also *Τα σταυροδρόμια του λαβύρινθου/Crossroads of the Labyrinth* (Athens: Ypsilon, 1991), 330–1.
13 Cornelius Castoriadis, *Η αρχαία ελληνική δημοκρατία και η σημασία της για μας σήμερα/Ancient Greek Democracy and Its Contemporary Significance* (Athens: Ypsilon, 1999), 25. Cf. his *Ο πολιτικός του Πλάτωνα: επτά σεμινάρια στην Ehess/ Plato's Politicus: Seven Seminars at Ehess* (Athens: Polis Publications, 2001).
14 Castoriadis, *Crossroads of the Labyrinth*, 329–33.
15 Castoriadis, *Ancient Greek Democracy and Its Contemporary Significance*, 22.
16 Terry Eagleton, *The Illusions of Postmodernism* (Oxford: Blackwell, 1997), 9.
17 William Desmond, *Ethics and the Between* (New York: State University of New York Press, 2001), 139–42.

Pacifist pluralism versus militant truth 145

18 Charles Taylor, *Hegel and Modern Society* (Cambridge: Cambridge University Press, 1979), 159, 167.
19 Charles Taylor, *The Malaise of Modernity* (Ontario, Canada: Anansi, 1991), 60–1, 66.
20 Charles Taylor, *Sources of the Self: The Making of the Modern Identity* (Cambridge, MA: Harvard University Press, 1996), 88.
21 Ibid., 88–9.
22 Alasdair MacIntyre, *Dependent Rational Animals: Why Human Beings Need the Virtues* (London: Duckworth, 1999). See especially his magnum opus, *After Virtue* (Notre Dame, IN: Notre Dame University Press, Third Edition, 2007). MacIntyre stands as a watershed in contemporary moral theory, and his work is considered to be of the same caliber as the philosophical output of Rawls and Habermas, i.e. sufficiently thought-provoking and original as to generate a new venue for ethics and moral reflection. But unlike these thinkers, he has sought to revive the long disdained philosophical strand of "virtue ethics," which lost ground to the "procedural" kind of moral discourse that has mainly dominated the field until this day. In that sense, MacIntyre has been a contrarian to the modern spirit of moral iconoclasm, which (by his own account) began as early as the Renaissance, when its philosophy broke free from the teleology of Aristotelian physics, only to gradually extend the rejection of that particular aspect of Aristotelianism to the realm of ethics as well – this, as already mentioned, in reaction to the medieval religious worldview, known for its perhaps intemperate and problematic (by many accounts) assimilation of Aristotelian metaphysics in Christian theology. Consequently, as MacIntyre would have it, the denunciation of teleological ethics, particularly in its religious apparel, was picked up and further worked out by the Enlightenment, and was to be given its final, decisive blow in the fuming prose of Nietzsche. As the key reason for the inevitable failure of the Enlightenment to make good on its promise to deliver emancipation, MacIntyre pinpoints the twin categories of *subjectivism* and *emotivism* that he believes replaced the underlying teleological bedrock of pre-modern morality, what Aristotle called judging and acting κατὰ τὸν ὀρθὸν λόγον, i.e., "according to the right reason" (*After Virtue*, 152–4. Aristotle's line is from *Nichomachean Ethics*, 1138b25.). In MacIntyre's assessment, this replacement could only have led, disastrously enough, to the advancement of a gross individualism, of the kind that Nietzsche would eventually hail in his startlingly frank celebration of the "will to power": this is the inevitable outcome of post-Platonic, post-Aristotelian and post-Christian ethics, according to MacIntyre (in upholding this view, incidentally, MacIntyre is the exact antithesis of popular moralist Ayn Rand, who glorified Nietzsche and vilified Plato in her promotion of what appears to the present writer as an overblown individualistic ethos that lent support to aggressive capitalism).

Richard Rorty's critical dismissal of MacIntyre's diagnosis concerning the (supposed) failure of the Enlightenment's project to emancipate is interesting in its own right, whether one agrees with Rorty's neo-pragmatist assault on it or not: "MacIntyre construes 'emotivism' as the only option left, once one abandons the Aristotelian ideas of man, because he retains a pre-Freudian [or, more generally, premechanist (and thus pre-Humean)] division of human faculties. In terms of this division, 'desire' or 'will' or 'passion' represents the only alternative to 'reason' (construed as a faculty of seeing things in themselves). But dividing people up this way begs the question against other ways of describing them – for example, Freud's way . . . if we take Freud to heart, we shall not have to choose between an Aristotelian 'functional' concept of humanity, one that will provide moral guidance, and Sartrean 'dreadful freedom.' For the Sartrean conception of the self as pure freedom will be seen as merely the last gasp of the Aristotelian tradition – a

146 Haralambos Ventis

self-erasing expression of the Cartesian determination to find something nonmechanical at the center of the machine, if only a 'hole in being.'" Richard Rorty, "Freud and Moral reflection," in *Essays on Heidegger and Others: Philosophical Papers Volume Two* (Cambridge: Cambridge University Press, 1991), 160.
23 Martha Nussbaum, "Non-Relative Virtues: An Aristotelian Approach," in *The Quality of Life*, ed. Martha Nussbaum and Amartya Sen (Oxford: Oxford University Press, 1993).
24 Charles Larmore, *The Morals of Modernity* (New York: Columbia University Press, 1996). See also Charles Larmore and Alain Renaut, *Débat sur l' éthique: Idéalisme ou realism*, in Greek, Περί Ηθικής, Λόγος και Αντίλογος: Ιδεαλισμός ή Ρεαλισμός (Athens: Polis Publications, 2006).
25 Before delving any deeper into the communitarian critique of the modern, liberal glorification of individualism (allegedly) ushered in and solidified by Kant, it might be wise to add a corrective, unbiased account of the way that Kant himself had envisioned autonomy, which was less crude and, in fact, more communally minded and responsible than usually presented by critics. As Robert B. Pippin indicates, "Kant's position . . . involves a rejection of such a classical ideal [of an ordered, hierarchical cosmos or Divine Order] and an assertion of an individualist model of freedom. But Kant claimed that I, as an individual agent, could only truly be said to be 'directing' my action, to be determining for myself what I should do, when I did not act primarily on the basis of any sensible motive, or desire for happiness, or contingent interest. This was 'heteronomy,' not autonomy. In a reformulation of Rousseau's romantic notion, Kant claimed that I could only be free as a practically rational agent, something that now meant much more than power or efficiency in achieving ends, as in the empiricist model of agency. Such views, for Kant, accepted the ends of action as given, *as not themselves self-legislated*, and so accepted a kind of unfreedom." Robert B. Pippin, *Modernism as a Philosophical Problem: On the Dissatisfactions of European High Culture* (Oxford & Cambridge, MA: Basil Blackwell, 1991), 63 (my italics).

Even Taylor, the premier communitarian theorist, concurs against a crude interpretation of Kantian autonomy as unduly individualistic and selfish: "Kant's theory in fact rehabilitates one crucial distinction, that between actions done from duty and those done from inclination. This is grounded on a distinction of motives: the desire from happiness versus respect for the moral law. Kant deliberately takes this stance in opposition to utilitarian thought, the '*Glückseligkeitslehre*' of which he speaks in scathing terms." Still, Taylor warns that "nevertheless Kant shares the modern stress on freedom as self-determination," as he (i.e. Kant) "insists on seeing the moral law as one which emanates from our will," a strong bone of contention for communitarian/neo-Aristotelian thinkers (Taylor, *Sources of the Self*, 83).
26 Larmore and Renaut, *Débat sur l' éthique*, 42.
27 Ibid., 44.
28 Ibid., 64.
29 As Robert Pippin correctly remarks, "Postmodernism would then be understood as the 'death of man' or of such humanism and its faith in human power and transcendence, as well as of God; the end of all attempts to discover ultimate 'origins,' or a certain method, or to revolutionize human consciousness"; Pippin, *Modernism as a Philosophical Problem*, 2.
30 "If those arrangements were to disappear as they appeared, if some event of which we can at the moment do no more than sense the possibility – without knowing either what its form will be or what it promises – were to cause them to crumble, as the ground of Classical thought did, at the end of the eighteenth century, then one can certainly wager that *man would be erased, like a face drawn*

in sand at the edge of the sea" (our emphasis); Michel Foucault, *The Order of Things: An Archaeology of the Human Sciences* (New York: Random House & Vintage Books, 1994), 386.
31 Paul Ricoeur, *Oneself as Another*, trans. Kathleen Blamey (Chicago, IL: University of Chicago Press, 1994), 43.
32 Ibid., 44.
33 Ibid., 3.
34 Ibid., 194.
35 Ibid., 169.
36 Ibid., 176, 181 (all italics, except for the word "mediating" at the last sentence, are mine). At bottom, Ricoeur is asking whether a so-called "freestanding" conception of justice conceived along liberal lines, i.e. as independent from a communal tradition, is possible: "*does a purely procedural conception of justice succeed in breaking all ties to a sense of justice that precedes it and accompanies it all along?*" His answer is clearly negative: "My thesis is that this conception provides at best the formalization of a sense of justice that it never ceases to presuppose." See Ricoeur, *Oneself as Another*, 230.
37 Michael Sandel, *What Money Can't Buy: The Moral Limits of Markets* (New York: Farrar, Straus, & Giroux, 2012).
38 Michael Ignatieff, "The Price of Everything," *New Republic*, June 7, 2012.
39 Jacques Le Goff, *The Birth of Europe*, trans. Janet Lloyd (Oxford: Blackwell Publishers, 2005).
40 Marcel Gauchet, *The Disenchantment of the World*, trans. Oscar Burge, introduction by Charles Taylor (Princeton, NJ: Princeton University Press, 1997); originally published in French as *Le Désenchantement du monde. Une histoire politique de la religion* (Paris: Gallimard, 1985).
41 Jürgen Moltmann, *The Experimental Hope*, ed. and trans. with a Forward by M. Douglas Meeks (London: SCM Press, 1975), 112ff.
42 Rorty, *Philosophy and Social Hope*, 203–4.
43 Ibid., 205.
44 Slavoj Žižek, *How to Read Lacan* (London: Granta Books, 2006), 38. Interestingly, in this book Žižek is trying to defend the worth of psychoanalysis through Lacan, as he has elsewhere tried to the same for Marxism, through Lenin.
45 Slavoj Žižek, *On Belief: Thinking in Action* (London & New York: Routledge, 2002), 2.
46 Ibid., 2–4.
47 Ibid., 4–5.
48 See especially George Steiner's short monograph *Nostalgia for the Absolute*, CBC Massey Lecture 1974 (Canada: House of Anansi, 1997).
49 Slavoj Žižek, *The Fragile Absolute: Or, Why Is the Christian Legacy Worth Fighting For?* (London & New York: Verso Books, 2000), 2 (italics are his).
50 Frédéric Lenoir, *Le Christ philosophe* (Plon, 2007), in Greek, *Ο Χριστός Φιλόσοφος* (Athens: Polis Publications, 2010).
51 Žižek, *The Fragile Absolute*, 120–1, 128–9.
52 Athanasios N. Papathanasiou, "An Orphan or a Bride? The Human Self, Collective Identities and Conversion," in *Thinking Modernity: Towards a Reconfiguration of the Relationship between Orthodox Theology and Modern Culture*, ed. Assaad E. Kattan and Fadi A. Georgi (Münster: St John of Damascus Institute of Theology, University of Balamand & Westphalian Wilhelm's University, Center of Religious Studies, 2010), 133–54. The cited passage comes from the paper's Greek version and was translated into English by myself.
53 This point is superbly analyzed in his Slavoj Žižek, *The Puppet and the Dwarf: The Perverse Core of Christianity* (Cambridge, MA: MIT Press, 2003).

148 *Haralambos Ventis*

54 Peter Thompson, "Introduction: Ernst Block and the Quantum Mechanics of Hope" in Ernst Bloch, *Atheism in Christianity* (ix-xxx, London: Verso Books, 2009), xxix.
55 Bloch, *Atheism in Christianity*, 14–15.
56 Žižek, *The Fragile Absolute*, 2.
57 Slavoj Žižek, *In Defense of Lost Causes* (London & New York: Verso Books, 2008), 1.
58 Ibid., 2. Here it must be added that cladding political programs with religious attires can be tricky and may well work counter to Žižek's emancipatory intentions. For example, Carl Schmitt is known for upholding the view that "all significant concepts of the modern theory of the state are secularized theological concepts," a belief which gave him the license to construct an influential political philosophy, structured along the lines of the new *theological* content that he gave to the category of the political – this for the purpose of lending support to Nazi ideology. See Carl Schmitt, *Political Theology: Four Chapters on the Concept of Sovereignty*, trans. George Schwab (Cambridge, MA: MIT Press, 1985; the original German version was published in 1922), 36. Worth mentioning as well is that for Schmitt, as for Žižek (despite their contrasting aims), *liberalism signifies the denial, the complete destruction of the political*, because the political in Schmitt's view thrives precisely on the alertness and rigor provided by one's (a group's, class' or nation's) juxtaposition against a rival X, Y and Z. Institutionalized tolerance, by contrast, of the kind espoused and promoted by western liberal democracies, in Schmitt's vision, weakens the spirit and only nurtures passivity and complacency, hence immobility, stagnation and, finally, decay.
59 Ibid., 30.
60 Ibid., 7.
61 It should be noted that Žižek's reading of Christianity is significantly different from those of Taylor, MacIntyre or Ricoeur.
62 Ibid.
63 Ibid., 289.
64 Ibid., 293.
65 Ibid., 282.
66 Ibid., 279 (my italics).
67 Ibid.
68 Ibid., 310–11.
69 Communitarians often romanticize traditional societies to the point of overlooking not only the ostracism suffered by those unable or unwilling to meet communal criteria of acceptance but also the restraints preventing members from leaving the community, following a revision of their goals or purposes in life. In *Liberalism, Community and Culture* (Oxford: Clarendon Press, 1991), 85–90, Will Kymlicka addresses the thorny issue of social exclusion, and goes one step further in defending the constitutional guarantee of a citizen's freedom to *exit* any given social or religious community/group, on top of the liberty to freely join it in the first place (Ibid., 59–60).
70 Karl Popper, *The Open Society and Its Enemies, Vol. 2: Hegel and Marx* (London & New York: Routledge, 1996), chapter 24, 237.
71 Edward Schilebeeckx, *The Language of Faith: Essays on Jesus, Theology, and the Church* (New York: Orbis Books, 1995), 97. Having said that, Fr. Schilebeeckx adds a correct and much-needed, in my view, qualification to Christendom's obligation to actively support the cause of human rights, by warning against the Church's absorption to political involvement at the expense of its sacramental and eschatological vision. In his own words, "it is possible for a critical [Christian] community to be politically committed, but to fail to provide this distinctively Christian perspective and to celebrate the promise in the liturgical language which prayerfully expresses the transcendent element. Such

a community might achieve very fruitful results, but it would not be acting as a Christian community. It would be in danger of becoming a purely political cell without evangelical inspiration – one of very many useful and indeed necessary political pressure groups, but not an *ecclesia Christi*" (Ibid., 78).

72 Schilebeeckx, *The Language of Faith*, 80.
73 Ibid., 81.
74 Pantelis Kalaitzides, *Orthodoxy & Political Theology*, trans. Gregory Edwards (Geneva: World Council of Churches, 2012), 48–50. Gutiérrez's passage is from his book *A Theology of Liberation: History, Politics, and Salvation*, Revised Edition with a New Introduction by the author, trans. Sister Caridad Inda and John Eagleson (New York: Maryknoll, Orbis Books, 1988), 103.
75 In the history of Christian theology, instances of protest against imperial abuses are not uncommon, and may be traced back as early as John Chrysostom and Basil the Great, both of whom (among other ancient Church writers) have drawn explicit demarcation lines between secular and spiritual authority. In spite of this, patristic literature mainly shows an interest not in political theory as such (it would be a gross anachronism to speak of this genre in the context of early and medieval Christianity, some notable exceptions notwithstanding) but in matters of social justice including a concern for inequality, which may be grouped under the rubric of philanthropy as an evangelical command. It is true that the problem of the tension between civic obedience and the limits placed upon it by the Christian moral conscience was a central issue for the early Church Fathers, who like all Christians living in the pre-Constantine period were called upon to worship the Emperor and submit themselves to the divinity of the State, i.e. the Roman Empire. Thus, Theophilus of Antioch epitomized the general Apostolic and post-Apostolic sentiment toward State authority when he posited clear-cut limits to the latter's demands for obedience:

> I shall honour the Emperor, I shall not, however, adore him but I shall pray for him. I give adoration only to the one true God, by whom I know the sovereign has been made. You will ask: Why then do you not adore the Emperor? Because it is his nature to be honoured with legitimate obedience and not to be adored: he is not a God, but a man whom God has ordained to administer justice, not to receive adoration. The administration of the State has in a certain sense been entrusted to him by God; and just as he does not permit any of his subordinates to bear the name of Emperor, which is proper to himself, and may not be lawfully applied to any other, just so no one may be adored except God. Honour, therefore, the sovereign with devotion, obeying him and praying for him; and in so doing, you will fulfill the will of God, whose law says: My son, honour the Lord and King: and do not disobey either one; for they will swiftly punish their enemies.
>
> (*Prov*. 24: 21–2)

Cited in Igino Giordano, *The Social Message of the Church Fathers* (Boston, MA: St. Paul's Editions, 1977), 118–19.
76 See Terry Eagleton, *Reason, Faith, and Revolution: Reflections on the God Debate* (New Haven & London: Yale University Press, 2009), and his more recent *Culture and the Death of God* (New Haven & London: Yale University Press, 2015).
77 David McLellan, *Marxism and Religion: A Description and Assessment of the Marxist Critique of Christianity* (London: The Macmillan Press, 1987).
78 Adolf von Harnack, *History of Dogma, Vol. II: Part Two*, English trans. Neil Buchanan (New York: Dover, 1971), and more concisely in his classic *What Is Christianity?* (Philadelphia: Fortress Press, 1986), 190–217.

150   *Haralambos Ventis*

79 Alain Badiou, *Saint Paul: The Foundation of Universalism*, trans. Ray Brassier (Stanford, CA: Stanford University Press, 2003), 5.
80 Nikos Mouzelis, *Η Θρησκευτική Διαμάχη: Σκέψεις Ενός Μη Ειδικού* (Athens: Themelio, 2003), 71–2.
81 Thomas Müntzer was the Thuringian leader of the Peasants' War, a self-professed theologian whose polemical grasp of revelation turned his energies against the "spinelessness" of Luther and his pacifist theology (Müntzer's so-called "Prague manifesto," dated November 1521, marks his rancorous break with Luther). The latter was denounced by Müntzer as espousing a reactionary submission to the landlords, a submission akin to a betrayal of the revolutionary character of the Gospel. Like Andreas Karlstadt, Müntzer subscribed to an ethic of "inner spiritual regeneration," that is known to accompany all movements of reform (religious and secular alike), and which prompts its followers to assume clear-cut codes of behavior, often accompanied by a messianic mission. Reformation scholar Carter Lindberg describes Müntzer as an ascetic reformer "whose self-understanding was that of a prophet – a chiliastic one at that – whose covenantal theology was oriented increasingly toward a theocratic christianizing of the world rather than renewal of the Church." See Carter Lindberg, *The European Reformations* (Oxford: Blackwell Publishers, 1996), 151.
82 *The Collected Works of Thomas Müntzer*, ed. and trans. Peter Matheson (Edinburgh: T&T Clark, 1988), 248–51; cited in *The European Reformations*, 153.
83 *Luther's Works*, ed. Jaroslav Pelikan and Helmut T. Lechman, vol. 40 (St. Louis: Concordia & Philadelphia: Fortress, 1955–86), 57; cited in *The European Reformations*, 154.
84 Luther's most refined political statement is made in "Temporal Authority: To What Extent It Should Be Obeyed," a treatise dealing squarely with questions of perennial social and political gravity. This text provides us with a helpful way into Luther's views on the legitimacy of secular governments, the relationship between Church and State, and the role of each in dealing with heresy and other matters religious. In its pages, Luther argues in favor of a categorical divide between the "heavenly" and the "earthly" kingdoms, inclusive of which is the assignment of distinct forms of authority to statesmen and prelate, respectively (a prerequisite for the subsequent emergence of the modern secular state). Having no doubt taken to heart the Lord's injunction in Mark 12:17 ("Give to the emperor the things that are the emperor's and to God the things that are God's," *NRSV*), Luther writes the following: "As nobody else can open or close heaven or hell to me, so nobody else can drive me to belief or unbelief. How [a person] believes or disbelieves is a matter for the conscience of each individual, and since this takes nothing away from the temporal authority the latter should be content to attend to its own affairs and let men believe this or that as they are able and willing, and constrain no one by force. For *faith is a free act*, to which no one can be forced. Indeed, it is a work of God in the spirit, not something which outward authority should compel or create. Hence arises the common saying, found also in Augustine, "No one can or ought to be forced to believe"; *Martin Luther's Basic Theological Writings*, ed. Timothy F. Lull (Minneapolis, MN: Fortress Press, 1989), 655–703, 682.
85 *Martin Luther's Basic Theological Writings*, 665.
86 Robert Cummings Neville, *Recovery of the Measure: Interpretation and Measure* (Albany, NY: State University of New York Press, 1989), 27.
87 For a thorough, challenging criticism of reductive materialism (written from a skeptic's point of view), see Thomas Nagel, *Mind & Cosmos: Why the Materialist, Neo-Darwinian Conception of Nature Is Almost Certainly False* (Oxford: Oxford University Press, 2011).
88 Žižek, *How to Read Lacan*, 99. The ontological externality of Christianity's truth-claims is beautifully related in John Updike's poem "Seven Stanzas at

Easter," particularly in the following verses affirming Christ's bodily Resurrection: "Make no mistake: if he rose at all/It was as His body . . . Let us not mock God with metaphor, / Analogy, sidestepping, transcendence, / Making of the event a parable, a sign painted in the faded Credulity of earlier ages: Let us walk through the door."

Bibliography

Badiou, Alain. *Saint Paul: The Foundation of Universalism*. Translated by Ray Brassier. Stanford, CA: Stanford University Press, 2003.

Bloch, Ernst. *Atheism in Christianity*. London: Verso Books, 2009.

Cornelius Castoriadis. *Ancient Greek Democracy and Its Contemporary Significance/ Η αρχαία ελληνική δημοκρατία και η σημασία της για μας σήμερα*. Athens: Ypsilon, 1999.

———. *Anthropology, Politics, Philosophy/Ανθρωπολογία, πολιτική, φιλοσοφία*. Athens: Ypsilon, 2001.

———. *Crossroads of the Labyrinth/Τα σταυροδρόμια του λαβύρινθου*. Athens: Ypsilon, 1991.

———. *Domaines de l' homme*. 1986, in Greek *Χώροι του ανθρώπου*. Athens: Ypsilon, 1995.

———. *L' Institution imaginaire de la societe*. Paris: Seuil, 1975, in Greek *Η φαντασιακή θέσμιση της κοινωνίας*. Athens: Rappas, 1981/2002.

———. *The Rise of Insignificance/Η άνοδος της ασημαντότητας*. Athens: Ypsilon, 2000.

Eagleton, Terry. *Culture and the Death of God*. New Haven & London: Yale University Press, 2015.

———. *The Illusions of Postmodernism*. Oxford: Blackwell, 1997.

———. *Reason, Faith, and Revolution: Reflections on the God Debate*. New Haven & London: Yale University Press, 2009.

Field, Harry. "Deflationist Views of Meaning and Content." In *Truth*, edited by Simon Blackburn and Keith Simmons, 351–91. Oxford: Oxford University Press, 1999.

Foucault, Michel. *The Order of Things: An Archaeology of the Human Sciences*. New York: Pantheon Books, 1970.

Gauchet, Marcel. *The Disenchantment of the World*. Translated by Oscar Burge. Introduction by Charles Taylor. Princeton, NJ: Princeton University Press, 1997.

Giordano, Igino. *The Social Message of the Church Fathers*. Boston, MA: St. Paul's Editions, 1977.

Le Goff, Jacques. *The Birth of Europe*. Translated by Janet Lloyd. Oxford: Blackwell Publishers, 2005.

Gupta, Anil. "A Critique of Deflationism." In *Truth*, edited by Simon Blackburn and Keith Simmons, 283–307. Oxford: Oxford University Press, 1999.

Harnack, Adolf von. *History of Dogma, Vol. 2: Part Two*. Translated by Neil Buchanan. New York: Dover, 1971.

———. *What Is Christianity?* Philadelphia: Fortress Press, 1986.

Kalaitzides, Pantelis. *Orthodoxy & Political Theology*. Translated by Rev. Gregory Edwards. Geneva: World Council of Churches, 2012.

Kondylis, Panagiotis. *Μελαγχολία και πολεμική: δοκίμια και μελετήματα/Melancholy and Polemics: Essays and Studies*. Athens: Themelio, 2002.

Kymlicka, Will. *Liberalism, Community and Culture*. Oxford: Clarendon Press, 1991.

Larmore, Charles. *The Morals of Modernity*. New York: Columbia University Press, 1996.

Larmore, Charles and Alain Renaut. *Débat sur l'éthique: Idéalisme ou realism*, in Greek, *Περί Ηθικής, Λόγος και Αντίλογος: Ιδεαλισμός ή Ρεαλισμός*. Athens: Polis Publications, 2006.
Lenoir, Frédéric. *Le Christ philosophe*. Plon, 2007, in Greek, *Ο Χριστός Φιλόσοφος*. Athens: Polis Publications, 2010.
Lindberg, Carter. *The European Reformations*. Oxford: Blackwell Publishers, 1996.
Lull, Timothy F., ed. *Martin Luther's Basic Theological Writings*. Minneapolis, MN: Fortress Press, 1989.
MacIntyre, Alasdair. *After Virtue*. Notre Dame, IN: Notre Dame University Press, 2007.
———. *Dependent Rational Animals: Why Human Beings Need the Virtues*. London: Duckworth, 1999.
Marsonet, Michele. "Linguistic Idealism in Analytic Philosophy of the Twentieth Century." In *Current Issues in Idealism*, edited by Paul Coates and Daniel D. Hutto, 83–120. Bristol, England: Thoemmes Press, 1996.
McLellan, David. *Marxism and Religion: A Description and Assessment of the Marxist Critique of Christianity*. London: The Macmillan Press, 1987.
Moltmann, Jürgen. *The Experimental Hope*. Edited and translated by M. Douglas Meeks. London: SCM Press, 1975.
Mouzelis, Nikos. *Η Θρησκευτική Διαμάχη: Σκέψεις Ενός Μη "Ειδικού."* Athens: Themelio, 2003.
Nagel, Thomas. *Mind & Cosmos: Why the Materialist, Neo-Darwinian Conception of Nature Is Almost Certainly False*. Oxford: Oxford University Press, 2011.
———. *The View from Nowhere*. Oxford: Oxford University Press, 1989.
Neville, Robert Cummings. *Recovery of the Measure: Interpretation and Measure*. Albany, NY: State University of New York Press, 1989.
Papathanasiou, Athanasios N. "An Orphan or a Bride? The Human Self, Collective Identities and Conversion." In *Thinking Modernity: Towards a Reconfiguration of the Relationship between Orthodox Theology and Modern Culture*, edited by Assaad E. Kattan and Fadi A. Georgi, 133–63. Münster: St John of Damascus Institute of Theology, University of Balamand & Westphalian Wilhelm's University, Centre of Religious Studies, 2010.
Pippin, Robert B. *Modernism as a Philosophical Problem: On the Dissatisfactions of European High Culture*. Oxford & Cambridge, MA: Basil Blackwell Publishers, 1991.
Popper, Karl. *The Open Society and Its Enemies, Vol. 2: Hegel and Marx*. London & New York: Routledge, 1996.
Putnam, Hilary. *Ethics without Ontology*. Cambridge, MA: Harvard University Press, 2004.
———. *Realism with a Human Face*. Cambridge, MA: Harvard University Press, 1990.
———. "Values and Norms." In *The Collapse of the Fact-Value Dichotomy and Other Essays*, 111–34. Cambridge, MA: Harvard University Press, 2002.
Rawls, John. "The Idea of Public Reason Revisited." *The University of Chicago Law Review* 64, no. 3 (Summer 1997): 765–807.
———. *Political Liberalism, With a New Introduction and a Reply to Habermas*. New York: Columbia University Press, 1996.
Ricoeur, Paul. *Oneself as Another*. Translated by Kathleen Blamey. Chicago, IL: University of Chicago Press, 1994.

Rorty, Richard. "The Contingency of a Liberal Community." In *Contingency, Irony, and Solidarity*, 44–71. Cambridge: Cambridge University Press, 1998.

———. "Failed Prophecies, Glorious Hopes." In *Philosophy and Social Hope*, 201–9. London: Penguin Books, 1999.

———. "Freud and Moral Reflection." In *Essays on Heidegger and Others: Philosophical Papers*, vol. 2, 143–63. Cambridge: Cambridge University Press, 1991.

Sandel, Michael. *What Money Can't Buy: The Moral Limits of Markets*. New York: Farrar, Straus, & Giroux, 2012.

Scanlon, Thomas Michael. "Metaphysics and Morals." *Proceedings and Addresses of the American Philosophical Association* 77 (2003): 7–22.

Schilebeeckx, Edward. *The Language of Faith: Essays on Jesus, Theology, and the Church*. New York: Orbis Books, 1995.

Schmitt, Carl. *Political Theology: Four Chapters on the Concept of Sovereignty*. Translated by George Schwab. Cambridge, MA: MIT Press, 1985.

Sourlas, Pavlos. "Philosophy and Democracy: The Fear of Platonism in Rawls and Habermas." *Isopoliteia* 4 (2000): 29–97.

Steiner, George. *Nostalgia for the Absolute*. Canada: House of Anansi, 1997.

Taylor, Charles. *Hegel and Modern Society*. Cambridge: Cambridge University Press, 1979.

———. *The Malaise of Modernity*. Ontario, Canada: Anansi, 1991.

———. *Sources of the Self: The Making of the Modern Identity*. Cambridge, MA: Harvard University Press, 1996.

Virvidakis, Stelios. "Afterword." In *Golfo Maggini, Ο Χάμπερμας και οι Νεοαριστοτελικοί: Η Ηθική του Διαλόγου στον Γιούργκεν Χάμπερμας και η Πρόκληση του Νεοαριστοτελισμού*, 343–74. Athens: Patakis, 2006.

Žižek, Slavoj. *The Fragile Absolute: Or, Why Is the Christian Legacy Worth Fighting For?* London & New York: Verso Books, 2000.

———. *How to Read Lacan*. London: Granta Books, 2006.

———. *In Defense of Lost Causes*. London & New York: Verso Books, 2008.

———. *On Belief: Thinking in Action*. London & New York: Routledge, 2002.

———. *The Puppet and the Dwarf: The Perverse Core of Christianity*. Cambridge, MA: MIT Press, 2003.

7 Rethinking universality
Badiou and Žižek on Pauline theology

Jack Louis Pappas

On the eve of our present century, the disintegration of the Soviet Union cemented the prevalence of an emergent consensus which interpreted the long catastrophe of the prior century as prelude to an age of permanent stability. This brave new world, established upon the sure foundations of global capitalism, liberal democracy and international cooperation, promised a post-ideological politics – embodied in a multiplicity of "third way" policy organizations and political parties, free of the dangerous extremities of left-right politics. Indeed, minor adjustment was all that would be necessary within a political order which perceived itself, in the now (in)famous words of Francis Fukuyama, as nothing other than the "end of history" itself. This secular-realized eschatology identified the expansion of U.S.-style suburban living and consumerism throughout the world as the fundamental force for the liberation of mankind and insisted upon the eternal and limitless power of science and technology as the means of achieving this utopia within our grasp.

In the wake of state communism's failure, meaningful critique could no longer be mounted by returning to exhausted forms of discourse. Creston Davis observes that

> the act of thinking was forced to find a new way forward, a new source of hope. It had to appeal to a tradition that could resist the hegemony of capitalism and its presupposition – the individual will to power. Thinkers could no longer appeal to the humanist–Marxist tradition alone, especially as the history of actual existing Marxism folded before the juggernaut of capitalism.[1]

So fundamental was this problem for the mere possibility of critical discourse that to remark that "it would be easier to imagine the end of the world than the end of capitalism," would hardly seem to be an overstatement.

However, imagining an end to neo-liberal hegemony seems increasingly easier in light of more recent events. Indeed, fundamental blows have been struck to the credibility of the global system and its corresponding messianic narrative, not merely along the margins of the international community, but within the heart of the "developed world" itself. The now ubiquitous presence of the very word "neo-liberalism," betrays a sense of its already being *past*, confirming Hegel's axiom that "the owl of Minerva spreads its wings only with the falling of the dusk."[2] The revitalization of leftist politics through the emergence of figures like Jeremy Corbyn, Bernie Sanders, Jean-Luc Mélenchon and parties such as Greece's SYRIZA are quite clearly indicative of a growing popular dissatisfaction with a generation of growing profits accompanied by stagnant wages, austerity and unemployment.

Yet, despite these developments, it is noteworthy that the greater political victories of recent years have been achieved not by the left but by a reinvigorated "populist" *right*. Though we should be wary of generalizing the ideological features of political movements separated by altogether distinct contexts, there is nonetheless a discernable common thread that can be drawn between Donald Trump's election to the U.S. presidency, the mainstreaming of Front National in France, and the Brexit crisis in the U.K. While it has been so consistently pointed out that these movements all share a deep distrust of globalization and immigration that it now seems facile to articulate the matter, what is most interesting about this phenomenon is that all along its various "fronts," the emergence of an anti-globalist right has unmistakably linked itself to a desire for recovering a more fundamental "center" for social and cultural life.

While an appeal to religious tradition is hardly novel within the broader history of political reaction, what is perhaps distinctive in these present movements is their clear rejection of dominant center-right politics, coupling together a repudiation of neo-liberal hegemony with a quasi-apocalyptic appropriation of national identity. Calling into question the dominant assumptions of Western humanism, they have sought to recover instead a starkly pre-modern conception of political engagement. In doing so, at least superficially, the radical right has exploited nothing other than the alienated ennui of the present order by appealing to (or at least to the superficial language of) transcendence. Though one might well agree that the appeal of these movements to a "deeper" source for our political and social imaginaries is warranted, the use of religion within this sphere is quite superficial (even if it is deeply affected). Far from being rooted in a recovery of a pre-Copernican cosmology, or even in the theological claims of the Christian tradition, the appeal to Christianity is thoroughly tribal and is more fundamentally ingrained in ethnic, national and cultural *identity*.

It is now, therefore, urgently necessary that philosophy once again engage religious discourse, for the sake of critiquing the present forms of oppressive socio-political organization manifested by neo-liberalism (however weakened it might apparently be), while also refusing to allow the language of religion to be claimed in service to an "identitarian" ethno-nationalist political program. That such a philosophical retrieval of theology would be undertaken by engaging the writings of the Apostle Paul is perhaps the most surprising trend in recent philosophy. No figure has been perhaps more previously unfashionable. Following Nietzsche, Paul has been long associated with the corruption of the radicalism of Jesus and identified as the proper founder of the oppressively institutional Church, the great genius of servile resentment.³ Nonetheless, Žižek locates within Paul's theology a singular possibility for overturning our prevalent conceptions of identity and universality, which reorients "transcendence" toward the disclosure of truth within the historical unfolding of what he calls the "Event." For Žižek, this re-orientation of transcendence renders possible a radical revision of the presupposed oppositions placed between transcendence and the immediate demands of political life.

In order to understand Žižek's radically revisionist understanding of Pauline theology, it is necessary not only to engage the manner in which Žižek approaches Paul within his own corpus but also to first examine the work of Alain Badiou to whom Žižek's reading of Paul is deeply indebted. Though Žižek's reading of Paul diverges from Badiou's in several key areas, both authors share an antipathy toward orthodox streams of Pauline interpretation (whether patristic, medieval or reformed) and do not wish to situate their recovery of Paul's theology within the usual theistic context. Žižek quite openly declares that he "is a complete atheist,"[4] and that despite his advocacy of the Christian theological legacy he must "make it very clear that this legacy today is not alive in the Catholic or any Christian church."[5] Likewise, Badiou declares in the prologue to his *Saint Paul: La Fondation De l'Universalisme* that

> I have never really connected to Paul as an apostle or saint, and I care nothing for the Good News he declares . . . I have never really connected Paul with religion. It is not in this register, to bear witness to any sort of faith, or even antifaith, that I have for a long time been interested in him.[6]

However, this does not mean that Žižek or Badiou have any desire to undermine Paul's thought from the vantage point of historical criticism, which might aim to retrieve a "purified" form of Christianity preceding Paul's perceived corruption of the content of the early Gospels.[7] Instead, Žižek identifies within Paul a certain destabilizing, liberationist discourse that is altogether distinct from the later institutionalized forms of theology as well as thoroughly destructive of pagan (and other monotheistic) expressions of religion. "For example, within a pagan attitude, injustice means a disturbance of the natural order . . . But the message that the Gospel sends is precisely the radical abandonment of this idea of some kind of natural balance."[8] This retrieval is similarly framed by Badiou, who understands Paul as a thinker of a paradoxical "subject without identity and a law without support which provides for the possibility of a universal teaching within history itself."[9]

For Badiou, Paul proclaims a universality placed over and against the abstraction of "the law," as well as a subjectivity liberated from the superficiality of identity. Holding these two paradoxes together and in tension, Paul shatters the enclosed ideological apparatus of the world, as it is constituted both politically and intellectually. This apparatus revolves around two dual axes which deceptively appear opposed and yet cannot be separated from one another: the simultaneous cultural appeal to a communitarian universal (such as capitalism, nationalism and so forth) and the appeal to particular identities of various groups, often in the mode of victimization (sexual orientation, gender or race). Yet, Paul instead succeeds in "subtracting truth from the communitarian grasp, be it that of a people, a city, an empire, a territory or a social class."[10]

Badiou characterizes the "core" of Paul's message to be a dramatic rupture, which cannot be subsumed or appropriated according to existing categories, either of community or identity. This "rupture" is the emergence of truth, which is disclosed in the manner of a historical "happening," what Badiou calls the "Event" of truth. It is in the wake of this Event that the subject arises, at once conscious of the absence of this truth in the (now transparent) apparatus of the past, and carries within itself the emergence of the truth as it discerns its trace within the present.

> If there has been an event, and if truth consists in declaring it and then in being faithful to this declaration two consequences ensue. First, since truth is eventual, or of the order of what occurs it is singular. It is neither structural, nor axiomatic, nor legal. No available generality can account for it ... Second, truth being inscribed on the basis of a declaration that is in essence subjective, no pre-constituted subset can support it.[11]

It is exactly this which Badiou understands to be signified for Paul by the death and Resurrection of Christ. The truth does not emerge from within the subject but rather is arrived at *through* the subject by the declaration of its universality which cannot be claimed by any identity or community. Consequently, this means that the meaning of the Event cannot be approached from the standpoint of neutrality, which would deny the concrete specificity of its emergence – for it is within the very concreteness of circumstance that its truth is disclosed. To approach the truth through neutrality would be a denial of truth *as* event. At the same time, this truth cannot be reduced to its "effect" as an objective fact disclosed in the mode of forensic evidence.

Instead, Žižek describes the relation of the subject to the Truth-Event in the following manner:

> The subject is thus, a finite contingent emergence: not only is truth not "subjective" in the sense of being subordinated to his whims, but the subject himself "serves the truth," since the subject always has to operate within a finite multiple of a situation in which he discerns the signs of truth.[12]

Paul is not making a *claim* about the truth of the death and Resurrection of Christ, rather, it is the Event of the Paschal mystery which *claims* Paul. He is not offering a forensic analysis of circumstantial evidence concerning the content of his claim. Rather, in the act of declaring the Event of Christ, Paul is calling into question the entire prior framework of truth as it has previously been constituted. The Christ-Event thus becomes the new measure of meaning and possibility *through* Paul's declaration of its Truth.

What is meant here is most easily illustrated in the words of Paul himself. For Paul, not only is the Gospel essentially unintelligible folly which cannot be subsumed within pre-existing categories, but any effort to subsume it would only serve to dissolve its radical center. As he says,

> [God] will destroy the wisdom of the wise, and will bring to nothing the understanding of the prudent. Where is the wise? where is the scribe? where is the disputer of this world? has not God made foolish the wisdom of this world? . . . For the Jews require a sign, and the Greeks seek after wisdom: But we preach Christ-Crucified, unto the Jews a stumbling block, and unto the Greeks foolishness.[13]

The Truth-Event (Christ-Crucified) does not merely lay claim to Paul (through his declaration), but also lays claim upon the prior categories of thought, whether Jewish or Hellenic.

According to Badiou, Paul is not referring to "Jews" or "Greeks" in a narrowly ethnic sense but is instead critiquing two pre-existing ideological modes of truth. Paul's identification of Jews with "signs" and Greeks with "wisdom" is intended exactly for the purpose of destabilizing these two forms of discourse. For Badiou, Jewish discourse is concerned primarily with radical individuation and alterity. "Jewish discourse is a discourse of exception, because the prophetic sign, the miracle, election, all designate transcendence as that which lies beyond the natural totality."[14] On the other hand, Greek discourse is concerned with assimilation and totalization. "[Greek wisdom] consists in appropriating the fixed order of the world, in the matching of the logos to being. Greek discourse is cosmic, deploying the subject with the reason of a natural totality."[15]

In service to the Event, Paul's declaration must coincide with an institution of an utterly new discourse which takes as its reference point no pre-existing center but refers instead constantly back to the horizon of the event and its historical emergence, which it embodies and carries within itself in the manner of a trace. It is all too easy to assume that this new discourse would constitute a synthesis between the "Greek" and "Jewish" modes. Yet Paul significantly departs from such an expectation and maintains a discourse which remains in suspended opposition. Rather, the prior categories are taken up within the new discourse but are negated. This is what is meant by Paul's utterance that,

> God chose what is foolish in the world to shame the wise; God chose what is weak in the world to shame the strong; God chose what is low and despised in the world, things that are not, to reduce to nothing things that are.[16]

Thus, the new discourse which Paul heralds not only destabilizes prior ideologies in such a way that the hold of such ideologies can no longer function, but they are "reduced to nothing." The Event imposes itself upon prior language in such a way that it requires a new discourse in order to be disclosed. However, the disclosure of the Event is precisely the disclosure of its uncircumscribable quality. "It is through the invention of a language wherein folly, scandal and weakness supplant knowing reason, order and power, and wherein non-being is the only legitimizable affirmation of being, that Christian discourse is articulated."[17]

In the *Ticklish Subject*, Žižek maintains the semblance of Badiou's radically anti-philosophical reading of Pauline discourse, and even deepens the proximity of his own analysis to the language of Paul himself. Indeed, Žižek argues that if the Event is not something which can be disclosed either "neutrally" or "factually," then one of the most decisive elements of its character *as Truth* is the sense that it emerges extrinsically from the subject who declares or "receives" it. The sense of the Truth's independent emergence means that it lays a claim upon us and demands a response. To accept the demand which this Truth requires is only suitably articulated in terms of *faith*. "What if the true fidelity to the Event is *dogmatic* in the precise sense of unconditional Faith, of an attitude which does not ask for good reasons, and which, for that very reason, cannot be refuted by any argumentation."[18]

This is especially highlighted by the absurdity of Paul's assertion not only of God's identification with both folly and weakness, but of the impossible claim of Christ's Resurrection from the dead. The scandal of the Truth-Event heralded by Paul renders us as contemporaries with the Greeks and the Jews whom Paul addresses in the text of his epistles despite the distance of two millennia.

> The Truth-Event designates the occurrence of something which, from within the horizon of the predominant order of Knowledge appears impossible . . . today, and location of the Truth-Event at the level of supernatural miracles necessarily entails regression into obscuration, since the event of Science is irreducible.[19]

Thus, the Truth of the Event is disclosed through the act of the *decisive* response of *faith*, rather than on the basis of the "content" of the Event itself.

In being faithful to the Truth-Event, we thus affirm that the Truth is not something which has been subjectively posited, but rather that the Truth-Event has emerged anteriorly to us, demanding our subjective proclamation of fidelity to its arrival. Žižek articulates the extrinsic dependency of fidelity explicitly by utilizing the Pauline language of *grace*:

> when I truly believe, I accept that the source of my faith is not myself; that in some inexplicable way, it comes from outside, from God Himself – in His grace, God addressed me, it was not I who raised myself to Him.[20]

Taking up the language of grace, Žižek distinguishes the sense of agency with which we might be tempted to engage the nature of both decision and fidelity. Žižek is careful to distinguish what he means by the act of "decision" from what he calls vulgar voluntarism or liberal "freedom of choice."[21] Thus, the Truth-Event's claim upon us extends to the manner of our response.

In a real sense, we are "pre-destined" for faith by the very imposition of the Event upon prior modes of discourse. "Predestination" should not be confused with strict necessity, however. According to Žižek, what is pre-destined is not what is being chosen but is our being "destined" to choose. This notion of "graced predestination" is emptied by Žižek of its explicit theological content and is identified with Heidegger's conception of *vorlaufende Entschlossenheit* [anticipatory resoluteness], which discloses to the agent the definitive finite horizon of its agency, compelling it to discern the condition of its response.

> Heidegger's decision, in the precise sense of anticipatory resoluteness, has the status of a *forced choice*, the Heideggerian decision . . . is not a "free choice" in the usual sense of the term . . . Rather, it is fundamentally the choice of "freely assuming" one's imposed destiny.[22]

This conception of a pre-destined (imposed) choice, displaces the "active" principle of election from within the agent and relocates it exteriorly within the Event (in the Pauline case, within God). Indeed, it is only in relation to being claimed by the Truth-Event that the subject is rendered an agent at all. This is a paradox which too easily loses its power upon clarification but is in this way revealed to be dependent upon the demand of the uncircumscribable revelation of the Truth and is altogether *gratuitous* in its emergence.

> It is fundamentally the choice of freely assuming one's imposed destiny. This paradox indicates the theological problematic of predestination and grace: a true decision/choice presupposes that I assume a passive attitude of "letting myself be chosen – n short, free choice and Grace are strictly equivalent, or, as Deleuze put it, we really choose only when we are *chosen*.[23]

In drawing upon *Entschlossenheit*, Žižek's conception of passive agency clearly resonates with the later development of the concept of *Gelassenheit* (releasement) in Heidegger's thought, and thus by extension to Meister Eckhart's notion of non-willing and its development within the radically Augustinian theology of Catholic Jansenism, as well as that of the Protestant Reformation. This is reflected in Žižek especially by his excursus on Kierkegaard as a consummate thinker of Pauline universalism.[24] For Žižek, in the thought of Kierkegaard, as in the thought of Paul, the claim of the Truth-Event is inexplicable and immediate, escaping every attempt at appropriation. Instead, it is only understood on the terms of the Event itself, disclosed only to the subject who has yielded to the demand of its claim.

Rethinking universality   161

The paradox of imposed choice is deepened and radically extended by Kierkegaard, who understands this paradox as being revelatory of the Event's simultaneous, extrinsic, universal quality and its intrinsic singularity carried *within* the believer.

> Kierkegaard determines faith as the pure internality which the believer is unable to symbolize/socialize, to share with others . . . this means that what, in his faith, is absolutely inner, what resists intersubjective symbolic mediation is [on the other hand] the very radical externality of the religious call . . . it is experienced as a radical traumatic intrusion which attacks the subject from outside.[25]

However, there are two distinct problems which emerge here for our consideration. First, it would appear that both Žižek and Badiou are advocating for a kind of fideistic conception of the Truth which is necessarily obscurantist and anti-philosophical. Indeed, as we have seen, Žižek has explicitly identified the Truth-Event as a dogmatic object of unconditional faith.[26] Badiou even asserts that Pauline discourse itself is necessarily "incompatible with any prospect of a Christian philosophy."[27] Second, if we follow this fideistic articulation of Pauline discourse, whereby every category has been negated, how is it that the Truth of the Event can be disclosed at all? Furthermore, if every possible ground of apprehending its content has been laid to waste by its arrival, how can a True event be distinguished from an apparent simulacrum of truth?

This is most obviously problematized by both Badiou and Žižek's denial of the Truth of the central Event to which Paul himself attests, and the ultimate Truth which he serves: the historical reality of the Resurrection of Christ. While Badiou refers to the Resurrection as a "fable," he asserts that regardless of this fabulous assertion, the essential "thought-form" which Paul institutes remains. It is precisely the thought-form of Pauline discourse which is consequential for distinguishing a Truth-Event from a mere semblance.

> What is important is the subjective gesture grasped in its founding power with respect to the generic conditions of universality. That the content of the fable must be abandoned leaves as its remainder the form of these conditions, and in particular the ruin of every attempt to assign the discourse of truth to pre-constituted historical aggregates.[28]

Even if we accept Badiou's assertion that the form of Paul's thought can be subtracted from its content, the question remains "of how it was possible for the first and still most pertinent description of the mode of operation of the fidelity to a Truth-Event to occur apropos of a Truth-Event that is a mere semblance, not an actual truth."[29]

Though Badiou affirms that it is specifically the fabulous quality of the Gospel which liberates Paul from the constraints of the ideologies he critiques and renders possible the institution of a new discourse of interruption and decision, there is nothing distinctively Christian (or even explicitly theological) about Badiou's philosophical (or anti-philosophical) reading of Paul. Up until this point, Žižek and Badiou's rendering of Paul can perhaps be summarized as being almost purely discursive, offering a critique of pervading ideology through a declarative claim of the Truth-Event and where "the universal must always be attained through the particular."[30] It is here, however, that Žižek departs rather significantly from the (perhaps self-imposed) limitations of Badiou's retrieval of Paul. Moreover, it is specifically through departing from these limitations, which have stressed the "form" of Pauline thought, that Žižek is equipped in overcoming the limitations of the irrational fideism that thus far have characterized our reading of the Truth-Event.

Žižek's aims are apparently more radical, insofar as he wishes to identify in the content of Paul's theological claims a constitutive center to the Truth-Event which is specific to Christianity. More radically still, by taking up Paul's theology, Žižek is capable of affirming the Truth of the Resurrection itself, albeit in a qualified sense. Žižek understands Christianity to be singular among the world's religions. On the one hand, Žižek distinguishes Christianity from classical paganism (including Greek philosophy) and from the Eastern religious traditions, by asserting, following Badiou, that Christianity thoroughly upends a conception of justice which is related to an underlying cosmic order.

> For example, within a pagan attitude, injustice means a disturbance of the natural order. In ancient Hinduism, or even with Plato, justice was defined in what today we would call almost fascistic terms, each in his or her place in a just order.[31]

In this conception, injustice comes about when this eternal law of balance is violated – when a mother abandons her station, when a king breaks faith with the gods or his people, when the soldier revolts against his king. The resulting cosmic disorder requires an intervention which restores this balance of justice and once again renders the cosmos wholly subordinate to the law.

On the other hand, Žižek understands God in both Judaism and Islam as being radically other both to the law (which He institutes) and the world which he creates. The biggest divergence between the other monotheisms and Christianity lies specifically in the absolute quality of this alterity within Islam and Judaism, and the Christian sublation of this presupposition within the person of the Christ. In both Judaism and Islam, God's radical alterity provides the basis for totalizing forms of election, whereby there are those who are within the proper relation to God (through obedience to Him) and those who are not – without exception. The Jewish and Muslim conception of God is

> the true God of Reason, He is wholly transcendent – not in the sense of frivolous irrationality, but in the sense of the supreme Creator who

knows and directs everything and thus has no need to get involved in earthly accidents.[32]

The fundamental divergence between Christianity on the one hand, and Islam together with Judaism on the other, arises from that radical condition upon which Paul's message depends, namely: Christ-Crucified.[33] As Žižek notes in the *Fragile Absolute*, in contrast to Judaism and Islam, in which the sacrifice of the son is prevented at the last moment (the angel intervenes to save Isaac), "*only Christianity opts for the actual sacrifice (killing) of the son.*"[34] For Žižek, Paul's proclamation of Christ's Crucifixion discloses the abolition of the transcendent cosmic order, as well as the possibility of reconciling disorder (sin) to it by way of a restorative subjugation to the law. Instead, the Crucifixion announces both the end of an omnipotent God who determines the natural order and the necessity of being subordinate to an external mediator for the sake of this order's preservation.

> We get a God who abandons this transcendent position and throws himself into his own creation, fully engaging himself in it up to dying, so that we, humans, are left with no higher Power watching over us, just with the terrible burden of freedom and responsibility.[35]

The consequence of this message, which the Crucifixion carries, is both atheistic and liberating. We are not only liberated from God by the death of God, but this Truth-Event is also made immediately present to us by virtue of the fact that the death of God coincides with annulment of the Law, granting the subject access to the universal claim of the Truth[36] in the mode of decision.

> The term "new creation" is revealing here, signaling the gesture of *sublimation*, of erasing one's past and beginning afresh from a zero-point: consequently there is also a terrifying *violence* at work in this uncoupling, that of the death drive, of the radical "wiping the slate clean."[37]

This terrifying violence is of course, the death of God (and with God, the prior order which was preserved in His name), but is also our own undergoing of a symbolic death.

This symbolic death, Žižek identifies with Paul's usage of the term "dead to the law."[38] The meaning of this symbolic death is that through the rupture of the natural order which Christ's death embodies, we are unburdened from our previous identities and ideology. We no longer identify with the station which we are born into, nor can we adhere to the structures of power which define our world. We thus become "uncoupled" from our communities and are individuated by the demand of the Christian Truth-Event. However, this does not mean that we remain in a state of fideistic suspension. The absolute negation of the Crucifixion contains within it the kernel of the new community and the new discourse. If Christ's death subverts the cosmic order (and together with it the pagan and Eastern religious traditions), it also subverts the absolutism of the other monotheistic traditions by disclosing a definitive *exception*.

Indeed, the whole Event of Christ is nothing other than exceptional: he is the suffering God, the innocent who is punished under the law, the Divinity who becomes human, and so forth. This exception is that which deprives Judaism and Islam of the Law's absolutism and inaugurates the overcoming of sin, not through reconciliation *with* the law but the replacement of the law by Love. "Christianity asserts as the highest act precisely what pagan wisdom condemns as the source of Evil: the gesture of separation, of drawing the line, of clinging to an element that disturbs the balance of all."[39] This disturbance is the rupture of individuating love which unravels the "cycle of the law"[40] and instead transgresses it in the concrete commitment of charity.

Finally, it is in charity that the content of the Truth-Event reveals itself. It is not, therefore, a conceptual abstraction but the transformative possibility of being uncoupled by the symbolic death of our ideological predeterminations and being reconstituted – *resurrected* – in relation to the rupture of the new within the horizon of the world. "Christianity is the miraculous Event that disturbs the balance of the One-All, it is the violent intrusion of difference that precisely *throws the balanced circuit of the universe off the rails*."[41] The intrusion of the impossible within the sphere of the possible accomplishes a fracture within one of philosophy's foundational problems, that of the relation between the One and the many. It forces us to revise our very notion of "singularity" and, by extension, *universality* itself. No longer can the "universal" be but a mere abstraction which seeks to annul any possibility of differentiation through unsparing assimilation. The meaning of the universal which emerges from the thought of Paul does not denote a sense of impersonal belonging which would sacrifice particularity in the name of a shared locus of identity. Instead, it is precisely the sacrifice of the *universal* for the sake of the *particular*. And, yet, the particular is no longer any sort of atomistic, subjective identity or individualism which sets itself over and against mere abstract universality. Instead, the particular itself is also transformed and emerges as an eccentric focal point of a new kind of universalism defined by the boundless and effusive demand of love for those who always necessarily remain on the margins of any impersonal system.

The intervention of a Christian imaginary within our simultaneously impersonal and hyper-identitarian age accomplishes for Žižek a revision of our very basis of the notion of the political. Theological language by its very nature upsets our conception of social and economic life, which expresses itself in the distant and dehumanizing language of "systems," and demands that we recover a concrete concern for our place within the world, particularly in relation to those which our systems exclude and marginalize. Moreover, Žižek recovers the apocalyptic dimension of Christian community as something not only utterly removed from but deeply opposed to the sense of tribal identification which has become an overwhelming feature of many Christian's conception of the role of their religion within society. Rather, Žižek insists that the very essence of Christianity is nothing other than the radical commitment to a kind of homelessness, which repudiates any system which would prioritize identity over the strange and irreducible presence of the particular.

Notes

1. Slavoj Žižek, John Milbank, and Creston Davis, eds., *The Monstrosity of Christ: Paradox or Dialectic?* (Cambridge, MA: MIT Press, 2009), 5.
2. G.W.F. Hegel, *Philosophy of Right*, trans. Thomas Malcolm Knox (Oxford: Oxford University Press, 1952), 13.
3. Nietzsche, Genealogy of Morals, 1.10.
4. Slavoj Žižek and Diana Dilworth, "Interview with Slavoj Žižek," *The Believer* 2, no. 7 (July, 2004).
5. Ibid.
6. Alain Badiou, *St. Paul: The Foundation of Universalism*, trans. Ray Brassier (Stanford, CA: Stanford University Press, 2003), 1–2.
7. Žižek, "Today, spirituality is fashionable. Either some pagan spirituality of tolerance, feminine principle, holistic approach against phallocentric Western imperialist logic or, within the Western tradition . . . You are allowed to do Christianity, but you must do a couple of things which are permitted. One is to be for these repressed traditions, the early Gnostic gospels or some mystical sects where a different non-hegemonic/patriarchal line was discernible. Or you return to the original Christ, which is against St. Paul." (Žižek and Dilworth, "Interview with Slavoj Žižek").
8. Žižek and Dilworth, *The Believer*.
9. Badiou, *St. Paul*, 5.
10. Ibid., 5.
11. Ibid., 14.
12. Slavoj Žižek, *The Ticklish Subject: The Absent Centre of Political Ontology* (London: Verso Books, 2009), 130.
13. 1 Corinthians 1: 19–20, 22–3.
14. Badiou, *St. Paul*, 41.
15. Ibid.
16. 1 Corinthians 1: 27–8.
17. Badiou, *St. Paul*, 47.
18. Žižek, *Ticklish Subject*, 144.
19. Ibid., 143.
20. Ibid., 211.
21. Ibid., 218.
22. Ibid., 18.
23. Ibid.
24. Ibid., 211.
25. Ibid., 211–12.
26. Ibid., 144.
27. Badiou, *St. Paul*, 47.
28. Ibid., 9.
29. Žižek, *Ticklish Subject*, 143.
30. Amy Hollywood, "Saint Paul and the New Man," *Critical Inquiry* 35, no. 4 (2009): 867.

31 Dilworth and Žižek, "Slavoj Žižek," *The Believer*.
32 Žižek, *The Monstrosity of Christ*, 85.
33 1 Cor 2:2.
34 Slavoj Žižek, *The Fragile Absolute: Or, Why Is the Christian Legacy Worth Fighting For?* (London: Verso Books, 2009), xviii.
35 Žižek, *The Monstrosity of Christ*, 25.
36 Žižek, *Fragile Absolute*, 129.
37 Ibid., 121.
38 Romans 7:4.
39 Žižek, *Fragile Absolute*, 112.
40 Ibid., 145.
41 Ibid., 112.

Bibliography

Badiou, Alain. *St. Paul: The Foundation of Universalism*. Translated by Ray Brassier. Stanford, CA: Stanford University Press, 2003.

Dilworth, Dianna and Slavoj Žižek. "Slavoj Žižek." *The Believer*, July 2004. Retrieved December 4, 2017 from www.believermag.com/issues/200407/?read=interview_zizek.

Hegel, G.W.F. *Outlines of the Philosophy of Right*. Edited by Stephen Houlgate. Translated by T.M. Knox. Oxford: Oxford University Press, 2008.

Hollywood, Amy. "Saint Paul and the New Man." *Critical Inquiry* 23, no. 4 (2009): 865–76. doi: 10.1086/599591.

Milbank, John and Slavoj Žižek. *The Monstrosity of Christ: Paradox or Dialectic?* Edited by Creston Davis. Cambridge, MA: MIT Press, 2009.

Nietzsche, Friedrich. *On the Genealogy of Morals & Ecce Homo*. Translated and Edited by Walter Kaufmann. New York: Vintage, 1989.

Žižek, Slavoj. *The Fragile Absolute: Or, Why Is the Christian Legacy Worth Fighting For?* London: Verso Books, 2008.

———. *The Ticklish Subject: The Absent Centre of Political Ontology*. London: Verso Books, 2009.

8 "Rühre nicht, Bock! denn es brennt"
Schelling, Žižek and Christianity

Sinan Richards

"Rühre nicht, Bock! denn es brennt"[1]

Schelling's main philosophical preoccupation at the turn of the nineteenth century was to resolve the tripartite deadlock inherent in his earlier identity philosophy. During the middle period between the publication of *Philosophy and Religion* in 1804 and the *Philosophical Inquiries into the Essence of Human Freedom* in 1809, Schelling clearly abandoned his earlier ideas of a rationalistic, idealistic monism.[2] Unlike Hegel, whose main task in the *Science of Logic* was to reground a form of rationalistic monism, Schelling moved away from idealism altogether. As he explained in the preliminary remarks to *Philosophy and Religion*, "those incapable of understanding science's mysteries distend the mass of borrowed thoughts, [. . .], into a caricature."[3] And it is this understanding of the mysteries of science that is a necessary step in Schelling's ultimate *struggle for the soul*. For Schelling, our entire being is in question and our souls can only be redeemed through the comprehension of these mysteries.

In our increasingly secular intellectual environment, the crisis of the immedicable soul has no obvious contemporary parallel. Insight into the dynamism of Schelling's "madness" requires us to first appreciate that Christianity was central to Schelling's entire philosophical project. Though it would be an overstretched interpretation to say that Schelling is a Christian philosopher, we could say that he is a philosopher deeply influenced by Christianity. Tracing the relationship between German philosophy and Religion, the German essayist Heinrich Heine parodied Schelling's philosophy of this period as a "folly," one whose failure makes room for the more coherent and rational Hegel. Heine says of Schelling in *Zur Geschichte der Religion und Philosophie in Deutschland* (1887):

> Schelling [. . .] goes cringing about in the ante-chambers of practical and theoretical absolutism, in the dens of Jesuitism he lends a hand in forging intellectual manacles, and all the while he tries to make believe he is still the same unperverted child of light that he once was; he apostatizes his apostasy, and to the shame of deserting his cause he adds

the cowardice of lying! [. . . Schelling] has become apostate to his own doctrine; he has forsaken the altar consecrated by his own hands; he has slunk back to the religious kennels of the past; he is now a good Catholic, and preaches an extra-mundane personal God, "who has committed the folly of creating the world."[4]

Heine's tone is irreverent; he is particularly scornful of Schelling's contribution to the history of German philosophy. Schelling is described as someone who "has become [an] apostate to his own doctrine," an unfortunate caricature that scholars of Schelling's philosophy will find difficult to shake off over the nineteenth and twentieth centuries.[5] Heine's description is not altogether false, as he accurately identifies Schelling's own dissatisfaction with his earlier philosophy (an "apostasy" and "desertion" I try to explain in the next part of this chapter). Furthermore, it is true that Schelling's middle philosophy *is* highly unorthodox. However, this philosophical unorthodoxy is not simply a Schellingian aberration but rather characteristic of the whole of German Idealism more broadly. Heine's mischaracterization of Schelling as someone who "tries to make believe he is still the same unperverted child of light that he once was" misses not just Schelling's contribution but the fundamental philosophical advance of German Idealism.

The legacy of German Idealism is that it was a concerted attempt to exploit the small intellectual gap that Kantian philosophy had created, enabling us to think from the position of darkness itself. As Žižek argues in *The Parallax View*, "only with Kant and German Idealism is the excess [of animal lusts and divine madness] "to be fought absolutely immanent [i.e.] the very core of subjectivity itself."[6] Žižek continues, "this is why, with German Idealism the metaphor for the core of subjectivity is Night, 'Night of the World,' in contrast to the Enlightenment notion of the Light of Reason fighting the darkness all around."[7] Schelling tried to give an account of the Absolute by employing a complex set of metaphysical machinery; that could, on the surface, take on the appearance of the convoluted thoughts of a madman. However, it would be a stretch to try and argue, as Heine does, that Schelling had "slunk back to the religious kennels of the past" when Schelling had evidently fallen into the abyssal darkness itself. As we will see, Schelling's middle philosophy is nothing short of a complete failure – a failure that he would try and rectify later. In the *Ages of the World*, which, alongside *Philosophy and Religion*, will be the primary focus of this chapter, Schelling ignites a shift in his philosophical project, seeking to rationalize the world from the position of God himself – a prophetic attempt to understand "the mysteries of science." In this chapter, I reconstruct Schelling's dissatisfaction with his earlier identity philosophy and elucidate Schelling's most speculative texts, drawing the link between this Schelling and Žižek's construction of God. Schelling's folly continues until the ailing Absolute is uncovered, a God who has irremediably fallen from himself. An injured and pernicious God, the very ground for the God that Lacan develops from *Seminar III* onwards.

The same God that Žižek deploys in his theological writings. Schelling in this middle phase is ready to risk it all, to make sense of these mysteries of science, and we should not doubt Schelling's bravery and sincerity in his desire to achieve complete truth:

> I am ready to admit [. . .] that these systems, which constantly hover between heaven and earth and are not brave enough to penetrate to the core of all knowledge, are much more secure against the most dangerous errors than is the system of a great thinker whose speculations take great flights, and who risks everything, either to achieve complete truth in all its greatness, or no truth at all. And please let me remind you that whosoever is not brave enough to follow the truth to its fullest height will never possess it even though he touch the hem of its garment, and that, in spite of tolerable errors, posterity will judge more justly the man who dares to meet the truth freely, than it will those who are afraid of shipwreck on the rocks or sandbars and prefer to drop anchor permanently in some safe cove.[8]

Schelling's philosophy attempts to eradicate "superficial understanding[s]," and Schelling critically dismisses the untrained minds, "[who] stirred up [by] their weak imagination" attempt to wander on this path unprepared.[9] Schelling's "desertion" of identity philosophy might have produced a "folly," but he is desperately trying to avoid "dropping the anchor permanently in some safe cove." Schelling obviously felt identity philosophy had failed, and he says of those too afraid to "follow the truth to its fullest height":

"*Rühre nicht, Bock! denn es brennt.*"[10]

Abandoning Fichte and absolute identity

Schelling's early work was heavily marked by the influence of Fichte's *Wissenschaftslehre* (1794). At this early stage, Schelling followed Fichte's methodology, used his vocabulary, and agreed with many of his conclusions.[11] However, Schelling did take some decisive steps to break away from Fichte. Schelling developed his *Naturphilosophie* between 1797 and 1799.[12] Schelling, like his Romantic contemporaries, believed that nature was more than just something "out there" in the world. There was more to nature than simply "a set of physical materials with diverse properties."[13] Schelling contended that nature ought to be construed as a "general medium for existence through which metaphysical, scientific, moral and spiritual questions could be explored."[14] By 1799, Schelling began to argue that natural philosophy and transcendental philosophy were of equal importance, claiming that each is separate from the other yet each rendering a different perspective on one singular reality.[15] Both transcendental and natural philosophy say something distinct about reality. They both have perspectives on "the activity of reason or intelligence."[16]

Schelling's grand intention was that his *Naturphilosophie* would be the counterpart to Fichte's *Wissenschaftslehre*, where *Naturphilosophie* would be able to treat nature as an autonomous realm. *Naturphilosophie* would have the exact same capacity to consider his "object as the absolute" as the transcendental philosopher of Fichte's *Wissenschaftslehre*.[17]

Schelling's conception of nature was born out of a belief that the thinking subject is not opposed to nature, but instead that "the subject is itself part of nature."[18] This idea emerged from Schelling's growing desire to disavow Kantian dualism. For Schelling, Fichte was wrong to have furnished natural phenomena with mechanistic explanations – rather, nature is self-determining and Schelling wanted to "extend naturalism to the Fichtean ego."[19] Indeed, much of Schelling's work was trying to "step beyond the Kantian limit," a move away from critical philosophy in a direction which embraced metaphysics.[20]

The duality that Schelling disavowed was one with which Kant himself, in his later philosophy, would begin to be dissatisfied and would try to bridge.[21] Kant's later philosophy sought to "bridge the gap between the metaphysical principles of natural science and empirical physics"[22] – using what Kant saw as the mediating principles of matter: cohesion, solidification, electric magnetism and chemical affinity. These mediating concepts, Kant claimed, resolved the "impossible" reconciliation between metaphysics and the natural sciences.[23] This is because these mediating principles, Kant believed, "are both a priori and a posteriori."[24] It is in this tradition, of resolving the antinomy of metaphysics and the natural sciences, that Schelling attempts to extrapolate an *a priori* subjective structuring of reality beyond the abstract and tries to push it into the natural sciences. This involved much empirical research on Schelling's part, gathering data on, for example, Lavoisier's and Priestley's investigations.[25] Schelling tried to "equate these results with his own transcendental deductions of the principles inherent in nature."[26] The intuition that there are "principles inherent in nature" in the first instance is born out of Schelling's Spinozistic turn – the return to the idea that "there must be something that exists unconditionally or absolutely."[27] Schelling specifically says: "in spite of all its errors, Spinoza's system seems to me more worthy of high esteem."[28]

In his *Presentation of My System of Philosophy* (1801),[29] Schelling again rails against Fichte. Schelling rejects Fichte's claim that the subject/object dichotomy, itself, had to be either subjective or objective. This is the idea that because we are grasping this whole (subject /object) from only one angle – in Fichte it is from the *Absolute-I* (the angle of subjectivity) – the dichotomy is therefore inescapable. Instead, Schelling's gambit was that the dichotomy was governed by something else; an absolute indifference point in which there is an absolute indifference of objectivity and subjectivity.[30] Schelling says, "this higher thing itself can be neither subject nor object, nor both at once but only the *absolute identity*."[31] Subjectivity and objectivity are, for Schelling, one and the same – but at a point which is neither subjective nor objective.[32] It is a combination of both/and and either/or. Schelling argues this by analogy to try and convince us that we can intuit an "absolute indifference point." Schelling posits that, for example, on a rectangular magnet, where one pole is positive and the other is negative, there must be a point in the middle where there is an indifference between positivity and negativity.[33] Similarly, Schelling uses this to try and persuade us that we must suppose that, in a sense, there can be a state of neither objectivity nor subjectivity.[34]

Governing Schelling's attempt to extrapolate an *a priori* subjective structuring of reality in his *Naturphilosophie* was also an attempt to reconcile his post-Kantian research with "Fichte's idea of nature as ultimately a construct of the human subject."[35] Simply put, Schelling's basic question is, "how must nature be thought, such that its appearing in products and processes can become comprehensible?"[36] Schelling believed that to answer this question, the bedrock of idealism had to be shifted from human reason to the "reciprocal relation between nature and subjectivity."[37] Schelling explains this in *Ideas for a Philosophy of Nature* as "Nature should be Mind made visible, Mind the invisible Nature. Here then, in the absolute identity of Mind *in us* and Nature *outside us*, the problem of the possibility of a Nature external to us must be resolved."[38] The basic insight here, and indeed the main idea from Schelling's *Naturphilosophie*, is that the structure of mind (*Geist*) is not absolutely separate to the structure of nature[39] – "the system of nature is at the same time the system of our mind."[40] This is where Schelling makes his "radical break with the Cartesian heritage,"[41] towards identity. Indeed, Schelling, Beiser argues, realized that epistemology, far from having a "presuppositionless" first principle, "had some dubious presuppositions" for itself.[42] The only starting point, for Schelling, ought to be nature in the first instance – i.e. "the universe as a whole – as opposed to beginning with Fichte's *I* – self-consciousness."[43]

Schelling moved away from Fichte's *I* in favor of a turn towards nature to allow "the terms in which individuality, freedom and certainty [are to] be thought."[44] Schelling's shift in focus from subject to nature does not now mean that we are unable to theorize the self – the self just needs to be theorized from within nature.[45] It should be noted that the subject is not raised to "a dangerous skepticism about its foundations [. . .] nor is it to become a passive reflector of external forms."[46] Rather, Schelling's ideas on nature are to be inserted "between the insupportable outside and inside."[47] It is to fill the gap where originally there had been nothing. The space in-between *things-in-themselves* and *things-for-themselves*, so Schelling says:

> One has, indeed, an idea even of nothing; one thinks of it at least as the absolute void, as something purely formal, and so on. One might think that the idea of things-in-themselves were a similar notion. But the idea of nothing can, after all, still be made palpable through the schema of empty space. Things-in-themselves, however, are expressly excluded from space and time, for the latter belong, of course, only to the peculiar form of representation of finite beings. So nothing is left but an idea

which floats midway between something and nothing, i.e., which does not even have the virtue of being absolutely nothing.[48]

This gap, that nature has filled in Schelling's construction, is the foundation for the nature of human identity – which he postulates in a move to grasp, in poetic terms, the "soul" of "freedom."[49]

Schelling proceeds in terms of *finitude* and *infinitude* in his *Naturphilosophie*, where nature should not be thought of as a series of causal chains. Instead, borrowing from Fichte's dialectic, progress is sought from the generative tension of polar nodes – *finitude /infinitude* or *the determined /the free*.[50] Schelling's dialectical process, that which makes up his system, is the *self* returning from "limitation to its original freedom and for the first time becomes for itself [. . .] what it already was in itself, namely pure freedom or activity."[51] In effect, by coming to what's real in consciousness, the subject of experience "is raised to the standpoint of philosophizing consciousness and the two coincide."[52] Therefore, for Schelling, nature has its own productivity through its own polarization. In nature, this polarity is typified by "gravitational force" on one end and what Schelling called "light essence" at the other end. The closer to the middle one gets, the closer one gets to the "more complex forms of objectivity."[53] Objectivity is characterized by the correlative features of unconsciousness, necessity and everything that represents the material world. Behind Schelling's elaborate construction is the simple idea that any and every entity in nature exists somewhere on the scale. The closer one gets to the middle, the closer one gets to accessing a new synthesis "and the stabilization of new forms of existence."[54] This is important to Schelling's system because at the absolute middle of the polarity "is the ultimate synthesis of freedom and necessity in an organism that is not only living, but self-reflecting – that is, human individuality."[55] Schelling's elaborate construction places humanity as independent of nature's determination (as one separate gradation), therefore, with the resultant effect of maintaining the possibility of freedom. However, this "resistance to determinate structures produces a paradoxical situation in which the ultimate nature of freedom remains suspended."[56] In a sense, freedom may not be constrained by the shackles of a system, but neither is it fully understood or appreciated, and there remains a fundamental problem with Schelling's account. While Schelling's identity philosophy has managed to preserve some minimal sense of real freedom, he nevertheless finds himself in a state of suspension. And it is this dissatisfaction, which I will further explain in the next section, that will lead Schelling to completely abandon identity philosophy.

Schelling's deadlock: abandoning identity

By 1804, Schelling viewed his earlier identity philosophy as a complete failure; it had failed to either establish or elucidate a real form of the principle of freedom. Of course, this is a hasty reduction since the failure to establish such a principle is in fact one effect, Schelling argues, of the original failure to establish the origin of the finite from the Absolute. "There can be no continuous passage," he tells us, "into the exact opposite, the absolute privation of all ideality, nor can the finite arise from the infinite by decrements."[57] This abstraction is necessary to grasp the core of the problem; for Schelling there might be a God, but how does the world come into existence? How can we comprehend the origin of the finite from the Absolute? This is the question that Schelling struggles to solve within the identity philosophy schema. It is also one aspect of a tripartite problem; the other two associated problems are that of human freedom and the problem of evil. Schelling attempts (and fails) to resolve these questions in the *Ages of the World* [henceforth *Weltalter*]. In this ambitious text, Schelling attempts to build a philosophical account of the nature of time and creation.[58] As Judith Norman notes, Schelling's three drafts of *Weltalter* are all fragmentary: "Schelling barely got further than book I, which treated the first 'age of the world,' the past. [And] he would eventually abandon the project."[59] This historical context exemplifies the hesitant nature of Schelling's endeavor. Indeed, as Jean-François Marquet put it in *Liberté et Existence, Études sur la formation de la philosophie de Schelling*, "the story of the *Ages of the World* is that of an unknown masterpiece – the story of enthusiasm, despair and sacrifice."[60] Schelling's task was to inaugurate a philosophical revolution which would in turn provoke a theological revolution, as Marquet argues:

> Schelling contended that a revolution in philosophy was merely a prelude to a revolution in Religion [. . .] his ambition remained the same – to overcome the unilateral vocabulary of philosophy and translate the truth into a popularized language; the only place where it could be really itself. An immemorial language which belongs to no-one.[61]

This explains why Schelling's language beyond 1809 becomes increasingly theosophical, as he employs "the only eternal language, the 'language of the people,' the biblical language of God."[62] However, Schelling only arrives at this point because of the failure of his earlier idealism, as outlined above. Why did Schelling decide on this theological direction?

Schelling's identity philosophy had only managed to elucidate a "principle" of freedom that relied on unstable foundations.[63] In *Schelling's Treatise on the Essence of Human Freedom*, Martin Heidegger explains Schelling's dissatisfaction with identity philosophy. For Schelling, a "system is the totality of Being in the totality of its truth and the history of the truth," yet the problem with such a system is that if freedom means the ability to break loose from any systematization, characterized by its intrinsic malleability, how can freedom be accounted for from within the very confines of a system?[64] Heidegger explains: if "freedom, [. . .] is groundless and breaks out of every connection, [how could it be] the center of [a] system?"[65] Therefore, Schelling's major dilemma with identity philosophy is that "a system of freedom appears to be impossible from both sides." Heidegger says, "there are two fundamental difficulties: (1) either 'system' is retained, then freedom must be relinquished; or (2) freedom is retained, which means renunciation of 'system'."[66] Schelling's motivation is to achieve a type of real freedom unbound by the confines of a system, and yet to ensure that it is not devoid of content. This is a task on which "[Schelling] is ready to stake everything."[67]

The deadlock Schelling confronts in his quest for human freedom is also tied to the problem of evil. For Schelling, real freedom is the kind of freedom that is exercised in moral choices; and if human beings are to have real freedom, it must also be that evil has reality. Schelling's gambit is that unless evil has reality, there is nothing sincere to choose between, and freedom becomes meaningless. Schelling thinks that a morally significant choice between alternatives means that there need to be at least two choices, Good and Evil. This deadlock of identity philosophy dominates Schelling's thought, and these three aspects are all, essentially, part of the same problem, which for Schelling is insoluble from within idealism.

To formulate a novel system, Schelling begins by setting himself the task of explaining the *origins* of the world; he argues that a historicization of "the beginning" would resolve all three problems. In *Philosophy and Religion*, Schelling follows Christian doctrine by arguing that since God (the Absolute) has created the world in his image, the image that he has created, what Schelling calls the *Gegenbild*, becomes a kind of counter-image of the Absolute itself. The implication is that the Absolute must share its Absolute freedom with something that is not itself – the *Gegenbild*, or counter-image. Therefore, there is a split at the heart of the Absolute:

> The exclusive particularity of the Absolute lies in the fact that when it *bestows its essentiality upon its counter-image* [*Gegenbild*], it also *bestows upon it its self-dependence*. This being-in-and-for-itself, this particular and true reality of the first-intuited, is *freedom*, and from that first self-dependence outflows what in the phenomenal world appears as freedom, which represents the last trace and the seal [*Siegel*], as it were, of divinity in the fallen-away world.[68]

Yet the underlying problem arises when God, who now wants to check the *Gegenbild*, finds that he can only do so from the position of the counter-image itself – the view that he desires needs to be immanent to the image. And so, in a flash, God *falls* from himself – he falls from the seat of the Absolute, into the abyss of the counter-image. Whereas previously Schelling had thought of all finite things in the world as remaining within God, suddenly the world, in becoming conscious of itself as something distinct from the absolute, falls from God:

> The counter-image, as an absolute entity and having all its attributes in common with the originary (*sic*) image, would not truly be in itself and

> absolute if it could not grasp itself in its selfhood [*selbstheit*], in order to have true being as the *other* absolute. But it cannot be as the *other* absolute unless it separates itself or falls away from the true Absolute.[69]

This is what Schelling means when he speaks of the split at the heart of the Absolute – in Schellingian terms; the need to separate *ground* from *existence*. Furthermore, there is a clear echo of the story of *The Fall*; God created Adam and Eve, and, somehow, they remained *within* him. However, since God must invest them with his own freedom, they are able to re-exercise their freedom to think of themselves as apart from God, to separate themselves from God. In Schelling's metaphysical construal of the *Fall of Man*, this is the condition in which the world remains. The created world has thought itself apart from God and has therefore fallen from God.

Contraction of Being

The fall of man from the clutches of God's care is, of course, to be understood as an originary catastrophe. Indeed, Schelling consistently used the word "contraction" to describe the split between ground and existence. Žižek explains that for Schelling, God *contracts* Being:

> God unavoidably, of blind necessity that characterizes the workings of fate, "contracts" Being, that is, a firm, impenetrable Ground. (Schelling, of course, plays upon the double meaning of the term *contraction:* to tighten-compress-condense *and* to catch, to be afflicted with, to go down with [an illness]; the primordial Freedom "contracts" Being as a painful burden that ties it down).[70]

Schelling suggests that Being is a sickness to be *contracted* – our human condition truly governed by a *condition*.[71] The ultimate account of the human subject is ominous, something must have "gone wrong" here – ontologically – at the very heart of being itself. It is evident that Schelling has clearly delineated himself from his earlier identity philosophy, and he revises his philosophy to argue that "the ultimate goal of the universe and its history is nothing other than the complete reconciliation [*Versohnung*] with and reabsorption [*Wiederaufladung*] into the Absolute."[72] This reconciliation should be understood as the condition for our redemption, the cure for our *condition/ sickness*. Schelling's wholesale re-articulation of philosophy is a clear deviation from standard rationalistic monism that, until 1801, he had thought possible.

On Schelling's account, the primordial wound is that God himself is irremediably lost to himself; he has fallen from the seat of the Absolute. Being able to comprehend the Absolute would mean going back to square one, in a sense, being lost once again, this time *as* God himself. God is nothing but a broken vessel. Here Schelling takes a speculative leap into attempting to think "pre-ontologically," and while this leap seems paradoxical and even nonsensical, his attempt results in a profoundly original set of metaphysical reflections. At the same time, this speculative leap also aims in the direction of the theological. Schelling's account is the radical disorientation of the human subject which can be thought *in* God himself. God is apprehensive, radically dis-unified, uncertain of himself and of his own act of Creation. Condemned to *his* absolute freedom, God is alienated, afraid and without excuse. Schelling's positioning of God yields an intrinsically pessimistic view of God as the original subject who is properly dethroned.

Accounting for God in this way is, no doubt, unfashionable to our contemporary intuitions, perhaps even objectionable to our atheistic sensibilities. However, for Schelling, these are not simply difficult philosophical problems that we are attempting to resolve, nor are they detours to entertain the human mind. These problems amount to the tension of irremediable non-self-coincidence of our subjectivity, the very schism found at the heart of God himself, which for Schelling is to be taken as a microcosm of our human condition. The "soul" is a serious concern, and it is precisely what is at stake. Schelling says in the second draft of his *Weltalter*:

> Man must be granted an essence outside and above the world; for how could he alone, of all creatures, retrace the long path of development from the present back into the deepest night of the past, how could he alone rise up to the beginning of things unless there were in him an essence from the beginning of times?[73]

Schelling further expands on why his task of elucidating the beginning of time, of the universe, is so crucial. It is, in a sense, the metaphysical goal which, if resolved, will alleviate the burden of our human condition – Man will be redeemed from the catastrophe of *The Fall*. With the characteristic drama of the German Romantic period, the freedom text – *Weltalter* – is constructed in accordance with tragic speech. Schelling urges a return to "the deepest night," abandoning the reason and rationalism of the Enlightenment. Yet this seemingly doomed act of probing the darkness is not as reactionary as it may appear – for Schelling's work develops in unexpected ways. For a brief moment there is an opening, and it is this glimpse of our dethroned God that makes Schelling important for Žižek's theological writings. As we will see, Schelling's conclusions open a gap that Žižek will exploit and develop in a direction that Schelling felt was too radical.

The beginning of the beginning

Schelling argued that by virtue of his essence, Man is privy to a glimpse of the origins of the world. However, Schelling deems this to be "the unfathomable."[74] Schelling says, the "prehistoric age rests in this essence; although it faithfully protects the treasures of the holy past, this essence is in itself *mute* and cannot express what is enclosed within it."[75] Thus we arrive at

"Rühre nicht, Bock! denn es brennt" 177

an impasse – we possess a vague knowledge of these treasures, but without being able to access their inner core. The entirety of knowledge, science and history, for Schelling, amounts to a success only because it allows us to unravel the "facts" about available "data." For Schelling, we are only able to describe the empirical world: "the history of nature has its monuments," which are "thoroughly researched, in part genuinely deciphered and yet they tell us nothing but rather remain dead,"[76] until such a time that we can think the inner core of the thing, the primordial "something to know," by which Schelling means the moment of creation, or the "holy past." Therefore, to explain the unfathomable Past, Schelling begins a discussion of time by arguing against its received linear understanding. Past is not, for Schelling, a linear succession of "presents"; "most know only of that [past] which grows within each moment through precisely that moment, and which is itself only becoming, not being."[77] Yet, when Schelling talks about the "Past," he means something closer to what we might describe as the Biblical past:

> Thus, everything remains incomprehensible to man until it has become inward for him; that is, until it has been led back to precisely that innermost [aspect] *(sic)* of his essence which for him the living witness of all truth.[78]

And so, for Schelling, to think this Past is to make great metaphysical inroads in philosophy. It is possible to think of the historical Past in this way: "these lofty representations might protect him [Schelling referring to himself as philosopher] from the belabored concepts of a sterile and dispirited dialectic."[79] It is to accept that "our knowledge is incomplete, that is, it must be produced piecemeal in sections and degrees."[80] Schelling is keen to ascribe modesty to these reflections, and to the achievability of the task at hand, first to think the "infinite manifold [that] is ultimately produced from the greatest simplicity of essence," man "must experience it in himself,"[81] yet Schelling knows this to be an extremely taxing task:

> But all experiencing, feeling and intuiting is in and of itself mute and requires a mediating organ to gain expression. If the intuiter [sic] does not have this, or if he intentionally pushes it away from himself so that he might speak immediately from his intuition, he thereby loses the measure necessary to him: he is one with the object and, to a third [party] [sic], like the object itself. For this reason, *he is not master of his thoughts; he is caught in a futile struggle, expressing without any certainty what is nonetheless inexpressible*; he encounters what he might, though without being sure of it, without being able to place it securely before him and, as it were, to reinspect it in the understanding as if in the mirror.[82]

Schelling's first decisive insight here is that the subject is "not master of his thoughts," and "he is caught in a futile struggle." So, Schelling says, to understand the Past, we must posit the unconscious grounds of the beginning, "unconscious presence [*bewußtlosen Daseyn*] of the eternal, science leads it up to the supreme transfiguration in a divine consciousness."[83] Ominously, Schelling adds, "this is still a time of struggle."[84] The general process is one of radical re-orientation, thus, with typical grandeur, Schelling announces that:

> The man who cannot separate himself from himself, who cannot break loose from everything that happens to him and actively oppose it – such a man has no past, or more likely he never emerges from it, but lives in it continually.[85]

Schelling's insight is clear; he simply asks for us to follow him in suspending the Present as constitutive in representing anything other than the appearance of day-to-day empirical reality – what we earlier called "data." Instead, Schelling's maneuver is that we must try and separate ourselves from ourselves, draw closer to our divine essence, and try to think the historical Past. This is already a radical subversion of philosophy as it stood in the early nineteenth century; Schelling is demanding from us a wholesale reconceptualization of philosophy and time, to re-orient ourselves towards a theosophy. This new conception of "the Past," for Schelling, is "what came before the world,"[86] and the evidence of this historical Past exists all around us. According to Schelling, if we are to understand the origins of the world, our historical Past, we must first posit the birth of the world, the oldest marks of the age of the world, as something which is unknown to us. Schelling refers to these unknown origins as "unconscious." Schelling exemplifies this by asking how it is that we can understand the oldest geological formations, which must have their birth before humanity, without first positing them as an unknown event, an "unconscious" beginning of the world?[87] In Žižek's essay on Schelling, *The Abyss of Freedom*, he explains this as: "Schelling's fundamental thesis is that, to put it bluntly, *the true Beginning is not at the beginning:* there is something that precedes the Beginning itself."[88] This intuition leads Schelling to proclaim that there exists a primordial "something to know," of which we obviously have an inkling, and that our task is to try and elaborate. However, this primordial thought is only to be contemplated via the Absolute. It is God who must learn to come to terms with himself and his origins. It is important to clearly state at this point that Schelling is clearly not advocating a God who is his own ground – *ens causa sui*. Schelling says: "nothing could live in this state, created things would be impossible, and the concept of a being of beings would be lost. This force of self-ness or individuality in God is captured in that barbaric term *aseity*."[89]

Schelling argues that to understand the Absolute Past we need to appreciate that time itself is constituted by two motions, one which propels time forwards, the other a slowing mechanism that attempts to prevent it from going too fast. "Whoever takes time only as it presents itself feels a conflict of two principles in it; one strives forwards, driving towards development, and one holds back, inhibiting [*hemmend*] [*sic*] and striving against development."[90] This is important for Schelling, since if this inhibiting element did not exist, then time would take place in an "uninterrupted flash."[91] And, if the inhibiting element were to exercise itself too much, then the world would be at total rest, and there would be only stillness. Therefore, it is in the dynamic interplay of the continual conflict between the two elements that allows for time to be characterized as it appears to us.[92] Crucially, this insight, adduced through time, is quickly enlisted to explain being; Schelling now argues that "it is necessary to conceive of these principles in everything that is – indeed, in being."[93] This idea, then, distilled from the speculation of time, has very clear bearings on our human subjectivity. The conflict at the heart of being, the conflicting relationship between the two incommunicable regions – *ground* and *existence* – is in Schelling's *Weltalter* the "original conflict of principles within being, which generates conscious subjectivity, and in so doing transposes itself into the relation of subject to world."[94]

The implications of Schelling's split in Being, combined with his tortuous struggle with theism and theosophy, become clearer when we consider the context of the *Weltalter*. Schelling's second draft, the one under consideration here, is characterized by its unfinished appearance. Indeed, roughly three-quarters into this draft, this editor's note appears: "according to the German editor, the printed manuscript ends here, and the rest of page 109 remains blank."[95] However, in the original manuscript the pages following this note form part of the rest of the second draft; these extra pages were discovered much later in the Munich University library and were almost destroyed by Allied bombings. The extra pages were published after the war.[96] Until 1946, the only known draft to exist of the *Weltalter* was Schelling's third draft, but it is in the final quarter of this second draft that Schelling makes some of his most audacious claims. The momentum of these ideas would lead Schelling to where he so clearly did not want to go and compel him to scribble in a marginal note towards the end: "the treatise falls into utter falsehoods *from this point forward*," and crossed out two pages.[97] It is the story of deep failure for Schelling: "the story of enthusiasm, despair and sacrifice."[98]

Is God hiding or lying?

Schelling's tempestuous uncertainty is instructive, and it is precisely what informs Žižek's view of Christianity and God. Žižek argues that we should historicize God in the same spirit as Schelling's failed attempt in *Weltalter*. Yet, whereas Schelling saw his conclusions as heading towards an unimaginable tragedy that, in effect, would end up blaming God for the world's many failures; Žižek sees Schelling's tragedy as an opportunity. Žižek's God is one that demonstrates the "destructive aspect of the divine, the brutal explosion of rage mixed with ecstatic bliss," the same God that "Lacan aims at with his statement that gods belong to the Real."[99] For Žižek, "this living god continues his subterranean life and erratically returns in multiple forms that are all guises of the monstrous Thing."[100]

In *Disparities*, Žižek accounts for this counterfactual God, the Real, that Lacan argues could be based on a lie. Žižek modifies Lacan's motif "*la vérité surgit de la meprise*" to "the truth that arises out of a lie."[101] The truth of God is an incomplete truth that is not governed by the totality of a universal. For Lacan, the gap is primary, at the ontological level, of being itself in relation to the transcendental logic of the phallic function. These insights, that Lacan developed more seriously in *Seminar XX*, find their origin in *Seminar III*. In *Seminar III* Lacan focuses on God and his potential deceit, starting with Descartes' *Fourth Meditation*. Descartes' theory considers that while human doubt renders ideas both incomplete and dependent, at the very least, we may form an idea of a clear, distinct God and conclude that he exists absolutely. We can know with certainty that God guarantees our existence. Descartes says:

> And when I consider the fact that I have doubts, or that I am a thing that is incomplete and dependent, then there arises in me a clear and distinct idea of a being who is independent and complete, that is, an idea of God. And from the mere fact that there is such an idea within me, or that I who possess this idea exist, I clearly infer that God also exists, and that every single moment of my entire existence depends on him.[102]

Descartes further argues that this God is not duplicitous, nor is he deceitful. God maintains the world as empirically stable; Descartes elaborates:

> To begin with, I recognize that it is impossible that God should ever deceive me. For in every case of trickery or deception some imperfection is to be found; and although the ability to deceive me appears to be an indication of cleverness or power, the will to deceive is undoubtably evidence of malice or weakness, and so cannot apply to God.[103]

Descartes argues that although God might have the ability to deceive us, he does not do so because, logically, a benevolent God would never do such a thing. Lacan questions this Cartesian logic, arguing that nothing protects us from God's potential malice. The key insight from Žižek, via Lacan and Schelling, is to historicize this God and to question the sincerity that Descartes attributed to him.

In *Seminar III*, Lacan makes a (very) rudimentary case for the logic of the "*non rapport sexuel*" and a corollary argument for the deceptiveness of the Big Other. There is, Lacan says, in the triad of the Real, Symbolic and Imaginary (RSI), "the basic condition of any relationship."[104] Lacan argues that the RSI reflect the registers of the subject, speech and order of alterity of the Other. "Vertically, there is the register of the subject, speech and the order of otherness as such, the Other."[105] The pivotal point of the function

"Rühre nicht, Bock! denn es brennt" 181

of speech is the subjectivity of the Other, who is capable of lying: "the hub of the function of speech is the subjectivity of the Other, that is to say, the fact that the Other is essentially he who is capable, like the subject, of convincing and lying."[106] Yet, the Cartesian wager is that there must be a non-deceptive core of reality at the heart of the Big Other. "The dialectical correlate of the basic structure which makes of the speech of subject to subject speech that may deceive is that there is also something that does not deceive."[107] Indeed, modern science has done much to demonstrate the repeatability and therefore perceived stability of the world,

> the notion that the real, as difficult as it may be to penetrate, is unable to play tricks on us and will not take us in on purpose, is, though no one really dwells on this, essential to the constitution of the world of science.[108]

But Lacan reminds us that the core of the Real is always already a function of speech and there is absolutely nothing that guarantees the original step of all scientific investigations as anything other than an act of faith – God maintaining the world as empirically stable:

> We have in fact never observed anything that would show us a deceiving demon at the heart of nature. But that does not prevent its being a necessary article of faith for the first steps of science and the constitution of experimental science. It need hardly be said that matter does not cheat, that it has no intention of crushing our experiments or blowing up our machines. This sometimes happens, but only when we have made a mistake. It's out of the question that it, matter, should deceive us. This step is not at all obvious. Nothing less than the Judaeo-Christian tradition was required for it to be taken with such assurance.[109]

Lacan does not share the certainty found in Descartes' *Fourth Meditation*. Lacan sees God as a potentially pernicious *in-itself* who forces the world to react maliciously and could manipulate the order of things to render our world duplicitous. For Lacan, every empirical development in modern science rests on that "little piece of the real" that we know nothing about, onto which we project stability and permanence; the phenomenological approach of "taking things as they are" is invalid, according to Lacan. Recall the opening lines of *Being and Nothingness*: "modern thought has realized considerable progress by reducing the existent to the series of appearances which manifest it."[110] Yet, Sartre's view does not take into account that there is always already the possibility of a deceptive God who is playing with the "apparitions" which manifest in the world. This is Žižek's theological approach, too. Žižek argues in *Some Thoughts on the Divine Ex-sistence*:

> How do we pass from the living gods of the Real to this dead god of the Word? The only consequent move is to make a step further from

describing historical changes in how we think about god and to historicize god himself. This idea was too strong for Schelling himself who introduced it: the key shift from the *Ages of the World* to late Schelling's philosophy of mythology and revelation is that the *Ages of the World* thoroughly historicizes God (the process of creation and revelation is a process into which God himself is caught, the becoming of the world is the becoming of God himself, his self-creation and self-revelation, so that the human awareness of god is the self-awareness of God himself).[111]

It is this radical idea that was too strong for Schelling himself that Žižek develops through Lacan. For Žižek, God himself is caught up in the division inaugurated with the catastrophe of *The Fall*,

> which proceeds in three steps, and the separation of the Son from the Father is only the last step in this process. First, God sets free his lowest potency, the egotist principle of contraction, what in God is not God, thereby creating matter as something actually existing outside Himself.[112]

Schelling ultimately gives up on this idea, because how can God have made such a great error? "Creation takes a wrong turn not intended by God, the created world becomes the fallen world of decay and sorrow, nature impregnated by melancholy."[113] Žižek paints the picture of a "homeless god wandering anonymously exiled from eternity and condemned to wander anonymously in his creation."[114] For Žižek, "Schelling's achievement is to show how the Christian Incarnation can be understood only against the background of this splitting."[115] The imperfection of God, and subsequent imperfection of man as an image of God, is Žižek's aim:

> The nature of this imperfection was indicated in the most radical reading of the "Book of Job" proposed in 1930s by the Norwegian theologist Peter Wessel Zapffe, who accentuated Job's "boundless perplexity" when God himself finally appears to him: expecting a sacred and pure God whose intellect is [. . .] infinitely superior to ours, Job: "finds himself confronted with a world ruler of grotesque primitiveness, a cosmic cave-dweller, a braggart and blusterer, almost agreeable in his total ignorance of spiritual culture./. . ./What is new for Job is *not* God's greatness in quantifiable terms; that he knew fully in advance/. . ./; what is new is the qualitative baseness."
>
> In other words, God – the God of the real – is like the Lady in courtly love, it is *das Ding*, a capricious cruel master who simply has no sense of universal justice. God-the-Father, thus, quite literally doesn't know what he is doing. [. . .] Only by falling into his own creation and wandering around in it as an impassive observer can God perceive the horror of his creation and the fact that the he, the highest Law-giver, is

himself the supreme Criminal. [. . .] in the core of Christianity, we find a different vision – the demiurge elevated above reality is a brute unaware of the horror he is creating, and only when he enters his own creation and experiences it from within, as its inhabitant, can he see the nightmare he fathered.[116]

The elaborate tragic division that Schelling ascribes to God ultimately allows Žižek to see in Christianity a God who is ultimately stupid and evil, "all powerful but stained by the indelible suspicion of being stupid, arbitrary, or even outright evil."[117] This is the conclusion that Schelling's piety had forced him to resist. Yet, Žižek could respond to Schelling's hesitation:

"*Rühre nicht, Bock! denn es brennt.*"

Notes

1. "Don't move, goat! Or you'll get burned." F. W. J. Schelling, *Philosophy and Religion* (1804), trans. Klaus Ottmann (Putnam, CT: Spring Publications, 2010), 5.
2. Schelling, *Philosophy and Religion*.
3. Ibid., 4.
4. Heinrich Heine, *Religion and Philosophy in Germany*, trans. John Snodgrass (Boston, MA: Beacon Press, 1959), 153.
5. We must partially credit Žižek for the renewed contemporary interest in Schelling among Anglo-American academics.
6. Slavoj Žižek, *The Parallax View* (Cambridge, MA: MIT Press, 2006), 22.
7. Ibid.
8. F. W. J. Schelling, *The Unconditional in Human Knowledge: Four Early Essays (1794–1796)*, trans. Fritz Marti (Putnam, Connecticut: Associated University Presses, Inc., 1980), 64.
9. Schelling, *Philosophy and Religion*, 4.
10. F. W. J. Schelling, Philosophy and Religion (1804), trans. Klaus Ottmann (Putnam, CT: Spring Publications, 2010), 5.
11. Frederick Beiser, *German Idealism: The Struggle against Subjectivism 1781–1801* (Cambridge, MA: Harvard University Press, 2008), 471–2.
12. Beiser, *Idealism*, 483–4.
13. Matt Ffytche, *The Foundation of the Unconscious: Schelling Freud and the Birth of the Modern Psyche* (Cambridge: Cambridge University Press, 2011), 78.
14. Ibid.
15. Beiser, *Idealism*, 487.
16. Ibid.
17. Ibid.
18. Andrew Bowie, *Schelling and Modern European Philosophy: An Introduction* (London & New York: Routledge, 1993), 31.
19. Beiser, *Idealism*, 487.
20. Jean-François Courtine, "Schelling," in *Blackwell Companions to Philosophy: A Companion to Continental Philosophy*, ed. Simon Critchley and William R. Schroeder (Malden, MA & Oxford: Blackwell Publishers, 1999), 83.
21. Bowie, *Schelling*, 31.
22. Beiser, *Idealism*, 185–6.
23. Ibid., 185.
24. Ibid.

184 *Sinan Richards*

25 Ffytche, *Foundation*, 79.
26 Ibid.
27 Will Dudley, *Understanding German Idealism* (Stocksfield: Acumen, 2008), 110.
28 Schelling, *Unconditional*, 64.
29 Translated by Michael Vater, "F. W. J. Schelling: Presentation of My System of Philosophy (1801)," *The Philosophical Forum* 32, no. 4 (December 2001): 339–71.
30 Terry Pinkard, *German Philosophy 1760–1860: The Legacy of Idealism* (Cambridge: Cambridge University Press, 2002), 175.
31 F. W. J. Schelling, *System of Transcendental Idealism (1800)*, trans. Peter Heath (Charlottesville, VA: University of Virginia Press, 1978), 209.
32 Ibid.
33 Ibid., 86–7.
34 Ibid., 209.
35 Ffytche, *Foundation*, 79.
36 Reinhardt Löw, "Das philosophische Problem der 'Natur an sich'," *Philosophisches Jahrbuch* 97 (1990), quoted in Bowie, *Schelling*, 34.
37 Ffytche, *Foundation*, 79.
38 F. W. J. Schelling, *Ideas for a Philosophy of Nature as Introduction to the Study of This Science (1797)*, trans. Errol E. Harris and Peter Heath (Cambridge: Cambridge University Press, 1988), 42.
39 Bowie, *Schelling*, 38.
40 Schelling, *Ideas*, 30.
41 Beiser, *Idealism*, 471.
42 Ibid.
43 Ibid.
44 Ffytche, *Foundation*, 82.
45 Ibid.
46 Ibid.
47 Ibid., 82–3.
48 Schelling, *Ideas*, 25.
49 Ffytche, *Foundation*, 83.
50 Ibid., 84.
51 Michael Vater, "Introduction," in F. W. J. Schelling, *System of Transcendental Idealism (1800)* (Charlottesville, VA: University of Virginia Press, 1978), xiii.
52 Vater, *Introduction*, xiii.
53 Ibid.
54 Ibid.
55 Ibid.
56 Ffytche, *Foundation*, 89.
57 Schelling, *Philosophy and Religion*, 17.
58 F. W. J. Schelling, "Ages of the World," in *The Abyss of Freedom, Ages of the World*, trans. Norman Judith (Ann Arbor: The Michigan University Press, 1997), 107.
59 Ibid.
60 Jean-François Marquet, *Liberté et existence, Études sur la formation de la philosophie de Schelling* (Paris: NRF Éditions Gallimard, 1973), 449. My own translation.
61 Ibid.
62 Ibid., 450. My own translation.
63 Slavoj Žižek, *The Abyss of Freedom* (Ann Arbor: The Michigan University Press, 1997), 3.
64 Martin Heidegger, *Schelling's Treatise on the Essence of Human Freedom*, trans. Joan Stambaugh (Athens, OH: Ohio University Press, 1985), 48.

65 Ibid.
66 Ibid., 49.
67 Žižek, *Abyss*, 3.
68 Schelling, *Philosophy and Religion*, 27–8. My emphasis.
69 Ibid., 28.
70 Žižek, *Abyss*, 16.
71 Marquet, *Liberté*, 541.
72 Schelling, *Philosophy and Religion*, 31.
73 F. W. J. Schelling, *Ages of the World [Weltalter]*, trans. Judith Norman (Ann Arbor: The Michigan University Press, 1997), 114.
74 Ibid.
75 Ibid., 114. My emphasis.
76 Ibid., 116.
77 Ibid., 120.
78 Ibid., 116.
79 Ibid., 117.
80 Ibid.
81 Ibid.
82 Ibid., 117–18. My emphasis.
83 Ibid., 119.
84 Ibid., 120.
85 Ibid.
86 Ibid., 121.
87 Ibid.
88 Žižek, *Abyss*, 14.
89 Schelling, *Weltalter*, 171.
90 Ibid., 123.
91 Ibid.
92 Ibid.
93 Ibid.
94 Sebastian Gardner, "Sartre, Schelling, and Onto-Theology," *Religious Studies* 42, no. 3 (2006): 253.
95 Schelling, *Weltalter*, 167.
96 Žižek, *Abyss*, 3.
97 Schelling, *Weltalter*, 180.
98 Marquet, *Liberté*, 449. My own translation.
99 Slavoj Žižek, "Some Thoughts on the Divine Ex-sistence," *Crisis and Critique* 2, no. 1 (2016): 14.
100 Ibid., 16.
101 Slavoj Žižek, *Disparities* (London: Bloomsbury, 2016), 298.
102 René Descartes, *Descartes Meditations on First Philosophy, with Selections from the Objections and Replies*, trans. John Cottingham (Cambridge: Cambridge University Press, 1996), 37.
103 Descartes, *Meditations*, 37.
104 Jacques Lacan, *The Seminar of Jacques Lacan: Book III: The Psychoses 1955–1956*, trans. Russell Grigg (New York: W.W. Norton & Company, 1997), 64.
105 Ibid.
106 Ibid.
107 Ibid.
108 Ibid.
109 Ibid., 64–5.
110 Jean Paul-Sartre, *Being and Nothingness*, trans. Hazel E. Barnes (London & New York: Routledge, 2003), 1.

111 Žižek, "Thoughts," 22.
112 Ibid., 23.
113 Ibid.
114 Ibid.
115 Ibid.
116 Ibid., 26.
117 Ibid., 27.

Bibliography

Beiser, Frederick. *German Idealism: The Struggle against Subjectivism 1781–1801*. Cambridge, MA: Harvard University Press, 2008.

Bowie, Andrew. *Schelling and Modern European Philosophy: An Introduction*. London & New York: Routledge, 1993.

Courtine, Jean-François. "Schelling." In *Blackwell Companions to Philosophy: A Companion to Continental Philosophy*, edited by Simon Critchley and William R. Schroeder, 83–93. Malden, MA & Oxford: Blackwell Publishers, 1999.

Descartes, René. *Descartes Meditations on First Philosophy, with Selections from the Objections and Replies*. Translated by John Cottingham. Cambridge: Cambridge University Press, 1996.

Dudley, Will. *Understanding German Idealism*. Stocksfield: Acumen, 2008.

Ffytche, Matt. *The Foundation of the Unconscious: Schelling Freud and the Birth of the Modern Psyche*. Cambridge: Cambridge University Press, 2011.

Fichte, Johann Gottlieb and Wilhelm G. Jacobs. *Grundlage der gesamten Wissenschaftslehre: als Handschrift für seine Zuhörer (1794)*. 4. Philosophische Bibliothek 246. Hamburg: Meiner, 1997.

Gardner, Sebastian. "Sartre, Schelling, and Onto-Theology." *Religious Studies* 42, no. 3 (2006): 247–71.

Heidegger, Martin. *Schelling's Treatise on the Essence of Human Freedom*. Translated by Joan Stambaugh. Athens, OH: Ohio University Press, 1985.

Heine, Heinrich. *Religion and Philosophy in Germany*. Translated by John Snodgrass. Boston, MA: Beacon Press, 1959.

Lacan, Jacques. *The Seminar of Jacques Lacan: Book III: The Psychoses 1955–1956*. Translated by Russell Grigg. New York: W.W. Norton & Company, 1997.

Löw, Reinhardt. "Das philosophische Problem der 'Natur an sich'. Anmerkungen zu einem aktuellen naturphilosophischen Problem." *Philosophisches Jahrbuch* 97 (1990): 53–68.

Marquet, Jean-François. *Liberté et existence, Études sur la formation de la philosophie de Schelling*. Paris: NRF Éditions Gallimard, 1973.

Pinkard, Terry. *German Philosophy 1760–1860: The Legacy of Idealism*. Cambridge: Cambridge University Press, 2002.

Sartre, Jean-Paul. *Being and Nothingness*. Translated by Hazel E. Barnes. London & New York: Routledge, 2003.

Schelling, F. W. J. "Ages of the World." Translated by Judith Norman. In *The Abyss of Freedom/Ages of the World*, by Slavoj Zizek and F. W. J. von Schelling. Ann Arbor: The Michigan University Press, 1997.

———. *Ideas for a Philosophy of Nature as Introduction to the Study of This Science (1797)*. Translated by Errol E. Harris and Peter Heath. Cambridge: Cambridge University Press, 1988.

———. *Philosophy and Religion (1804)*. Translated by Klaus Ottmann. Putnam, CT: Spring Publications, 2010.

———. *System of Transcendental Idealism (1800)*. Translated by Peter Heath. Charlottesville, VA: University of Virginia Press, 1978.

———. *The Unconditional in Human Knowledge: Four Early Essays (1794–1796)*. Translated by Fritz Marti. Palinsboro, NJ: Associated University Presses, Inc., 1980.

Vater, Michael, trans. "F.W.J. Schelling: Presentation of My System of Philosophy (1801)." *The Philosophical Forum* 32, no. 4 (December 2001): 339–71.

———. "Introduction." In *System of Transcendental Idealism (1800)*, by F.W.J. Schelling, xi–xxxvii. Charlottesville, VA: University of Virginia Press, 1978.

Žižek, Slavoj. *The Abyss of Freedom*. Ann Arbor: The Michigan University Press, 1997.

———. *Disparities*. London: Bloomsbury, 2016.

———. *The Parallax View*. Cambridge, MA: MIT Press, 2006.

———. "Some Thoughts on the Divine Ex-Sistence." *Crisis and Critique* 2, no. 1 (2016): 13–34.

9 Murder at the vicarage
Žižek's Chesterton as a way out of Christianity

Bruce J. Krajewski

> *Tutti hanno la vaga intuizione che facendo del cattolicismo una norma di vita sbagliano, tanto è vero che nessuno si attiene al cattolicismo come norma di vita, pur dichiarandosi cattolico. Un cattolico integrale, che cioè applicasse in ogni atto della vita le norme cattoliche, sembrerebbe un mostro.*
>
> All people have a vague intuitive feeling that when they make Catholicism a norm of life, they are wrong [*sbagliano*], so much so that nobody adheres to Catholicism in a normative way, even when declaring himself a Catholic. A full Catholic, one, that is, who applied the Catholic norms in every act of life, would seem a monster.
>
> – Antonio Gramsci[1]

> Nor is there ever any suggestion that Father Brown possesses any particular supernatural insights. The reason for this insistence is not just because Chesterton wants all the emphasis to fall upon Father Brown's experience of human nature. At least as important is the idea that Catholicism and Catholic theology are entirely consonant with common sense and reason, while false religions dabble in the mysterious and occult.
>
> – Ian Ker[2]

> "YES," said Father Brown, "I always like a dog, so long as he isn't spelt backwards."
>
> – Father Brown[3]

Slavoj Žižek's political instability with regard to practical politics causes confusion among those who look to his work to further some of the ideals of those dedicated to a communal, global alternative to capitalism, an alternative that would bring about egalitarianism.[4] At one point, Žižek was running for political office, at another writing that Martin Heidegger's Nazi engagement was "the best thing he [Heidegger] did,"[5] and at another point when Žižek had left practical politics to become a "rock star" public speaker he endorsed Donald Trump for president in what some later attributed as a gesture toward a certain brand of accelerationism,[6] the hastening of the end of capitalism by any means. It's Todd McGowan who presents succinctly the difficulty of looking to Žižek for answers: "Those who hold onto the idea of communism, like Alain Badiou and Slavoj Žižek, have no concrete account of what this idea would look like in practice."[7] This "inability to envision the communist future," as McGowan has it, seems linked to Žižek's holding onto another idea that communism, for one, had abandoned – religion, specifically Christianity.

While McGowan paints his position about Žižek in mainly neutral tones, perhaps with a shade of disappointment,[8] Ronald McKinney finds Žižek's lack of engagement with practical politics to be unsurprising, a natural outcome of negative dialectics.

> That neither Žižek's nor Milbank's position seems to offer a particularly concrete and inspired socio-political vision should not surprise us. Negative dialectics is good at seeing what is wrong but not so good at seeing what ought to be done in the real world.[9]

The first section of Gregory Fried's "Where's the Point?" also examines in detail some of Žižek's bizarre shifts in political utterances over the years.[10]

For a collective response to capitalism, one does not need Catholicism, religion in general or an understanding of the psychic dynamics at work with belief. Empirical evidence for this claim is plentiful, one political example being the U.S. Green Party, which has adopted a platform that includes an anti-capitalist statement. The U.S. Green Party is not affiliated with a religious party, nor does it attempt to ground its activities in any psychological account of belief. For Žižek to return continually to issues of belief and religion (and not just any religion) when addressing overtly political issues, especially at a time when the religious right of several religious communities is at war with democracies in Europe and elsewhere, makes it appear as if he is aiding and abetting a regressive enemy. I will label this complicity World War Ž (the "Ž" for Žižek). As in the film to which the phrase alludes, an infection is spreading across the globe that must be undone; in the case of World War Ž, that infection is the symbiotic relationship between religion and war and its various manifestations, including Nietzschean and Heideggerian manifestations. Žižek is complicit in the war[11] and claims Chesterton as an ally in his philosophical war.[12] Žižek is happy to do away with a transcendent God, a figure Žižek labels a "master-mind criminal,"[13] but not with the Holy Spirit, "the spiritual substance of the religious community," according to Žižek, who sees the Holy Spirit as a Hegelian synthesis of Father and Son.[14] Žižek permits himself this move, in part, because he posits that orthodox Christianity has done away with God.[15] It's not clear whether the Holy Spirit retains the characteristic of "master-mind criminal," given homologies among the members of the Trinity.

Žižek's multiple references to G. K. Chesterton's works makes for a dilemma for communists and other Leftists who might wonder about Žižek's apparent deference to Christianity while he simultaneously seeks ways to undermine capitalism and expresses profound concerns about capitalism's *telos*. The universalism Žižek latches on to in Christianity, and admired by people like Milbank, is of a different stripe from the universalism of egalitarianism sought by communists, most of whom would prefer to jettison religion from the picture. One need think here only of the differences between hierarchical structures in Christianity, especially Roman Catholicism, as opposed to the suggestions of someone like Kojin Karatani in *Transcritique*, who posits choosing leaders by lottery, not by ordination. In *The Monstrosity of Christ*, Žižek bows to Peter Sloterdijk's claim that "atheism bears the mark of the religion out of which it grew through its negation,"[16] and I plan to repeat that structure by showing, through Chesterton's Father Brown and Žižek's own Lacanian model of the detective described elsewhere in *Looking Awry*, that Christianity bears the mark of the anti-hierarchical polytheism out of which it grew by negation, if only by being Janus-faced in the way Jan Assmann describes in *Religio Duplex*. "They [religions] have an outer face, in the form of the official religion, and an inner face, in the form of mysteries."[17] This two-world picture in Christianity contains proposed consequences that run counter to communism's egalitarianism, for while the Gospel is preached to all, "those who accept it will gain entry into heaven; those who reject it will be consigned to hell."[18] The negation that exists as part of atheism is, in large part, a negation of a world in which those who do not buy into the religion are damned to hell or hemlock. Father Brown does not seem to hold to this traditional Christian view of what happens to non-Christians. For example, in "The Honour of Israel Gow," Father Brown remarks in a moment of allegiance to polytheism, "Devil-worship is a perfectly genuine religion."[19]

The primary issue with Žižek continues to be his on-again, off-again engagement with practical, party politics. As Will Self has written in the *Guardian*, "Žižek certainly makes like he really wants us to abandon the last vestiges of our discredited value system, and march with him (and Bernie Sanders) towards some yet-to-be-constructed barricades." But that does not happen. Instead, we get more prose unfolding the nuances of Hegel and Lacan, and not a full-throated endorsement of a global party politics, like communism, that would help to organize disparate groups, especially those in the United States mired in identity politics. As someone who once ran for political office, Žižek could shift from a "thought leader" to a political strategist. With his capacities for linking complex ideas to familiar cultural products, he could be a powerful force for moving large groups of people out of the problems generated by global capitalism.

Critics like Peter Paik make the case that Žižek helps to remind the general public about "the roots of communism in the Christian tradition."[20] Paik asserts that Žižek is advancing "the argument that the Christian conception of faith, or something like it, is essential to the militant activity of revolution." My twist on Paik's position is to latch on to the "or something like it," while jettisoning faith from the picture, as well as the militancy (soldiers tend to defend the capitalists), retaining the revolutionary characteristic of Paik's assertion. Think of it as the difference between invoking "Christian Warriors" as opposed to invoking Spartacus.[21] In reconfiguring Žižek for the political struggle against global capitalism, Paik works through some of Žižek's theological ruminations, such as Žižek's appeal to Kierkegaard's interpretation of the Abraham story as one of admirable militancy. Žižek prefers that we forget about questioning a model for political activity that involves a person hearing a voice from God and carrying out commands from that voice, even though the requested murder does not take place. We are meant to concentrate on the philosophical lessons of duty and absolute relationships. Žižek steers his readers toward thinking about Abraham's militancy, not the action's genesis in voices from heaven. Paik notes that Abraham's actions lack "any kind of distinct political direction."[22]

Žižek senses the need to address the "murderousness" associated with revolution (it's questionable whether the Abraham and Isaac narrative corresponds to a revolutionary moment) and to reframe the violence in religious analogies and theological abstractions, as if those tactics are prerequisites to a mass movement against global capitalism that would probably involve the capitalists in a bloody defense of greed. Paik is not entirely sure why Žižek seems to want to anticipate a call for justification of revolutionary violence, what Paik calls "the political suspension of the ethical"[23] that will be part of the emancipatory force of revolution. Paik's essay predates Žižek's discussion of "divine violence" in *Disparities* (2016), where he states bluntly that we are "to simply accept the fact that divine violence is brutally unjust,"[24] which ought to serve as a response to those who wish to bring up the point that the victims of revolutionary violence do not receive satisfactory justification from the revolutionaries. It also seems to undo Ian Ker's point in the epigraph about Catholicism's consonance with reason.

The linkage among violence, capitalism and Christianity plays itself out as well under Žižek's umbrella of "living in the end times." The capitalists have their own "last days" in mind, as do some Christian groups who are busying themselves to bring about "the end times," not simply waiting for prophecies or capitalist ecological catastrophes to play themselves out of their own accord. The capitalists will be the agents of their own version of the rapture, for they will be in a position to afford the supplies, the remote real estate, and the extraordinary protections against nuclear fallout, anarchy, revolution.[25] We should not forget, as Bosteels has it, via León Rozitchner, that capitalism simply would not have been possible without Christianity.[26] Bosteels calls it "collusion."

The reliance on prophecy/divination (especially if rooted in any kind of scriptures, like the ones linked to the rapture) calls for a level of caution. North Americans and Europeans have been through unexpected/unprophesied political developments (e.g. Brexit, Donald Trump's election) that should serve as warnings against counting on any particular outcome, even seemingly divinely ordained ones. Caution is called for by some on the religious right who, unlike

Žižek, do have practical, non-egalitarian, political ends in mind bound up in scriptural prophecies. Timothy Weber (2004) explains in the *On the Road to Armageddon: How Evangelicals Became Israel's Best Friend* that after 9/11, "dispensationalists believed that it was necessary to leave the bleachers and get onto the playing field to make sure the game ended according to the divine script." Dispensationalism is a theory that Biblical history is divided deliberately by God into defined periods, and for each of those periods or ages, God has allotted distinctive administrative principles that are to be carried out by believers.

Some on the left were hoping for Žižek to get onto the playing field and to show others the steps for bringing about the "end times" of global capitalism. Hampering the emergence of a more strategic Žižek is his inability to divorce himself from religion, particularly orthodox Catholicism. In *The Fragile Absolute*, Žižek writes, "Christianity and Marxism should fight on the same side of the barricade against the onslaught of new spiritualisms – the authentic Christian legacy is much too precious to be left to the fundamentalist freaks."[27] It is Fredric Jameson who posits that Žižek and Chesterton are "fellow traveler[s] in the perilous effort of coordinating passionate belief with orthodoxy."[28] Žižek's fascination with G. K. Chesterton and Father Brown constitutes part of the problem. That same part, however, could lead us toward a solution, if it becomes possible to follow Žižek in his view of Father Brown as representative of the common person capable of bringing about good in oneself and for others. Before that, we must remember Žižek's interest in using Chesterton's writings on orthodoxy to valorize orthodoxy, though Father Brown hardly represents orthodoxy across the board. Chesterton's biographer Ian Ker contends that Father Brown is "on the fringe of society"[29] as a Roman Catholic in a land dominated by the Established Church. In this sense, Father Brown does not count as orthodox even among clergymen.[30]

Ker wants his readers to notice that Father Brown embodies the kind of social criticism of a class society that represents, in part, Chesterton's views. Ker sees Chesterton as anti-capitalist, but not necessarily socialist or communist. My aim is to push for the view that Father Brown, unlike a Sherlock Holmes or Auguste Dupin,[31] does not claim superiority in intelligence, but attributes his success with criminality to understanding people in general, partly stemming from, as Ker puts it, Father Brown's "pastoral concern, which gives him an intimate access to people that the ordinary detective would not have." As we learn in the story of "The Queer Feet," Father Brown pays attention to all people, unlike plutocrats who "could not bear a poor man near to them."[32]

Father Brown's empathy seems to be a more important characteristic than a Holmes-like IQ, and Holmes is the character who is frequently subject to charges of a lack of empathy and human understanding, most poignantly by his friend Watson. Father Brown's linkages to commoners and his insistence that his skills at detection are based in common sense,[33] and not in some unearthly power answering his prayers, allow for a case that Father Brown is fulfilling a structural requirement of communism – treating people equitably, finding power from within collective existence. Finding power within the collective describes how the character of Father Brown emerged. Chesterton based the character of Father Brown on his actual friend, Father O'Connor, whom he met in 1906.

A non-religious reading of Father Brown's activities could be interpreted as a reversal of Žižek's aims in appropriating Chesterton. Such an interpretation would sustain my Žižekian framing. A leitmotif in Žižek's works is the reversal (counterfactuals might be considered a synonym for reversals). The counterintuitive becomes almost a fetish in the course of Žižek's body of work. Things appear to be one way but are really another. Reality is a dream, or vice versa. "For what followed was so improbable, that it might well have been a dream."[34] Žižek admires Chesterton's *The Man Who Was Thursday*, which includes an almost laughable number of reversals, with policemen imagining that they are in a struggle with master criminals who are members of a secret society, only to learn that their death struggle with a particular criminal is with another undercover policeman disguised as a member of the secret society. The enthusiasm animating the police through much of the novel is the fear that the anarchists will be detonating bombs at any moment. The novel participates in the "last days" motif as well.[35] As Chesterton describes the scene in the first pages of the novel, we learn that: "This particular evening, if it is remembered for nothing else, will be remembered in that place for its strange sunset. It looked like *the end of the world*."[36]

From another angle, what I propose is not so much a reversal as a reconfiguring of Father Brown. Part of that figuration brings Agatha Christie's *Murder at the Vicarage* into play. The murder at the vicarage is a symbolic one; the killing of a clergyman in the context of this essay is the dissolution of the churchly Father part of Father Brown, allowing Father Brown to be uncoupled from his priestly role, and to view him as a model political actor *sans* his Catholicism. Father Brown rejects respectability, esotericism and intellectualism. As Ker puts it, Father Brown "has no time for intellectuals,"[37] and so I do not mind divorcing Father Brown from Žižek, an intellectual who, despite the lesson he could have learned from Father Brown, chooses superstition over reason, philosophical and theological disputation over action on behalf of a common good. The Agatha Christie novel shocks some people because it includes a vicar who says that doing away with another person, Colonel Protheroe, would be a service to the community. Doing away with the religion Žižek has in mind might also be a service to the community. Žižek wants his audience to think otherwise, which is why he reads the final pages of Chesterton's *Orthodoxy* as a statement that sacrificing religion will result in "the gray universe of egalitarian terror and tyranny."[38] Rather than fashion a word-for-word counter-argument about the concluding lines of Chesterton's *Orthodoxy*, I conclude with something far less contentious in *The Man Who Was Thursday*. The characters in the novel warn readers about a kind of Nietzschean violence perpetrated by philosophers.[39] Yet, it is the policemen/philosophers who go to war during the novel. For some of the characters, war provides a "spark of life,"[40] as if human vitality is dependent on Nietzsche's (and Heidegger's) *polemos*. My conclusion arrives now with a character named Bull (interpret his name expansively, meaning whatever emanates from Bull falls under the category of Bull), who says, "You have not wasted your time; you have helped to save the world. We are not buffoons, but very desperate men at war with a vast conspiracy."[41] Chesterton's vision of war in *The Man Who Was Thursday* deserves the reading Žižek gave to the last bit of Chesterton's *Orthodoxy*, meaning that leaving readers with policemen/philosophers will result in "terror and tyranny," capitalism unshrugged. How would Žižek refute Gramsci's claim that a "full Catholic" would be a monster? In light of Gramsci's quotation at the start of this essay, the most chilling words in *The Man Who Was Thursday* remain, "We are all Catholics now."[42]

Notes

1 Antonio Gramsci, "What Is a Human Being?," in *Quaderni del carcere*, vol. 2 (Turin, Italy: Einaudi, 2014), 1344. I accept the homology of Gramsci's description of a full Christian with Žižek's use of "monstrosity" in his essay in which that word becomes part of the essay's title. Žižek is retroactively confirming Gramsci's point in Žižek's essay: "Reconciliation cannot be direct; it has first to generate (appear in) a *monster* – twice in the same page Hegel uses this unexpectedly strong word, 'monstrosity,' to designate the first figure of Reconciliation, the appearance of God in the finite flesh of a human individual"; *The Monstrosity of Christ: Paradox or Dialectic?*, ed. Creston Davis (Cambridge, MA: MIT Press, 2009), 74. This equation (normative Christian = Christ) should not be surprising, and then it would follow that if Christ is a monstrosity, a normative Christian would be a monster. What Žižek fails to explain in his description of the Trinity as a kind of Hegelian "synthesis," which appears later in my chapter, is why Christ is subject to laws/commandments (part of the path to becoming a normative Christian) to which the Father was not subject. It should also be noted the Gramsci quotation comes from an essay entitled "What Is a Human Being?" ("*Che cos'è l'uomo?*"), but Žižek asserts that Christ is monstrous because Christ is "more than human."
2 Ian Ker, *G.K. Chesterton: A Biography* (Oxford: Oxford University Press, 2011), 285.
3 G. K. Chesterton, *Father Brown: Selected Stories* (London: Collector's Library, 2003), 265.
4 Agon Hamza, *Repeating Žižek* (Durham, NC: Duke University Press, 2015), 227. Hamza excuses Žižek's waffling, but acknowledges the problem: "The standard reproach to Žižek's conception of politics is that he constantly changes his positions in relation to concrete situations."
5 Gregory Fried, "Where's the Point?: Slavoj Žižek and the Broken Sword," *International Journal of Žižek Studies* 1, no. 4 (2007): 2.
6 See Steven Shaviro's *No Speed Limit: Three Essays on Accelerationism*. Shaviro seems to have given up on Žižek, utopia, and on revolutionary aims in general: "The hope driving accelerationism is that, in fully expressing the potentialities of

capitalism, we will be able to exhaust it and thereby open up access to something beyond it"; Shaviro, *No Speed Limit: Three Essays on Accelerationism* (Minneapolis, MN: University of Minnesota Press, 2015), 3.
7 Todd McGowan, *Capitalism and Desire: The Psychic Cost of Free Markets* (New York: Columbia University Press, 2016), 173.
8 McGowan concludes his book by forgiving capitalism: "Capitalism is not the worst economic system that the world has produced, and it is not the cause of all our woes" (242). Like Žižek, McGowan seems trapped in the prison-house of psychoanalysis and cannot imagine a political alternative to capitalism that does not involve a simultaneous fixing of psychic structures and mechanisms. Note the tone of his "of course" in the following quotation: "Of course, the end of capitalism requires a political act, but a change in the psyche must inform this act" (242–243).
9 Ronald H. McKinney, "Žižek's Atheistic Reading of Chesterton: A Paradoxical Hermeneutic," *Philosophy Today* 57, no. 4 (2013): 417.
10 My positive appeal to the first portion of Fried's essay needs to be accompanied by a warning about my objections to Fried's allegiance, later in his essay, to the Platonic philosopher-king model for contemporary politics, a model based on the presupposition that there should be rulers and those ruled. That viewpoint is not compatible with the political model suggested by Karatani at the end of *Transcritique*. That model has the virtue of offering the concrete political advice missing from Žižek's writings, as numerous critics have noted.
11 For more about how this infection is subcutaneous for Žižek, see the discussion in Geoff Waite's *Nietzsche's Corps/e: Aesthetics, Politics, Prophecy, Or, the Spectacular Technoculture of Everyday Life* (Durham, NC: Duke University Press, 1996), especially 54–5, and 439, where Waite quotes Antonio Negri: "The dialectic is certainly to be rejected whenever, as Negri notes, it is 'the form in which bourgeois ideology is always presented to us in all its variants – even in those of the purely negative dialectics of crisis and war.'" The quotation is from Negri's *The Savage Anomaly: The Power of Spinoza's Metaphysics and Politics* (Minneapolis, MN: University of Minnesota Press, 1999), 20. See also Waite's essay on violence in the Heideggerian/Nietzschean tradition with its citing of Heidegger's statement: "Only when we grasp that the use of violence [*Gewaltbrauchen*] in language, in understanding, in building co-creates [*mitschafft*] the violent act [*Gewalt-tat*] of clearing paths into surrounding Being – only then do we understand the uncanniness of all that does violence", quoted in Waite, "Heidegger, Schmitt, Strauss: The Hidden Monologue, or, Conserving Esotericism to Justify the High Hand of Violence," *Cultural Critique* (Spring 2008): 121.
12 Slavoj Žižek, *Disparities* (London: Bloomsbury, 2016), 5.
13 Ibid., 264.
14 Žižek, *Monstrosity of Christ*, 33.
15 See ibid., 31–3. "Once God became man, there was no longer a God one could return to or become – so one would have to paraphrase Irenaeus's motto: 'God made Himself man, that man might become God *who made Himself man*.' The point of Incarnation is that one cannot become God – not because God dwells in a transcendent Beyond, but because God is dead, so the whole idea of approaching a transcendent God becomes irrelevant."
16 Žižek, *The Monstrosity of Christ*, 48.
17 Jan Assmann, *Religio Duplex* (Cambridge, UK: Polity Press, 2014), 4.
18 Ibid., 5.
19 G. K. Chesterton, *The Innocence of Father Brown* (Harmondsworth: Penguin Books, 1982; original 1911), 121.
20 Peter Paik, "The Pessimist Rearmed: Žižek on Christianity and Revolution," *Theory and Event* 8, no. 2 (2005): 2.

21 While I am at pains to say which bits of Marxism are missing from Žižek's account of Christianity, Bruno Bosteels approaches the matter from the other end: "What is missing from Marxism's account of Christianity according to Žižek is an understanding of the overlap between the two forms of alienation, or two forms of what in theology is called kenosis, that is, the self-emptying of both man and God"; "Žižek and Christianity: Or the Critique of Religion after Marx and Freud," in *Žižek Now: Current Perspectives in Žižek Studies*, ed. Jamil Khader and Anne Rothenberg, (Cambridge, UK: Polity Press, 2013), 72.
22 Paik, "The Pessimist Rearmed," 4.
23 Ibid., 3. Žižek's comments from a 2009 BBC show entitled "Terror! Robespierre and the French Revolution" have upset some of his critics. In that BBC broadcast, Žižek seems to be endorsing democratic violence in the name of revolution. Does that viewpoint require a defense different from the Christian and Augustinian "just war" tradition, which according to one of its students, exceeds rational thought but is grounded in the aim of eventual peace? See John Mattox's book.
24 Žižek, *Disparities*, 378.
25 See Evan Osnos, "Doomsday Prep for the Super-Rich," *The New Yorker*, January 30, 2017.
26 Bruno Bosteels, "Žižek and Christianity: Or the Critique of Religion after Marx and Freud," in *Žižek Now: Current Perspectives in Žižek Studies*, ed. Jamil Khader and Anne Rothenberg, (Cambridge, UK: Polity Press, 2013), 54–83.
27 Slavoj Žižek, *The Fragile Absolute* (London: Verso Books, 2001), 2.
28 Fredric Jameson, *An American Utopia: Dual Power and the Universal Army*, ed. Slavoj Žižek (London: Verso, 2016), 94.
29 Ker, *G.K. Chesterton*, 288.
30 Žižek's attention to orthodoxy aligns him potentially with another philosopher who does not seem to be on Žižek's radar, Hans Blumenberg. "Right opinion," the etymological rendering of "orthodoxy," might be the best humans can do in some important circumstances. Blumenberg's rhetorical anthropology recognizes the importance of *doxa* for human flourishing. Blumenberg points his readers to the "provisionality of reason" in his famous essay "An Anthropological Approach to the Contemporary Significance of Rhetoric." Philosophy cannot provide foundational truth, and so we are left to convince, to persuade others to act on something less than foundational truth. Rhetoric is, in part, getting others to act on opinions (*doxa*). Rhetoric's task is to discover the best options and present those for action, a version of orthodoxy, but one not necessarily tied to religious considerations.
31 See Slavoj Žižek, *Looking Awry: An Introduction to Jacques Lacan through Popular Culture* (Cambridge, MA: MIT Press, 1991), 48–50, where Žižek links explicitly Chesterton and Conan Doyle. In that section of *Looking Awry*, Žižek wants to keep Agatha Christie and Chesterton apart, since his purpose is to make some points about differences in the historical developments that accompanied the detective story as opposed to the detective novel. Žižek admits indirectly that the salient differences in genre are elided by a rhetorical concern, viz., improbability. Highlighting the rhetorical element at this point is meant to reinforce the point made in the previous note.
32 Ker, *Chesterton*, 289.
33 G. K. Chesterton, *The Innocence of Father Brown* (Harmondsworth: Penguin Books, 1982; original 1911), 61.
34 G. K. Chesterton, *The Man Who Was Thursday* (New York: Barnes & Noble Classics, 2004; original 1908), 7.
35 Ibid., 37. "The Last Crusade" pops up at that point in the narrative.
36 Ibid., 3, my emphasis.
37 Ker, *Chesterton*, 287.

38 Slavoj Žižek, "The 'Thrilling Romance of Orthodoxy'," in *Theology and the Political: The New Debate*, ed. Creston Davis, John Milbank and Slavoj Žižek (Durham, NC: Duke University Press, 2005), 53.
39 Chesterton, *The Man Who Was Thursday*, 15, 33–4, 100.
40 Fried, "Where's the Point?," 13.
41 Chesterton, *The Man Who Was Thursday*, 100.
42 Ibid., 9.

Bibliography

Assmann, Jan. *Religio Duplex*. Cambridge, UK: Polity Press, 2014.
Blumenberg, Hans. "An Anthropological Approach to the Contemporary Significance of Rhetoric." Translated by Robert Wallace. In *After Philosophy: End or Transformation?*, edited by Kenneth Baynes, James Bohman and Thomas McCarthy, 429–58. Cambridge, MA: MIT Press, 1987.
Bosteels, Bruno. "Žižek and Christianity: Or the Critique of Religion after Marx and Freud." In *Žižek Now: Current Perspectives in Žižek Studies*, edited by Jamil Khader and Anne Rothenberg, 54–83. Cambridge, UK: Polity Press, 2013.
Chesterton, G. K. *Father Brown: Selected Stories*. London: Collector's Library, 2003.
———. *The Innocence of Father Brown*. Harmondsworth: Penguin Books, 1911/1982.
———. *The Man Who Was Thursday*. New York: Barnes & Noble Classics, 1908/2004.
Fried, Gregory. "Where's the Point? Slavoj Žižek and the Broken Sword." *International Journal of Žižek Studies* 1, no. 4 (2007): 1–25.
Frisby, David. "Between the Spheres: Siegfried Kracauer and the Detective Novel." *Theory, Culture & Society* (1992): 1–22.
Gramsci, Antonio. *Quaderni del carcere, II*. Turin, Italy: Einaudi, 2014.
Hamza, Agon, ed. *Repeating Žižek*. Durham, NC: Duke University Press, 2015.
Jameson, Fredric. "An American Utopia." In *An American Utopia: Dual Power and the Universal Army*, edited by Slavoj Žižek, 1–96. London: Verso Books, 2016.
Karatani, Kojin. *Transcritique: On Kant and Marx*. Cambridge, MA: MIT Press, 2005.
Ker, Ian. *G.K. Chesterton: A Biography*. Oxford: Oxford University Press, 2011.
Mattox, John Mark. *St. Augustine and the Theory of Just War*. London: Continuum, 2006.
McGowan, Todd. *Capitalism and Desire: The Psychic Cost of Free Markets*. New York: Columbia University Press, 2016.
McKinney, Ronald H. "Žižek's Atheistic Reading of Chesterton: A Paradoxical Hermeneutic." *Philosophy Today* 57, no. 4 (2013): 408–19.
Negri, Antonio. *The Savage Anomaly: The Power of Spinoza's Metaphysics and Politics*. Minneapolis, MN: University of Minnesota Press, 1999.
Osnos, Evan. "Doomsday Prep for the Super-Rich." *The New Yorker*, January 30, 2017.
Paik, Peter. "The Pessimist Rearmed: Žižek on Christianity and Revolution." *Theory and Event* 8, no. 2 (2005). doi: 10.1353/tae.2005.0031.
Self, Will. "Review of *The Courage of Helplessness*." *The Guardian*, April 28, 2017. Retrieved May 16, 2017 from www.theguardian.com/books/2017/apr/28/courage-of-hopelessness-slavoj-zizek-review.
Shaviro, Steven. *No Speed Limit: Three Essays on Accelerationism*. Minneapolis, MN: University of Minnesota Press, 2015.

Waite, Geoff. "Heidegger, Schmitt, Strauss: The Hidden Monologue, or, Conserving Esotericism to Justify the High Hand of Violence." *Cultural Critique* (Spring 2008): 113–44.

———. *Nietzsche's Corps/e: Aesthetics, Politics, Prophecy, or, the Spectacular Technoculture of Everyday Life*. Durham, NC: Duke University Press, 1996.

Weber, Timothy. *On the Road to Armageddon: How Evangelicals Became Israel's Best Friend*. Grand Rapids, MI: Baker Academic, 2004.

Žižek, Slavoj. *Disparities*. London: Bloomsbury, 2016.

———. *The Fragile Absolute*. London: Verso Books, 2001.

———. "From Job to Christ: A Paulinian Reading of Chesterton." In *St. Paul among the Philosophers*, edited by John Caputo and Linda Alcoff, 39–58. Bloomington, IN: Indiana University Press, 2009.

———. *Looking Awry: An Introduction to Jacques Lacan through Popular Culture*. Cambridge, MA: MIT Press, 1991.

———. *The Puppet and the Dwarf: The Perverse Core of Christianity*. Cambridge, MA: MIT Press, 2003.

———. "The 'Thrilling Romance of Orthodoxy'." In *Theology and the Political: The New Debate*, edited by Creston Davis, John Milbank and Slavoj Žižek, 52–71. Durham, NC: Duke University Press, 2005.

Žižek, Slavoj and John Milbank. *The Monstrosity of Christ: Paradox or Dialectic?* Edited by Creston Davis. Cambridge, MA: MIT Press, 2009.

10 Žižek and the dwarf
A short-circuit radical theology

Mike Grimshaw

How does one think theologically in the twenty-first century? While there are of course many options, in this discussion I want to ask how can we engage with theology more than a century after Nietzsche's proclamation of the death of God and half a century after the challenge of death of God theology? Who can we turn to, who can we engage with to make our way, haltingly, provisionally in this century when religion in all its political and violent glory is seemingly on the increase, when theology seems to have splintered to so many inward-looking varieties of identity politics and those of us who seek to hold fast to a secular and radical identity in our theology are seemingly increasingly a minority? The following discussion is a self-consciously radical theology that is positioned against traditional (or orthodox) Christian readings of the Incarnation and Crucifixion. It also situates Christianity as a type of radical, materialist knowledge that calls for a new understanding of humanity. While the claim of a radical knowledge does open up the challenge of being labeled Gnostic, it is the materialist focus of this knowledge that prevents the retreat into Gnosticism. The call is not to flee this world or our bodies, but rather live fully and only in this world, in the one life we have, in the name of revolutionary Love.[1]

Increasingly it seems that, to deliberately misuse Heidegger, only an atheist Lacanian Hegelian–Marxist can – if not save us – then perhaps point us in the right direction. As I have stated elsewhere, Žižek is perhaps the leading radical theologian of this new century, precisely because he is not a theologian but one who engages with theology and then expands on from that engagement. It is Žižek, I believe, who most consistently reminds us that to think philosophically is also to think theologically – most often against theology and its institutional expressions and limitations.[2] This is perhaps most apparent in *The Puppet and the Dwarf*,[3] which proceeds from Žižek's reversal of Benjamin's first thesis on the philosophy of history.[4] Noting the recession of historical materialism and the return of theology "in the guise of the 'post-secular' Messianic turn of deconstruction," Žižek offers his own short-circuit reversal of Benjamin using Benjamin's analogy of the chess-playing Turk automaton:

> The puppet called "theology" is to win all the time. It can easily be a match for anyone if it enlists the service of historical materialism, which today, as we know, is wizened and has to keep out of sight.[5]

In response, what follows is my short-circuit reading of *The Puppet and the Dwarf* via what I term an annotative hermeneutics. In this reading strategy, I literally annotate and interpret the text as I read and then write out of my annotations. In terms of the short-circuit, I am the minor author who in my reading and annotating writes a minor text of the major text and author via my act of hermeneutics.

In my short-circuit, Žižek's text is read not only through Christianity, but through a radical, secular theology that short-circuits both Žižek and his own reading of and via the orthodox Christianity of Chesterton. What eventuates is a deliberatively non-orthodox, in fact unorthodox, Christianity – and that is deliberate, for it pushes through the death of God to the death of man. I also want to raise a further short-circuit that sits underneath this reading where I ask, what if Žižek is the Puppet and we have the dwarf of Christianity, or more so, the dwarf of theology within him: a decentering not only of the text but of Žižek himself? Framing my question and engagement is a statement T. S. Eliot made in 1946 in a broadcast to post-war Germany. Eliot emphasizes that while the unity of European culture as expressed in arts and ideas arose out of a history of a common Christian culture, this did not necessitate nor mean there was a contemporary, unified Christian culture in the modern world. Rather, as he observed, the acknowledgment of a shared heritage did not necessarily involve a shared belief. However, this also meant that:

> It is against a background of Christianity that all our thought has significance. An individual European may not believe the Christian faith is true, and yet what he says, and makes, and does, will all spring out of his heritage of the Christian faith for its meaning.[6]

On this level Christianity, and Christian theology, is indeed the dwarf that sits inside Žižek, just as it sits within all of us who continue to work and think in the European tradition – in all our intellectual, cultural and social activity. In the manner of the short-circuit reading, is this not the confrontation of Žižek – and indeed of all of us – with our "own hidden presuppositions" and so the revelation of our "disavowed truth"?[7]

To begin, I wish to state what, in my reading, Žižek gets wrong, as that frames the rest of my response. In saying this I acknowledge Žižek's reading is informed by Chesterton's Christian orthodoxy, while my reading is informed by a radical, death of God theology arising in particular from the work of Thomas Altizer and Gabriel Vahanian – and more latterly, that of Gianni Vattimo. Therefore, in responding to Žižek, I wish to push on further from Christian orthodoxy which, in my reading, hides the central radicalness of the secular nature of Christianity. In short, Christianity is even more radical than either Žižek or Chesterton express it.

What Žižek (but of course not only Žižek) gets wrong is that with Paul's theology and the event of Eternity (that is, of God) entering time, the imperfectability of humanity, the temporality of human existence became the driver of history due to the theology of this event. For if Eternity, that is, if God declared a radical identification with temporality and with imperfection, we have entered a new time oriented to imperfection and temporality. What we may have previously considered the Eternity of God – that is, that God is timeless – is radically undone. God entering human time is the timeless becoming timebound: Eternity becoming temporal. The question that a radical theology asks is, why have we not orientated ourselves to this when God has? Perhaps to push this further: why do we wish to keep God as that which God chose to no longer be? My answer is simple: we wish to keep God as that which keeps us *as we were*: that is, we do not want to be materialist Christians of the death of God. Here I am reminded of Graham Ward's statement in *Cities of God* that the question theology "does not handle" is the question concerning "'what time is it'?"[8] Theology, of course, may not want to handle the answer I seek to discuss, which is the time of a radical identification with imperfection and temporality, that is, the time of the death of God. What I term Paul's rupture event is a new theology arising from the universal imperfection and temporality of existence, an existence chosen by God unto death.

Žižek begins by laying out the ground from which he will proceed, a ground mapped, a ground framed by a definition of modernity in which religion can globalize as "the same religion in different cultures" wherein religion exists as either "*therapeutic* or *critical*."[9] From this, Žižek articulates a possible, Hegelian-derived "downward synthesis" which expresses the "lowest point" as "a kind of negative synthesis."[10] What this means is that we need to rethink religion and theology for our society, for our time. What time is it? The time to rethink theology and the question of belief. Here I wish to acknowledge that, like Žižek, I identify that it is *only* through a materialist approach that "the subversive kernel of Christianity"[11] is accessible; but I want to ask not whether Žižek has really "gone through the Christian experience," as he states a true dialectical materialist must, but more so can *anyone* go through it to the point of a total exit? Or, is one, if a European, part of the European and/or Christian diaspora or as part of the European cultural and intellectual tradition, *always* in some way, as Eliot suggests, *within* the Christian experience, especially within the Christian experience of the death of God?

It is here that I wish to ask what happens if we take Christianity seriously, a Christianity of the death of God seriously. For while, in his text, Žižek certainly takes Christianity in its Chesterton-derived orthodox expression seriously, I want to push Žižek on, to prod him to consider what happens if we take the death of God seriously. It is this that makes theology the dwarf, and as such, this also perhaps means a reversal in Žižek's labeling, for is it not Lenin who is therefore a great Paulist, who seeks to organize the new party, the new party that breaks from that which has already arisen? For, whether it is Paul then or Lenin later, it is the materialist here and now that matters, not the belief of what had been done that seeks to impose a new orthodoxy of the party line. So, what does Paul do? Paul is the outsider who replaces *history* with *Christianity* to the extent that even today we live in history divided by Christianity; history as that before the event of Christianity and history that lives after the event and in the revolution of Christianity. It is here that we can signify the puppet as: History ÷ Christianity. It is this that also, via Lacan, symbolizes the Holy Spirit, that which "cancels (or, rather, suspends) the entire domain of 'life',"[12] for it is also Paul who makes the Holy Spirit as not only signifier of the divine but also of humanity, a signifier whereby *everything* (i.e. history) is now the puppet of the dwarf. Therefore, it is not that the dwarf of theology enters history, but rather that the dwarf resignifies the puppet; it is this event that sits at the center of Paul's identification of and emphasis on the rupture, the break with Judaism.

In discussing this, Žižek raises the question:

> What if God's descent to man, far from being an act of grace toward humanity, is the only way for God to gain full actuality, and to liberate Himself from the suffocating constraints of Eternity? What if God actualizes Himself only through human recognition?[13]

To this we respond by pushing on through the question of actuality and temporality to state: God enters into history and in so doing not only gains actuality but also fully experiences temporality. This means that this is not the puppet of Benjamin whereby historical materialism enters theology. Rather, it is an inversion of Benjamin's first thesis that undermines all that is built on the tradition of the puppet and the dwarf. History is the temporality of the human that God enters and the temporality in which God actualizes Himself. This means the imperfection of humanity is the imperfection that God chooses to experience and identify with – *to death* – in Christ. We can describe this as the ethical act whereby God undertakes *total* identification with the imperfection of humanity. But, as Žižek posits contra Schelling, this act is not only the ethical one that I would posit, but also, perhaps first and foremost, an act for divine freedom where the fall into time is the escape from and the rejection of Eternity. This introduces an ontological opening into human experience, "the time when Eternity reaches into time."[14]

We can express this by stating Paul makes time the time of the imperfect, *the time of and for the imperfect* and therefore universal, for the true universal human experience is that of imperfection. This imperfection is that which God chooses to enter into, an imperfection whereby God experiences the reality of forsakenness expressed in the cry from the Cross. It is in this cry of forsakenness that the Pauline event, in this cry the rupture of Eternity, is completed. It is in this cry that theology, the truly radical theology of Christianity, becomes the dwarf – even to Žižek and to all atheists; it is in this cry and the death that follows that Christianity became the universal dwarf. For in the cry of abandonment, as Žižek notes, the normal act of atheism is perverted; the "normal" atheism of man not believing in God is, in Christianity, preceded from its origin by God not believing in God.[15] The death of God that occurs when humanity stops believing is, in Christianity, the death of a God *who has already died*. This death, the event that gives rise to Christianity, is the death of God that Christianity wishes to deny – and in so denying denies its origin and its perverse universalism. For there is, as discussed by Žižek, a perverse core to Christianity: the forbidden tree of the knowledge of good and evil, the prohibition of law that creates sin, the necessity of the betrayal of Judas.[16]

How might we understand this last act, that of betrayal? We need to proceed from that which Christianity makes clear: God cannot die unless humanity acts to undertake the act that leads to death and so *only* in the event of Christianity can God die. Without the betrayal, there is no central event. The betrayal is therefore necessary because without the death there is no universal Messianic community – only a particular Messiah of God doomed to fail. It is perversely the death of Messiah, that itself is the death of God, that makes Christianity the universal Messianic community of atheism. It is the death that creates Christianity, the death that via Paul frees Christianity from the particular and makes it into the universal singular. This death could only be set in motion by the necessary betrayal, a betrayal that is itself betrayed when calls for the particularity of Christianity emerge.

The betrayal of Christ is necessary because, as stated, otherwise Christ would have only been yet another failed, living "messiah" who accomplishes nothing and dies a merely human death, believing unto death, in God. What occurs *because of* the act of betrayal, is the perverse failure of Christianity, for Christ *needs* to be betrayed so that the cry from the Cross can be made. If, in response to the cry, God *had* acted, then Christianity would have been exposed as a non-perverse failure: nothing more than the *performance* of the Messiah, the *performance* of incarnation, the *performance* of the event whereby Eternity enters time. If God had acted, had been able to act, then that would have been the act that exposed the continuation of the old reality and expectation and the continuation of God separate from time: *nothing would have changed*. But because God *did not* act, for God *could not* act, in the cry and the death, *everything changed* – but perversely and crucially in a way that, for most, it seemed *nothing* had changed. At the moment I want to leave this as a hanging statement, one not yet ready to be answered. But I will say that the experience of Holy Saturday, that day between the cry and death and then the claim of resurrection, is the day when it seemed that nothing had changed, except for that inner core of the original circle of Christ for whom the failure of Christ was experienced – if not understood; and nor is it properly understood by Žižek.

In saying this I am by no means seeking to dismiss the centrality of Žižek as a theologian of the death of God, for in his discussion he goes to the point where most death of God theologians get to. But if we are to take the death of God seriously as a *Christian* event, then we need to take seriously what occurs when Eternity enters time, and that means taking the claim of incarnation seriously. This is why the Trinity is so problematic, even if as Žižek observes, it is the Trinity that enables Christianity to be the one true monotheism. Yet does not the Trinity, does not Christianity as monotheism, one true monotheism or not, resurrect the God who died? Is not the Trinity that which seeks, in a monotheistic perversity, precisely to undo the central perversity of Christianity? For, as Žižek does, to situate Christ as the gap, "the gap which simultaneously separates God from God and man from man,"[17] is to undo the death and abandonment that is, in its universal event, the perverse good news of Christianity. Because the perverse good news of Christianity is that via the event *God and man* are no more – and therefore *there is no gap*. It is this that truly exposes "what is false about Levinasian–Derridean Otherness":[18] yes, it is as Žižek pinpoints, the very opposite of his identified gap in the One – and in the logic of Žižekian Christianity, this is as far as we need to go. But what if the perverse core of Christianity is the end of monotheism itself and therefore there is no One for the gap to be in? It is this that makes the theology of Christianity universal, for it is the theology that arises *after the end of any theism*, mono or otherwise.

What, then, is Christianity left with? It would be very easy to follow in the wake of Dostoevsky and Camus and argue that now both "everything is permitted" and that we have to "live without appeal."[19] That is indeed where we might get to if we continue to think that *man that was* continues *as is* after the death of God. But I argue that the death of God results in a new humanity that exists in the materialist demand of universal love. Perhaps a way forward is via an extension of Žižek's discussion of the work of love as expressed by Che Guevara and Žižek's associated mention of Lenin's acts of revolutionary violence as "works of Love."[20] I want to raise the possibility that the original act of the revolutionary violence as work of Love was the abandonment that resulted in the cry of despair from the Cross. This work of Love was revolutionary in that it overturned everything, including the existence of God and the existence of man; it was violent in that not only did it result in the death of both God and man, it was an act of ontological and teleological violence, a violence done to both time and Eternity.

It is this that then raises the question of how we can read and respond to Žižek's engagement with Chesterton. The way forward that I propose is to take orthodoxy seriously and push it to its true conclusion. What is this true conclusion? Nothing more or less than the Easter faith wherein God dies via the revolutionary act of violent love. This in turn makes the atheist's "not believing in God" always secondary to the atheist act of God as expressed and experienced on the Cross. Christianity, true Christianity, is therefore atheist from the beginning.

How might we then understand the atheist who, within what can be expressed as the orthodoxy of Christianity or more latterly the culture that arose from Christianity, finds herself not believing in that which has already, and from its event of origin, been *self-negated*? My answer is that Christianity has not wanted to be *Christianity* but rather sought to be the monotheism of the resurrected God. For the Event of Easter reveals Christianity as universal atheism expressed as revolutionary Love. Christianity is where revolutionary Love becomes the responsibility of the new humanity that exists *after God and after man*. No longer do we exist in reference and in response to the external Other, nor can we expect that external Other to intervene on our behalf. This is what I term living in Holy Saturday, that day after Good Friday but before – and not even expecting – Easter Sunday. For Easter Sunday is not the resurrection of the external Other but rather that Event whereby we realize that atheism, that Christian atheism, is the situation of hope and revolutionary Love, the event whereby we realize that the death of the external Other is that which frees us. Here we may make use of both Chesterton and Žižek and their emphasis that *it could have been otherwise*.[21] The "*otherwise*" is the central lesson of the Crucifixion, for it was "otherwise" to that which was expected – even by Christ – and because of this we get the new universal of Christian atheism.

It is this "*otherwise*" that also raises the question of happiness and the noting that happiness is a pagan category. For the Christian narrative is not about happiness or the happy life – and only becomes so when it is paganized. If it not about happiness, how might we read the issue of confronting the consequences of desire for Christianity? Here I draw upon Žižek's discussion of Lacan, for if true desire is to get what we really desire, and yet we pretend to desire that which we do not really desire, what is it that Christianity desires? What happens if the true desire is that which will not eventuate, nor eventuate as we desire it to? Here we can ask, is not the end of capitalism a desire like that of the Kingdom of God? Whether as anti-capitalists or Christians (or perhaps even both), we wish to critique the current situation in the name of a desire for that which will not eventuate. To push this further, did or does Christianity *really* want the Kingdom and the return of the Messiah – or are these claimed and desired as a type of hypocritical happiness? Are not the demands for the Kingdom and the return of the Messiah actually hysterical demands, a hysterical provocation that address the Master with a demand that is impossible to meet, impossible because the Master is *not there*. For the Christian demand, the desire for the impossible desire is nothing less than a pagan demand and desire that does not and cannot face up to the central atheism of Christianity: there is no Master, there is no One to address these demands and desires to, there is no One to enact that desired and demanded.

As Žižek observes, conservatives are opposed to radical knowledge because "ultimately, knowledge makes us unhappy."[22] Therefore, Christianity, that is non-radical Christianity, non-atheist Christianity, is conservative because it seeks happiness and denies the radical knowledge that sits within as its perverse core: *the death of God and the death of man*. But even if Christianity did not want to confront its perverse core, what of the statement from Matthew 10:34–36 (KJV):[23]

> Think not that I am come to send peace on earth: I came not to send peace, but a sword. For I am come to set a man at variance against his father, and the daughter against her mother, and the daughter in law against her mother in law. And a man's foes shall be they of his own household.

If happiness is a pagan category, then it is this statement that positions Christianity as anti-pagan in ethos and, furthermore, positions Christianity as knowledge and not happiness. What is it, then, that Christianity "knows"? Of course, the answer Žižek and I will offer is obvious: the death of God. But this is only one part of the knowledge, for the death of God is the event that the anti-happiness knowledge of Christianity emerges from. This knowledge is also linked to the central Christian category of reason, a claim of reason that itself is central to the claim of Imago Dei. This reason is what enables us to ascertain and understand that which the death of God makes stark, that which brings not happiness but knowledge.

The response to the death of God is not a reversion to a pagan pleasure principle but rather the knowledge of what desire actually is – and involves: the perverse nature of desire. The knowledge that Christianity offers is that which we can see as also expressed in Žižek's stating of the ethical nature of the status of desire: "'not to compromise one's desire' ultimately equals 'do your duty'."[24] It is here my inner Calvinist comes out, for the Calvinist is suspicious of desire precisely because he is aware of how easy it is to betray it. Similarly, the Calvinist has no carnival, no time letting go "to indulge in hitherto forbidden pleasures";[25] or, rather, the Calvinist has no carnival as holy day; rather, we have the holiday in which trivial desire is often indulged, along with feelings of guilt, for there is no confession or absolution. The only absolution is that the holiday letting go occurs away from our everyday location and community, that particular Protestant perversity of locational transgression whereby the others that see the transgression is not known to us.

Here is not the place to go into a discussion of what social media, Facebook and the like have done to this Protestant attitude; but perhaps they have made Protestants digital catholics who seek a perverse confession via social media? Or rather, is this not the pagan pleasure principle in digital hegemony? For is there not a deeply melancholic expression and experience sitting at the heart of social media transgression?

What, however, of Christian transgression? I want to start by first engaging with Žižek's discussion of symbolic castration as "the loss of something that one never possessed"[26] and ask if this is actually a way to think of secularization as the loss of faith, the loss of religion that *we never possessed*? The fundamentalist is therefore "staging the spectacle of a desperate search"[27] for faith and religion they never possessed.

But let us also push the discussion further into the central perverse notion of the Crucifixion as a sacrifice, for how can we think of the Crucifixion as sacrifice if "one sacrifices not in order to get something from the Other, but in order to dupe the Other, in order to convince him or it that one is still missing something, that is *jouissance*"?[28] The death of God in the Crucifixion therefore cannot be, despite Christian orthodoxy's insistence, a sacrifice – or even the sacrificial event that ends sacrifice – because the question arises: who is duped? Is it the self-duping of God – or the duping of humanity? The death of God, the Crucifixion, is therefore not a sacrificial act but rather the duty that expresses the desire of God: the act of love that ends both God and man. That Eternity enters time is desire, not sacrifice; it is duty as the *jouissance* of God and man. It is this that makes Christianity the ethical knowledge of atheism;[29] it is through the death of God that Christianity occurs as the event of ethical duty. This also means that with no Big Other, the ultimate transgression is now that of our acting *as if* the Big Other does exist; our ethical duty is to live out the event of the death of God and the death of man.

I am aware I have made reference to a second death alongside the death of God, and I will make clear what I mean by this, but first I need to take Žižek's discussion of the universal and the universal singular and situate Christ as, post-death of God, the *Universal Singular*. More so, is not the Real that which is made manifest by the death of God, but not the abyss opened up by Good Friday and the abyss lived in as Holy Saturday. The Real is not this abyss, for in response to this we all too easily seek either a monstrous God or New Age self. Rather, the Real is the Lacanian Real, the Real as obstacle. How might we apply this to our inversion, our perversion of the puppet and the dwarf? What if the dwarf (that is, death of God theology) is the Real – is then the puppet (that is, historical materialism) which conceals the dwarf actually itself the very notion of the dwarf? Does this not explain why within every dialectic materialist (such as Žižek) is the Christianity of the death of God? As Žižek states, "the Real is not external to the Symbolic: the Real is the Symbolic itself in the modality of non-All, lacking an external Limit/Exception."[30] Is this not the centrality of my perverse, inverse reading of the puppet and the dwarf: that the puppet is the Symbolic of the dwarf? Therefore, is not Žižek's symbolic engagement with theology that which exposes him *as* theologian? Dialectical materialism is therefore the Symbolic of Christian atheism.

I have, a couple of times, stated that the death of God is also the death of man. To understand what I mean by this radical extension of death, we need to go back to what is claimed to occur in the Incarnation, that is Christ is fully God and fully man. In Christ, God and man meet. So, while I agree with Žižek's statement that "it is the very radical separation of man from God that unites us with God, since in the figure of Christ, God is thoroughly separated from himself,"[31] I want to push this to the other side of what is involved; that is, in the figure of Christ, man is thoroughly separated from himself. For in the figure of the Christ, those who were separated from each other unite; but just as God is separated from himself in Christ, so is man separated from himself in Christ. Otherwise what we get is the divine visitor who takes on human form. What this means is that if "the gap that separates us from God" is "*internal to God himself*," then the internal Gap is that made present not by Christ but by the death of God. Therefore, the site of truth in Christianity is the gap between God and man, the Gap that is Christ *as* the death of God.

But to speak as we too often do only of the death of God is to not fully understand what occurs in the death of Christ, in the death of the Incarnation. For, if we want to use the language of orthodoxy, Christ is *fully Human* and *fully Divine*. That is, Christ is where separated God and man meet – *and die*. This death, if it is really, truly to be death, cannot be only the death of God; it must, if it is not to be a one-sided theocide, also be the death of separated man – otherwise, there is a division between the "human" and "divine" parts of his nature. What is interesting is that while many who claim to be orthodox Christians are all too willing to concentrate on the death of the human part of the nature of Christ, all too many death of God thinkers concentrate only on the death of the divine part of the nature of Christ. In both accounts there is the failure – and perhaps the fear – to truly engage with what is the most radical, revolutionary truth of the death of Christ: *God and man die*.

It is this dual death that makes Christ the *Singular Universal*. Christianity is atheistic not only toward God, but toward man, who lives in reference to God. As the Singular Universal Christ is the Thing in itself as Gap rupture, the Gap rupture at the heart of both man and God. The Singular Universal is therefore that pointed to by the Singular Universal of Christianity: the Gap between the Thing of Christ and that which follows Him. It is via this that we can properly understand what is meant by Christianity as subtraction. The subtraction is not just from God, but also a subtraction from man. The Gap itself subtracts from both and is the overcoming of the Gap (God from man and man from God) into the New. Both God and man are dead: that is Christian atheism. This death, this double death, coincides with its direct opposite: the rebirth of God and humanity in what is the Christianity of the death of God, expressed as the Holy Spirit.

If we push on from Žižek's use of the Hegelian matrix of development then the death of God as wound is its own healing, but so (yet forgotten or refused to be thought) is the death of man, that is, the death of humanity separated from God. To push further, this combined death of God and death of man is itself the dwarf within Christianity, the dwarf within theology, the dwarf within history – and the dwarf within Žižek (as representative European) himself. This dwarf of death is the dwarf that is the perverse kernel of freedom that has, as identified by Žižek, the task "not to return to a previous 'higher' existence, but to transform our lives in *this* world."[32] Therefore, the Christian atheism that emerges from the death of God that also involves the death of man results in a secular theology, which is the true identity of the dwarf. How might we think of this? A way forward is offered by the understanding of the "secular" offered by the radical theologian Gabriel Vahanian, who, tracing secular back to *saeculum*, observes "in a pluralistic world, it is not religion we have in common. What we have in common is the secular,"[33] a secular that is the world of shared experience. As Clayton Crockett notes:

> For Vahanian, a *saeculum* is a theological notion which implies we live in a world of immanence which functions as the location of human and divine meaning and value.[34]

The secular theology that sits at the heart of Christianity is a secular theology of the Incarnation, cry from the Cross and Crucifixion. The world of shared experience, that which we have in common, is *this* world, a world of imperfection and imperfect beings, a world and experience that God chose to be part of – against Godself. The death of God is the universal, shared experience, an experience now shared by God. God died to Godself. But, remember, man also died. The shared experience is now to live *after* God and *after* man, that is, after man who lived in reference to God, to Eternity. This is the negation that Žižek is pointing towards, the negation of Adam that is also the self-negation of God. If we wish to use the term redemption, then this world, our world, our life has been redeemed as being now the sole focus and experience. There is no longer God to divide us; our shared experience is that in Christ: the shared experience of the death of God and the death of man. The gap that was, the gap that separated us from the Absolute, is overcome in the death of Christ who held that gap within him. The gap is now no longer between man and God; the gap is now only *between us as humanity*, a gap that we must now, in a new atheistic *imitatio Christi*, strive to overcome in ethical action: the ethical action that in the name of redemption, of redemption in this world, brings not peace but a sword. This is the revolutionary kernel of secular Christianity: the sword of the dwarf in the puppet of peace. I realize that for many the puppet and dwarf analogies may be being stretched too far, but I wish to argue that an analogy should be stretched to its extreme – for it is *only an analogy*. This is how we short-circuit analogies, by continually extending them past their original use and intension, to rethink and reuse them to see what may become apparent.

Is not Christianity therefore a failure? A claim of peace in the call to the sword, a call to revolution that is yet to fully manifest? Indeed, Christianity seems too often obstructed by its own institution and its collusion with power. But centrally, the failure arises from the failure of the self-negated God who could not, would not act to save himself – or humanity. This is, Žižek notes, "the properly *Christian* form of identification: it is ultimately *identification with a failure*."[35] While Žižek rightly identifies this failure as God failing, we must also extend the failure to the failure of man. Otherwise this is only a one-sided failure – and redemption. What we get with the failure of God but not of man is the redemption of God but not of man. This is why the failure is actually the double death: the death of God and the death of man. It is this that enables the new event of secular Christianity and secular theology. This is how we can truly understand Žižek's statement: "We are one with God only when God is no longer one with Himself, but abandons Himself."[36] It is separation from God that we share, "the infinite pain of separation"[37] that is the pain felt by Christ on the Cross. But, as challenging to orthodoxy as this is, we must push past separation to death, for what we share is not only separation but death: the death of what was, the death that ends the old identities and relationship.

The experience we share is therefore not just the separation and pain of Good Friday, but the mundane day after death, the secular world of Holy Saturday. The day after the Event when everything changed, but life continues *as if it has not*. The day after the death of God and the death of man when almost all live as if old God and old man continue *as they were*. The failure to really engage with the event of Good Friday means, despite all claims to the contrary, we have been living in variations of Holy Saturday ever since.

To understand that, we must engage with Žižek's discussion of revolution. The question of when we are most alive, when we are "really alive" is, Žižek suggests, answered "only if and when we engage ourselves with an excessive intensity with puts us beyond 'mere life'."[38] To apply this to the Christian Event, it is in the Crucifixion, in the despair and abandonment, that God and man were "most alive." It is this death that is the revolutionary act, the act of the death of God and the death of man; and just like all revolutionary acts the issue, the problem, is not the revolutionary act, not the revolution but what is to be done *after it*. In the Christian Event, in the Christian revolution, *after the revolution* is the mundane experience of Holy Saturday. This is the day that is not and cannot be "what was before" but perversely seeks a return to what was before the Event, before the act. Holy Saturday is where we do not want to face up to what the revolution, the revolutionary act has done. Holy Saturday is whereby we either engage in counterrevolutionary nostalgia for what was before or expose ourselves as not believing fully in the necessity of on-going revolution. Only by acknowledging that *both* God and man died is the revolution able to be accomplished; otherwise we, at best, engage in the Stalinist line of centrist Christianity and theology, a Stalinist Christianity of orthodox theology and the institutional, centrist power of the Church.

It is here we must stress the revolutionary nature of the Crucifixion. It is not that God is dead nor God doesn't exist; rather it is God is dead *and* man is dead. This is the revolutionary Event in that a new beginning has occurred: God is dead and man in relation to God separate from human existence, the God of Eternity, is dead. *Nothing is what it was before*; it is now Holy Spirit and humanity, the Holy Spirit who acts though the actions of new humanity. But because we do not understand this, because we do not want to engage in the reality of what occurred and what it means, we carry on as if the deaths have not occurred. We live therefore in Holy Saturday. What Easter Sunday means, the Event of a new hope and new beginning, is the Event whereby we acknowledge *our* responsibility for the world and for all who live in it.

There is no God to intervene, no God to resurrect, no self-resuscitation of dead Christ; to be a Christian atheist means there is only us to now live out the ethics of love in this world.

This also means we need to rethink Saint Paul and how we respond. For Paul's writings are on how the community created out of the death are to live *after the Event*; Paul is about how to live *after* the revolutionary Event. Yet while Christianity thinks it is Pauline, it actually betrays Paul constantly in its focus on the life and death of Jesus; it is as if after the revolution the Party spends its time focusing on the life and death of Lenin *before* revolution, not on the on-going revolution itself. In such a circumstance we get the church as Stalinist force, for what is orthodoxy if not the following of the correct party line against "rightist" or "leftist" deviations?

What I want to offer is a deviation, a deviation away from the centrist line, a deviation that states the revolution was more revolutionary than we imagined. For the revolution was not just done to God, that is, to authority, the power over our lives but done to us who lived under and in, reference to the power and authority. Not only did the authority, the power overthrow itself (the death of God), but this Event also overthrew who we used to be. That is, no longer are we man in reference to God.

What is the revolutionary offer? Nothing less than the universal offer of the new Humanity *without* "God." This is what could be expressed as the real meaning of "the true communion with Christ" that Žižek references, the participation being not just participation in "Christ's doubt and disbelief,"[39] but participation in the death of the old self who "believes." For in the cry from the Cross, Christ takes on *our* doubt and exposes the reason to doubt in what we did believe. For Salvation *is not* divine intervention; it is *Event* that enables a new beginning for all, not an action *for me*.

It is here that we also need to reconsider sin, for sin is, at source, estrangement from God. What if now we live *after* sin, that is, after separation, after estrangement, from God? We live after sin because in Christ, God and man estranged die. Therefore, it is the death of God and the death of man *combined* that free us from sin as ontological condition. It is now not estrangement from God that causes us to act in certain ways; it is estrangement from each other. In Christ we now live in the radical universality of love, where the only estrangement is that which we choose to enact and to impose against others.

It is from here that we can rethink who is the Remainder, those who have "no proper place in the 'official' universality grounded in exception."[40] The Remainder are those whom we decide to exclude in the name of our particular interests.

It is Christ who is the basis of the absolute, pure difference; Christ who was *neither just estranged God nor just estranged man*. That is, Christ who was the overcoming of the opposition based in the mutual estrangement of God and man. Christianity, that is, radical death of God *and* man secular Christianity, is therefore the faith of the new *who are neither estranged from God nor who seek to estrange man from man*; Christianity is the faith of those who seek to live out a true, revolutionary universality. The liberation theologian Gustavo Gutierrez proclaimed the central tenet of liberation theology as "the preferential option for the poor";[41] here I wish to extend this and state the central tenet of radical, secular theology is "the preferential option for the *Remainder*," for this politicizes the poor and all others excluded as – via Laclau and Rancière – "the properly democratic subject."[42]

It is Žižek who proposes how this might be undertaken by asking, via Saint Paul and the Law, what it would mean to suspend the Law in the name of Love, a state of exception: "In short, what if Romans has to be read together with Corinthians"?[43] What we get can be termed the rupture of Romans, the rupture of the Law that suspends in the name of Love, a Love in which there is no Remainder to the Universal act and Event. For does not Paul seek to suspend the Law by that which acts as Universal Law within (the transgression within) that is Love? Is not the basis the God who transgresses his own laws to the extreme by undertaking the ultimate transgression as the God who dies? For in dying, God self-transgresses all that is created and expected in response to God. Therefore, the Love beyond the Law is that inaugurated by the death of God, the death of the God of the Law, the death of man who lives by that Law. This Love beyond the Law is now to be enacted by the new humanity who, in so acting, constitute the community of the Holy Spirit. It is this new humanity which takes the "Love beyond the Law" from the particular to the universal; for the transgression of the Law is the love-act that makes the new Law of Love beyond Law universal in itself. And what is this new Law of Love? It is the preferential option for the Remainder.

It is Love that also makes clear that knowledge "remains, in a way, non-all, incomplete."[44] For it is not just knowledge that is incomplete, but also all claims to knowledge; for now – in the death of God and of man – there is no completion and no final referent, for there is no singular but only the *incompletion* of Love. It is this incomplete Love, the love of the incomplete being that is, as Žižek notes, "the kernel of Christian experience."[45] This imperfection is what is revealed in the mutual death, the death of God and the death of man, for all that is left, all that is revealed, is imperfection: the imperfection, the *necessary imperfection* of humanity. For imperfection is *all there is* and *all we are* – but that imperfection is to be encountered and experienced as Love. The kernel of Christianity, the kernel of secular Christianity, is that we exist in a world of universal imperfection, but that this is also the world of the call to universal love.

This is also how we can extend Žižek's discussion on how "the Fall is *identical* to Redemption,"[46] in that in both there is the "explosion of freedom."[47] In the fall, man fell *into* the world, fell into the knowledge of Good and Evil, fell into that whereby that which separated God and man was now *only*, it seems eternal life. This is what Genesis 3: 22–24 warns of: man is now only seemingly separated from God by mortality;[48] man is therefore expelled from the garden; and the tree of Life is guarded by cherubim and a flaming sword. Man has fallen into knowledge, fallen into this world, fallen into freedom, fallen into a world of secular, mundane mortality. It is the Eternity of God that separates God and man. But human freedom is not divine freedom, and yet Eternity seeks to fully join with mortal man, to fall into freedom in the world unto death. Therefore, if God dies, what difference is there now between man and *non*-God, for both now experience death? If we do not acknowledge the death of God, what we have is man who continues to die – yet living in reference to a God who is now dead. This is no freedom; this is no redemption. Redemption therefore only occurs if *both* God and man die in Christ and the explosion of freedom is freedom *from all that was* in the Event of the new Universal: victory over death that kept God and man in estrangement. For death is no longer that which estranges, but that which overcame estrangement. In death, the death of God and death of man, occurs the explosion of freedom that is redemption.

It is this explosion of freedom via death that also provides the true meaning of the Christian assertion of "the direct identity of God and man."[49] With the redemptive fall of God that completed the redemptive fall of man, in the death of Christ occurs this direct identity that negates the oppositional stance of God and man that preceded it. It is a negation not in the sense that it opposes the oppositional stance but that it negates in the sense that it *ends it*. The oppositional stance is often, as indeed Žižek does, referenced to the suffering figure of Job. The provocation of Job is his insistence "on the utter *meaninglessness* of his suffering."[50] But Job is only able to do so because of his belief in the *meaningfulness* of that which imposes his suffering, even if the suffering itself is meaningless. The provocation of Christ is also a meaningless suffering,[51] but now a meaningless suffering imposed by God upon Himself and man in Christ: a meaningless suffering from which there is no answer to the cry of abandonment. No answer, for there is no meaning. What the meaninglessness of the suffering death of God and man in Christ exposes is that there is no meaningfulness in the imposition or experience of suffering. Suffering has no meaning for either God or man: suffering is only the sign of estrangement.[52]

What the death of God and man in Christ explodes as freedom is the redemption of the end of any claim to meaningful suffering. Suffering only ever was – and is – the sign of estrangement. It *was* the sign of the estrangement of God and man; it is *now* the sign of the estrangement of humanity from itself, an estrangement that we are called upon to overcome in the name of Universal Love, which is the community of the Holy Spirit. This is the basis of what Žižek identifies as Paul's "fighting collective grounded in the reference to an unconditional universalism."[53] Why is it an unconditional universalism? Precisely because God and man died. For it is the death of man as separate, as estranged from God, *and* the death of God separated, as estranged from man, *that combined* is the explosive freedom of the Event which *allows* the breaking forth of unconditional universalism. There is not the separated because there is no God to be separated from: *all* is now the secular. This is why Christianity is the religion of the death of God: *Christianity is atheism.*

But we must also be clear that Christianity is atheism as Event *within* Judaism, an Event that is *no event* for Judaism except in its perverse effects. Yet for Christianity to deny Judaism is for Christianity to deny that which hosts the Event, for without Judaism there is no Christianity, because the Universal Event is that which occurred within the particular. So, Christianity is not the end or the negation or the supersession of Judaism, but rather, as Paul signals, the break *with* Judaism that does not end it. It is the break that occurs from within Judaism, the break that occurs from within God and man. It is the break that seeks to make universal that which was particular within Judaism: that the bond of God and man is enacted in what we do to one another as fellow humans. It is the break that seeks to make universal the limitation of the Law in the Event of Universal Love.

The Event of Universal Love is what we can term the Messianic; it is a revolutionary Event because it occurred before the expected right moment and not as the expected right manner. The question that Christianity asks is: what revolutionary act do we undertake in response to the revolutionary Event? This is how we understand Žižek's statement that "the Time of the event is not another time beyond and above the 'normal' historical time, but a kind of inner loop within this time."[54] This is also how we can understand that secular Christianity is an Event within Judaism, for it is the death of God and man that ruptures, in repetition, all who still live, Christian or Jew, within the belief of the estrangement of God and man. The Event *occurs*; it has not just occurred: it is a repetition Event that occurs in our time, in my time. This means the faith of the Christian atheist is a personal apocalypse in response to the Messianic event encountered in *my* time. For the apocalypse is never universal, never communal, but always personal, always singular – as is the apocalypse of the Crucifixion.

For the Crucifixion was the apocalyptic Event for God and man that then engenders the personal, singular apocalypse for the one who responds because "there is no Event outside the engaged subjective decision which creates it – if we wait for the time to become ripe for the Event, the Event will never occur."[55] This is also why the revolutionary Event of the death of God is an Event for us here today, for "Authentic revolution . . . always occurs in an absolute Present, in the unconditional urgency of a Now."[56] So the authentic revolution of the death of God *and* man is the event of *our* time, that is of *my* time. The Event occurs and I live in Holy Saturday. How we respond, how I respond, is whereby Easter Sunday occurs – which is the revolutionary Event *for* us, the revolutionary, universal Event *of* us. This is our "earnest work" that occurs "*after* the Event"; that is, on Holy Saturday, *what do we do*? For while the universal Event of Easter Friday and Easter Sunday are particulars that individuals respond to, it is Saturday that we all share. It is from Holy Saturday that we are called to respond: in the aftermath of the Event of Good Friday and before the Event of Easter Sunday.

This raises the question of what is meant by fidelity to the Event. What does fidelity mean when the Event is the death of God and death of man? It is fidelity to living in the Universal after – and before – the particulars. For the death of God that also involves the death of man throws open, via the Event, the question of who we are and what we are to do. This is because the death of God is the Event of pure – and only – materialism that exposes there is now *only* us, *only* this world – and *no God*. Yet it is this Event that also exposes the death of man estranged and in relation to God. This, is how "the Event is a pure-empty sign, and we have to generate its meaning"[57] whereby in the death of God and man we are confronted, on Holy Saturday, with "the openness of a New Beginning, and it is up to humanity to live up to it, to decide its meaning, to make something of it."[58]

It is from Holy Saturday that the impotence of God becomes clear, for God has fallen into history, has fallen into the secular, and in his death and the death of estranged man made clear that it is now new humanity who, as the community of the Holy Spirit, must act, must intervene – in the name of the Event of Love. This is what is meant by "the suspension of Otherness":[59] the collective of new humanity who live in fidelity to the Event. This new humanity lives both *after* God and *after* man who was separated, was estranged from God. The central kernel of Christianity is that the Other is Other no longer and that the Messiah is not a promise or expectation but an on-going event within New Humanity *for the world. Christianity is therefore the politics of revolutionary emancipation in the name of the Event.*

This is why Christianity is the dwarf in the puppet of historical materialism; this is why Christianity is the dwarf in Žižek, the dwarf in all who are materialists, in all who seek a revolutionary emancipation in the name of the Event.

Žižek's concluding question is "do we really need God"?[60] As should be now clear, the answer, his answer, my answer is that in the Event the answer is provided by God: NO! For the Event is the death of the Big Other – *and* – what Žižek and almost everyone else misses – the death of that man who existed in relation to and expectation of the Big Other. What we have now is the new community of the Holy Spirit, who seek to live out the ethics of revolutionary love. The Holy Spirit is therefore the community of atheist Christians that abandons both "the shell of its institutional organization (and, even more so, of its specific religious experience)."[61] Žižek and those of us who align ourselves with him stand revealed as Christians who are not part of Christianity, theologians who are not part of theology: our dwarf revealed in the secular universalism of living Holy Saturday in fidelity to the Event.

Notes

1. I thank the anonymous reviewer of an earlier version for this paper their careful reading and comments that have resulted in the addition of this positioning statement and other clarifications of what is, admittedly, a radical re-reading of Christianity.
2. Mike Grimshaw, "Review of *Absolute Recoil: Towards a New Foundation of Dialectical Materialism* by Slavoj Žižek," *International Journal of Žižek Studies* 10, no. 2 (2016): 108–9.

216 Mike Grimshaw

3 Slavoj Žižek, *The Puppet and the Dwarf: The Perverse Core of Christianity* (Cambridge, MA & London: MIT Press, 2003).
4 In Walter Benjamin's First thesis on the Philosophy of History (from his *Theses of the Philosophy of History/On the Concept of History* [1940]) he states:

> It is well-known that an automaton once existed, which was so constructed that it could counter any move of a chess-player with a counter-move, and thereby assure itself of victory in the match. A puppet in Turkish attire, water-pipe in mouth, sat before the chessboard, which rested on a broad table. Through a system of mirrors, the illusion was created that this table was transparent from all sides. In truth, a hunchbacked dwarf who was a master chess-player sat inside, controlling the hands of the puppet with strings. One can envision a corresponding object to this apparatus in philosophy. The puppet called "historical materialism" is always supposed to win. It can do this with no further ado against any opponent, so long as it employs the services of theology, which as everyone knows is small and ugly and must be kept out of sight.

www.marxists.org/reference/archive/benjamin/1940/history.htm
5 Žižek, *Puppet*, 3.
6 T.S. Eliot, *Notes towards a Definition of Culture* (London: Faber & Faber Ltd., 1948), 122.
7 Žižek, *Puppet*, Series preface.
8 Graham Ward, *Cities of God* (London & New York: Routledge, 2000), 2.
9 Žižek, *Puppet*, 3.
10 Ibid.
11 Ibid., 6.
12 Ibid., 10.
13 Ibid., 13.
14 Ibid., 14.
15 Ibid., 15.
16 Ibid., 15–16.
17 Ibid., 24.
18 Ibid.
19 I want to again thank the anonymous reviewer of the earlier draft, for, in their comments, pushing me on this point.
20 Žižek, *Puppet*, 30.
21 Ibid., 41.
22 Ibid., 44.
23 I acknowledge that any resort to what could be viewed as proof-texting opens up the fraught possibility of counter-proof-texting *ad infinitum*. I therefore use this text as part of my claim for a revolutionary Christian love, albeit noting in particular also the claim of "blessed are the peacemakers" (Matthew 5:9). But peace in a context of radical, revolutionary love does not precede conflict, it resolves it. Conflict manifests out of structural conflict that then assumes revolutionary form. We should not, and must not, confuse the structural conflict and its oppression for peace. This is especially so for we who are bourgeois and who benefit from current structural conflict which we mistake for peace.
24 Žižek, *Puppet*, 49.
25 Ibid.
26 Ibid., 51.
27 Ibid.
28 Ibid.
29 What makes Christian atheist ethics different from other ethical options such as consequentialism, virtue ethics or even possibly Stoicism is its foundation in

the act of revolutionary, universal love. This is ethics that constantly seeks to change the world, not moderate it. That is, it is an atheistic ethics of constant, revolutionary struggle in the name of a materialist universal love. Again, I thank the anonymous reviewer for pushing me on this point.
30 Žižek, *Puppet*, 69.
31 Ibid., 78.
32 Ibid., 87.
33 Gabriel Vahanian, *Tillich and the New Religious Paradigm* (Aurora, CO: The Davies Group Publishers, 2005), 21.
34 Clayton Crockett, "Introduction," in *Secular Theology: American Radical Theological Thought*, ed. Clayton Crockett (London & New York: Routledge 2001), 1.
35 Žižek, *Puppet*, 89.
36 Ibid., 91.
37 Ibid.
38 Ibid., 94.
39 Ibid., 102.
40 Ibid., 109.
41 See Gustavo Gutierrez, *A Theology of Liberation* (New York: Maryknoll, 1973).
42 Žižek, *Puppet*, 109.
43 Ibid., 112.
44 Ibid., 115.
45 Ibid.
46 Ibid., 118.
47 Ibid.
48 Or, as again spurred by the anonymous reviewer, we could also state that the difference is between the timeless and the timebound, for human life is timebound. This of course is overcome when God chooses to enter into the limitations of timebound life.
49 Žižek, *Puppet*, 123.
50 Ibid., 125.
51 Ibid.
52 By suffering, I mean that which arises out of preventable human action, including structural violence, or from a lack of adequate human response to the suffering of natural disasters. Pain I would qualify as something different, something which includes non-human animals. Suffering is therefore retained as a theological, as an anthro-theological condition.
53 Žižek, *Puppet*, 130.
54 Ibid., 134.
55 Ibid., 135.
56 Ibid.
57 Ibid., 136.
58 Ibid.
59 Ibid., 138.
60 Ibid., 169.
61 Ibid., 171.

Bibliography

Benjamin, Walter. "On the Concept of History [1940]" [Theses of the Philosophy of History]. Retrieved December 27, 2017 from www.marxists.org/reference/archive/benjamin/1940/history.htm.

Crockett, Clayton. "Introduction." In *Secular Theology: American Radical Theological Thought*, edited by Clayton Crockett, 1–9. London & New York: Routledge, 2001.

Eliot, T.S. *Notes towards a Definition of Culture*. London: Faber & Faber Ltd, 1948.
Grimshaw, Mike. "Review of *Absolute Recoil: Towards a New Foundation of Dialectical Materialism* by Slavoj Žižek." *International Journal of Žižek Studies* 10, no. 2 (2016): 108–17.
Gutierrez, Gustavo. *A Theology of Liberation*. New York: Maryknoll, 1973.
Vahanian, Gabriel. *Tillich and the New Religious Paradigm*. Aurora, CO: The Davies Group Publishers, 2005.
Ward, Graham. *Cities of God*. London & New York: Routledge, 2000.
Žižek, Slavoj. *The Puppet and the Dwarf: The Perverse Core of Christianity*. Cambridge, MA & London: MIT Press, 2003.

Afterword
The antinomies that keep Christianity alive
Slavoj Žižek

Pope Francis usually displays the right intuitions in matters theological and political. Recently, however, he committed a serious blunder in endorsing the idea, propagated by some Catholics, to change a line in Lord's Prayer where the prayer asks God to "lead us not into temptation":

> It is not a good translation because it speaks of a God who induces temptation. I am the one who falls; it's not him pushing me into temptation to then see how I have fallen. A father doesn't do that, a father helps you to get up immediately. It's Satan who leads us into temptation, that's his department.

So, the pontiff suggests we should all follow the Catholic Church in France, which already uses the phrase "do not let us fall into temptation," instead.[1]

Convincing as this simple line of reasoning may sound, it misses the deepest paradox of Christianity and ethics. Is God not exposing us to temptation already in paradise where he warns Adam and Eve not to eat the apple from the tree of knowledge? Why did he put this tree there in the first place, and then even draw attention to it? Was he not aware that human ethics can arise only after the Fall? Many most perspicuous theologians and Christian writers, from Kierkegaard to Paul Claudel, were fully aware that, at its most basic, temptation arises in the form of the Good – or, as Kierkegaard put it apropos Abraham, when he is ordered to slaughter Isaac, his predicament "is an ordeal such that, please note, the ethical is the temptation."[2] Is the temptation of the (false) Good not what characterizes all forms of religious fundamentalism?

Here is a perhaps surprising historical example: the killing of Reinhard Heydrich. In London, the Czechoslovak government-in-exile resolved to kill Heydrich; Jan Kubiš and Jozef Gabčík, who headed the team chosen for the operation, were parachuted in the vicinity of Prague. On 27 May 1942, alone with his chauffeur in an open car (to show his courage and trust), Heydrich was on his way to his office when, at a junction in a Prague suburb, the car slowed; Gabčík stepped in front of the car and took aim at it with a submachine gun, but it jammed. Instead of ordering his driver to speed away, Heydrich called his car to halt and decided to confront the attackers. At this moment, Kubiš threw a bomb at the rear of the car as it stopped, and the explosion wounded both Heydrich and Kubiš. When the smoke cleared, Heydrich emerged from the wreckage with his gun in his hand; he chased Kubiš for half a block but became weak from shock and collapsed. He sent his driver, Klein, to chase Gabčík on foot, while, still with pistol in hand, he gripped his left flank, which was bleeding profusely. A Czech woman went to Heydrich's aid and flagged down a delivery van; he was first placed in the driver's cab of the van, but complained the van's movement was causing him pain, so he was placed in the back of the van, on his stomach, and quickly taken to the emergency room at a nearby hospital . . . (Incidentally, although Heydrich died a couple of days later, there was a serious chance that he would survive, so this woman may well have entered history as the one who saved Heydrich's life.) While a militarist Nazi sympathizer would emphasize Heydrich's personal courage, what fascinates me is the role of the anonymous Czech woman: she helped Heydrich, who was lying alone in blood, with no military or police protection. Was she aware who he was? If yes, and if she was no Nazi sympathizer (both the most probable surmises), why did she do this? Was it a simple half-automatic reaction of human compassion, of helping a neighbor in distress no matter who he or she (or ze, as we will be soon forced to add) is? Should this compassion win over the awareness of the fact that this "neighbor" is a top Nazi criminal responsible for thousands (and later millions) of deaths? What we confront here is the ultimate choice between abstract liberal humanism and the ethics implied by radical emancipatory struggle: if we progress to the end of the side of liberal humanism, we find ourselves condoning the worst criminals, and if we progress to the end of partial political engagement, we find ourselves on the side of emancipatory universality – in the case of Heydrich, for the poor Czech woman to act universally would have been to resist her compassion and try to finish the wounded Heydrich off . . .

Such impasses are the stuff of actual engaged ethical life, and if we exclude them as problematic we are left with a lifeless benevolent holy text. What lurks behind this exclusion is the trauma of the Book of Job where God and Satan directly organize the destruction of Job's life in order to test his devotion. Quite a few Christians claim the Book of Job should be therefore excluded from the Bible as a pagan blasphemy. However, before we succumb to this politically correct ethic cleansing, we should pause for a moment of consider what we lose with it.

The almost unbearable impact of the Book of Job resides not so much in its narrative frame (the Devil appears in it as a conversational partner of God, and the two engage in a rather cruel experiment in order to test Job's faith), but in its final outcome. One should precisely locate the true greatness of Job: contrary to the usual notion of Job, he is *not* a patient sufferer enduring his ordeal with the firm faith in God – on the contrary, he complains all the time, rejecting his fate (like Oedipus at Colonus, who is also usually misperceived as a patient victim resigned to his fate). When, after his livelihood is destroyed, the three theologians–friends visit him, their line of argumentation is the standard ideological sophistry: if you suffer, it is by definition that you *must have* done something wrong, since God is just . . . However, their argumentation is not limited to the claim that Job must be somehow guilty: what is at stake at a more radical level is the meaning(lessness) of Job's suffering. Like Oedipus at Colonus, Job insists on the utter *meaninglessness* of his suffering – as the title of Job 27 says: "Job Maintains His Integrity." As such, the Book of Job provides what is perhaps the first exemplary case of the critique of ideology in the human history, laying bare the basic discursive strategies of legitimizing suffering: Job's properly ethical dignity resides in the way he persistently rejects the notion that his suffering can have any meaning, either punishment for his past sins or the trial of his faith, against the three theologians who bombard him with possible meanings – and, surprisingly, God takes his side at the end, claiming that every word that Job spoke was true, while every word of the three theologians was false.

And it is with regard to this assertion of the meaninglessness of Job's suffering that one should insist on the parallel between Job and Christ, on Job's suffering announcing the Way of the Cross: Christ's suffering is *also* meaningless, not an act of meaningful exchange. The difference, of course, is that, in the case of Christ, the gap that separates the suffering desperate man (Job) from God is transposed into God himself, as His own radical splitting or, rather, self-abandonment. What this means is that one should risk a much more radical than usual reading of Christ's "Father, why did you forsake me?" than the usual one: since we are dealing here not with the gap between man and God, but with the split in God himself, the solution cannot be for the God to (re)appear in all his majesty, revealing to Christ the deeper meaning of his suffering (that he was the Innocent sacrificed to redeem humanity). Christ's "Father, why did you forsake me?" is not the complaint to the *omnipotent* capricious God–Father whose ways are indecipherable to us, mortal humans, but the complaint which hints at the *impotent* God. It is like the child who, after believing in his father's powerfulness, with a horror discovers that his father cannot help him. (To evoke an example from recent history: at the moment of Christ's Crucifixion, God-the-Father is in a position somewhat similar to that of the Bosnian father made to witness the gang rape of his own daughter and to endure the ultimate trauma of her compassionate–reproaching gaze: "Father, why did you forsake me?") In short, with this "Father, why did you forsake me?," it is God-the-Father who effectively dies, revealing his utter impotence, and thereupon rises from the dead in the guise of the Holy Ghost, the collective of believers.

Why did Job keep his silence after the boastful appearance of God?[3] Is this ridiculous boasting (the pompous battery of "Were you there when . . ." rhetorical questions: "Who is this whose ignorant words / Smear my design with darkness? / Were you there when I planned the earth, / Tell me, if you are so wise?"; Job 38:2–5) not the very mode of appearance of its opposite, to which one can answer by simply saying: "O.K., if you can do all this, *why did you let me suffer in such a meaningless way?*" Do God's thundering words not render all the more palpable his silence, the absence of answer? What, then, if *this* was what Job perceived and what kept him silent: he remained silent neither because he was crushed by God's overwhelming presence, nor because he wanted thereby to signal his continuous resistance, i.e. the fact that God avoided answering Job's question, but because, in a gesture of silent solidarity, he perceived the divine impotence. God is neither just nor unjust, but simply impotent. What Job suddenly understood is that *it was not him, but God himself who was effectively on trial in Job's calamities*, and he failed the test miserably. Even more pointedly, one is tempted to risk a radical anachronistic reading: Job foresaw God's own future suffering – "Today it's me, tomorrow it will be your own son, and there will be no one to intervene for *him*. What you see in me now is the prefiguration of your own passion!"

So, if we want to keep the Christian experience alive, let us resist the temptation to purge from it all "problematic" passages – they are the very stuff which confers on Christianity the unbearable tensions of a true life. Martin Luther was fully aware of this when, referring to Jesus' claim that a good tree does not bring forth evil fruit (i.e. a good tree produces only good fruit), he concluded from it that "good works do not make a good man, but a good man does good works." One should fully assume the "static" anti-performative (or anti-Pascalean) aspect of this conclusion: we do not create ourselves through the meanders of our life-practice; in our creativity, we rather bring out what we already are. It's not "act as if you are good, do good works, and you will become good," it is "only if you are good you can do good works." The easy way to read this claim is to interpret it as a "necessary illusion": what I am is effectively created through my activity; there is no pre-existing essence or essential identity which is expressed/actualized in my acts; however, we spontaneously (mis)perceive our acts as merely expressing/actualizing what we (already) are in ourselves. However, from a properly dialectical standpoint, it is not enough to say that the pre-existing self-identity is a necessary illusion; we have here a more complex mechanism of (re)creating the eternal identity itself. Let's clarify this mechanism with an example. When something crucial happens, even if it happens unexpectedly, we often get the impression that it *had* to happen, that it would violate some higher order if it were not to happen. More precisely, once it *does* happen, we see that it had to happen – but it may *not* have happened. Let's take a case of desperate love: I am deeply convinced that my love is not reciprocated, and I silently resign myself to a gloomy future of despair; but if I all of a sudden discover that my love is reciprocated, I feel that this had to happen and I cannot even image the despair of my life without it. Or let's take a difficult and risky political decision: although we sympathize with it, we are skeptical, we don't trust the scared majority; but when, as if by a miracle, this decision *is* taken and enacted, we feel it was destined to happen. Authentic political acts take place like this: in them, (what was considered) "impossible" happens and, by way of happening, it rewrites its own past and emerges as necessary, "pre-destined" even. This is why there is no incompatibility between predestination and our free acts. Luther saw clearly how the (Catholic) idea that our redemption depends on our acts introduces a dimension of bargaining into ethics: good deeds are not done out of duty but in order to gain salvation. If, however, my salvation is pre-destined, this means that my fate is already decided and my doing good deeds does not serve anything, so if I do them, it is out of pure duty, a really altruistic act:

> This recognition that only as one was freed from the paralyzing need to serve one's own self, could acts of love become altruistic, was one of Luther's most positive contributions to Christian social ethics. It enabled him to view good deeds as ends in themselves, and never as a means of salvation.[4]

Luther realized that a love that sought no reward was more willing to serve the helpless, the powerless, the poor, and the oppressed, since their cause offered the least prospect of personal gain. But did Luther draw all ethico-political consequences from this key insight? His great pupil and opponent Thomas Müntzer accused Luther of betrayal: his basic reproach to Luther's social ethics concerns the perverse application of the Law–Gospel distinction. The rightful use of the law was to bring "destruction and sickness to the healthy," and that of the Gospel to bring "comfort to the troubled." Luther had turned this application on its head by defending the presumptuous and tyrannical rulers with the gracious words of the Gospel, while bringing the "grim sternness" of the law to bear against the God-fearing poor and oppressed peasants. The result was a total misuse of Scripture.

> Thus the godless tyrant says to the pious, "I must torture you. Christ also suffered. Therefore you are not to resist me." (Matthew 5) This [is] a great perversion . . . one must forgive with the Gospel and the Spirit of Christ, to the furtherance and not the hindrance of the Gospel.[5]

With this perversion, "the elect were no longer envisioned as directly active or forceful instruments of that retribution" against those who violate the spirit of the Gospel. This critique of Luther is clear, but it nonetheless seems to court the danger of succumbing itself to the perverse position of perceiving oneself as the direct instrument of Big Other's will. How to avoid this danger? Let us begin at the beginning, with the triad of Orthodoxy, Catholicism and Protestantism.

Central to the Orthodox tradition is the notion of "theosis," of man becoming (like) God, or, to quote Saint Athanasius of Alexandria, "He was incarnate that we might be made God." (De incarnatione 54.3) What would otherwise seem absurd – that fallen, sinful man may become holy as God is holy – has been made possible through Jesus Christ, who is God incarnate. St. Maximus the Confessor wrote:

> A sure warrant for looking forward with hope to the deification of human nature is provided by the Incarnation of God, which makes man god to the same degree as God Himself became man . . . . Let us all become the image of the one whole God, bearing nothing earthly in ourselves, so that we may consort with God and become gods, receiving from God our existence as gods.[6]

This Orthodox formula – "God became man so that man can become God" – is totally wrong: God became man *and that's it*, nothing more, everything already happens here, what needs to be added is just a new perspective on this. There is no resurrection to follow; the Holy Spirit already *is* the Resurrection. Only Protestantism (not even Catholicism) enables us to think Incarnation as an event in God himself, as *His* profound transformation: He was incarnate that *He* became God, i.e. He became fully God only through His self-division into God and man. This may sound paradoxical since God is an unknown Beyond, *deus absconditus*. We thus seem to have three incompatible positions: God is an absolutely impenetrable Beyond; God is the absolute Master of our fate which is pre-destined by Him; God gave us freedom and thereby made us responsible for our deeds. The unique achievement of Protestantism is to bring together these three positions: everything is pre-destined by God, but since God is an impenetrable Beyond for me I cannot discern what my fate is, so I am left to do good deeds without any calculation and profit in view, i.e., in total freedom,

True freedom is not a freedom of choice made from a safe distance, like choosing between a strawberry cake or a chocolate cake; true freedom overlaps with necessity; one makes a truly free choice when one's choice puts at stake one's very existence – one does it because one simply "cannot do it otherwise." When one's country is under a foreign occupation and one is called by a resistance leader to join the fight against the occupiers, the reason given is not "you are free to choose," but: "can't you see that this is the only thing you can do if you want to retain your dignity?" This is why radical acts of freedom are possible only under the condition of predestination: in predestination, we know we are pre-destined, but we don't know how we are pre-destined, i.e., which of our choices is predetermined, and this terrifying situation where we have to decide what to do, knowing that our decision is decided in advance, is perhaps the only case of real freedom, of the unbearable burden of a really free choice – we know that what we will do is pre-destined, but we still have to take a risk and subjectively choose what is pre-destined.

Freedom, of course, disappears if we locate a human being into objective reality, as its part, as one among objects – at this level, there is simply no space for freedom. In order to locate freedom, we have to make a move from the enunciated content (what we are talking about) to our (the speakers') position of enunciation. If a scientist demonstrates we are not free, what does this imply for the position from which he (and we) speaks? This reference to the subject of enunciation (foreclosed by science) is irreducible: whatever I am saying, it's me who is saying it, so apropos of every scientific reduction to objective reality (which makes me a biological machine) a question is to be raised of the horizon from which I see and say this. Is this not why psychoanalysis is exemplary of our predicament? Yes, we are decentered, caught in a foreign cobweb, overdetermined by unconscious mechanisms, yes, I am "spoken" more than speaking, the Other speaks through me, but simply assuming this fact (in the sense of rejecting any responsibility) is also false, a case of self-deception – psychoanalysis makes me even more responsible than traditional morality; it makes me responsible even for what is beyond my (conscious) control.

This solution works on one condition: the subject (believer) is absolutely constrained by the unsurpassable horizon of its subjectivity. What Protestantism prohibits is the very thought that a believer can, as it were, take a position outside/above itself and look upon itself as a small particle in the vast reality. Mao was wrong when he deployed his Olympic vision reducing human experience to a tiny unimportant detail:

> The United States cannot annihilate the Chinese nation with its small stack of atom bombs. Even if the US atom bombs were so powerful that, when dropped on China, they would make a hole right through the earth, or even blow it up, that would hardly mean anything to the universe as a whole, though it might be a major event for the solar system.[7]

There is an "inhuman madness" in this argument: is the fact that the destruction of the planet Earth "would hardly mean anything to the universe as a whole" not a rather poor solace for the extinguished humanity? The argument only works if, in a Kantian way, one presupposes a pure transcendental subject non-affected by this catastrophe – a subject which, although non-existing in reality, *is* operative as a virtual point of reference (recall Husserl's dark dream, from his *Cartesian Meditations*, of how the transcendental *cogito* would remain unaffected by a plague that would annihilate entire humanity). In contrast to such a stance of cosmic indifference, we should act as if the entire universe was created as a backstage for the struggle of emancipation, in exactly the same way that, for Kant, God created the world in order to serve as the battleground for the ethical struggle of humanity – it is as if the fate of the entire universe is decided in our singular (and, from the global cosmic standpoint, marginal and insignificant) struggle.

The paradox is that, although (human) subjectivity is obviously not the origin of all reality, although it is a contingent local event in the universe, the path to universal truth does not lead through the abstraction from it in the well-known sense of "let's try to imagine how the world is independently of us," the approach which brings us to some "gray" objective structure – such a vision of the "subjectless" world is by definition just a negative image of subjectivity itself, its own vision of the world in its absence. (The same holds for all the attempts to picture humanity as an insignificant species on a small planet on the edge of our galaxy, i.e. to view it the same way we view a colony of ants.) Since we are subjects, constrained to the horizon of subjectivity, we should instead focus on what the fact of subjectivity implies for the universe and its structure: the event of subject derails the balance, it throws the world out of joint, but such a derailment *is* the universal truth of the world. What this also implies is that the access to "reality in itself" does not demand from us that we overcome our "partiality" and arrive at a neutral vision elevated above our particular struggles – we are "universal beings" only in our full partial engagements. This contrast is clearly discernible in the case of love: against the Buddhist love of All or any other notion of the harmony with the cosmos, we should assert the radically exclusive love for the singular One, a love which throws out of joint the smooth flow of our lives.

Notes

1 Harriet Sherwood, "Lead Us Not into Mistranslation: Pope Wants Lord's Prayer Changed," *The Guardian*, December 8, 2017. Retrieved from www.theguardian.com/world/2017/dec/08/lead-us-not-into-mistranslation-pope-wants-lords-prayer-changed.
2 In *Fear and Trembling*, Søren Kierkegaard, *Fear and Trembling/Repetition*, trans. Howard Vincent Hong and Edna Hatlestad Hong (Princeton, NJ: Princeton University Press, 1983), 115.
3 Editorial note: There would be a valid philological question here on whether "silence" is an accurate rendering of the Book of Job's text, and since this is a crucial part of Slavoj Žižek's argument, particularly in view of his later remark that "in a gesture of silent solidarity, [Job] perceived the divine impotence," a short note might be in order. Providing one is not literalistic, "silence" is a reasonable way of construing Job 40:4–5, "I lay my hand on my mouth. I have spoken once, and I will not answer; twice, but will proceed no further" (NRSV). However while "silence" fits the response to the first of God's speeches, it does not necessarily fit that to the second speech about Behemoth and Leviathan, a response which extends in slightly garbled fashion from Job 42:1–6. The earlier part of this latter passage can no doubt be read in a manner more or less aligned with that of the first response, but the interesting challenge comes with verses five and, especially, six. NRSV gives a traditional translation: Job 42:5–6, "I had heard of you by the hearing of the ear, but now my eye sees you; therefore I despise myself, and repent in dust and ashes." This rendering of the crucial verse six is psychologically not far from that of the Septuagint which, literally translated, gives "I esteem myself dust and ashes." Now, of course one could simply maintain that the second response, together with the second of God's speeches, should be ignored as later interpolations (though it is more often held that while the Behemoth/Leviathan speech may well be an interpolation, it has been interpolated between the two halves of Job's response). Given that Žižek does not otherwise challenge here the integrity of the received text, rather more promising would be the fact that Job 42:6 is a notorious textual crux for translators. There are at least six plausible renderings, and one of the most defensible of these might be thought to fit rather well into the overall scheme of Žižek's text at hand. Forty years ago Dale Patrick argued in "The translation of Job

XLII 6" (*Vetus Testamentum* 26, no. 3 (July 1976): 369–71) that verse six should be translated "therefore I repudiate and repent of [that is, 'forswear'] dust and ashes." When the final disaster struck, Job "sat among the ashes" (Job 2:8); on this reading, hearing and "seeing" the Lord led him "to cease wallowing in dust and ashes," to abandon "the posture of mourning" (Patrick, 370–1).
4 Paul P. Kuenning, "Luther and Muntzer: Contrasting Theologies in Regard to Secular Authority within the Context of the German Peasant Revolt," *Journal of Church and State* 29, no. 2 (March 1, 1987): 306, https://doi.org/10.1093/jcs/29.2.305.
5 Thomas Müntzer, *Schriften und Briefe*, ed. Gerhard Wehr, Fischer-Taschenbücher 1378 (Frankfurt am Main: Fischer, 1973), 330, as quoted in Kuenning, "Luther and Muntzer," 319.
6 Maximus the Confessor, "Various Texts on Theology, the Divine Economy, and Virtue and Vice, First Century," in *The Philokalia. The Complete Text, Compiled by St. Nikodimos of the Holy Mountain and St. Makarios of Corinth*, trans. G. E. H. Palmer, Philip Sherrard and Kallistos Ware, vol. 2 (London: Faber & Faber Ltd., 1990), 177–8, 171 (I.62 and I.28 respectively).
7 Mao Tse-tung, "Selected Works of Mao Tse-tung: The Chinese People Cannot Be Cowed by the Atom Bomb, January 28, 1955. Main Points of a Conversation with Ambassador Carl-Johan (Cay) Sundstrom, the First Finnish Envoy to China, When He Presented His Credentials." Retrieved January 4, 2018 from www.marxists.org/reference/archive/mao/selected-works/volume-5/mswv5_40.htm.

Bibliography

Kierkegaard, Søren. *Fear and Trembling/Repetition*. Translated by Howard Vincent Hong and Edna Hatlestad Hong. Princeton, NJ: Princeton University Press, 1983.
Kuenning, Paul P. "Luther and Muntzer: Contrasting Theologies in Regard to Secular Authority within the Context of the German Peasant Revolt." *Journal of Church and State* 29, no. 2 (March 1, 1987): 305–21. https://doi.org/10.1093/jcs/29.2.305.
Maximus the Confessor. "Various Texts on Theology, the Divine Economy, and Virtue and Vice, First Century." In *The Philokalia: The Complete Text, Compiled by St. Nikodimos of the Holy Mountain and St. Makarios of Corinth*, translated by G.E.H. Palmer, Philip Sherrard and Kallistos Ware, vol. 2, 165–87. London: Faber and Faber, 1990.
Müntzer, Thomas. *Schriften und Briefe*. Edited by Gerhard Wehr. Frankfurt am Main: Fischer, 1973.
Sherwood, Harriet. "Lead Us Not into Mistranslation: Pope Wants Lord's Prayer Changed." *The Guardian*, December 8, 2017. Retrieved from www.theguardian.com/world/2017/dec/08/lead-us-not-into-mistranslation-pope-wants-lords-prayer-changed.
Tse-tung, Mao. "Selected Works of Mao Tse-tung: The Chinese People Cannot Be Cowed by the Atom Bomb, January 28, 1955. Main Points of a Conversation with Ambassador Carl-Johan (Cay) Sundstrom, the First Finnish Envoy to China, When He Presented His Credentials." Retrieved January 4, 2018 from www.marxists.org/reference/archive/mao/selected-works/volume-5/mswv5_40.htm.

Index

abyss 4, 5, 30, 60, 69, 73, 78, 88, 95, 97, 120, 121, 174, 207
Aquinas, Thomas 28, 32, 92
Ascension 8, 18
atheist 1, 9, 10, 12, 14, 15, 19, 20, 21, 22, 23, 24, 27, 28, 33, 40, 41, 42, 46, 47, 67, 86, 137, 156, 199, 204, 205, 211, 214, 215, 216
Augustine 3, 6, 8, 37, 67, 150, 197

Badiou, Alain 2, 3, 15, 16, 18, 28, 37, 38, 44, 115, 118, 126, 129, 133, 136, 138, 150, 151, 154, 156, 157, 158, 159, 161, 162, 165, 166, 189
Balibar, Etienne 17
Benjamin, Walter 3, 42, 58, 64, 65, 82, 84, 199, 202, 216, 217
Bible 220
Big Other 6, 10, 11, 29, 30, 31, 32, 207
Buddhism 15, 46, 130, 131, 141
Butler, Judith 4, 87

capitalism 9, 15, 16, 17, 18, 19, 26, 36, 37, 54, 57, 58, 59, 64, 129, 131, 135, 142, 145, 154, 157, 188, 189, 190, 191, 192, 194, 195, 205
Caputo, John D. 14, 22, 43, 44, 101, 102, 198
Castoriadis, Cornelius 35, 118, 119, 120, 121, 143, 144, 151
Catholic 31, 41, 73, 86, 90, 137, 156, 160, 168, 188, 189, 190, 191, 192, 193, 194, 219, 223, 224
Chesterton, G. K. 15, 41, 62, 188, 189, 190, 192, 193, 194, 195, 196, 197, 198, 200, 201, 204, 205
Cross 1, 3, 5, 7, 8, 9, 10, 11, 13, 15, 17, 18, 19, 21, 23, 25, 26, 27, 29, 31, 33, 35, 37, 39, 41, 42, 43, 45, 89, 221
Crucifixion 3, 8, 13, 14, 16, 18, 23, 27, 28, 29, 30, 41, 42, 98

Davis, Creston 1, 43, 44, 45, 66, 79, 85, 97, 102, 103, 116, 154, 165, 166, 194, 197, 198
decaffeinated 1, 13
Depoortere, Frederick 22, 43, 44
Derrida, Jacques 4, 19, 73, 81, 83

Eagleton, Terry 35, 121, 144, 149, 151
Eckhart, Meister 3, 4, 28, 32, 33, 38, 86, 87, 89, 91, 92, 93, 94, 95, 96, 97, 98, 99, 100, 101, 102, 103, 160
event 3, 11, 16, 38, 42, 53, 88, 90, 146, 151, 156, 157, 158, 159, 160, 161, 162, 163, 164, 178, 195, 197, 200, 201, 202, 203, 204, 205, 206, 207, 210, 211, 212, 213, 214, 215, 224, 225, 226

Father Brown 41, 188, 190, 192, 193, 194, 195, 196, 197
Feuerbach, Ludwig 3, 13, 24, 26, 27, 28, 48, 49, 54, 55, 57, 58, 64, 65, 117
free will 4, 5, 49
Freud, Sigmund 3, 4, 7, 17, 28, 29, 50, 64, 65, 67, 69, 72, 79, 80, 81, 83, 84, 117, 135, 145, 146, 153, 183, 186, 196, 197
fundamentalism 46, 47, 64, 134, 219

German Idealism 3, 4, 5, 168, 183, 184, 186
God 1, 4, 5, 7, 8, 10, 12, 13, 14, 15, 17, 18, 20, 22, 23, 27, 29, 30, 31, 32, 33, 37, 38, 39, 41, 42, 43, 44, 45, 47, 48, 50, 51, 53, 60, 61, 62, 63, 64, 67, 73, 74, 75, 76, 77, 78, 81, 83, 85, 89, 91, 92, 93, 94, 95, 96, 97, 98, 100, 101, 103, 110, 117, 119, 121, 127, 130, 132, 139, 143, 144, 146, 149, 150, 151, 158, 159, 160, 162, 163, 164,

168, 169, 173, 174, 175, 176, 178, 179, 180, 181, 182, 183, 189, 191, 192, 194, 195, 196, 199, 200, 201, 202, 203, 204, 205, 206, 207, 208, 209, 210, 211, 212, 213, 214, 215, 216, 217, 218, 219, 220, 221, 222, 223, 224, 225, 226
gotheit (Godhead) 95
Gramsci, Antonio 194, 197
Gunjević, Boris 1, 22, 43, 44, 45, 85

Hegel, G.W.F. 3, 4, 20, 22, 24, 26, 27, 28, 33, 34, 38, 45, 49, 50, 54, 60, 61, 62, 63, 64, 65, 66, 86, 98, 103, 104, 107, 108, 110, 111, 112, 113, 114, 115, 118, 121, 145, 148, 152, 153, 155, 165, 166, 167, 190, 194; Hegelian 1, 4, 15, 16, 18, 20, 27, 31, 34, 62, 63, 64, 67, 79, 85, 86, 88, 90, 97, 98, 103, 104, 108, 109, 110, 111, 112, 113, 114, 115, 124, 189, 194, 199, 201, 208
Heidegger, Martin 37, 79, 133, 146, 153, 160, 173, 174, 184, 186, 188, 194, 195, 198, 199
history 3, 5, 15, 16, 23, 35, 36, 39, 43, 48, 54, 76, 86, 110, 112, 117, 118, 119, 121, 127, 129, 131, 135, 138, 140, 149, 154, 156, 168, 173, 175, 177, 192, 199, 200, 201, 202, 208, 215, 216, 217, 220, 221
Holy Spirit 2, 3, 8, 9, 15, 17, 19, 24, 27, 31, 32, 33, 41, 43, 62, 63, 67, 79, 89, 90, 96, 98, 107, 108, 110, 111, 114, 189, 202, 208, 210, 212, 213, 215, 221, 224

ideology 2, 7, 10, 11, 12, 13, 26, 28, 59, 79, 138, 148, 162, 163, 195, 221
Israel 190, 192, 198
Isticheit (is-ness) 95, 96

Jesus Christ 1, 2, 3, 7, 10, 11, 12, 13, 14, 15, 17, 18, 19, 20, 21, 22, 23, 26, 27, 29, 30, 31, 36, 37, 39, 40, 41, 42, 43, 44, 45, 62, 63, 65, 66, 67, 68, 72, 73, 74, 75, 76, 77, 78, 79, 82, 85, 86, 87, 89, 90, 95, 97, 102, 103, 107, 110, 115, 116, 126, 129, 130, 132, 137, 138, 139, 140, 141, 147, 148, 151, 152, 153, 155, 157, 158, 159, 161, 162, 163, 164, 165, 166, 190, 194, 195, 198, 202, 203, 204, 205, 207, 208, 209, 210, 211, 213, 221, 222, 223, 224

jouissance 29, 30, 67, 69, 71, 72, 76, 78, 207
Judaism 4, 7, 9, 10, 15, 16, 17, 18, 22, 32, 62, 162, 163, 164, 202, 214

Kierkegaard, Søren 3, 133, 160, 161, 191, 219, 226, 227
knowledge 12, 13, 34, 78, 82, 87, 88, 107, 108, 110, 111, 112, 123, 127, 169, 177, 199, 203, 205, 206, 207, 212, 219
Kotsko, Adam 22, 43, 45

Lacan, Jacques 2, 3, 4, 5, 7, 9, 11, 14, 24, 27, 28, 29, 32, 33, 34, 39, 50, 62, 67, 69, 70, 71, 72, 74, 75, 77, 79, 80, 81, 82, 83, 84, 104, 107, 112, 114, 132, 147, 150, 153, 168, 179, 180, 181, 182, 185, 186, 190, 196, 198, 202, 205
Law 3, 6, 7, 8, 9, 17, 18, 32, 37, 87, 88, 89, 90, 126, 143, 152, 163, 164, 182, 212, 214, 223
Lenin, Vladimir 3, 46, 147, 201, 204, 211
Levinas, Emmanuel 4, 28, 32, 88, 89, 90, 95, 97
liberal 28, 35, 36, 37, 46, 117, 118, 125, 127, 128, 129, 132, 133, 134, 135, 138, 142, 143, 146, 147, 148, 154, 155, 160, 220; liberalism 2, 29, 35, 112, 118, 125, 126, 148, 155
Luther, Martin 3, 28, 42, 139, 140, 150, 152, 222, 223, 227

MacIntyre, Alasdair 35, 122, 124, 145, 148, 152
Marion, Jean-Luc 28, 29, 31, 73, 77, 80, 81, 82, 83, 84
Marxism 2, 19, 33, 34, 35, 36, 47, 61, 63, 104, 117, 118, 128, 129, 132, 134, 141, 147, 149, 152, 154, 192, 196
Marx, Karl 3, 13, 24, 25, 26, 27, 28, 33, 47, 49, 50, 51, 52, 53, 54, 55, 56, 57, 58, 59, 61, 64, 65, 78, 104, 114, 115, 117, 135, 148, 152, 196, 197
Maximus the Confessor 24, 43, 224, 227
metamorphosis 67, 68, 69, 71, 73, 74, 75, 76, 77, 78, 79, 81, 82, 85
Milbank, John 1, 14, 20, 22, 28, 31, 40, 43, 44, 45, 65, 66, 85, 86, 97, 98, 101, 103, 115, 116, 165, 166, 189, 190, 197, 198
Milner, Jean-Claude 28, 34, 104, 105, 106, 107, 108, 109, 110, 113, 114, 115

Moltmann, Jürgen 74, 126, 136, 147, 152
Müntzer, Thomas 139, 150, 223, 227

neighbor 8, 9, 18, 19, 24, 32, 33, 86, 87, 88, 89, 90, 91, 95, 96, 97, 98, 220
New Age 15, 46, 47, 131
Nietzsche, Friedrich 12, 13, 18, 23, 29, 69, 80, 83, 87, 115, 116, 118, 121, 122, 144, 145, 155, 165, 166, 189, 194, 195, 198, 199

objet petit a 6, 9
Old Testament 88, 130
Orthodox 1, 15, 18, 20, 22, 23, 24, 31, 41, 42, 44, 45, 86, 90, 130, 138, 147, 149, 151, 152, 193, 194, 197, 198, 223, 224

pagan 6, 32, 129, 130, 131, 156, 162, 164, 165, 205, 206, 220
Papathanasiou, Athanasios N. 147, 152
Pentecost 3, 8, 16
perversion/perverse 1, 2, 11, 16, 72, 73, 76, 77, 78, 79, 203, 204, 206, 207, 208, 214, 223
psychoanalysis 1, 2, 3, 4, 8, 12, 16, 17, 19, 29, 30, 31, 33, 34, 36, 38, 67, 68, 69, 70, 71, 72, 73, 74, 75, 77, 78, 79, 81, 83, 85, 104, 106, 110, 112, 128, 147, 195, 225

Rancière, Jacques 3, 17, 28, 115, 212
real 4, 6, 17, 18, 29, 30, 31, 34, 39, 42, 80, 83, 104, 109, 111, 113, 114, 115, 132, 179, 180, 181, 207
religion 2, 7, 8, 11, 13, 15, 16, 17, 18, 19, 20, 24, 25, 26, 27, 30, 40, 42, 46, 47, 48, 49, 50, 51, 52, 54, 55, 57, 58, 59, 60, 61, 62, 63, 64, 72, 79, 107, 108, 111, 114, 117, 118, 119, 120, 126, 140, 143, 147, 155, 156, 165, 189, 190, 192, 193, 199, 201, 206, 209, 213

Resurrection 2, 3, 8, 9, 16, 20, 23, 27, 28, 29, 31, 42, 79, 83, 97, 102, 161
Ricoeur, Paul 35, 124, 147, 148, 152
Rorty, Richard 35, 118, 120, 127, 128, 129, 131, 141, 142, 143, 144, 145, 146, 147, 153
Rousseau, Jean-Jacques 46, 64, 65, 123, 146
Russell, Bertrand 117, 185, 186

Schelling, F.W.J. 3, 4, 5, 28, 38, 39, 40, 43, 167, 168, 169, 170, 171, 172, 173, 174, 175, 176, 177, 178, 179, 180, 182, 183, 184, 185, 186, 187, 202
symbolic 4, 6, 7, 10, 17, 18, 30, 31, 34, 42, 69, 104, 180, 207

theology 1, 2, 3, 5, 7, 8, 10, 12, 14, 15, 18, 19, 20, 21, 22, 23, 26, 29, 30, 31, 33, 39, 41, 42, 47, 48, 54, 59, 67, 68, 72, 73, 74, 78, 83, 87, 89, 91, 97, 137, 138, 145, 149, 150, 154, 155, 156, 160, 162, 188, 196, 199, 200, 201, 202, 204, 207, 208, 209, 210, 212, 215, 216
Thing 4, 6, 7, 8, 9, 17, 18, 27, 29, 32, 41, 88, 89, 107, 111, 180, 208
Triadology 15, 17, 18, 23
Trump, Donald 41, 155, 188, 191

universalism 15, 33, 40, 104, 160, 164, 190, 203, 213

Ward, Graham 20, 43, 44, 45, 201, 216, 218
West/Western 10, 15, 17, 23, 24, 46, 126, 128, 129, 134, 135, 141, 155, 165

Yannaras, Christos 18, 44, 45

Zupančič, Alenka 109, 110, 114, 115, 116